The Dutch
Republic in the
Eighteenth Century

# The Dutch Republic in the Eighteenth Century

## DECLINE, ENLIGHTENMENT, AND REVOLUTION

EDITED BY

Margaret C. Jacob
*and* Wijnand W. Mijnhardt

*Cornell University Press*

ITHACA AND LONDON

First published 1992 by Cornell University Press.

International Standard Book Number 0-8014-2624-3 (cloth)
International Standard Book Number 0-8014-8050-7 (paper)
Library of Congress Catalog Card Number 91-55551

Printed in the United States of America

*Librarians: Library of Congress cataloging information*
*appears on the last page of the book.*

⊗ The paper in this book meets the minimum requirements
of the American National Standard for Information Sciences—
Permanence of Paper for Printed Library Materials, ANSI Z39.48-1984.

# Contents

v

## THE DUTCH REPUBLICAN TRADITION

## THE DUTCH ENLIGHTENMENT

## DUTCH CULTURE IN ITS SOCIAL SETTING

# Acknowledgments

Multiauthored volumes are never easy to bring off. We did it because of some remarkable assistance. We are grateful to Herbert Rowen, the leading American historian of the Dutch experience, who helped put together the conference at which early versions of these chapters were read. Undaunted by that labor, he provided important editorial assistance. So too did John Ackerman of Cornell University Press, who had the faith to keep seeking. Of course, all infelicities that remain are entirely our responsibility.

Always a friend to republics, John Pocock also helped in the planning of the Folger Shakespeare Library conference in 1987. It was generously funded by the National Endowment for the Humanities, the Koninklijke Nederlandse Akademie van Wetenschappen, the Netherlands-American Amity Trust, The Royal Netherlands Embassy, and the Stichting Nederland-Amerika. Lena Orlin and her assistant, Gregory Barz, at the Folger did everything we could ever have wished for to make the conference, and hence this volume, a success. Finally, we thank each other and the other contributors for patience, forbearance, and good humor. Het was voor ons een groot plezier.

M.C.J.
W.W.M.

# Introduction

## Margaret C. Jacob and Wijnand W. Mijnhardt

Two centuries after a precipitous decline, and within the remarkable context provided by the Netherlands of the late twentieth century—peaceful, intensely stable, enriched by the benefits of postwar international cooperation through the EEC—the Dutch found themselves in 1987, somewhat uncomfortably, celebrating a revolution. It was the two hundredth anniversary of the only modern revolution in Dutch history. Faced with the late eighteenth-century events that created a division between the ancien régime and the modern world, the Dutch, like their American, French and Belgian counterparts, confronted a revolutionary past and sought to make sense of it.

Postwar Dutch historians, and their American colleagues, many of whom were born during or after World War II, rose to the occasion represented by this two-hundredth anniversary. But the Dutch historians, who are the principal contributors to this historical discussion, spoke from a rather unique perspective. One celebratory volume published in the Netherlands in 1988 was titled *De Nederlandse revolutie?*[1] The question mark would be unthinkable in any present-day historiography concerned with the late eighteenth-century French and American revolutions.

To a certain extent this uneasiness about the 1787 Dutch revolution

---

1. Th. S. M. van der Zee, J. G. M. N. Roosendaal, and P. G. B. Thissen, eds., *De Nederlandse revolutie?* (Amsterdam, 1988).

may be explained by the vicissitudes of Dutch history itself. From the seventeenth to the late twentieth century, no European country, with the possible exception of Great Britain in the postwar era, has experienced such profoundly different degrees and circumstances of power and prosperity as has the Netherlands. In the middle of the seventeenth century it was probably, per capita, the richest nation in the world and the most influential in international politics; by the end of the eighteenth century its international stature had declined to that of a second-rate power, and equally apparent was a concomitant poverty in almost all former commercial and industrial areas of the country.[2] The nineteenth century brought industrialization to the Netherlands decades later than in Belgium and even parts of France. This delay only furthered Dutch decline as an international power. The twentieth century was no less ironic. World War II, which brought about the destruction of Dutch Jewry and economic disaster, left the Netherlands in 1945 a deeply troubled nation. Yet, once again, fate reversed itself. By 1987, from any perspective, the Netherlands had become one of the most prosperous nations in the world.

How were historians to make sense of phenomena no less contradictory or confusing? What was to be made of the corruption and decline that eighteenth-century commentators attributed to their age, or of a revolution that was neither as violent nor, at first sight, as decisive in its outcome as its French counterpart and that, in the short term, resulted in invasion and occupation by foreign armies, first Prussian in 1787 and then French in 1795? The answers given by earlier generations of Dutch historians may be considered a mirror of the country's vicissitudes. The Leiden historian H. T. Colenbrander, who at the turn of this century opened the debate, questioned the very existence of a Dutch revolution. He treated the 1780–1787 events chiefly as a by-product of international conflict fought on Dutch soil. Deploring decline, he saw the Patriots, as the 1787 revolutionaries called themselves, and their adversaries, the Orangists, first of all as puppets operated by the French, English, and Prussian ambassadors in The Hague.

By the middle of this century, Colenbrander's essentially international and negative reading of the Dutch revolutionary experience had dramatically shifted. The challenge came from Pieter Geyl, who sought to rescue the Dutch dimension of the drama. For Geyl, as Nicolaas van Sas in his chapter here shows, the Patriot movement was a decisive

2. See, for example, H. A. Diederiks et al., *Armoede en sociale spanning: Sociaal-historische studies over Leiden in de achttiende eeuw* (Leiden, 1978).

phase in an authentic Dutch reform movement that had its roots in the upheavals of 1672, 1702, and 1747. This essentially political interpretation was itself challenged during the 1960s by C. H. E. de Wit. Offering a social interpretation, De Wit saw the Patriot revolution as the beginning of a long and bitter struggle between aristocrats and democrats which ended only with the introduction of a democratic constitution in 1848. Alliances between regents and burghers in this struggle were simply impossible because, for De Wit, bourgeois political emancipation was the driving force behind the revolution. Simon Schama's *Patriots and Liberators* of 1977 should be considered a synthesis of these older social and political interpretations.[3]

For present-day Dutch historians, the problems of interpretation are framed differently. In the context of the roller coaster that is late twentieth-century Dutch history, what is one to make of revolutions that lead to invasions? How does one grapple with the reality of economic decline and the loss of international prestige, or with the perception of corruption and atrophy, when one's own experience has been largely about the reverse? One can think of no period in subsequent Dutch history as remote from the eighteenth century as is the present.

The eighteenth century in the Dutch Republic was a deeply troubled time. In 1747–1748, some enlightened reformers agitated for change and instigated a brief and hardly successful—yet the only— revolution in a Western European power between 1689 and 1787. The revolution of 1747—discussed in full detail in this volume by Jan de Jongste—restored the stadholderate in the person of William IV. Some radical reformers in a movement known as the *Doelistenbeweging* sought to go farther, to democratize the institutions of local government and to address contemporary economic decline by calling for the application of science to the problems of industry. But to no avail; in

3. H. T. Colenbrander, *De Patriottentijd: Hoofdzakelijk naar buitenlandse bescheiden*, 3 vols. (The Hague, 1897–1899); P. Geyl, *De Patriottenbeweging, 1780–1787* (Amsterdam, 1947); C. H. E. de Wit, *De strijd tussen aristocratie en democratie in Nederland, 1780–1848* (Heerlen, 1965), and *De Nederlandse revolutie van de achttiende eeuw, 1780–1787: Oligarchie en proletariaat* (Oirsbeek, 1974); S. Schama, *Patriots and Liberators: Revolution in the Netherlands 1780–1813* (New York, 1977). For recent reviews of Dutch historiography on the Patriot revolution, see N. C. F. van Sas, "De Nederlandse revolutie van de XVIIIe eeuw," *Bijdragen en Mededelingen betreffende de Geschiedenis der Nederlanden* 100 (1985): 636– 646; G. J. Schutte, "Van verguizing naar eerherstel: Het beeld van de patriotten in de negentiende en twintigste eeuw," in *Voor vaderland en vrijheid: De revolutie van de patriotten*, ed. F. Grijzenhout, W. W. Mijnhardt, and N. C. F. van Sas (Amsterdam, 1987), and A. E. M. Janssen, "Over Nederlandse patriotten en hun historie: Enige historiografische kanttekeningen," in *De droom van de revolutie: Nieuwe benaderingen van het Patriottisme*, ed. H. Bots and W. W. Mijnhardt (Amsterdam, 1988).

the second half of the century, the republic's problems were only aggravated and tensions continued to mount.

The complexity of the republic's machinery of state had frequently resulted in an inability to reach decisions. In the seventeenth century the necessities of almost continuous war and economic prosperity had resulted in a rich flow of taxation money. Both money and imminent danger permitted the governing elite to overcome the problems inherent in the highly localized structure of politics in the Dutch Republic. In the eighteenth century, however, these stimuli were lacking. Especially the continuous shortages of money, caused by the enormous war debts incurred at the beginning of the eighteenth century, further complicated the decision-making process, often bringing it to a halt. Neither of the eighteenth-century stadholders, William IV (d. 1751) and his son William V (1751–1795), succeeded in addressing these problems.[4] Despite their strong, almost monarchic position, neither stadholder pursued the creation of a strong executive. Both preferred to exert their power through the traditional, slow-working channels of the established political machinery. Tensions between regents and the governed also grew. Both stadholders were content to control the elections of regents, a right they had secured for their office in the 1672 and 1747 upheavals, but they did little else to curb the regents' power. To the regents they presented themselves as *primus inter pares* without trying to put an end to the process of aristocratization that estranged the governmental elite from the governed.[5]

Economic decline brought old conflicts into the open, and with decline came a fundamental shift in the regional and social balance. From the seventeenth century onward, there had been conflicts of interest between industrialists and merchants. Dutch industrial entrepreneurs had to pay their workers high wages because of the high taxes levied on the first necessities of life such as bread and beer. Confronted with sharpening foreign competition in the eighteenth century, Dutch factory owners did not succeed in promoting measures that would protect their home markets. Such measures were invariably opposed by the merchants, who considered tariffs damaging to trade. Economic decline was a selective process as well. While industrial cities like Haar-

---

4. Herbert H. Rowen, *The Princes of Orange: The Stadholders in the Dutch Republic* (Cambridge, 1988).

5. D. J. Roorda, "Het onderzoek naar het stedelijk patriciaat in Nederland," in *Kantelend geschiedbeeld: Nederlandse historiografie sinds 1945*, ed. W. W. Mijnhardt (Utrecht-Antwerp, 1983), pp. 118–142.

lem and Leiden were severely hit after 1750, resulting in sharp drops in population, the Rotterdam economy boomed. The collapse of the economy of northern Holland sharply contrasted with the economic growth of the agrarian provinces. Despite the decrease of international commerce, Amsterdam for much of the century remained the world's financial center, enabling many banking families to acquire huge fortunes. Only in the last quarter of the century was Amsterdam forced to cede its first place to London.

Nevertheless, the social and human cost of decline was huge. As a result of the polarization of incomes, many middle-class families were forced along the road to poverty and, especially in the commercial and industrial regions, large numbers of workers were driven into pauperism. Then, toward the turn of the century, population growth came to a standstill. Politically, socially, and economically the republic presented the gloomy picture of a stagnant society.

These problems arose in a century characterized by unprecedented "public opinion." The high degree of literacy found in the republic coincided with the cultural movement known by the second half of the eighteenth century as the Enlightenment. Its hallmark was an explosion of printed matter and, as Jeremy Popkin points out in this volume, the growth of a new reading public. Books, pamphlets, journals, newspapers, broadsides, clandestine manuscripts, and spectatorial literature—so called after the London *Spectator*—all of it written in the vernacular, created a new "republic of letters" which, unlike its seventeenth-century predecessor, was populated by a nationally oriented, educated public instead of by scholars with a cosmopolitan outlook. All this literature possessed one common purpose, amid a diversity of perspectives: to shape and influence, as well as to inform, the new public opinion. Put another way, the Enlightenment began in England and the Dutch Republic because in both places by the 1690s the presses were freer than anywhere else. Throughout the eighteenth century that freedom continued. Major works of the Enlightenment were published in French in the Dutch Republic, making it the production center, although not necessarily the intellectual center, of this new secular culture.

Any discussion of the Dutch revolution of 1787 inevitably requires constant reference to the major cultural shifts experienced by the republic in the eighteenth century: Enlightenment and decline. Their coupling makes the Dutch context unique to its century. The fact of decline relative to the progress and inventiveness of the seventeenth century, the Golden Age, vexed eighteenth-century reformers just as it continues to vex contemporary historians—but for profoundly different reasons. As E. H. Kossmann notes in the opening chapter of this volume, eighteenth-century critics wanted the decline to be halted by a return to the principles and practices of that earlier, golden age. In his chapter, Frans Grijzenhout, discussing eighteenth-century art, questions the overall importance attached to the seventeenth-century past. He presents instead a picture of eighteenth-century Dutch art that emphasizes its neoclassicist roots and its richness. Some art historians, such as Arthur Wheelock of the National Gallery in Washington, tend to disagree. It is one thing to postulate decline; it is quite another to find agreement as to its component parts, even on its existence. However we measure it, decline was real enough in the eighteenth-century Dutch Republic.

Nostalgic idealism became widespread at least from the 1730s onward, and it permeated all political, religious, and intellectual debate. But looking to the past does not dampen passions in the present. Indeed, the disruptive power of Patriot rhetoric derived precisely from an obsession with the past. Expositions of the loss of virtue and a longing for a long-lost golden age were, of course, quite common among European commentators in the eighteenth century. But, for the Dutch, the Golden Age was a recent reality, and this very fact provided their discourse with a peculiar moralism. With the benefit of hindsight, present-day Dutch historians see decline as a process that was inevitable once British and French rivals mustered their resources against the smaller and less centralized republic. Such a consoling insight should not obscure the vexation that fed into Patriot as well as Orangist discontent, both in 1747 and more profoundly in 1787. Nor should the insight remove us from the responsibility of assessing the Dutch republican experience in relation to the Italian, English, and American tradition of republican discourse explicated by J. G. A. Pocock. The questions he raises in his chapter are among the most difficult all historians of the republican experience seek to understand.

American readers of this volume may be challenged by this eighteenth-century Dutch approach to the appearance of decline within their republic. Just their efforts to define it, never mind to treat it, anticipate a debate with which we in the late twentieth century grow increasingly familiar. The Dutch experience is relevant to our pressing concerns for a variety of reasons. We are now witness, once again in Western history, to the dramatic decline of empires. The Dutch experience of decline shows us that it can be combined with progressive and enlightened cultural movements, with the impulse to reform and even to revolt. After spectacular growth and hegemonic authority over parts of the globe, the Dutch experience tells us something about the ability to survive, and even to prosper, without having to remain a world power or without succumbing to the creation of authoritarian and repressive regimes. The story of the Dutch Republic is displayed in this volume as what in fact it has always been: an inherent, yet distinctive, part of early modern (and modern) Western history.

The revolutionary upheavals that transformed the West in the late eighteenth and early nineteenth centuries began in the American colonies in the 1770s, only to be transferred a decade later to the Dutch Republic, one of the United States' first allies. Thus, it is by no means accidental that Dutch and American historians find the paradox of the Dutch Republic in the eighteenth century—Enlightenment, and then revolution, amid a perceived decline—such a tantalizing, even compelling, historical phenomenon. Where, then, in the effort to reconcile the paradox presented by Dutch history do the essays in this collection take us?

All the contributors to this volume are aware of recent historiographic developments, particularly in studies of the French Revolution, but also in the historiography of Anglo-American republicanism. The unifying feature in much contemporary historical writing is the attack—largely successful, we would argue—against the classical Marxist insistence on the existence of a revolutionary bourgeois class poised by the 1780s to assault the old regimes in Europe. The loss of the Marxist paradigm brings special problems to eighteenth-century Dutch historiography. The "bourgeois" postulate once permitted an easy solution to the central paradox of the age. The decline brought about by the corruption of the old order was attributed to the decline of a class, an aristocracy wedded to birth and title, and to the monopolizing of its power, which was based on an outmoded system of production. Eighteenth-century capitalism undid that system, and with its demise came the rise of a new bourgeoisie. Concomitant with belief in the existence of the market-oriented class came the assumption that, if culture mattered, then enlightened culture was for the most part generated by, and certainly for, the edification of the bourgeoisie. Almost no aspect of that explanation now remains intact.

The one great strength of the older Marxist historiography, or of its liberal variations, lay precisely in its ability to offer explanations of the events in Paris, Amsterdam, or Brussels. Thus it transcended the local and the particular and sought to anchor politics, as well as culture, in patterns of property ownership, birth, title, or rank in society, which possessed meaning and displayed similar characteristics in every Western European language, in every ancien régime. As William Reddy observes, we are at a point in our understanding of the French Revolution where we can describe events and mentalities leading up to it, but the present demise of classical Marxism leaves us, at first sight, with no explanation of the causes of that revolution.[6]

We are in a similar place in Dutch historiography. Although it is true that a strong Marxist historiography never came into being in the Netherlands, none of the essays in this volume follow even a liberal Marxist rendering of the class basis for the Patriot revolution, first offered by C. H. E. de Wit in 1965. Ideological allegiance is no longer held to be contingent on social origin or occupation, and the Patriots are no longer identified with a revolutionary bourgeois movement. In the place of an identifiable bourgeoisie, Dutch historians now prefer to identify a variety of interest groups, from wealthy merchants ready to emulate the regent aristocracy to journalists and publishers who would print anything for a profit, not to mention reforming aristocrats and a vast Orangist populace.

Amid this diversity stands culture, a seamless web of language that mediated the interests of these various groups and at moments gave coherence to their loyalties and discontents. In the eighteenth century, as Willem Frijhoff's chapter on enlightened attitudes toward the populace explains, culture meant something very different to its elite consumers from what they imagined their plebeian neighbors possessed. Bearing this division between high and low culture in mind, present-day historians are increasingly cautious about how democratic those late eighteenth-century revolutions could possibly have been.

Most important, however, as Nicolaas van Sas is quick to point out, postulating the relative autonomy of culture, as well as of politics as a process, separable from (but not unrelated to) social class has certain advantages. In this radical departure from the Marxist canon, which Van Sas advocates, the politics and political culture of the 1780s in the Netherlands replace class interest as the explanatory mechanism that brings us to 1787. Local issues, print culture, pamphlet warfare, Patriot and Orangist ideologies converge in the chapters of this volume

6. William Reddy, *Money and Liberty in Modern Europe* (Cambridge, 1987).

to explicate a process by which the stadholder and his supporters lose the initiative. With it slips away their ability to govern or to monopolize the offices of local government. In that sense, both Enlightenment and decline made revolution possible.

Seeing political culture as dynamic and transforming does not imply that it is free floating. The Dutch may have had a relatively bloodless upheaval in the later 1780s and 1790s, but it was not for want of material interests or class antagonisms. We must remember the hatred foreign invasion provoked as well as all those Dutch exiles in France during the 1790s who became Jacobins in the crucible of another revolution. When they came home, they did so seasoned by exile and Terror, with their will to reform galvanized. They embarked, however, not on Terror but on a massive overhaul of Dutch institutions. By 1795, there was a nearly universal sense in the republic that some reform was necessary. The Enlightenment, however moderate, had worked its magic among regents as well as Jacobins.

In this book, two important factors in both the Dutch revolution and the old order are given new explanatory power: Dutch politics, more than French or British, were local politics, and the oligarchy of the regents and the stadholder alike resisted all attempt at reform until their opponents, now styling themselves "the nation," took their political opposition to the level of a national revolutionary movement in the spring of 1787. This coupling of nationalist ideology with localized politics provided the Patriot movement with its success as well as with its demise. That it failed to transform the institutions of the republic, as Wayne te Brake ruefully observes, owes as much to the local and fragmented nature of politics in the republic as it does to foreign invasion. In this highly political and cultural approach, the fact of war exposed the weaknesses in the prevailing order and stirred the wrath of critics and reformers. War was responsible for an extreme nationalism which, in its search for remedies, had to express itself through local channels. It is therefore in local and provincial politics that we must look first for the social background of the revolution, for answers to the questions, What did property and money, title and lineage, beliefs and ideologies have to do with revolutionary actions? Having reasserted the integrity of the cultural and the political, it does, however, remain for the historiography of the 1990s to explain how the social and economic will correlate with political postures and cultural values.

The emphasis on local government also stemmed from the Patriots' own stand in the debate, which focused on the problems caused by the complexity of the decision-making process in the republic. Both Patriot and Orangist political commentators agreed on the necessity of reforming that process if they were to be able to attack the issue of decline. The Patriots suggested that matters would improve by making the regents into dependent instruments of the popular will through a system of government by representation. By contrast, Orangist theorists, as early as William Bentinck in the 1740s and 1750s, proposed the strengthening of the executive, in the Dutch context personified by the stadholder. In Dutch historiography the classic position articulated some years ago by I. Leonard Leeb has been to argue that Patriot political thought—especially in its main tract, the 1784 *Grondwettige herstelling* (Constitutional Restoration; see Glossary)—was too involved in a historical mode of thinking and too dependent on historical precedent to be able to produce a truly modern notion of popular sovereignty.[7] The same would apply to their opponents, the Orangists.

In several of the present chapters, however, the modern, though not necessarily fully democratic, elements of Patriot political thought are stressed. The reform of local government in various cities, as urged by the *Grondwettige herstelling*, led to experiments no longer inspired by historical precedent but rather by the desire for new definitions for the political nation. Patriot local reform proposals created new types of political representation, though often disguised in traditional language, and thus paved the way for a more democratic approach to politics, rendering it impossible after 1787 to return to the policies of the old order. Both Wyger Velema and I. J. H. Worst in their chapters also emphasize the modernity of Orangist theorists. Elie Luzac attempted to adapt the state to new circumstances and to find a way out of the narrow boundaries imposed by traditional constitutional practices, without, however, jeopardizing stability. Such Orangists as F. W. Pestel and Adriaan Kluit, through their discussions of the nature of the Dutch constitution, equally developed a new vision of politics as a substantial activity.

Then there is that elusive phenomenon of the Enlightenment. Both Patriots and Orangists claimed their dependence on Enlightenment thought. This volume begins the enterprise of giving social and political meaning to the Dutch Enlightenment. The essay on science and the first essay in English to tackle the question of the origins of the Dutch novel are all contributions to that enterprise. They begin to address the para-

7. I. L. Leeb, *The Ideological Origins of the Batavian Revolution: History and Politics in the Dutch Republic 1747–1800* (The Hague, 1973).

dox presented by Dutch science and literature in the eighteenth century, the relative decline of the former and the relative lateness of the latter. H. A. M. Snelders describes the character of Dutch scientific decline and the reasons Dutch scientific lay education was only minimally successful in implementing industrial applications of the new science. Christine van Boheemen-Saaf alerts us to the alliance between liberal theology and the rise of the Dutch novel and offers a subtle reading of the novel's relationship to the Patriot vision. This chapter is, as well, the only one here to deal with religiosity. Perhaps we need to know more about the religiosity of various social groups, as well as of Orangists and Patriots, before we can locate the various ideological postures that enlightened discourse in the republic might have taken. The Enlightenment cannot be understood apart from religiosity. Before they were anything else, deism, Spinozism, materialism, freethinking, and pantheism were religious battle cries. How did Dutch Calvinism fare in the century that, by and large, made impiety fashionable? This seems a particularly appropriate question to ask of the country that acted as a Calvinist bulwark while at the same time publishing some of the most impious books of the Enlightenment. Can we still assume that these texts belong only to the French Enlightenment? In the university town of Leiden and in Middelburg, the capital of the province of Zeeland, for example, elite families evinced little interest in either the scientific or the impious.[8] By contrast, internationally oriented booksellers such as the Luchtmans dynasty in Leiden distributed works written in French by, or about, freethinkers, Vanini, Anthony Collins, Toland, not to mention Locke, Bayle, Descartes, Leibniz, and the English latitudinarians.[9]

In the Dutch Republic this enlightened, and even radical, literature mingled with the vastly more popular works by the pious or by the vulgarizers of a moderate version of the Enlightenment. Both were available and sold. And perhaps the surest sign that part of the international Enlightenment must have caused anxiety was the periodic outbreak of censorship, usually of a local character, brought to bear against Socinianism (in Amsterdam in 1710), against pantheistic and anonymous works such as the *Treatise on the Three Imposters* (in The

8. M. Prak, *Gezeten burgers: De elite in een Hollandse stad, Leiden 1700–1780* (Amsterdam, 1985), pp. 222–225; J. J. Kloek and W. W. Mijnhardt, *Leescultuur in Middelburg aan het begin van de negentiende eeuw* (Middelburg, 1988), chap. 4.

9. See the manuscripts in the Luchtmans archives at the Bibliotheek van de Vereeniging ter bevordering van de belangen des boekhandels, University Library, Amsterdam, which also show Luchtmans supplying dealers all over Holland.

Hague in 1720), against La Mettrie at mid-century, and against Voltaire in the 1760s and Rousseau as late as 1787. Most of the Dutch historiography that deals with the warfare between the pious and the impious, between religious moderates and radicals, was, interestingly enough, written before World War II.

The definition of religious postures was once thought to have little to do with political affiliation. In British historiography, at least, that has changed as more is now known about the filiations of freethinking and radical Whiggery, and of liberal Anglicanism and the Whig oligarchy. What were those comparable affinities in the Dutch Republic between Enlightenment heresies and political ideology? Questions like these loom large, especially if we would now assert the integrity of political culture, and hence of ideology, as immensely useful concepts.

This volume offers a variety of approaches to the ideological postures available within eighteenth-century Dutch culture. Margaret Jacob stresses the importance of a radical undercurrent in the Dutch Enlightenment at work in the revolutions of both 1747 and 1787. Defining radicalism in terms of adherence to the new science and to a theoretically anchored form of republicanism derived ultimately from ancient as well as Italian sources, she locates its political manifestations in various forms of Amsterdam sociability, especially in freemasonry. Emphasizing the link existing in the Dutch Republic between political radicalism and a new industrial vision, the radicals of 1747 and once again in the 1780s offered solutions drawn from the Enlightenment and intended to address the problem of economic decline as well as the political future. Once again the culture of sociability, this time among the scientifically inclined, became a force for change and reform.

A different perspective is stressed by Wijnand Mijnhardt, who distinguishes between the radical version of Enlightenment, sponsored by the many refugees and exiles on Dutch soil, and a moderate variety supported by Dutch intellectuals and adapted to the religious, political, and intellectual values of the republic. The backing of the radical variety by the Dutch publishing industry, until mid-century at least, made it into one of the clearinghouses of the European Enlightenment. The moderate and indigenously Dutch variety of the Enlightenment had its origins in the new, nationally oriented republic of letters dominated by the new, cultivated reading public.[10] The vast literature circulating in this community stressed the perfectability of humanity and offered vir-

10. For the concept of national varieties of the international Enlightenment, see R. Porter and M. Teich, eds., *The Enlightenment in National Context* (Cambridge, 1981).

tue as an outstanding means of fighting decline. Dutch commentators diagnosed the ultimate cause of this predicament as moral. The coincidence of decline amid Enlightenment produced a new national consciousness that drew its inspiration from the past. Its aim was to restore the morals that were thought to have been the very basis of the seventeenth-century Golden Age. What was needed, the writers of the Dutch Enlightenment argued, was the infusion of a nationalized version of universal Enlightenment ideas, a massive inculcation of ideas such as virtue, knowledge, and the pursuit of happiness. The heavy dependence of eighteenth-century Dutch historians on seventeenth-century intellectual and religious traditions is also stressed in E. O. G. Haitsma Mulier's chapter. Dutch historians were well acquainted with the new international and philosophical history, but they showed a marked tendency to subordinate those trends to their concern about fortifying Dutch morale in a world that seemed increasingly to exclude the republic from its center.

All contributors to this volume agree on the enormous importance to be attached to Dutch organized sociability. The popularity of a wide variety of literary and cultural societies reached its apex in the 1770s and 1780s and acted in its various manifestations as the organized public opinion. To a large extent this movement, political or apolitical, was responsible for a new element in Dutch political culture. By venturing the idea that the pursuit of literature, the arts, and the sciences was at least an acceptable alternative to political participation, and of immense benefit to the nation, the Dutch Enlightenment fostered the notion that all citizens should seek to serve the public good.

As W. van den Berg in his contribution on Dutch literary sociability—the term now widely used to describe the phenomenon of secular fraternizing—points out, the meaning of the poetry produced in these organizations did not lie in its literary value but in its emphasis on serving the nation's welfare. The most influential Dutch society, supported toward the end of the century by thousands of enlightened citizens, had aptly named itself *Maatschappij tot Nut van 't Algemeen* (Society for Public Welfare). The *Nut*, as it was generally called, offered a wide range of Enlightenment-inspired reform proposals, varying from compulsory education to a standardization of the Dutch language. More important, it succeeded in bridging the gap between the new national consciousness and the traditional local and regional loyalties. From its beginning, the *Nut* was active on two levels: the national society, with its base in Amsterdam, developed new reform proposals; the various departments, firmly entrenched in local and regional communities, were responsible for implementing new measures and for taking care of the cultural needs of its members by providing lectures, libraries, and discussion.

Thus, both decline and Enlightenment seem to have constituted major ingredients precipitating the 1787 Dutch revolution. Crucial, however, was the outbreak of the fourth Anglo-Dutch war of 1780, which was responsible for arousing a fierce nationalism that transformed the widespread but vague criticisms of the governing elite and the numerous proposals for reform into a political program stipulating a restoration of the republic's international power, moral rearmament, and political representation. Undeniably, the revolution was finally crushed by foreign invasion. This did not, however, entail a crushing of the ideals and concepts put forward in these crucial years. In the long term, the effects of the 1787 revolution and the Enlightenment debates that preceded it would prove to be lasting.

First and foremost, the eighteenth century was instrumental in the creation of what has been termed by Ernest Gellner a "universal high culture."[11] Dutch Enlightenment reformers of the 1780s were extremely active in standardizing language and in reforming the school and university systems. They spoke of the need for universal education and, much more important, of the duty of every citizen, high and low, to contribute to the welfare of the nation. The majority of these proposals were realized during the Batavian period, from 1795 to 1806, when, supported by invading French revolutionary armies, the Patriots finally succeeded in implementing their 1787 program. Second, the political innovations of the Batavian period equally had their origins in the preceding revolutionary period. Modern politics, with its new concept of the political nation and politics as a choice between alternatives, were decidedly Patriot inventions. In all these respects the Batavian revolution was a brilliant first night that could not have succeeded without the extremely important rehearsal provided by the failed revolution of the 1780s.

Certain unifying assumptions are at work throughout this book. The contributors were willing to nuance and dispute about the truly revolutionary character of a revolution interfered with almost before it itself could address, indeed even formulate, its agenda for reform. Nevertheless, we affirm the validity of the revolutionary process as the

11. See Ernest Gellner, *Nations and Nationalism* (Oxford, 1983).

shaper of Dutch national identity. In the process, we open the Dutch Enlightenment as a fertile area for research and inquiry. We lay before our colleagues in the other national histories the paradox of the culture of Enlightenment amid the reality of economic decline and political inertia. The pages that follow present a revolution distinctive in its relative bloodlessness yet no less indebted to the political culture of the Enlightenment. Students of eighteenth-century Europe must contend with these phenomena because they are part of our common inheritance. The Dutch experience was distinct as well as paradoxical; it was moderate in tone yet revolutionary in action, national in vision yet intensely local in execution. We commend it to your attention.

# V R Y E
# GEDACHTEN
## VAN EEN'
# BURGER
### OVER HET VERVAL VAN 'T GEMEE-
### NEBEST DER VEREENIGDE
# NEDERLANDEN.

## IN HOLLAND.
## 1782.

*Vrije Gedachten van een Burger.* Free thoughts of a citizen concerning the decline of the Commonwealth of the United Netherlands. Title page of a pamphlet on the violations of the Dutch constitution (1782). Private Collection.

# THREE DUTCH REVOLUTIONS:
## 1747, 1787, 1795

# I

# The Dutch Republic in the Eighteenth Century

## E. H. Kossmann

IT is estimated that the total population of the seven provinces of the
Dutch Republic grew from about one million in 1500 to two million
in 1800. All that growth took place in the sixteenth and seventeenth
centuries; in the eighteenth century the figure virtually did not rise.
Compared with France, which had eighteen million inhabitants in
1700 and more than twenty-eight million in 1800, or Great Britain,
which grew from nine million in 1700 to sixteen million in 1800, this
demographic stagnation is an exceptional case. There were also interesting differences in the development of the various provinces. In some
of the eastern and southern agrarian provinces the population grew. In
the province of Holland it declined substantially. In 1500, almost 29
percent of the total population of the provinces that were later to form
the republic lived in Holland. In 1650, this figure had risen to 48.2
percent; in 1795 it was 37.7 percent. Between the middle of the seventeenth century and 1795, Holland lost 120,000 inhabitants. The
smaller towns were hit hardest. Leiden and Haarlem, once famous for
their textile industry, lost almost half of their population. Of the eighteen towns with a vote in the estates of Holland, only the bigger
ones—Amsterdam, The Hague, and Rotterdam—kept growing, mainly
in the second half of the eighteenth century.

Phenomena of this kind are complicated. It would be unwise to
ignore the historical demographers who warn us that this depopulation
did not simply reflect the decline of Holland's commercial and indus-

trial prosperity and the flourishing of agriculture in some of the more rural provinces. But whatever the precise connections between these trends, it is a fact that in the eighteenth century the Dutch economy came to lean somewhat more on the agricultural than on the commercial and industrial sectors, thus adapting itself to the virtually inevitable decline of Holland's market as an entrepôt. The socioeconomic position of the republic and specifically that of the province of Holland had undergone profound changes.

From its inception in the 1580s, the Dutch republic had become one of the greatest economic powers of the world, far surpassing France, England, or the German states. One usually explains this strength by referring to the impotence of the bigger neighboring countries, the closure of the Scheldt, and the exhaustion of Spain and Portugal, which allowed the Dutch to grasp the opportunities offered by the expanding world economy in a much larger measure than could normally have been expected. From the middle of the seventeenth century, however, the Dutch economic hegemony and, in some areas, monopoly was no longer tolerated by England and France, which succeeded first in stopping Dutch expansion and then in building up an economic power more solidly based on their own inherent possibilities—on the wealth of their soil, the energy of their growing population, the productivity of their agriculture.

The economic greatness of the Dutch was due to their role as mediators. But when the countries among whom the Dutch mediated developed means to bypass Dutch intervention and services, the republic was forced to adapt itself to the circumstances. Apart from its connection with its own colonies in East India and to a smaller degree with those in the West Indies, it abandoned many of its global responsibilities. In the early nineteenth century Holland's most important trading partners were the neighboring countries, which provided outlets for its agrarian products. At the end of the nineteenth century the Dutch would transform their economy through a gradual process of industrialization, and after World War II they would do so once again. But there is a significant difference between these later economic achievements and those in the early seventeenth century: the Dutch in the early seventeenth century were able to take the lead and prosper because they were ahead of their neighbors; in the nineteenth and twentieth centuries they were essentially followers. It was then, in fact, the economic growth of Britain, France, and above all Germany that helped the Dutch, situated between such highly industrialized nations, to modernize their economy and take part in the general European upswing.

Such a fundamental change in the economic position of a country entails consequences in other fields, social, political, and cultural. It is not at all easy, however, to indicate precisely how these different elements are related and how the whole mechanism of change actually worked. Perhaps the chapters in this book will bring us somewhat farther than I feel myself able to go at the moment. The matter is of the greatest complexity. The Dutch were on the whole not aware of the nature of their economic difficulties. In the second half of the eighteenth century they complained loudly that the wealth and greatness of their country were in danger of disappearing. They were inclined to try to restore them rather than to realize that their so-called decline was in certain sense inevitable and signaled the need for them to adapt their social, cultural, and political ambitions to a new era. Eighteenth- and even nineteenth-century observers were obviously incapable of analyzing the phenomenon dispassionately.

However this may be, in the eighteenth century the Dutch did not revise their political traditions or habits. They continued practices that in the seventeenth century had worked more or less satisfactorily, although some modern historians criticize them for a lack of logic and efficiency. It is true that the political system was ambiguous, suffered from internal contradictions, seemed old-fashioned compared to the absolutist style developed in other European countries, and could be easily manipulated to postpone critical decisions. Sovereignty was supposed to reside with the estates of the seven provinces that together formed the republic. These estates were in theory representatives of the people, but in fact they were governing bodies appointed by the aristocratic or patrician corporations, namely, the nobility and the regents or patricians ruling the towns. In the largest and most influential province, Holland, the towns had eighteen votes and the nobility only one. It was not always easy for the provincial estates to make decisions. The towns and the other constituents of the estates enjoyed much independence. Each of them had its own interests to defend, and each was reluctant to contribute to the common means and to further the common good. This reluctance would not have mattered so much if the Dutch had been willing to overrule recalcitrant parties in the decision-making process before having exhausted all possibilities to bring about a consensus. Instead, the usual result was interminable discussion, bickering, and delay.

On the level of the Estates General, the situation was sometimes even more awkward. In theory each of the seven provinces was sovereign and had one vote in the Estates General. In theory, therefore, the seven provinces were equal partners in the alliance, the seven votes carried equal weight, and no one member could be overruled. Unanimity was supposedly required for the most important decisions. In practice, the system worked poorly as soon as the seven sovereign provinces felt themselves obliged by circumstances to act not as members of a mere alliance but as members of a real state, and this they could hardly avoid. In that situation, the enormous dominance of the province of Holland, which contained almost half the population of the republic and which contributed more to the general taxes than all the other provinces together, made the theory seem unrealistic. It is not at all astonishing that, from the point of view of Holland, the rest of the country except for Zeeland and the geographic center, the province of Utrecht, belonged to the outer provinces, politically important because they could not be overruled in the Estates General but otherwise dependencies rather than equal partners in the Seven United Netherlands. Holland put up with a system apparently so inimical to its interests for many reasons, the major one being that an alteration would have undermined the principle of provincial sovereignty and left Holland less influence in its relations with that other republican officer, the stadholder. For Holland to seek constitutional reform for the purpose of institutionalizing its hegemony would entail the establishment of greater unity in the loosely constructed state and might provide the stadholder with more opportunities to increase his power.

The stadholder's position was complicated. Appointed by the various estates, he held a provincial function dependent on the sovereign will of his principals, but several elements bestowed on him a much higher status. The office derived great importance from the fact that during the seventeenth century in Holland, Zeeland, and most of the other provinces only the direct heirs of the immensely popular tradition of William the Silent were appointed as stadholders. In Friesland and sometimes also in Groningen and Drenthe, however, the descendants of a younger brother of William held the office. In the eighteenth century the situation changed. William III had no children, and in the provinces of which he was the stadholder no successor was appointed at his death in 1702. In the ensuing years only the stadholder of Friesland continued the office; but in 1718 this man was also appointed stadholder in the province of Groningen, in 1722 in Drenthe and Gelderland, and finally in 1747 in all other provinces. From that mo-

ment until the fall of the republic in 1795, there was only one stadholder in the state, holding the same hereditary office in the whole
country and acting at the same time as federal general and admiral. It is
easy to see why his function was interpreted both by contemporaries
and historians as a counterweight against the tendencies inherent in the
system of provincial sovereignties, as a unifying force in a state that
lacked a real center. And, although the office included several sovereign
rights such as those of electing urban magistrates, appointing some
provincial officials, and granting pardon or remission of penalties, it
did as a whole not possess sovereign status and would never acquire it
as long as the patriciate of Holland on which the whole republic depended for its survival saw no advantage in replacing its own hegemony with an emerging semimonarchic and unitary power.

During the eighteenth century thoughtful members of the patriciate
as well as more radical agitators considered this system to have become
unworkable, and historians are inclined to agree with them. Yet for all
its deficiencies and ambiguities it had its charms. If it was often inadequate on the national level, it had the merit of leaving a great deal of
autonomy to provinces and towns—the real centers of authority for
the inhabitants. In France the better-equipped and legitimized central
power wrought havoc in provincial and urban government by its spasmodic, inefficient interference in local matters. Without idealizing the
state of affairs and underrating the oppressive character of rule by local
patricians and nobles eager to further their own interests, one may insist on the generally peaceful and quiet nature of their regime. The
fairly coherent and efficient system of local government and local or
provincial jurisdiction kept the country from anarchy; indeed, state
and society were relatively well ordered. Moreover, although a major
aspect of all European eighteenth-century social history was the phenomenon called aristocratization, the Dutch patricians were bourgeois
and remained so for all their pomposity. And it was they who set the
standards and determined the meaning of private and social life, not
merely for their own caste but for the inferiors who imitated their example and repeated their professed ideals. Next to the aristocratization
of parts of the oligarchy, the phenomenon pervading Dutch society as a
whole was *embourgeoisment* of the entire population. Orderliness, re-
spectability, material success, and quiet family life formed the main
elements of the eighteenth-century Dutch concept of happiness, and the
Dutch valued the Enlightenment, or much in the Enlightenment, for
stressing these practical virtues.

A second merit of the traditional system was its flexibility. Political upheavals were certainly not rare. The decisions taken in 1650 and 1702 not to appoint a new stadholder in Holland represented a fundamental change, and the decisions in 1672 and 1747 to appoint a stadholder were no less fundamental. In the seventeenth century the events prompting the regents to take these decisions were dramatic. Both in 1650 and 1672, Holland was on the verge of civil war, yet in both years the changeover from one from of government to another, though far from peaceful, did not develop into turmoil even remotely comparable to the Fronde or the English Revolution. One of the reasons may have been the ambiguity of the whole political system and the vagueness of the constitution, of which the opportunistic patriciate made use to legitimize both the abolition and the reestablishment of the stadholdership. In the eighteenth century the passage from a stadholderian into a non-stadholderian regime in 1702 and out again in 1747 was surprisingly smooth. It is as if the Dutch elites had come to accept this sort of change as a natural element in their constitutional history and no longer worried much about its significance. During the first non-stadholderian period in the 1650s and 1660s, some highly interesting work on the value of republicanism was written, published, and discussed. During the second non-stadholderian period, from 1702 to 1747, there was virtually nothing of the kind.

In the second half of the eighteenth century all this changed. It is not my purpose to give a narrative of the main events, but it is useful here to summarize what happened to the stadholderate during this period because it was in that office that all problems concentrated.

During the 1730s it became clear that the Orange dynasty was gradually building up its position in the republic. In 1729 William, the heir of the Frisian branch of the family, celebrated his eighteenth birthday and took up government in the provinces where the office of stadholder had been preserved: Friesland, Gelderland, Groningen, and Drenthe. Although he had little power there, his presence was felt. In 1734 he married Anne of Hanover, the daughter of King George II, thus continuing the British link first established almost a century before, in 1641, when the young Prince of Orange, William II, married Mary Stuart, the daughter of Charles I. The marriage to Anne indicated that William IV was ambitious to become stadholder of Holland and that the British expected him to succeed. Developments were, however, slow. In the late 1730s, William IV saw no easy access to the highest political and military posts in the republic and there were moments when he and his ambitious wife despaired of ever achieving their aims.

This is not the place to sketch the complicated maneuvers by which some members of the Orange party—first and foremost William Bentinck, son of one of William III's most intimate friends—succeeded in playing the English card with the purpose of furthering William IV's interests. Bentinck persuaded the British government in 1746 to appoint as its ambassador in The Hague a man committed to involving the republic more actively in the War of the Austrian Succession. From 1744, Britain was at war with France, and France began conquering parts of the Southern Netherlands. The Dutch, whose foreign policy had for a generation been preoccupied with preventing the French from taking Belgium, saw the Barrier, which they had built there with Austrian and Belgian money in accordance with the Treaty of Utrecht of 1713, easily overrun. The French, who tried unsuccessfully to keep the republic officially neutral, crossed the Dutch frontier in Zeeland on 17 April 1747. The adherents of the Orangist party reacted promptly. Just as in 1672, there was war again. Just as in 1672, they said, it was inconceivable that war could be won without a stadholder to carry all political and military responsibilities. These opinions, proclaimed loudly and vehemently and reinforced by popular unrest in the towns, worked marvelously. The estates of Zeeland decided on 28 April to appoint William IV as their stadholder. On 3 May those of Holland and Utrecht, and on 10 May those of Overijssel, followed suit; on 12 May the prince made his entry into The Hague.

William IV's rise to power was caused by popular unrest following a French invasion into Dutch territory, as had been William III's seventy-five years previously. The effective Orangist propaganda emphasizing this similarity made the population believe that the new stadholder would soon bring the war to a victorious close and restore Dutch self-respect. This did not happen. Army and fleet were in poor condition and were badly led. Although the Orangists succeeded in making the Holland towns provide substantial financial means, they were unable to equip the military forces adequately, and in 1748 the inconclusive Peace of Aix-la-Chapelle ended a war in which the republic, faced with far less danger than in 1672, had appeared impotent and untrustworthy.

William IV died in 1751 after a short and ineffective reign. This simple fact is of the greatest importance. It is as if during the four years of his reign the predicament of the Dutch state and Dutch society became for the first time so painfully clear that one could no longer ignore the urgency of the problems. Yet, it was extremely difficult to define the nature of these problems. In retrospect it may seem obvious that, although the republic was probably no less prosperous in the mid-eighteenth century than in the mid-seventeenth, it should nevertheless have stepped down from its positon as a major power, reorganized its fiscal system, reduced its expenses, and paid some of its debts. Why should this have been impossible for a country where so much wealth was still available? It was not, however, in these terms that the situation was presented by contemporaries. Both the Orangists and anti-Orangists who strove for reform dreamed not of transforming the republic into the small neutral nation it was to become but of restoring ancient Dutch greatness and power.

William IV was a capable man, well-educated, able to converse in various languages, and willing to concentrate on his political duties, but he was no innovator. It was his destiny to imitate his predecessor. William III had made no attempt to reform the Dutch system of government. He confined himself to collecting as many rights and as much influence as possible without revising the constitution, without trying to redress abuses, without risking a fundamental discussion about the role and place of the regent patriciate. His priority was foreign policy. He needed power and money to fight Louis XIV. William IV, following his example, also succeeded in obtaining much power. He grasped all opportunities to appoint his protégés to important offices and to make the urban administrations obey his orders. The practice of his government did not differ much from that of William III, but he did not use his power for any concrete purpose. The republic could no longer play a great role in international affairs. The growth of other European countries and Dutch demographic and economic stagnation reduced its size. Traditionally, foreign affairs and war had preoccupied all stadholderian regimes and dominated all major clashes between the Orangists and the Estates party. In fact, all the transformations of the Dutch government between stadholderian and non-stadholderian periods had a single cause—a crisis in foreign affairs. In the eighteenth century this was still the case, with one exception in 1702 when circumstances were somewhat different. But in 1747 and during the 1780s, foreign policy and war mattered enormously. And yet, as I have already suggested, there was a fundamental difference between the functioning of these elements in the second half of the eighteenth century and in the previous periods. The power stadholder William IV and later his son William V obtained, which was in theory even greater than that of Frederick Hendrik or William III, was no longer needed to enable the republic to take decisive action in international affairs.

The tragedy of the last two stadholders of Holland was that their education, the precedents, the whole tradition of the dynasty prevented them from drawing any clear conclusion from the basic fact of Dutch impotence—from trying to use their authority for other aims, that is, for reform. The necesssity of reform was urged on them from inside as well as outside their own party, and there was no lack of realistic proposals. Nothing helped. The stadholders refused to become the Dutch equivalent of enlightened despots. Contemporaries as well as historians have regretted this stubbornness and blamed them for missing brilliant opportunities. With the help of that part of the bourgeoisie that had not been able to rise to the ranks of the patrician regents, and of the lower classes of the population among whom they were traditionally most popular, they could, so runs the argument, have reduced the financial, political, and social privileges of the urban ruling class and thus made possible the initiation of policies to distribute fiscal charges more equitably, to reorganize the public debt, to develop schemes for employing paupers in public works, to abolish regulations hindering free trade, to support industrial innovation, to improve public education, to admit dissenters and the middle classes to political offices, and so forth. In doing so, they would have modernized the state and made its subjects happier. The whole complex of enlightened reform put forward by the anti-Orangists could have been realized by the stadholders if they had possessed the intelligence and the courage needed for such bold policies. They would have found sufficient support in the whole population beneath the small oligarchy.

This is an extremely shortened and simplified version of the case against William IV and William V. Before considering it, I summarize the career of William V. He was three years old in 1751 when his father died. In 1766, at the age of eighteen, he assumed the tasks he had inherited, and until his flight in 1795—when the republic was conquered by the French—he performed his duties conscientiously and industriously. A well-educated man, trained in French, German, English, and Latin, he was knowledgeable about military affairs and about the minutest details of Dutch institutions, and he had a lively interest in his collection of paintings and objects relating to the natural sciences. He was a loyal and simple member of the Reformed church. He worked hard, as his father had done and his son, King William I, would do later, but he was inclined to concentrate on details, unable to distinguish the essentials of a problem; he clung to precedent even in semi-revolutionary situations, with the result that he rarely knew what to do in difficult circumstances. He possessed such a doggedness and profound distrust of other people's sincerity that his advisers and even his much more determined wife, Wilhelmina of Prussia, found it hard, or even impossible, to lead him to the decisions he must, but could not, take. He was obviously not the man to deal adequately with the so-called revolt of the Patriots that arose in the republic during the 1780s. His mind was impervious to the idea of reform. Not only did he not tolerate any reduction of his own power, which is understandable enough, he also rejected the suggestion that his office be elevated to semimonarchic, sovereign status. He wanted to preserve the tradition as he saw it, and to use his power not for ruling subjects but for influencing people. He wanted only to exercise his right to appoint friends and clients to high offices and to work for consensus during times of vehement controversy.

The subjects of this volume are decline, Enlightenment, and revolution. What do we understand by "decline"? Usage of this concept in the eighteenth century was the broadest possible. Decline was thought to be total, on all levels, in all human endeavor—moral, economic, social, cultural, political. Moral decline, luxuriousness, idleness, of course formed the deepest cause of the phenomenon; only by returning to the sober, uncorrupted style of the seventeenth century could the Dutch find their way back to a more satisfactory existence. Contemporaries saw nothing fundamentally inevitable in Dutch decline. If the Dutch reverted to their ancient ways, their history would rise again to the high peaks of prosperity and power reached in the seventeenth century. It is clear that William IV and William V made no concrete contribution to solving the problem of a decline defined in this way. They did not use the power they had collected for reform, and with the help of Prussia and Britain William V prevented the Patriots from carrying out designs for enlightened reform. The case against the last two stadholders, formulated by some contemporaries and by some historians, is therefore that as a result of their stubborn and shortsighted conservatism the republic lost the little vitality it still possessed and was doomed to collapse.

Is this a useful proposition? Probably not. The stadholders were asked to initiate reforms not only with the limited purpose of redressing abuses but in order to reestablish Dutch greatness. The republic was still considered a power that mattered, however decrepit it might in fact have become. No longer a major power, it was nevertheless one that could not be ignored, one useful to have as an ally or satellite. It is therefore not at all astonishing that contemporary discussion about reform was not only about a more equitable or, broadly, more democratic distribution of power but also about the consequences such reform would have for the international stature of the state. Some of the suggested reforms had a modernizing character, yet they were expected to contribute to the enhancement of Dutch influence and independence, the restoration of seventeenth-century greatness. Of course, there need not be a contradiction between such elements. It is not unlikely that some of the reforms would have increased the state's potency; the development of the French state after the revolution of 1789 proves this possible. The case of the Dutch Republic was, however, different from that of France. The republic had to adapt itself to the inevitable reduction of its status; this process was by no means what the reformers of that age intended to initiate or to further.

I think we have now touched on the fundamental ambiguity of eighteenth-century Dutch attitudes, an ambiguity that makes it difficult for us to understand the motives and passions of both Patriots and Orangists and to grasp the essence of the concept of decline as defined by contemporary commentators. However imprecise their usage—and how else could it be when the phenomenon it referred to was supposed to encompass the whole of Dutch life?—it had connotations that seem to distinguish it from our own usage. To us decline represents, I think, an inexorable process of diminishing power, health, or energy that may be stopped or slowed for a while but rarely if ever reverses itself. A state, an economy, or a culture in decline may succeed in halting the process, but in such a case we expect it to survive at the lower level, not at the previous high. If we see that a state, a culture, or an economy is merely passing through difficult circumstances but may become vigorous again, we do not, or perhaps should not, use the word "decline." "Setback," "stagnation," or "recession" are probably more appropriate; they are gloomy enough but do not suggest outright doom.

In Dutch, two of the terms used to characterize such situations are *achteruitgang* and *verval*. *Verval*, the stronger one, means "decline, decay, decadence." *Achteruitgang* is less dramatic, equivalent to "retrogression." A person who *achteruitgaat* moves backward, with his face turned toward the point he had reached and from which he now withdraws. Why should he not be able to stop receding and force his legs to go forward again? The movements of a person who *achteruitgaat* are more easily reversible than those of one whose life is declining.

These admittedly frivolous reflections make us more cautious than usual when writing about Dutch decline. But if we accept that the *achteruitgang* that eighteenth-century observers complained about and criticized so much is not equivalent to what we tend to call decline, how then do historians nowadays characterize the development of Dutch society in that period? Are historians, who are better able to analyze the whole phenomenon than their predecessors, justified in using the term "decline" in characterizing the eighteenth-century republic? Modern research has made it abundantly clear that the War of the Spanish Succession (1701–1713) saddled the republic and above all the province of Holland with such an exorbitant debt that political leaders were obliged to reduce miliary and international commitments and to withdraw from the international scene as much as they could. In the 1740s, the War of the Austrian Succession demonstrated that the republic was no longer the great power it had been in the first decade of the century. The Anglo-Dutch war of 1780–1784 was a catastrophe in all respects—a terrible military defeat, a political and economic disaster of awful magnitude, an unprecedented humiliation for a nation that in the seventeenth century had fought three wars against England and won two of them. And if ever decline was made almost palpable, it was surely in 1787 when a Prussian army was needed to restore William V's power in The Hague, a century after the republic supported William III to carry out his Glorious Revolution in England. In 1795 the curtain fell. The Dutch Republic, which for four decades (1672–1713) had successfully repelled the expansionism of the French king, was totally helpless before the army of the French revolutionaries. Why should we not give the Dutch Republic its due place in the long row of ruins we trace through modern history, from seventeenth-century Spain to eighteenth-century Sweden or Poland, to nineteenth-century Turkey or twentieth-century Austria or Britain? On the scene of European history, the corpses of glorious lost empires lie about in sad confusion. Why not acknowledge that the Dutch Republic is one of them?

The difficulty is that, just as Spain or Poland or Britain, Holland is still present—and also wealthier, more prosperous, and, with a population of fourteen million, seven times larger then in the seventeenth century. Nothing today reminds one of the so-called decline of two centuries ago—with one crucial exception: the Netherlands has become an even smaller power than it was in the late eighteenth century. The reduction of its international influence has gone on inexorably in spite of the remarkable economic and demographic growth. Whereas the phenomena indicating that the eighteenth-century republic was losing its vitality turned out not to be durable, its decline as a great power was lasting. In other words, in the eighteenth century the Dutch state "declined" to what was apparently a more normal stature, given its size, than it had been able to adopt in the seventeenth century as a result of the transitory demands of that age. The fact that eighteenth-century observers did not see it this way is easy to explain. The Dutch simply had no experience with small-nation status. Shortly after their state had come into existence in the late sixteenth century, it acquired the responsibilities of a great power. It is not astonishing that its inhabitants felt deeply uncomfortable about the state's chance to survive as an independent entity after its reduction to a much lower status. It is not astonishing either that their desire for reform sprang from a passionate hope to avoid this reduction. For them the ultimate goal of reform was the elimination of the only lasting element in the decline they thought they observed.

This was a formidable paradox. Would William IV and William V have been able to solve the problem by using their excess power for enlightened reform? In a sense, William V's son, the first King William of the Netherlands, was in 1814 given the opportunity to rule a state which, thanks to the incorporation of the industrializing Southern Netherlands, was much stronger than the late eighteenth-century republic. With the support of former members of the Patriot party, he was able to do so vigorously as an enlightened and reforming despot. He indeed used his power for reform policies, and his kingdom possessed international prestige. The two elements that might be considered antagonistic in the eighteenth century—reform and national power—were now seemingly reconciled. And yet William I did not achieve his aims. The Belgians seceded in 1830 and the Kingdom of the Netherlands that remained was an impotent and rather old-fashioned state. Dutch reform movements succeeded only after all dreams of former greatness had evaporated. The Dutch elites had still to learn through humiliation following on humiliation that modernity was attainable only after they had reconciled themselves to the state's new status as a minor power. I suggest that this reconciliation happened only in 1848, when at last a liberal constitution was introduced by which the power of the dynasty was greatly limited. Only then did the Dutch, now generally aware of and resigned to the relative smallness of their influence, permit themselves the luxury of liberal freedom and renewal.

# 2

# The Restoration of the Orangist Regime in 1747: The Modernity of a "Glorious Revolution"

## Jan A. F. de Jongste

O N 17 April 1747, French troops crossed the southern borders of the Dutch Republic. With little effort they overran the neglected Scheldt fortifications and within a few days also overran the southern province of Staats-Vlaanderen. Horror stories told by eyewitnesses and rumors of treason were willingly believed, just as they had been in 1672. And just as in the previous invasion, fear turned the population of Zeeland toward panic and uncertainty. The Orangists, intent on revolution, took advantage of the situation and benefited from the arrival of an English squadron in Zeeland's waters on 19 April. During the night of the 24th, uprisings started in a few cities. Other towns followed, some pushed along by violence. After a few days of incidents and intimidation, the estates of Zeeland appointed Willem Karel Hendrik Friso stadholder and captain general. Thus began the brief stadholderate of Prince William IV.

The Orangist movement spread from Zeeland to the province of Holland, where Rotterdam led the way. In touch with an English agent, a group of artisans assembled a crowd in front of the town hall on 29 April. This was too much pressure for the *vroedschap* (town council), which on that same day proposed to the estates of Holland that the prince be made stadholder. The Hague, too, had become a center of unrest. Within a few weeks, Holland, the most important province in the republic, seemed destined for the Orangist cause.

The Orangists directed their indignation especially at the grand pensionary of Holland, Jacob Gilles, who was said to have bargained away the country in the negotiations with France in 1746. Everywhere things now went smoothly for the Orangists; more and more cities settled for the inevitable, Amsterdam (and Enkhuizen) being the last to accept the stadholder. On 3 May the estates of Holland unanimously accepted the proposal of Rotterdam. The provinces of Utrecht (3 May) and Overijssel (10 May) also seemed willing to follow Zeeland. In Utrecht, some problems did arise, because the regents desired to bind the stadholder with an instruction that would not restrict their own freedom. But William IV refused to agree and demanded completed adoption of the governmental regulation of 1674, which gave generous powers to the stadholder. On 18 May the States of Utrecht also gave in.

Remarkably, William IV contributed little to this revolution. The urgent summonses of advisers, such as Count William Bentinck, begging him to use his personal influence failed. He disliked popular disturbances, although he eagerly accepted the powers handed over to him by the legal authorities. With that his personal ambitions had been fulfilled; from his perspective the revolution should be considered completed for the time being. The only important matter now was simply the continuation of the war. Such opinions did not suit the conceptions of his adviser, the energetic Bentinck, who in an extensive memorandum (summer 1747) urged the reform of government and sought the dismissal of the local republican and anti-Orangist bosses. Soon the adherents of Orange wished to consider the installation of William IV as only a first step to what was generally called, in vague terms, redress. The brief period of William IV's stadholderate (1747–1751) became a time of revolutionary movements, and within them opponents of the sociopolitical order briefly surfaced. Although short, the period merits our attention; it reveals much about the nature of Orangism, the weaknesses of the oligarchic state, and, not least, the conflicting impulses and desires of reformers who looked back to a golden age while attempting the creation of a different and enlightened order.

For a better insight into the nature of the disturbances of 1747, it is important to understand the complicated problem of preconditions, triggers, and precipitants. It is also necessary to analyze the numerous remonstrances and grievances recorded in a multiplicity of petitions, without, it is hoped, devoting too much attention to local grievances. Finally, there is the important problem of modernity. Was this mid-eighteenth-century revolution a mere reprise of the glorious Orangist restoration in 1672, or did it herald the future? Did it look forward to

1787 or backward to an earlier pattern of early-modern rebellions dominated by local interests and the privileges of traditional elites?

## PRECONDITIONS AND PRECIPITANTS

The socioeconomic situation in the middle of the eighteenth century is our starting point. As is well known, the year 1740 witnessed an important change in the long-term trend of prices and wages within the republic. A general price increase set in, and one that was more difficult to absorb because it had been preceded by a long period of downward pressure on prices. For large groups of the population with unchanged or reduced wages, this meant a rapid deterioration of living conditions. Declining employment in a few labor-intensive branches of industry, already evident in the second half of the seventeenth century, added to the level of unhappiness. Research by Jan de Vries, Hubert Nusteling, and others points out that only later in the eighteenth century did a real catastrophe occur. But the 1740s were definitely years of crisis and decline. Nusteling's recent study on prosperity and employment in Amsterdam indicates that, on the basis of migration numbers, the years between 1741 and 1745 formed the lowest point in a larger period of economic decline.[1]

The unfavorable social and economic developments were strongly connected to the European crisis that started in 1739 and became severe in 1740–1741.[2] Insufficient grain supplies and some extremely severe winters caused *taxation populaire* and food riots in the strongly urbanized province of Holland.[3] As a result of the sudden pressure on relief and subsidies, the town governments faced great financial problems. Figures for the cost-of-living index suggest that after 1741 conditions improved, until 1745 when, once again, deterioration set in. Survivors could only fear further decline.[4] The 1740s thus display the

---

1. J. de Vries, *Barges and Capitalism: Passenger Transportation in the Dutch Economy, 1632–1839* (Wageningen, 1978); H. Nusteling, *Welvaart en werkgelegenheid in Amsterdam, 1540–1860: Een relaas over demografie, economie en sociale politiek van een wereldstad* (Amsterdam-Dieren, 1985), pp. 41, 95, 260–261.

2. W. Abel, *Massenarmut und Hungerkrisen im vorindustriellen Europa: Versuch einer Synopsis* (Hamburg-Berlin, 1974). See also J. A. Faber, "Times of Dearth and Famines in Pre-industrial Netherlands," *Acta Historiae Neerlandicae* 13(1980): 51–64.

3. R. Dekker, *Holland in beroering: Oproeren in de 17de en 18de eeuw* (Baarn, 1982), pp. 23–28.

4. Nusteling, *Welvaart en werkgelegenheid*, pp. 260–261, offers price index figures constructed by Jan de Vries on a fixed weighing system.

marks of social disorientation, doubt and fear, not only among people in decaying inner towns in the province of Holland, but also among those in the countryside and rural areas. Cattle plague broke out in 1744 for the second time in the eighteenth century and lasted until 1755, bringing catastrophe to many farmers. It hit after a long period of low prices for agrarian products and high production costs, and rural Holland lacked any financial reserves. As a result, the provincial governments suffered a drastic decrease in tax income.

Pressure increased on government finances as the result of other problems as well. In the 1730s, the government had come to the financial aid of some territories. The cause of their distress lay in the damage to the wooden poles supporting the sea dikes caused by the shipworm. In addition, after 1740 international complications related to the War of the Austrian Succession and the resulting need to strengthen defense caused the republic great difficulty. The rural provinces, unwilling or unable to support the army, expected Holland to equip warships. Holland, however, seemed increasingly less able to meet its obligations. To pay interest and redemption on a loan of three million guilders, the province resorted to an extraordinary exaction, the *personele quotisatie*, a tax on estimated annual income with a minimum of 600 guilders, amounting to a total of 966,000 guilders in 1744—of which Amsterdam paid nearly half. This measure put pressure especially on the upper strata of society, which helps explain why aversion to the system of impositions and excises was not restricted to those of low income.[5]

As a result of these various taxes and calamities, the tax farmers of the 1740s—who were the pivot of the fiscal system—faced diminishing incomes. Out of self-interest they squeezed the population, which in turn resisted. The "tease taxes" were the most unpopular. The lower middle class, formerly taxed only indirectly and then solely on the basis of real consumption, now received an additional assessment. The tax farmers simply adjusted the unfixed line between assessable and non-assessable income or property.

As is not surprising, the belief became widespread that members of the governing elite enjoyed unlawful benefits under the operating fiscal system. Certainly members of the government could dispose of important emoluments on this tax system. In consequence, the oligarchy of the first half of the eighteenth century was not held in high esteem. The

5. W. F. H. Oldewelt, "De Hollandse imposten en ons beeld van de conjunctuur tijdens de Republiek," *Jaarboek Amstelodamum* 47 (1955): 48–80.

highly critical notes of Simon van Slingelandt (1664–1736), as well as sharp criticism from the Orangists (especially after the restoration of the stadholder in 1747), provide important evidence of contemporary perceptions. It is certainly easy enough to infer an extremely bleak picture of legal and governmental abuses. Yet, there are certain imponderables in the historical record. We simply do not know if abuses increased in the first half of the century, nor do we know if the political system was actually affected by what corruption there was. It is essential to attach no overarching value to negative judgments and assertions of victims and opponents. What is obvious, however, is that in the 1740s the ruling regime failed to govern and was unable to solve national or provincial problems.

One of the characteristics of the first half of the century was the growth of the oligarchic system. The number of families competing for power and control of the distribution of administrative offices decreased. It is hard to avoid the impression that the pursuit of posts (*douceurs*) controlled political activity and paralyzed decision making. The oligarchic system was maintained through *contracten van correspondentie* (secret agreements), an office rotation system, and "eternal" calendars for the distribution of offices. In a unique situation in Friesland, for example, a diminishing oligarchy seized power by a systematic control of votes.[6] The concentration of power in this province peaked in the first half of the eighteenth century and was influenced by the fact that a few patrician families had died out. Studies about Zierikzee (Zeeland) and some towns in the province of Holland indicate that the old local governing groups had difficulty sustaining their power as the result of demographic shifts.[7] Sometimes it was necessary to manipulate the traditional admission standards for the *vroedschap* or even set them aside in order to save oligarchic principles. But saved they were.

Oligarchization created ill feelings among the upper class, particularly among those who harbored resentments against oligarchic poli-

6. J. A. Faber, "De oligarchisering van Friesland in de tweede helft van de zeventiende eeuw," *A.A.G.-Bijdragen* 15 (1970): 39–64. See also H. Spanninga, "De regeringsvorm alhier is een van de beste soorten: Oer stimrjocht en regintebewâld yn Fryslân yn de 18de ieu," *It Beaken* 45 (1983): 116–156, and H. Spanninga, "De Friese politieke elite in de 17de en 18de eeuw," in *Frieslands verleden verkend*, ed. J. Frieswijk et al. (Leeuwarden, 1987), pp. 120–133.

7. H. van Dijk and D. J. Roorda, "Sociale mobiliteit onder regenten van de Republiek," *Tijdschrift voor Geschiedenis* 84 (1971): 306–328; H. van Dijk and D. J. Roorda, "Het patriciaat van Zierikzee tijdens de Republiek," in *Archief: Mededelingen van het Koninklijk Zeeuwsch Genootschap der Wetenschappen* (Middelburg, 1980).

cies. Amsterdam merchants and entrepreneurs wished to participate in government. They claimed to have a better understanding of the needs and interests of business than the professional oligarchy. In the nearby shipping town of Hoorn, the local oligarchy terminated all civilian influence by eroding the electoral college of the *boongangers*; in the 1740s these electors were recruited almost exclusively from ex-aldermen and their number was drastically diminished.[8] Even more radical was the earlier (October 1717) decision of the estates of Gelderland to appoint municipal magistrates for life instead of for three years or less, and so to restrict civilian influence. All these measures undertaken decade after decade plus the violent suppression of resistance left deep traces.

In many town councils in Holland, forms of oligarchization developed in which even a minority of the local regents were excluded from power and profits. Sometimes, as in Haarlem, this happened when burgomasters and ex-burgomasters imposed their will on the other regents. More often, the dividing line between power and impotence was rather accidental and whimsical. Apart from that, an alliance between two power groups or factions within a local elite could keep peace within the government.[9]

Neither objections from outsiders nor quarrels among oligarchs posed a real threat to oligarchic power, especially in those provinces that cherished the ideology of *Waare Vrijheid* (True Liberty), of local interests unencumbered by the interventions of a stadholder. One such defense of republican liberty can be read in the posthumously published *Verhandeling van de vrijheit in den burgerstaat* (A Treatise on Liberty in a Civil Society, 1736) of Lieven de Beaufort (1675–1730), a regent from Tholen (Zeeland). De Beaufort argued that sovereignty rested with the people and went on from there (we might think somewhat remarkably) to argue that therefore no reason existed to complain about insufficient influence on government. In opposition to the blessings of the freedom-loving and mixed form of government, he set a monarchy based on slavery and despotism. Defendants of the rights of the House of Orange, of course, protested against De Beaufort's eulogies on True Liberty. Two Frisian adherents of the stadholder

8. L. Kooijmans, *Onder regenten: De elite in een Hollandse stad, Hoorn 1700–1780* (Amsterdam-Dieren, 1985), pp. 52–55.
9. J. A. F. de Jongste, *Onrust aan het Spaarne: Haarlem in de jaren 1747–1751* (Amsterdam-Dieren, 1984), pp. 102–116; J. J. de Jong, *Met goed fatsoen: De elite in een Hollandse stad, Gouda 1700–1780* (Amsterdam-Dieren, 1985), pp. 49–64; M. Prak, *Gezeten burgers: De elite in een Hollandse stad, Leiden 1700–1780* (Amsterdam-Dieren, 1985), pp. 63–86.

wrote their conversational *Schuite-* and *Jagtpraatjes,* which were in turn widely read.[10] Orangists consistently protested the monopoly that adversaries of the stadholderate claimed for the term "Patriots."

Revival of the debate between Orangists and anti-Orangists in the 1730s arose from the apparently favorable prospects of the stadholder of Friesland, the future William IV. On his coming of age, this Frisian Nassau had accepted the stadholderate in Gelderland and Groningen (and Drenthe), as well as in Friesland. In the northern provinces his power was traditionally limited, and it was marginal even in Gelderland, where the instruction of 1722 prevented him from carrying out military and civil functions. The latter especially restricted traditional possibilities of enlarging power in a functional system of patronage. For someone possessing sufficient qualifications to continue the traditions and rights of the House of Orange, this modest position was too small. It remained to be seen only which way William would choose to reach his larger goal, that of becoming stadholder in each of the seven provinces.

The termination in 1732 of the conflict with the Prussian king Frederick William I over the inheritance of the deceased William III increased the prestige of the Frisian stadholder. Committed republicans considered the agreement as proof of the political aspirations of the new Nassau heir, who saw his rights to the Orange title confirmed. Ironically in light of what would happen in 1747, the strongest negative reaction came from Zeeland, which, with Holland's support, thwarted the prince by nullifying the marquisate of Veere and Flushing. So the estates of Zeeland deprived Orange of the chance to build a new and powerful position through the domination of votes in both cities. The possibility that control of a fourth province would put a majority of the provinces under control of the stadholder explains why the Hollanders supported their Zeeland colleagues so strongly in their rejection of Orange. All of this would dramatically change in 1747.

A second personal success that further enhanced William's claim on the stadholderate of all seven provinces was his marriage in 1734 to Anne, a daughter of England's George II. The Frisian Nassaus, who until this time had found their spouses in minor German dynasties, saw their increasing prestige consolidated. Marriage to the daughter of the English king immediately suggested the connection with the previous

10. See I. J. H. Worst, Chapter 6, this volume, and W. R. E. Velema, "God, de deugd en de oude constitutie: Politieke talen in de eerste helft van de achttiende eeuw," *Bijdragen en Mededelingen betreffende de Geschiedenis der Nederlanden* 102 (1987): 476–497.

two Oranges. This, as well as the English expectation for restoration of the stadholderate in *all* provinces and a greater docility on the part of the Dutch Republic, scared even moderate republicans. In a polite, official letter of congratulations to George II, the Estates General made it very clear that the regents embraced continuation of the present condition of the government (*de tegenwoordige gesteldheid onzer Regeeringe*), that is, the condition of being stadholderless. How serious they were became evident when, as stadholder of three provinces, William failed to gain admission to the council of state and did not obtain the highest army post. Thus by 1740 the prince was disillusioned and considering retirement to his German dominions, which had enlarged because some other Nassau branches had died out. His despair in 1740 could hardly have foretold the turn of events in 1747.

All would change, however, as the result of the War of the Austrian Succession. Although the republic tried to avoid the conflict and to give no offense to France, after Walpole's downfall the English pursued an aggressive war policy. Dutch politicians realized that they could not restrict themselves to mere subsidy but had to give military support to Austria. The republic maneuvered itself into an impossible position when, on the one hand, it tried to meet its obligations toward Maria Theresa and, on the other hand, followed a spasmodic neutrality toward France. The untenable nature of the policy became clear when France officially declared war on England and Austria and announced in The Hague in April 1744 that the Southern (Austrian) Netherlands would no longer be spared. The Barrier appeared to be of no worth; fortresses surrendered, some without struggle, and the campaign of 1745 against the French also failed to progress smoothly. The English, preoccupied with the attack launched in Scotland by the Stuart pretender, left the republic entirely to its own defenses. Negotiations with France were attempted in 1746, first alone (in Paris), and later with England (in Breda). There, it became clear to republican leaders that the British had changed policies; they now aimed at the restoration of Orange.

In the republic, the Orangist party had recently recovered its strength. We can sense the renewal of its fortunes from the favorable reception given a particularly sharp piece of Orangist propaganda, *Leonidas* (1742), a battle cry against Dutch neutrality written by the Orangist (and active freemason) Willem van Haren. Despite the vociferous loyalty of some of his followers, William IV could not activate his divided supporters; he merely concentrated on the problem and issues of control and command. This uninspiring attitude annoyed William Bentinck, son of the Duke of Portland, who had once been confidant to William III. The younger Bentinck's origins, coupled with his admiration for the English political system, seemed to destine him for a central part in the new mid-century drama around William of Friesland. His first visit to William and his English wife, toward the end of 1743, signified to outsiders a clear choice in favor of the restoration of the stadholderate. In Bentinck's mind this would lead to a remodeling of Dutch government and the opportunity of installing an anti-French foreign policy. On the basis of these goals, he gradually coordinated the scattered and heterogeneous supporters of Orange and inspired them to make a choice. In 1746, he finally convinced England of the value of intervention. When the earl of Sandwich was sent to the republic as ambassador, it became clear that England had changed its policy: his instruction to get the republic involved in the war meant practical support for the conspiring Orangists.

In the flush of victory after the 1747 restoration, affection for Orange was dominant, although there was a critical undercurrent. This criticism did not come only from republican regents in the tradition of the ideology of True Liberty but also from the socially differentiated Protestant nonconformists (Mennonites, Remonstrants, Lutherans) as well as from Catholics, who still had to be content with second-class citizenship. The Calvinist lower classes traditionally sympathized with Orange; so too did their many Calvinist ministers. Most of the nobility chose in favor of Orange, but some wavered in part because the province of Holland controlled the distribution of many profitable positions, particularly the military ones. Personal motives were important for regents in the cities as well. Those who were kept out of power or could not move up sufficiently in their careers were easy targets for Orangist propaganda. In their frustration, they could envision themselves in the small group of "well-intentioned" Patriots.

TOWNS AND PROVINCES IN UPHEAVAL

Numerous pamphlets glorifying the revolution of 1747 strengthened expectations that war would end and that redress would be available everywhere. When nothing happened, impatience and discord quickly followed. After the conquest of Bergen-op-Zoom by the French in September 1747, pointless acts of violence occurred against Catholic citizens, whose quite understandable lukewarmness or distrust toward the Orangist regime was immediately explained as sympathy for the French. Publicist Jean Rousset de Missy (1686–1762), of Huguenot origin, strongly anti-French and well-known in court circles, seemed to play the main role in the Orangist press campaign. Public opinion was enlisted in the call to reenforce the stadholder's power, according with Bentinck's idea of using popular dissatisfaction to further the goals of the House of Orange. Contacts between court and discontented citizens were used mainly to avoid, or to bring under control, an unacceptable radicalism.[11]

An extraordinary new capital tax, the so-called Liberal Gift, became the concrete starting point for demands and protests in a few towns in Holland (Rotterdam, Amsterdam, Gouda, Haarlem). The demands included the public sale of offices in order to improve the poor financial situation of the republic, as well as the succession of the stadholderate in both male and female lines. Although William IV rebuked his supporters by rejecting the idea of selling public offices, in fact these proposals were an effective way to put pressure on the regents. As a result, the estates of Holland agreed under pressure not only to an arrangement concerning the municipal offices but also to succession in both lines of the stadholderate. This last point, especially succession in the female line, was the object of much criticism and discussion.[12]

Holland's acceptance of female succession was in turn followed by acceptance in Zeeland, Utrecht, and Overijssel. In these provinces, where the stadholderate had been restored a few months earlier, the oligarchy seemed willing to make the best of the inevitable. In Gelderland, Friesland, and Groningen the power of the stadholder had always been limited by tradition or rules. There the opposition against female succession was much stronger than in other provinces. In Gelderland, riots precipitated by the Orangists forced the diet to approve the hereditary stadholderate and return to the regulation of 1675. With the January 1748 amendment that William IV could adjust or change that

11. A. J. Zondergeld-Hamer, "De houding van de Rotterdammers tijdens de gebeurtenissen van 1747 en 1748," *Rotterdams Jaarboekje* (1971): 259; P. Geyl, "De agent Wolters over de woelingen van 1747 en 1748," *Bijdragen en Mededelingen van het Historisch Genootschap* 43 (1922): 66.

12. De Jongste, *Onrust aan het Spaarne*, pp. 145–148, 155–169.

regulation at his discretion, he acquired more power than William III, a position that was confirmed in the governmental regulation of 1750.[13]

A similar development occurred in the northern provinces. The ambition to consolidate the stadholder's power in Groningen, Friesland, and Drenthe was associated, however, with a broad protest and redress movement. The poor economic situation, resulting from the persistent pressure of heavy taxation, brought on disturbances in 1748. In addition to making the stadholderate hereditary and curbing the power of the oligarchy, issues centered on the reform of the tax system and a better check on finances. The joy surrounding the birth of William Batavus, the future William V, in March 1748 brought Groningen to open resistance against the regime of the republican town government and against the unbridled power of the noblemen in the Ommelanden.[14] Representatives of citizens and peasants from the Ommelanden, meeting in Appingedam, put heavy pressure on the estates for a range of demands concerning government, jurisdiction, and taxes. When William IV refused to keep soldiers garrisoned in Groningen and called them away to the war front, the estates relented because they were being deprived of their final support. Here, too, the prince received considerable power to clear away abuses. Here, too, a *reglement reformatoir* shaped the excessive growth of the stadholder's power. This was expressed in a multitude of rights of appointment in November 1749. The main result was probably the admission that a more independent jurisdiction was urgently needed, for the town as well as for the Ommelanden, which took shape in the foundation of the high chamber of justice as court of appeal for the region as a whole. These reforms remained strongly dependent on the wishes of the stadholder to repair inequities in the oligarchic power system. Although there was no talk of actually broadening the social basis of government, the uprisings in this thoroughly divided province curbed some oligarchic excesses.

In Friesland, demolition of the homes of tax controllers was the signal for attacks on the system of oligarchic rule.[15] A June 1748 meeting of about three hundred deputies of cities and *grietenijen* under the guidance of a Mennonite clergyman in the Church of the Jacobines in

---

13. A. H. Wertheim-Gijse Weenink, *Democratische bewegingen in Gelderland, 1672–1795* (Amsterdam, 1973), pp. 96–100.

14. For a recent overview of the developments in the province of Groningen, see W. J. Formsma et al., eds., *Historie van Groningen: Stad en land*, 2d ed. (Groningen, 1981).

15. C. J. Guibal, *Democratie en oligarchie in Friesland tijdens de Republiek* (Assen, 1934), pp. 138–189.

the capital, Leeuwarden, was impressive. The demands made in this meeting—hereditary stadholderate, return to the so-called *poincten reformatoir* of 1672 and 1673, replacement of the system of tax farming by a system of poll taxes, controls on financial conduct—all were sanctioned by the hard-pressed estates of Friesland. Pressure became even greater after deputies from the whole province set up regular meetings in the *Doelen* in Leeuwarden, where they pressed the estates with proposals and demands and advocated the formation of a permanent organ of control.

The court of William IV did not appreciate these kinds of democratically colored experiments and ideas. At the end of July 1748, troops appeared to bring the deputies back into the Orange harness. Meanwhile, the regents were sufficiently broken and thus forced to accept the intervention of the stadholder without complaint. A new instruction granted him nearly boundless nomination rights. Finally, in December 1748, William IV came personally to Friesland, where he proposed a new regulation to the estates that was accepted as a "fundamental and undissoluble law." This *reglement reformatoir*, although containing a few improvements, stayed mostly within the prevailing sociopolitical framework. In case of disagreements, it offered the stadholder the exclusive right of "explication and interpretation," which made the future of reform his responsibility and that of his representatives. Disappointment was everywhere. The oligarchy had to resign itself to the powerful position of the stadholder and to the privileges of a small nobility. There was apparently no room left for new views about representation and control.

Disturbances occurred in Drenthe, too, at first in the north bordering on Groningen, and subsequently elsewhere.[16] Much against the wishes of the government, representatives from all over the district gathered in Schoonlo in June 1748, including men not normally represented in the diet. In fifty-two points of redress, they demanded the hereditary stadholderate in both lines as well as the elimination of all abuses in the financial system and the distribution of offices. An extraordinary session of the diet was forced to accept these demands. Now the movement became more radical. A group of freeholders claimed control of financial management by two independent lawyers, who were also to investigate the behavior of former governments.

16. For Drenthe, see M. G. Buist, "Van oude vrijheid naar nieuwe eenheid, 1748–1850," in *Geschiedenis van Drenthe*, 2 vols., ed. J. Heringa et al. (Meppel, 1985), vol. 1, pp. 475ff.

Moreover, they sent invitations to all parishes for a general meeting on finances.

In reply to cries of distress from the hard-pressed authorities, William IV at last sent word that he would allow no one to arbitrarily convene such meetings and reserved for himself the right to make improvements. He supported his words with troops. Another meeting of representatives in Schoonlo in November 1748 provided William IV with great powers—with which the diet agreed—despite opposition from the nobility. Only in the fall of 1749 did deliberation with three commissioners of the prince lead to the formulation of a regulation that brought some improvements, mainly in the sphere of finances and offices, but ignored many other demands. Abuses in the distribution of offices (cumulation and appointment of minors) were not positively forbidden and the freeholders did not get a better hold of financial management. Continuation of the system of tax farming met no opposition. Public expenditures had begun falling after the Peace of Aix-la-Chapelle, and economic conditions were improving. Another important factor was that, especially in these typical rural areas, tax farmers could not allow themselves excesses in the region where they also lived. In the disturbances in Drenthe, the most active role was played by wealthy peasants who, though sufficiently qualified for the diet, were not part of the government in their own region.

Despite these events in Drenthe and elsewhere, those in Holland and especially in Amsterdam in the summer and fall of 1748 have drawn most of the historiographic attention.[17] They were of greater interest for internal political relations than were the disturbances in the country provinces. Because of the unrest of the north, a fierce outburst arose against the houses and offices of the tax farmers. The troubles began in Haarlem, a textile city in decline, and jumped successively to Leiden, also hit by unemployment, The Hague, and Amsterdam (all within a few days of one another), which had been restless for several days. Trouble also affected parts of the countryside. Civic militia in the towns failed; the soldiers, mainly members of the lower middle class, refused to protect the tax farmers and in fact found fault with the tax

---

17. F. G. Slothouwer, *Bijdrage tot de geschiedenis der Doelisten* (Leiden, 1875); N. J. de Voogd, *De Doelistenbeweging te Amsterdam in 1748* (Utrecht, 1914); P. Geyl, *Revolutiedagen te Amsterdam (Augustus-September 1748): Prins Willem IV en de Doelistenbeweging* (The Hague, 1936); A. Porta, *Joan en Gerrit Corver: De politieke macht van Amsterdam (1702–1748)* (Assen, 1975), especially pp. 226–268. F. J. L. Krämer published some documents in the *Bijdragen en Mededelingen van het Historisch Genootschap* 23 (1902), 26 (1905), and 28 (1907).

system. Their refusal to apply force caused the governments of Leiden and Haarlem abruptly to change tactics. Tax farming was to be abolished and collection suspended.

With the sudden illness of the prince and the absence of Bentinck, decision making at court bore an inprovisational character. A Frisian court dignitary sent to Haarlem in great haste tried to get the situation under control by encouraging all companies of the civic militia to record their grievances and wishes. A few days later he returned to The Hague with a whole series of divergent and even contradictory demands regarding taxes, the position of the *krijgsraad* (commanding officers of the civic militia), civic offices, and guilds; most of them were closely related to the decline of the textile industry.[18] Because unrest continued as long as tax farming existed, the experiment of an organized petition movement was not repeated in Leiden.

In Amsterdam, burgomasters asserted that there could be no consideration of abolishing tax farming as long as there was no agreement about a new tax system. Here too the civic militia refused to protect tax farmers' homes against plunder. Yet, after the homes of other civilians were threatened, the officers renewed their control over the militia. A shooting occurred and two ringleaders were captured and hanged after a short investigation. In contrast to the lenient policies of the bewildered Haarlem and Leiden regents, the Amsterdam authorities took a firmer course. Haarlem's weak and irresponsible management was sharply condemned in the estates of Holland. Bentinck returned hastily from Aix-la-Chapelle and succeeded, with the help of a few members of the Orange party (among them the pastry cook Laurens van der Meer), in keeping Rotterdam quiet.[19] There was an increasing chance for more unrest here and elsewhere. People were nevertheless surprised when on 25 June William IV personally proposed in the estates of Holland that tax farming be abolished immediately. This proposal became fact on the following day, when it appeared that Amsterdam did not want to oppose it at all.

A variety of grievances and demands arose during the troubles in the northern provinces and in Haarlem. In coffeehouses and in pamphlets, the ruling oligarchy was sharply criticized by a small group of Orange activists. In Amsterdam, questions the prince had broached regarding the distribution of offices and the transfer of the postal service

18. De Jongste, *Onrust aan het Spaarne*, pp. 179–236.
19. Zondergeld-Hamer, "De houding van de Rotterdammers," p. 275; see also Porta, *Joan en Gerrit Corver*, p. 255.

(on which point Amsterdam had refused to give in) became starting points for more radical demands. The Eleven Articles stipulated that the *krijgsraad* should be chosen by and from the citizenry, which also was to appoint the directors of the East India and West India companies. The apparent object of this program, which allowed prominent nonregent citizens to participate in government, was to deal a heavy blow to the power of the Amsterdam regents. This aim fit well with the opinions of Bentinck, who in mid-July 1748 attacked the stubborn attitude of the Amsterdam regents and pointed out the need for action.[20]

Many Orangists objected to the radicalism of the Eleven Articles. To give the movement a more moderate character, they called on Laurens van der Meer of Rotterdam, who was a moderating influence and who evidently developed some useful contacts in Amsterdam. His intervention resulted in the transfer of the postal service to the prince, elimination of abuses in the distribution of offices, and the restoration of the rights of the guilds and election of the *krijgsraad* from among the citizenry. After some minor changes, Princess Anne gave her approval to this moderate program. Conflicts arose over the question of how strong the demands would have to be; after 9 August this battle was fought in meetings in the Kloveniersdoelen, formerly the building of the civic militia. Thus the Amsterdam Orangist supporters of radical persuasion have come to be known as *Doelisten*.

Most prominent among the *Doelisten* was the Haarlem designer Hendrik van Gimnig, who in bombastic speeches avowed his belief in radical solutions. He got the majority of the audience on his side through oratorial talent. He derived his inspiration from contacts with Rousset de Missy (see Chapter 10), who himself kept in the background. Van der Meer won the support of Daniel Raap, who played an active role during the fall of 1747. The latter soon acquired personal contacts at court, which greatly benefited the moderate program. The minimal cooperation of the Amsterdam town council was in fact advantageous to the radical *Doelisten*. Van Gimnig and his followers organized throughout the city at the various meetings of delegates and, moreover, they found allies among the ships' carpenters.[21] Their marches through the town created a great deal of pressure on the regents. Increasingly, they sought the removal of the old cliques by a

20. *Archives ou correspondance inédite de la Maison d'Orange-Nassau*, 4th series, vol. 1, ed. Th. Bussemaker (Leiden, 1908), p. 220.
21. A. J. Deurloo, "Bijltjes en klouwers," *Economisch- en Sociaal-historisch Jaarboek* 34 (1971): 4–71.

personal act of the stadholder. The burgomasters opposed the radicals' program as long as possible, but late in August they realized the futility of any further resistance. Burgomasters and town councillors put their seats at William's disposal and invited him to restore law and order. On 31 August, official authorization came to change the magistracy, if necessary, according to town privileges.

In the final phase, Bentinck, the power behind the scenes, maneuvered skillfully. During a brief visit to Amsterdam he explained to Van der Meer, Raap, and Van Gimnig that they should be available for service to the cause when needed but that the prince would solve all problems himself. When the latter arrived in town by 2 September, he realized that the movement would grow more radical each day. Forced by Bentinck and civic delegates, William had to intervene more strongly than he previously thought necessary. With the changes in magistracy, the leading group was discharged and newcomers, selected from wealthy merchants outside the oligarchy, came into the town council. Some of them maintained close relations with the court or with the leaders of the *Doelisten*. The stadholder acquired a limited right of recommendation for the appointment of burgomasters and alderman, but this was not affirmed on paper. William IV caused great confusion in connection with the position of the *krijgsraad*. For a time, he gave the impression that he accepted the principle of independence with respect to town government, and during his stay uproarious elections even took place. In a last, notorious proclamation he acknowledged the election results, but the future council composition was to be positively linked to existing "privileges, old constitutions, regulations and traditions," and no meetings could be held without permission of the burgomasters.[22] Still, the issue of reform did not end with this proclamation.

Unrest developed in other towns in Holland, too. As in 1672, two commissioners, authorized by the estates, traveled from town to town to remove the old magistracy, to nullify institutional changes made during the period without a stadholder, and to adjudicate the numerous local grievances and claims that had arisen in the petitions. It was often within the civic militia that dissatisfaction took shape. Moreover, unrest was often combined with sharp controversy within the circle of regents (in Haarlem and Gouda, for instance), where connections developed between a discontented minority of regents and rebel-

22. Geyl, *Revolutiedagen*, pp. 127–130.

lious citizens outside their ruling circle.[23] In Leiden, civic delegates ("speakers" from the sixty-four quarters of the city, with ten "chief speakers") dominated the streets for a while. At first William IV intervened only mildly, but he was forced to commit troops to restore order in November 1748.[24] More than a year later, a similar disturbance happened in Haarlem, where the return of the old consumption taxes—now collected by officially appointed collectors—was sharply opposed.

William IV died in October 1751, at just forty years of age. Next to nothing was left of the élan of his initial years or of his personal popularity, especially in the middle classes and probably within some intellectual circles as well. The reform movements that had crystallized around William—however much he sought to avoid change—may be said to have died with him. Neither radicals nor moderates had accomplished their goals, and that failure had implications decades to come.

### REDRESS AND REFORM: A SERIES OF RELATED DEMANDS

A few general remarks provide context for an analysis of the program of redress as it appeared in petitions and pamphlets. Hundreds of grievances and demands, not just one program, were put forward. People frequently acted and reacted in response to local and possibly regional circumstances, and a brief survey can scarcely do justice to the diversity of these small-scale developments. Nevertheless, the different demands had a common character, which originated in organizational contacts between the Orangist supporters and a reform-minded court circle. After the consolidation of power, these contacts were to find their ideological expression in an Orangist patronage and clientage system.

In contrast with later decades, newspapers did not play a significant role in the spread of ideologies. In 1747–1748, their existence and content were subject to governmental scrutiny. The mostly anonymous pamphlets and some monthly magazines had some influence, although exactly how much is difficult to estimate. The *Nederlandsche Jaerboeken*, which had started in 1747, focused on all of the United Provinces and gave monthly information complete with documents and

---

23. For Haarlem, see De Jongste, *Onrust aan het Spaarne*, pp. 242–253. For Gouda, see De Jong, *Met goed fatsoen*, pp. 59–77.
24. P. J. Blok, *Geschiedenis eener Hollandsche stad*, vol. 3, *Onder de Republiek* (The Hague, 1916), pp. 155–163.

moderate republican comments. The local *Groninger Nouvellist*—Orange-minded, though not without criticism—was also eagerly bought elsewhere.[25] Great surveys such as *Het ontroerd Holland* and *Nederlands wonder-toneel* certainly contributed to a sense of collectivity and coherence.[26]

One of the major issues addressed by all these publications was the extent of the stadholder's power. In the fall of 1747, a hereditary stadholderate in both lines was part of a Orangist policy. Bentinck expected a lot from it: "If you consider all the consequences of this step, how it puts an end to all hopes of future cabals and partys, in case the Prince should come to fail, what additional strength it gives to our party, what a dependency it puts the magistrates of the towns . . . , you will judge that this is as great a *coup de parti* as the election of the Stadholder."[27] These words are significant. They tell us about the spirit with which Bentinck tried to influence the stadholder's policy; they also suggest why republican regents disapproved of a hereditary stadholderate. Even among some Orange supporters, heredity in the female line was controversial mainly because it was seen as an uncertain bill drawn on the future. In Orangist ideology, however, there was no doubt concerning female succession. Both the appointment rights and heredity were part of the plan to reduce the power of the oligarchy. In Orangist circles, the possibility was also raised of offering William IV the title of Count of Holland. This idea, however, was put aside as unrealistic.

A strong stadholdership meant a counterweight to the oligarchy, as numerous Orangist propagandistic writings had always claimed. Many activists, however, saw it also as an instrument to break the oligarchy. For his part and in contrast, William IV merely used his accumulated power to establish a completely dependent and therefore pro-Orangist oligarchy that could be forced to act according to directions given by intermediaries (the so-called premiers). This patronage system permitted neither a widening of the social basis nor a control system as

---

25. See Geyl, *Revolutiedagen*, p. 157; De Jongste, *Onrust aan het Spaarne*, p. 310.

26. *Het ontroerd Holland, of kort verhaal van de voornaamste onlusten, oproeren en oneenigheden die in de Vereenigde Nederlanden in voorige tijden en allerbijzonderst in deze laatste jaaren zijn voorgevallen*, 3 vols. (Harderwijk, 1748–1750); *Nederlands wonder-toneel, geopent in de jaren 1747 en 1748*, 2 vols. (Leiden, 1749).

27. *Briefwisseling en aantekeningen van Willem Bentinck, Heer van Rhoon (Tot aan de dood van Willem IV, 22 oktober 1751)*, ed. C. Gerretson and P. Geyl, Werken uitgegeven door het Nederlands Historisch Genootschap, 3d series, 85 (The Hague, 1976), p. 301.

had been desired by radical reformers. As a result, the name of Orange soon lost popularity.

The many petitions and demonstrations in 1748 give clear evidence of a widespread desire that government no longer be the prerogative of a privileged small group. In Drenthe the main purpose was to broaden the oligarchy into an aristrocracy of freeholders with greater influence in financial management. In this effort to redistribute power, the lower classes (small peasants, day laborers, craft workers, and the inhabitants of the peat colonies) provided the activists.[28] People in the city of Groningen, recalling the past, claimed restoration of the rights of the *taalmannen* and *gezworen gemeente*, which were seen as real representatives of the citizenry set against the decadent oligarchy.[29]

From the viewpoint of the modernity of the Orangist revolution, the events in Friesland appear to be of greater relevance than those in the other provinces.[30] With regard to local matters in the countryside (such as the election of Protestant ministers), petitioners asked for an increase in the number of people entitled to vote but no alteration in the administrative structure. Essential changes were proposed on the provincial level. First of all, the Frisian *Doelisten* demanded that the composition of the estates be changed to give the freeholders, together with the members of the town councils, a majority in the diet. The reformers also sought the establishment of a committee of representatives (two *burgergecommitteerden* from each *grietenij* and town) to check whether the governmental regulation was observed, to oversee the finances, and to present measures in different fields to the estates. This totally new democratic institution would operate along with the traditional representational institution, the States.

In Holland, where a limited number of committee elections were held (Leiden; Amsterdam, 1748; Haarlem, 1750), no action on a provincial level occurred. A few contacts existed between *Doelisten* from the different towns, but these were largely the result of initiatives taken by the court, which used the activists for its own purposes.[31] In some towns, including Haarlem, Schiedam, and Brielle, there was a call for expansion of the town council. The purpose was, in fact, only to roll back the reductions in its size that had been made in the stadholderless period. The claim had nothing to do with democratization.

28. Buist, "Van oude vrijheid," p. 481.
29. *Nederlands wonder-toneel*, p. 497.
30. Guibal, *Democratie en oligarchie*, p. 162ff.
31. For example, the Rotterdam Orangist Laurens van der Meer was sent to Amsterdam.

More revolutionary than the proposals to expand the town councils were some propositions from the radical Amsterdam *Doelisten,* grouped around Rousset de Missy. These included election of the town council by the citizenry from the wealthiest and richest citizens and of the burgomasters from that council. For Rousset this was the embodiment of an enlightened political radicalism.[32] His less intellectual supporters based legitimacy on the past. That past was idealized by citing the role of the civic militia in the year of the *Satisfactie* (1578), when Amsterdam became part of the revolt against Spain, and by the fact that in the 1672 Orangist restoration such claims were also made. The democratic quality of the radical demands was later somewhat mitigated; civic delegates (*burgergecommitterden*) would be allowed to act as electors for the town government together with the captains of the militia.[33] The claim was probably no more than an attempt to create a permanent role for the civic delegates, the shibboleth of the Amsterdam radicals.

Representative of the effort to limit oligarchic practice was the demand for a free *krijgsraad.* Militia officers would then no longer be elected from the *vroedschap* but from the citizen nonregents. In the most extreme proposals, they would be elected by the civic militia. Without the regents, the *krijgsraad* would become an independent organ alongside the town government and as a representative institution would serve the interests of the citizens. The creation of such a political structure, based on the dualism of *vroedschap* and *krijgsraad,* would have been unfortunate. For many citizens in the mid-eighteenth century, however, its realization was the highest political ideal, not only because of its democratic character but more so because the claim was legitimated by vague reminiscences of a past when the militia, as a civic organization, had been consulted in political matters. This practice had officially come to an end in 1581 by a resolution of the estates of Holland.[34] Its memory, however (as also was evident in 1672), survived in a troubled and vague form. In Holland the impulse for democratic reform progressed differently from that in the northern provinces, where a democratic tradition (as in Friesland) and even democratic in-

---

32. Margaret C. Jacob, *The Radical Englightenment: Pantheists, Freemasons and Republicans* (London, 1981), p. 237ff.

33. De Voogd, *De Doelistenbeweging te Amsterdam,* p. 169.

34. J. C. Grayson, "The Civic Militia in the County of Holland, 1560–81: Politics and Public Order in the Dutch Revolt," *Bijdragen en Mededelingen betreffende de Geschiedenis der Nederlanden* 95 (1980): 35–64; also, de Jongste, *Onrust aan het Spaarne,* pp. 132, 220–223, 287–288.

stitutions—however much deteriorated and eroded—directed the call for reform.

If the power of the oligarchy could not be checked, then at least its networks of patronage could be eliminated or curtailed. The regents' distribution of governmental and high military functions as well as numerous municipal offices became the target of sharp criticism, focused mainly on nepotism and favoritism, the appointment of minors, unqualified persons, and foreigners, and other abuses. The conviction that this system of simply giving accrued wealth to the regents led, in Holland in the fall of 1747, to the advocacy of the public sale of offices.[35] The provisional arrangement set up in Holland (November 1747–January 1748) forced the town governments to supply a complete list of all municipal offices and demanded that the appointees fulfill their posts themselves. As an investment fund, the small municipal offices lost appeal when substitutes were no longer allowed. The regents were indeed restricted in their influence on the conferral of offices, but they suffered no substantial defamation of rights. They could still acquire a clientele.

In the northern provinces the *Doelisten* joined the battle against bestowal of the highest political and military functions and against abuses in payment. In Friesland they asked for a commission to investigate the problem of surplus offices and professional salaries.[36] By advocating a system of public sale rather than private patronage, reformers sought to open offices to the economically qualified, not simply to the well born or well connected. Like so many demands, this one came to nought.

## FINANCES, TAXES, TRADE, AND INDUSTRY

It is understandable that, in these years of diminishing revenues and high expenses, financial management came under scrutiny. In Leiden a

35. In Antwerp and other towns in the Austrian Netherlands, public sale of offices was common practice; see P. Geyl, *Geschiedenis van de Nederlandse stam*, 6 vols. (Amsterdam-Antwerp, 1962), vol. 4, p. 1108. In the fall of 1747, the idea of public sale was popular, especially in Rotterdam, which led the way; see Zondergeld-Hamer, "De houding van de Rotterdammers," pp. 258–264. The historian Jan Wagenaar opposed the demand in his *De Patriot* (10 October and 14 November 1747); see *Verzameling van historische en politieke tractaaten*, vol. 2 (Amsterdam, 1780), pp. 154–163, 191–199. After condemnation by William IV, the idea of public sale generally disappeared, although it still found adherents in Haarlem up to January 1750; see De Jongste, *Onrust aan het Spaarne*, pp. 225, 316.

36. *Nederlands wonder-toneel*, 518, XI (Groningen), 514, VI (Friesland), 623–624, XXIII and XXXVIII (Drenthe).

yearly financial accounting was called for; in Gouda the request was for an official inquiry into deductions from the *personele quotisatie* (an extraordinary tax from 1742) and the *verponding* (real estate tax). That this mistrust was justified became obvious in Gorinchem, where some regents fraudulently benefited themselves.[37]

The years 1748 and 1749 were a golden time for the financial planners, who distinguished themselves by their inventiveness as they juggled population numbers, classifications, and figures. All projects started from an assessement of wealth, without consideration of consumption. There was no coherent system in which theoretical premises and economic results contributed.[38] In Holland the new *provisioneel middel* (provisional tax) seemed to have no success. The provinces, which under pressure had hastily discarded the old system, simply retraced their steps.[39] The tax farmers were replaced with collectors paid by the government. Agitation against the tax farmers did not result in abolition of the farming system in Zeeland (where no unrest occurred after the revolution), Gelderland, or Drenthe. The stimulus to inventiveness was diminished by improved economic prospects and successful retrenchment. Modernization of the tax system nationally would be settled only half a century later. Trade and industry did not fare much better.

Against the background of a deteriorating economic climate in the 1740s, citizens of Haarlem and Leiden insisted on support for the textile industry, which was suffering.[40] The Haarlem petitioners in particular opposed contracting to rural areas of Brabant the most labor-intensive stages of production. They also turned against the board of *geauthoriseerden* (authorized people), which settled conflicts between manufacturers and laborers over wages and conditions of employment, since it consisted solely of factory owners and was not impartial. The insertion of "foreigners" in the production process was sharply criticized as not conforming to the old charters and ordinances. If the charters and regulations were not honored, the basis for the relationship between laborers and manufacturers would vanish. The Haarlem

37. For Leiden, see Blok, *Geschiedenis eener Hollandsche stad*, vol. 3, pp. 158–159, and *Nederlands wonder-toneel*, 701, VIII. For Gouda, see *Nederlands wonder-toneel*, 731, VI. For Gorinchem, see *Nederlands wonder-toneel*, 739–743, and *Memorien van Mr. Diderik van Bleyswijck, burgemeester van Gorinchem, 1734–1755*, ed. Th. Jorissen, Werken Historisch Genootschap, new series, 45 (Utrecht, 1887).

38. Guibal, *Democratie en oligarchie*, pp. 179–182, 185–187.

39. For general information on the provisional tax, see De Jongste, *Onrust aan het Spaarne*, pp. 288–293.

40. Ibid., pp. 228–232; Blok, *Geschiedenis eener Hollandsche stad*, pp. 158–159.

petitioners regarded the restoration and strengthening of the guild system as a means of regaining a secure living and preventing further economic deterioration. Especially in the export-directed textile industry, the guild pattern was deeply affected by the appearance of early capitalistic industry under the management of export-providing entrepreneurs.

Restoration of the guilds, mainly the craft guilds, was an issue in the northern provinces as well. Vaguely formulated in petitions, the issue was how to avoid abuses such as corruption in the admission of new members, the bungling and poor trading practices of street vendors, and the predominant influence of the regents in the boards of guilds. It is likely that vague notions about former political influence played a minor role. It was believed that the strict maintenance of the guilds would lead, by itself, to the return of the former golden times. How dazzled these reformers were by the ostensible splendor of an idealized past!

There was also a free-market–oriented and therefore future-looking vision. The Frisians claimed that a good regulation must ensure "that the guilds be no burden but a comfort on the common people and to the benefit of artists and craftsmen." This suggests support for the guild structure but hints that not everyone was convinced of its usefulness. There was also a desire in Friesland that all be free "to start such factories as they please." Haarlem asked not only for the unobstructed establishment of industries, which would advantage employment, but also for a system of *free* weekly markets, where prices would be set through free competition and admission for merchants from other places would be unlimited. This meant regulating and legalizing all sorts of sales methods.[41]

The protest against the lack of freedom and openness pointed clearly to the future. In this connection, a manuscript note from Van Gimnig calls for special mention. Van Gimnig wanted to restrict the guilds' rigid exclusiveness and monopolistic character and advocated a more democratic structure. This is a more critical attitude toward the guilds than was expressed in the petitions, one probably originating in Van Gimnig's professional contacts as a designer with textile factory owners, who strongly opposed restrictive guild regulations. In another note, Van Gimnig acknowledged the worth of trade activities but argued that industry and agriculture should be the bases of economic life.

---

41. Guibal, *Democratie en oligarchie*, pp. 169, 162; De Jongste, *Onrust aan het Spaarne*, pp. 163–165, 231–232, 273.

The effort to lower production costs would benefit from the application of "mechanics of toolcraft" as well as from scientific methods developed in new "scientific academies."[42] These issues of the free market and mechanical inventiveness would be raised again in later decades.

Both of Van Gimnig's notes are part of an extensive list of proposals, most of which reached the court after the Peace of Aix-la-Chapelle and promised redress in many fields of economic activity. Many figured in the preparation of the "Propositie voor een gelimiteerd porto franco" (proposition for a limited free zone) for which Amsterdam and Rotterdam merchants acted as advisers (1751). Thomas Hope of Amsterdam gave a definite shape to this ambitious plan to consolidate the staple market.[43] After ample discussion and sharp differences, the proposition disappeared. The economic Patriots would choose another way to redress the situation.

## RELIGION AND REVOLUTION IN THE AGE OF ENLIGHTENMENT

The revolution of 1747 and the subsequent agitation bore a significantly Calvinist character. Just as in 1672, Dutch Reformed ministers ostentatiously chose the side of Orange, and anti-Catholic riots took place in many areas in May and September. In the petition movement there repeatedly emerged an outspoken Reformed point of view; Rotterdam supporters of the public sale of administrative offices claimed in autumn 1747 that buyers should be members of the Dutch Reformed church.[44] High on the list of demands was the observance of existing rules concerning religion. Not only in Drenthe and the city of Groningen, but also in Leiden and Schiedam, cursing, swearing, and desecration of the Sabbath were considered evils. Groningen was unique in insisting on measures against the influx of Catholic foreigners, mostly

---

42. National Archives, The Hague (ARA), Stadhouderlijke secretarie, 579: *Generaele regel op welke men alle kamers of gildens zoude kunnen schikken, overgegeeven door H. Gimnigh*, 6 April 1749; 532: *Generaale gronden, op welke men de negotie, alsmede het algemene welzyn door het opregten van een Commercie Raad zoude kunnen herstellen en bevorderen, alsmeede verschyde aanmerkingen tot redres opgedragen* (6 April 1749). Van Gimnig's notes are mentioned in J. Hovy, *Het voorstel van 1751 tot instelling van een beperkt vrijhavenstelsel in de Republiek (Propositie tot een gelimiteerd porto-franco)* (Groningen, 1966), pp. 280–281, 290, 315–316.

43. See J. Hovy, *Het voorstel van 1751*.

44. Zondergeld-Hamer, "De houding van de Rotterdammers," pp. 259–260.

from Westphalia.[45] There was undoubtedly a Reformed contribution in the unrest of these years. But did Protestant nonconformists (that is, non-Calvinists) and Catholics keep to the side in emphatic aloofness?

Although no quantitative information is available, it seems certain that the Mennonites played a prominent role in Friesland. They provided the chairman for the meeting of delegates in the Church of the Jacobines in Leeuwarden. They were no doubt worried about Calvinist fanaticism, since one of their clergymen had gotten into trouble as a result of Calvinist accusations. In Holland, Catholics voiced their concerns in general petitions. In Leiden as well as in Gouda, they attempted to free funds spent to ensure their freedom of worship and wanted to use them instead on Catholic poor relief.[46] In Haarlem, they grew from critical reserve in 1747 to evident participation in the movement of January 1750. At that time, one of the eight civic delegates was a Catholic tobacconist. It is remarkable that in 1754 a prominent Catholic penetrated the *krijgsraad* of the totally reorganized civic militia. Some lower officers' ranks were also filled by Catholics. These appointments brought intentional exclusion of Catholics in the management of the civic militia to an end.[47] In other towns in Holland, this was only possible in the 1780s.

## CHARTERS AND PRIVILEGES

In the northern provinces as well as in Holland, there was a call for maintenance of the old laws, charters, and privileges and also of guild bylaws. In a few towns in Holland, there was a call to publicize these documents in order to protect their effectiviness through the vigilance of the citizenry.[48] In 1672, too, such reforms had been heard, and William III had even agreed in a single case, although no authorized editions appeared. In 1748, renewed interest caused publication of some volumes with charters and privileges for various towns, among them Amsterdam (a reprint of a pamphlet from 1672) and Haarlem. The demands for restoration and publication of the privileges are the most striking testimony of the traditionalism that directed public thinking.

45. *Nederlands wonder-toneel*, 621 (Drenthe), 497–498 (Groningen), 700 (Leiden), 747 (Schiedam).

46. Ibid., 700 (Leiden), 732 (Gouda).

47. De Jongste, *Onrust aan het Spaarne*, pp. 200–203, 259–262, 317, 355.

48. *Nederlands wonder-toneel*, 690 (Haarlem), 701 (Leiden), 731 (Gouda), 746 (Schoonhoven), 748 (Schiedam).

Other sounds, though weaker, could be heard for which no thoughts of the past formed a guideline. Sometimes these progressive voices were guided exclusively by what the "law of nature and of the peoples" prescribed, by what was "reasonable" or "fair" or "good and useful in the common interest." In this way the "novelty" of an independent board of the civic militia was defended. In pamphlets from 1747 and 1748, they cited Voltaire and the sovereignty of the people in a plea for the right to choose a new government. Also invoked were William Temple (*Essay on the Origin and Nature of Government*) and John Locke.[49] By order of Bentinck, Rousset de Missy tried to reprint the French edition of Locke's *Two Treatises*.[50] The *Doelisten* leader Van Gimnig, not publicly but in his memorandum about the guilds in 1749, dismissed the traditional and quasi-historical arguments rampant in previous years: "Everyone, more blind than a mole, searched for his salvation there where it could not be found or lost." Do we hear the echo of Montesquieu in the opinion "that one has to adapt the laws to the circumstances and the character of the people and not the people and its circumstances to the laws"? Not the antiquity of the laws but their intrinsic "merits and usefulness" should tip the scales.[51] However awkwardly it may have been formulated, here the future glimmered.

In 1747 and later, both the reform-minded citizens and the Orangist court was inspired by the events of 1672–1674. The restoration of William III, the uprisings and petitions, the removal of local political leadership, the governmental regulations, and the establishment of a well-organized system of patronage were taken as leading examples. In 1742, the year of Willem van Haren's *Leonidas*, a reprint of Petrus Valkenier's *'t Verwerd Europa* (1675) presented a positive and flattering description of the events of 1672. A knowledge of those events, it was believed, would give the radical elements a chance to avoid the errors of the past. In Friesland, the regulations of 1672 and 1673 were considered the basis of reform, but there were important adjustments and corrections. There was no question of a mere reprise of 1672.

Dominant in the movements and demands of 1747–1748 was a premodern mentality. People looked back to a lost golden age rather than forward to a better life. Revitalization, renovation, and redress were the key words of their essentially conservative ideology. The glory

---

49. N. Japikse, "De aard der volksbewegingen van 1747 en 1748," *De Gids* 4 (1910): 322ff.; Hovy, *Het voorstel van 1751*, p. 289.
50. Jacob, *The Radical Enlightenment*, p. 236.
51. ARA, Stadhouderlijke secretarie, 579: *Generaele regel*, especially 1–4.

of the past inspired and legitimized their actions and program. Perez Zagorin has called this "the ideology of the normative past." He is, however, fully aware that this is not the only sort of ideology to be found in premodern revolutions, and that the relation between renovation and innovation is a rather complicated one.[52]

The backward-looking demand for reform of the *krijgsraad* was actually an imaginative effort to create an independent, "democratic" institution beside the oligarchic *vroedschap*. In spite of the dominant role of the regulations of 1672 and 1673 in the Frisian movements, the requirement of an elected committee of representatives to keep a check on the provincial estates was a real innovation. Thus, conservative ideology could lead to innovative demands. As John Elliott once put it, "renovation in theory does not of itself preclude innovation in practice; and the deliberate attempt to return to the old ways may lead men, in spite of themselves, into startlingly new departures."[53] The regime restored in 1747, however, did not leave room for experiments and innovative initiatives.

The efforts to broaden the social basis of government had only a limited objective. Government should no longer be considered the privilege of a closed oligarchy, but principally the task and responsibility of the upper stratum of society. The middle classes, from which most activists were recruited, lacked cohesion and the driving power of an ideology of progress. The self-consciousness of these groups was thoroughly conservative.

The impact of the Enlightenment on the revolutionary movements was negligible, in spite of Rousset de Missy's committed activities in Amsterdam. The establishment in the second half of the century of societies and clubs where an exchange of ideas could take place was to become of the utmost importance for the genesis of new and more coherent ideals, for the formation of a political culture that would lead to 1787.

In their different demands for redress, the people of 1747 asked for improvements in their own village, city, region, or province. They gave no attention to reforms on a supraprovincial level. Yet, in the long run, patriotism would form the core of a national consciousness. In 1747

---

52. P. Zagorin, "Prolegomena to the Comparative History of Revolution in Early Modern Europe," *Comparative Studies in Society and History* 18 (1976): 151–174.

53. J. Elliott, "Revolution and Continuity in Early Modern Europe," in *The General Crisis of the Seventeenth Century*, ed. Geoffrey Parker and Lesley M. Smith (London, 1978), p. 130.

and after, the Orangists attempted to monopolize the term "patriotism." They called themselves "Patriots" or "the true Patriots," suggesting that their republican adversaries neglected or even betrayed the real interests of the country.[54] In the 1750s, however, this much disputed appellation passed to the republican regents. Under its mantle they seized the ideological initiative and in the 1780s turned patriotism against the Orangists who had once claimed it as their own.

54. See also the comment in Jan Wagenaar's weekly *De Patriot* (8 August, 1747) in *Verzameling van historiesche en politike tractaaten*, vol. 2 (Amsterdam, 1780), pp. 87–94; E. H. Kossmann, "In Praise of the Dutch Republic: Some Seventeenth-Century Attitudes," in *Politieke theorie en geschiedenis* (Amsterdam, 1987), pp. 161–175.

# 3

# Provincial Histories and National Revolution in the Dutch Republic

## Wayne Ph. te Brake

THE political struggles of the Dutch Patriot revolution remain enigmatic to historians. Accustomed as we generally are to judging revolutionaries by the fruits of their labors, the dramatic defeat of the revolutionary Patriots in the fall of 1787 leaves us conspicuously empty-handed. Since, as R. R. Palmer observed, the Dutch had the misfortune of being a small country and thus easy objects of foreign intervention, the immediate consequence of the Patriots' revolutionary action was Orangist counterrevolution sponsored by English money and Prussian troops.[1] To fill the obvious void, historians have often turned to assessments of the Patriots' political objectives. Beyond the general problem that the announced intentions of revolutionary leaders are notoriously bad predictors of the actual outcomes of revolutions, there is no general agreement on which of several general programmatic statements issued by various groups between 1784 and 1787 we should take most seriously.[2]

The research for this chapter was funded jointly by the Netherlands-America Commission for Educational Exchange and the Nederlandse Organisatie voor Zuiver-wetenschappelijk Onderzoek. Thanks to Marjolein 't Hart for her thoughtful and informed criticism of an earlier draft.

1. R. R. Palmer, *The Age of the Democratic Revolution*, vol. 1, *The Challenge* (Princeton, 1959), p. 369.
2. There is a large and contentious literature on the Patriots' ideology. For a review of the literature, see E. G. O. Haitsma Mulier, "De geschiedschrijving over de Patriottentijd en de Bataafse Tijd," in *Kantelend geschiedbeeld*, ed. W. W. Mijnhardt (Utrecht-Amsterdam, 1983), pp. 206–227.

But revolutions are not only to be judged by their outcomes or by the intentions of their leaders. As Perez Zagorin argues, "in a deep and therefore non-tautological sense, it is true that every people gets the revolution it deserves and equally true that it gets only the revolutions of which it is capable."[3] In this light, revolutions can be as revealing of the old regimes they seek to replace as the new ones they try to build. By extension, too, the comparative study of revolution can be an important adjunct to the comparative study of long-term political and social change. Indeed, in the broader comparative context of the so-called democratic revolutions of the last decades of the eighteenth century, the Dutch revolution deserves careful analysis for at least two reasons: on the one hand, it was the most forceful challenge to Europe's old regime before the French revolution of 1789 altered the very meaning of the word "revolution"; on the other hand, it occurred in a decentralized republic rather than in a centralized monarchy.[4]

From a comparative point of view, perhaps the most revealing feature of the Dutch revolution is its diffuse and episodic character. Like the polity in which it took place, the Dutch revolution was fragmented and decentralized—a revolution without a center within a state without a center. In fact, if we view revolution as an essentially political process, as a struggle for state power in which the various contenders strive to make good their mutually exclusive claims for political sovereignty,[5] then the Dutch revolution comes more clearly into focus as, at bottom, a series of more or less discrete municipal and provincial revolutions. To be sure, the "piecemeal" quality of the Dutch revolution, to borrow Simon Schama's characterization, has not escaped attention, but historians have usually treated it as a problem or deficiency—as an explanation of the revolution's failure. Thus, E. H. Kossmann suggested that the revolutionary Patriots were "enfeebled by the organization of the Republic," while to Schama the "subdivisions" of the conflict looked like a political handicap because they diffused the energies the Patriots needed to resist violent counterrevolution.[6] In general,

3. P. Zagorin, "Prolegomena to the Comparative History of Revolution in Early Modern Europe," *Comparative Studies in Society and History* 18 (1976): 151; see also P. Zagorin, *Rebels and Rulers, 1500–1660*, 2 vols. (Cambridge, 1982).

4. See Palmer, *Democratic Revolution*, pp. 323–340.

5. I borrow this definition from C. Tilly, *From Mobilization to Revolution*, (Reading, Mass., 1978), and R. Aya, "Theories of Revolution Reconsidered," *Theory and Society* 8 (1979): 39–99.

6. E. H. Kossmann, *The Low Countries, 1780–1940* (Oxford, 1978), p. 44; S. Schama, *Patriots and Liberators: Revolution in the Netherlands, 1780–1813* (New York, 1977), p. 134.

however, the historiography of this period—which is overwhelmingly concerned with the emergence of the unitary Dutch state after 1795— has actually obscured the fragmentation of the political process by looking for "parties" that transcended the "particularisms" of the old republic.[7]

In this chapter I explore the extent to which the Dutch got, in Zagorin's terms, the revolution they deserved and the only one of which they were capable. To do this, I must invert the older historiography and view the revolution prospectively from the view of the early-modern republic rather than retrospectively through the lens of the nineteenth-century monarchy. Using the provinces of Holland, Friesland, and Overijssel as examples, I show how the variations evident in the character and fate of the Patriots' provincial revolutions in the 1780s are reflections of the distinctive political development of the Dutch provinces under the old regime. In comparing these provinces, I hope to illustrate the broad range of political experience that was accommodated under the umbrella of the Dutch confederation; at the same time, I argue that these distinctive provincial histories nevertheless converged in the second half of the eighteenth century to produce what might well, in the final analysis, be considered a national revolution.

To set the problem for analysis, we might well begin with the political standoff that paralyzed the republic in the summer of 1787.[8] After years of slowly escalating conflict between Patriots and Orangists, the first element of a political deadlock emerged in August 1786, when a new popularly elected Patriot magistracy was sworn into office in the city of Utrecht. The estates of the province of Utrecht, refusing to recognize the legitimacy of the elections, packed up for safer haven in the Orangist city of Amersfoort, whereupon the magistrates of the city convened their own Patriot version of the provincial estates and effectively divided the province into two warring camps. Early in 1787, similarly contested elections in the cities of Zwolle and Deventer gave the Patriots less equivocal control of the province of Overijssel, allowing them to eliminate the last vestiges of the stadholder's influence in

7. See Haitsma Mulier, "Geschiedschrijving."

8. General accounts of the Patriot revolution on which I am dependent throughout are H. T. Colenbrander, *De Patriottentijd*, 3 vols. (The Hague, 1897–1899); P. Geyl, *De Patriottenbeweging 1780–1787* (Amsterdam, 1947); C. H. E. de Wit, *De Nederlandse revolutie van de achttiende eeuw 1780–1787* (Oirsbeek, 1974); Schama, *Patriots and Liberators*. See also W. Ph. te Brake, "Popular Politics and the Dutch Patriot Revolution," *Theory and Society* 14 (1985): 199–222.

the province and to send an unchallenged Patriot delegation to the Estates General. Frustrated by the inconsistent policies of the traditionally anti-Orange province of Holland, militant Patriots purged the magistracy of Amsterdam in April 1787 and those of Rotterdam, Schiedam, and Gorcum shortly thereafter. But firm Patriot control of the provincial estates of Holland was not assured until a rapid-fire series of seven other municipal purges was accomplished in the summer of 1787.

Meanwhile, in Friesland, militant Patriots, having been consistently frustrated in their attempts to deflect the increasingly reactionary policies of the provincial estates in Leeuwarden, convened a rival meeting of the provincial estates in Franeker and began preparing for a military confrontation with their Orangist enemies. In the province of Groningen, Patriot control of the dominant city of Groningen assured their control of the province's delegation to the Estates General but could not disguise deep divisions between the city and the Ommelanden within the estates of the province. For their part, Orangists managed to maintain their dominant and apparently unassailable position in the provincial estates of Zeeland, and they consolidated their control of the provincial estates of Gelderland by executing purges of the magistracies of Zutphen and Arnhem, supported by violent crowd action against leaders of the Patriot movement.[9] Everywhere, however, local populations were thoroughly divided, and between two organized and armed movements there was little room left for political neutrality.

The result of all this division was the essential paralysis of Dutch politics at the national level. If, as in American sports, control of the political destiny of the Dutch Republic amounted finally to a best-of-seven series, then on the eve of the Prussian invasion in September one might well have declared the Patriots to be winners—with a record of three wins, two losses, and two draws. But even in more tranquil times, when the great powers of Europe were less likely to interfere, simple majorities (and much less pluralities) could not rule in Dutch politics. Had the numbers been as narrowly in favor of the Orangists, the political result would have been the same; as long as the constituent provinces were as deeply divided as they were, the United Provinces of the Netherlands ceased to function as a collectivity. Given the apparent unwillingness of either side to compromise, the republic seemed to be headed for civil war.

9. Earlier, in September 1786, William V had also, at the request of the provincial estates of Gelderland, used regular troops to attack and capture the small, dissident cities of Elburg and Hattem, which set off the first wave of counterrevolutionary violence.

The confluence of so many political conflicts is both remarkable and problematic. It is remarkable because all parts of the republic— even Drenthe, the so-called eighth province, which was not part of the Estates General, and the Generality lands, conquered sections of Brabant and Limburg that were ruled jointly by the seven constituent provinces—were torn simultaneously by serious conflict between groups identified as Patriots and Orangists. It is problematic because, as local archival research on the Patriot period has begun to show, the conflicts arose from quite diverse social and political circumstances, involved the full range of old-regime political actors, and offered the revolutionary Patriots variable chances for success. The provinces of Holland, Friesland, and Overijssel illustrate the major themes as well as the contrapuntal variations.[10]

In all three provinces, the Patriots mounted strong challenges to the existing regime based on a broad foundation of popular support, depended on alliances with disaffected elements of the regent elite, and were united by a common enmity for the stadholder, Prince William V of Orange. Provincial variations on these important themes produced, however, strikingly different patterns of conflict in the course of 1787. In Overijssel, for example, the Patriots quickly and decisively seized control of provincial government early in the year, while in Holland they only gradually came to control the provincial government by virtue of a long series of municipal revolutions in the spring and summer. In Friesland, by contrast, the Patriots were unable to establish direct control of the existing institutions of provincial government and instead created an alternative set of governing institutions. To clarify and account for these distinctive patterns of revolutionary conflict, I propose to make an excursion into the political history of the Dutch Republic with special emphasis on the geography of Dutch state formation under the old regime. The goal is not simply to outline the structure of Dutch republican politics but to discern the pace and direction of political change under the republican regime. In conclusion, then, I return to the problem with which I began: the relationship of

10. For the history of the Patriot revolution in these provinces, see, in addition to the general literature, W. Ph. te Brake, *Regents and Rebels: The Revolutionary World of an Eighteenth-Century Dutch City* (Oxford, 1989); M. A. M. Franken and R. M. Kemperink, eds., *Herstel, hervorming of behoud? Tien Overijsselse steden in de Patriottentijd, 1780– 1787* (Zwolle, 1985); W. W. van der Meulen, *Coert Lambertus van Beijma: Een bijdrage tot de kennis van Frieslands geschiedenis tijdens den Patriottentijd* (Leeuwarden, 1894); W. Bergsma et al., ed., *For uwz lân, wyv en bern: De Patriottentijd in Friesland* (Leeuwarden, 1987). There is no general survey for the province of Holland.

the diffuse and episodic Patriot revolution to the distinctive patterns of Dutch political development.

## THE FOUNDATION OF THE REPUBLICAN REGIME

I take as my point of departure Johan de Witt's description in 1652 of the United Provinces as, at bottom, a confederation of sovereign republics rather than a single sovereign state. To be sure, De Witt's remarks were contentious, but as G. de Bruin has argued, the question of sovereignty was not simply an abstract issue of interest to political theorists; during the Dutch Revolt and the Eighty Years' War, it was a practical and urgent question of political power and authority.[11] Earlier, in 1587, De Witt's predecessor as pensionary of the province of Holland, Johan van Oldenbarnevelt, had argued for the political primacy of the Estates General over his own province. But the political and religious conflicts that resulted in Van Oldenbarnevelt's execution during the truce with Spain, the painful struggles over the terms of peace with Spain leading up to 1648, and finally young William II's unsuccessful coup d'etat in 1650 had all helped to establish the contrary principle—the sovereignty of the provinces—as the undisputed foundation of Dutch politics by the 1650s.[12]

It is hardly original to suggest that the precise geographic and political configuration of the Dutch Republic, as De Witt knew it, was something of a historical accident.[13] Though at first resistance to Habsburg centralization and religious intolerance was strongest in the most prosperous provinces of the Southern Netherlands, the outcome of the long war effort was the independence of eight northern provinces plus parts of Brabant and Limburg. The combination of territories thus united for the next two centuries by the Union of Utrecht had diverse roots and relatively little political experience in common. The counties of Holland and Zeeland had come to be known as among the best

11. G. de Bruin, "De soevereiniteit in de republiek: Een machtsprobleem," *Bijdragen en Mededelingen betreffende de Geschiedenis der Nederlanden* 94 (1979): 27–40.

12. See J. den Tex, *Oldenbarnevelt*, 2 vols. (Cambridge, 1973); Jonathan I. Israel, "The Holland Towns and the Dutch-Spanish Conflict, 1621–1648," *Bijdragen en Mededelingen betreffende de Geschiedenis der Nederlanden* 94 (1979): 41–69; and Herbert H. Rowen, *John de Witt, Grand Pensionary of Holland, 1625–1672* (Princeton, 1978).

13. For a review of the general literature of the Dutch Revolt, see G. de Bruin, "De geschiedschrijving over de Nederlandse Opstand," in *Kantelend geschiedbeeld*, ed. W. W. Mijnhardt, pp. 48–82. On the politics of the republic in the seventeenth century, see G. de Bruin, "De geschiedschrijving over de Gouden Eeuw," ibid., pp. 83–117.

governed of the ministates of northwestern Europe even before they became part of the core of the Burgundian domain in the Netherlands in 1427. By contrast, the other provinces in the east and north were added only later by the Habsburgs—Friesland first in 1523 followed by Groningen and Drenthe; Overijssel in 1528 along with Utrecht; Gelderland finally in 1543. In many ways they remained peripheral territories within the Habsburg Netherlands up to the time of the revolt.[14]

In retrospect, one is necessarily impressed by the economic and political preponderance of Holland, one province among the United Provinces. But it is wise to remember that such peripheral provinces as Friesland and Overijssel were important and distinct in their own right. In late antiquity and in the early medieval period, the intrepid and fiercely independent Frisians had been the dominant traders along the North Sea coast. To be sure, in the wake of Frankish expansion northward the Frisians gradually lost much of their commercial function, but at its inclusion into the Habsburg domain the Dutch province of Friesland remained a relatively advanced and prosperous agrarian society.[15] By contrast, much of Overijssel seems like an agrarian backwater, but during the late middle ages the province's three cities along or near the IJssel River—Deventer, Kampen, and Zwolle—had developed lucrative and important trading functions under the aegis of the Hanseatic League. In time, the commerce of the "IJsselsteden" would pale by comparison with the enormous growth of the international markets of Antwerp and, later, Amsterdam, but at the time of the revolt these cities still had vital functions in the region's overland and river traffic with the interior of Westphalia and the Rhineland.[16]

Still it is true that Holland and Zeeland were the driving force in the successful revolt, and in the fledgling republic Holland stood head and shoulders above the other provinces. This is not surprising given Holland's significantly larger size and rapidly expanding commercial economy. Even more, under Habsburg rule Holland had undergone an

14. W. Prevenier and W. Blockmans, *The Burgundian Netherlands* (Cambridge, 1986); see especially the useful chronologies (pp. 374–386) and the map (pp. 390–391).

15. W. Ph. te Brake, "Economy and Ecology in Early Medieval Frisia," *Viator: Medieval and Renaissance Studies* 9 (1978): 1–29; J. A. Faber, *Drie eeuwen Friesland*, 2 vols. (Wageningen, 1972).

16. According to one estimate, at the end of the fifteenth century, 48 percent of the population of the province of Overijssel was urban; this is actually higher than the estimates for Holland (45 percent), Flanders (36 percent), and Brabant (31 percent); see Prevenier and Blokmans, *Burgundian Netherlands*, p. 392. See also W. Jappe Alberts, *De Nederlandse Hanzesteden* (Bussum, 1969).

enormously important financial revolution by which its provincial estates could mobilize the resources of a host of small investors.[17] This meant that, during the long years of war with Spain, Holland was able to foot its own 58 percent share of the budget of the Generality as well as advance money for such poorer provinces as Overijssel, all the while maintaining the confidence of its creditors. But Holland not only bankrolled the war effort; through the leadership of Van Oldenbarnevelt, it also guided the process by which an unlikely collection of diverse provinces were gradually shaped into a workable confederation. The making of this distinctive state is still very much understudied, but two complementary features of Dutch republican state making are nevertheless clear.[18] In the first place, all the provinces underwent significant political changes when they abjured their sovereign *landsheer* and took on the new responsibilities of republican self-government. Second, although Holland clearly played a dominant role, especially with regard to the defense and, more generally, foreign policies of the Generality, the leaders of Holland and the Generality did not seek to dominate or rule the lesser provinces directly; rather, they fostered the creation of institutional arrangements everywhere, except in the conquered sections of Limburg and Brabant, for meaningful provincial self-government.

The kinds of institutional transformation that were necessary to sustain self-government—that is, government in the absence of a recognized *landsheer*—were first evident in the county of Holland following the rebels' first military victories there in 1572, well before the official abjuration of Philip II in 1581.[19] In the first place, the provincial estates had to begin meeting regularly in their own name and on their own authority to deal with the exigencies of the war effort, and the estates in turn recognized William of Orange, rather than Philip II's appointee, as their stadholder. At the same time, the revolutionary government of Holland significantly broadened its political base by inviting twelve smaller cities to send delegations to the estates in addition to the six

---

17. J. D. Tracy, *A Financial Revolution in the Hapsburg Netherlands* (Berkeley, 1985); M. 't Hart, *In Quest for Funds, Welfare and State Formation in the Netherlands, 1620–50* (dissertation, Leiden, 1989).

18. The best general work on the institutions of the Dutch Republic is still Robert Fruin, *Geschiedenis der staatsinstellingen in Nederland tot den val der Republiek* (The Hague, 1922/1980); S. J. Fockema Andreae, *De Nederlandse staat onder de Republiek* (Amsterdam, 1960), is more recent but much less useful. For a welcome, new interpretation, see M. 't Hart, "Cities and Statemaking in the Dutch Republic, 1580–1680," *Theory and Society* 18 (1989): 663–687. See also De Bruin, "Gouden Eeuw."

19. Fruin, *Staatsinstellingen*, pp. 55–63, 78–82, 160–164, 214–227, 230–241.

largest, or oldest, which had been traditionally summoned by the count to sit alongside the higher nobility, the *ridderschap*. Also, it was soon clear that the urgency of the situation demanded that some form of provincial council take on the necessary tasks of provincial government when the estates were not in session. After several experiments on this score, the estates finally created an executive council (the *gedeputeerde staten*), led by the by the so-called *landsadvocaat*, a provincial appointee. This group provided William of Orange with the kind of continuous, authoritative support he needed to carry on as leader, on much broader diplomatic and military fronts, of what gradually became a war of independence.[20]

By contrast with Holland, much larger political transformations were necessary to make Overijssel into a self-governing "republic."[21] Prior to its inclusion in the Habsburg domain under Charles V, Overijssel, which consisted of three diverse rural districts plus the three important trading cities along the IJssel River, had been subject to the bishopric of Utrecht. The bishops were hardly proto-monarchic autocrats, and under their relatively benign and unintrusive policies the province, or rather its constituent parts, enjoyed a great deal of autonomy and developed provincial estates (called the *landdag*) that served, when summoned by the bishop, essentially to preserve that autonomy. Under the Habsburgs, the estates—composed of the *ridderschap* and delegates of the three IJsselsteden—took on an increasingly important role as provincial bargaining agent vis-à-vis a much more aggressive *landsheer*. But the estates never developed a clear institutional identity prior to the revolt because the cities in fact determined the policies of the estates in a separate caucus prior to the estates meetings and were able to enforce their "majority" decisions with the support of just one nobleman. In Overijssel, then, government, in the sense of day-to-day responsibility for and administration of public affairs and justice, was essentially local—in the cities under chartered councils and magistracies and in the countryside in various kinds of local jurisdictions under the auspices of the nobility.

Ill-equipped institutionally to take on the important role of sovereign in the first place, the provincial government of Overijssel was fur-

20. Ibid., pp. 162–163. The province actually maintained two distinct executive councils—one for the bulk of the province and the largest cities and one for the small towns of the northern district, which feared the domination of the south.

21. R. Reitsma, *Centrifugal and Centripetal Forces in the Early Dutch Republic: The States of Overijssel, 1566–1600* (Amsterdam, 1982).

ther paralyzed by the almost continual warfare that kept major portions of the province under Spanish occupation from 1580 to 1597. What remained of the province fell effectively under the tutelage of the Generality (that is, Holland, Zeeland, and generally Utrecht) and the council of state. As Prince Maurice's reconquest of the northeastern provinces proceeded, the council of state, working especially with the Calvinist minority of the political elite, carefully nurtured political and institutional reforms that would make provincial self-government possible. The principal changes, in place by 1605, were the creation of an executive committee of the estates, composed of three representatives of the nobility and delegates from the three IJsselsteden, which, like its counterpart in Holland, took on important administrative and judicial functions when the *landdag* was not in session; the imposition of a uniform system of taxation, which had always been resisted under the Habsburgs, to ensure that the province would be able to meet its financial obligations to the Generality; and the formation of a uniform judicial system for the countryside under the control of the provincial estates. Thereby, the conditions were created for Overijssel, too, to take its place as a sovereign and equal republic under the umbrella of the Union of Utrecht, even though it contributed only 3.5 percent of the Generality budget.

In Friesland, the institutional changes brought on by the revolt were equally important, but they worked in an entirely different context.[22] Prior to its inclusion into Charles V's Netherlands domain, Friesland had had little experience with sovereign overlordship, and even under the Habsburgs the province had stubbornly retained its distinctive government. The province was composed of three "quarters," which were, in turn, divided into a total of thirty *grietenijen*, each administered by a *grietman*. The *grietman* had originally been elected by the eligible landowners of the *grietenij*, but under the Habsburgs they were appointed by the provincial governor, the stadholder, in cooperation with a council of advisers. The provincial estates (*landdag*), which like its counterparts elsewhere served as a provincial bargaining agent with the *landsheer*, was organized along the lines of the three quarters, each composed of delegates from the constituent *grietenijen* as well as delegates from the towns in the quarter and individual prelates and noblemen who might appear in their own right.

22. J. J. Woltjer, *Friesland in hervormingstijd* (Leiden, 1962); Fruin, *Staatsinstellingen*, pp. 96–104, 247–251.

Following the conquest of Maurice in 1598, Friesland's provincial institutions changed in several important ways. As perhaps befits a province under the influence of bourgeois Holland, the new provincial estates now organized the delegates from the eleven towns as a separate quarter—an emancipation the towns gained in return for a pledge to bear a relatively higher proportion of the province's financial burden. At the same time, the estates also created an executive council consisting of two representatives from each of the rural quarters and three from the towns' quarter. For the rest, the annual electoral system for representatives of the thirty *grietenijen* to the provincial estates was retained, and the *grietmannen* were appointed for life by the stadholder and the executive council of the estates from nominations by the electors of the *grietenij*.

Ironically, of the three provinces discussed here, the Frisians with their fiercely independent, even anarchic, reputation began their life as a constituent part of the Dutch Republic with the most unitary and uniform of institutional arrangements. In Holland, the eighteen enfranchised towns jealously guarded their varying degrees of independence and self-governance, and the countryside looked like a patchwork quilt of seignorial jurisdictions. In Overijssel, the three IJsselsteden even claimed a certain degree of municipal sovereignty, which was not simply a matter of hollow rhetoric since, unlike the towns of Holland, each had a judicial system not subject to higher appeal outside the city's jurisdiction. By comparison, the eleven Frisian cities, while now collectively enjoying a separate voice and vote in the provincial estates, nevertheless functioned administratively and judicially much like the rural *grietenijen*, clearly subject to the sovereignty of the provincial estates; in Friesland, all criminal prosecutions and all civil cases on appeal were handled by a single provincial court.[23]

## THE PATHS OF PROVINCIAL DEVELOPMENT

Having thus embarked on their collective political life from diverse starting points, Holland, Overijssel, and Friesland continued to develop along distinctive lines. One can usefully trace that development in terms of three broad political themes that are particularly relevant to

23. See A. H. Huussen, Jr., "Jurisprudentie en bureaucratie: Het hof van Friesland en zijn criminele rechtspraak in de achttiende eeuw," *Bijdragen en Mededelingen betreffende de Geschiedenis der Nederlanden* 93 (1978): 241–298.

an understanding of the politics of the Patriot revolution: the evolution of consensual decision making at the provincial level, the trend toward aristocratization of local government, and the changing role of the stadholder in provincial politics.

The creation of institutions for provincial self-government was an important step, but this in itself could not ensure political stability in the Dutch Republic. In the absence of centralized authority, decision making within the union regarding foreign and defense policy was an exceedingly complex process in which consensus or unanimity was required on all important issues. Likewise, at the provincial level, consensus among the constituent parts of the provincial estates was considered essential to the efficient and harmonious governing of provincial affairs. The creation of executive committees in each province enabled the routine execution and administration of provincial policies, but these bodies generally could not at the same time ensure that the estates arrived at workable and agreeable policies to begin with. Thus, one of the characteristic features of the Dutch political process was the creation of special commissions to pave the way for consensus before formal deliberations in the provincial estates.[24] Because the provinces were so differently constituted, however, the search for political consensus also naturally took a variety of forms.

That special efforts were required to arrive at political consensus is especially evident in Friesland. Besides the provincial court and the executive council of the estates, Friesland developed something called the *mindergetal*, whose sole function was to promote consensus at the meetings of the *landdag*.[25] The four quarters of the estates, once assembled in Leeuwarden, held their deliberations in separate sessions, where the delegates voted by head and convened as a whole body only to cast their final votes by quarter. Before and during the meetings, then, the function of the *mindergetal*, which was composed of representatives of each of the quarters, was to receive the various positions of the quarters and to produce, where possible, compromises that were generally acceptable. Overijssel had no equivalent to the *mindergetal* but depended on a permanent commission on finances, composed of three noblemen and delegates of the three cities.[26] Typically, when controver-

24. See G. de Bruin, "Gouden Eeuw," p. 95.
25. J. H. Grever, "The State of Friesland: Politics and Society during the 1660s," *Parliament, Estates, and Representation* 9 (1989): 1–25.
26. G. J. ter Kuile, "Rechtspraak en bestuur in Overijssel ten tijde van de Republiek," *Verslagen en Mededelingen voor Overijsselsch Recht en Geschiedenis (VMORG)* 67 (1952): 141–168, and 68 (1953): 69–97.

sial issues came before the meetings of the estates, they were immediately referred to the commission on finances, or occasionally to a
special ad hoc commission; if compromises could not be found, the
issues generally died in committee. The remarkable result of this political arrangement was that, in approximately two centuries of provincial
self-government, the issue of what might constitute a decision by simple majority vote (*overstemming*) within the estates of Overijssel was
never resolved.[27] In neither Friesland nor Overijssel, however, could division and conflict always be avoided. Thus, especially in the early
years of the republic, the Estates General was often called on to ar-
bitrate particularly divisive issues, as provided for in the Union of
Utrecht.[28]

Probably the most curious feature of the provincial government of
Holland was the office of *raadpensionaris*, which must also be seen in
the context of the perceived need for political consensus in the republic.[29] Even before the revolt, the *ridderschap*, like the most important
cities severally,[30] had an appointed jurist (*pensionaris* or *advocaat*) who
functioned as permanent legal adviser, spokesman, or even ambassador; but under the republic, the *pensionaris* of the nobility served
also as *raadpensionaris* (council pensionary) of the estates as a whole.
He would became a central figure in both provincial and national politics. Because the *raadpensionaris* was the spokesman for the powerful
voice of Holland in the Estates General, he is often likened to an all-
powerful minister of state, but he remained in fact a servant of the
estates of Holland. The *raadpensionaris* was, nevertheless, the effective
leader of the meetings of the provincial estates and the person in charge
of the preparation, the execution, and even the formulation of the decisions of the estates. Thus, although the position lacked an independent
power base, men such as Van Oldenbarnevelt and De Wit, who were
clearly possessed of the requisite skills of persuasion and political ma-
neuver, demonstrated how the position could be used to broker the
compromises and deals that were necessary in a body that had no less
than nineteen independent votes. In effect, in the absence of a *mind-*

27. The cities, under pressure from the Patriots, finally forced the issue in 1784, bringing
provincial government to a standstill until mediation by the Generality resolved the issue in
favor of the cities.

28. For examples, see Fruin, *Staatsinstellingen*.

29. De Bruin, "Gouden Eeuw," pp. 96–97; Fruin, *Staatsinstellingen*, 236–238.

30. On the role of the city pensionaries, see J. A. F. de Jongste, "Hollandse stadspen-
sionarissen tijdens de Republiek: Notities bij een onderzoek," in *Bestuurders en geleerden,
opstellen . . . aangeboden aan prof. dr. J. J. Woltjer* (Amsterdam, 1985).

*ergetal* or its functional equivalent, Holland turned again and again to the informal political brokerage of its *raadpensionaris*.

By the time more or less stable patterns of provincial politics had begun to emerge, it was also clear that the provincial governments would everywhere be controlled by relatively well defined oligarchies.[31] The fragmentation of political power meant that more than two thousand officials of one sort or another were directly involved in the deliberation of even the most weighty matters of state—the declaration of war and the ratification of peace treaties—in various local, provincial, and national corporations and assemblies.[32] This arrangement not only ensured that the republican oligarchy would be broadly based but also presented a bewildering variety of avenues to political power and influence. There is a certain measure of intellectual solace involved in calling all these direct participants in the Dutch political process "regents," connoting especially the self-perpetuating, patrician quality of corporate municipal government. To be sure, these urban oligarchies were everywhere important, but there were in Holland, Overijssel, and Friesland several alternative modes of access to political power that were essential to the development of Dutch republican politics.

If we are anywhere justified in focusing on urban oligarchies, it is surely in Holland. The broadening of the province's urban political base at inception of the republic (by admitting twelve smaller towns to the estates alongside the original six) set the stage for an enormously complex and variable political process. Membership in one of the eighteen self-perpetuating municipal corporations (the *vroedschappen*) made one in some sense a true regent, a member of the elite for whom politics was an ongoing and exclusive activity. But becoming a regent in this sense was only a first step toward political power, influence, and income; it merely opened the possibility of preferment to a myriad of important political offices, within the local magistracy (as, for example, burgomaster or *schepen*) and at the provincial and national level (as a delegate to the estates or one of the Generality bodies), as well as a welter of revenue-producing administrative posts. Since the competi-

31. For what follows I am especially dependent on the work of D. J. Roorda; for a review and summary of the research on oligarchies, see D. J. Roorda, "Het onderzoek naar het stedelijk patriciaat in Nederland," in *Kantelend geschiedbeeld*, ed. W. W. Mijnhardt, pp. 118–142. In English, see H. van Dijk and D. J. Roorda, "Social Mobility under the Regents of the Republic," *Acta Historiae Neerlandicae* 9 (1978): 76–102.

32. On this bewildering complexity, see, for example, John H. Grever, "Committees and Deputations in the Assemblies of the Dutch Republic, 1660–1668," *Parliaments, Estates, and Representation* 1 (1981): 13–33.

tion for these offices was intense, the urban oligarchies, or subgroups within them, often negotiated contracts or complex schedules that attempted to regulate the appointment process and to distribute the available patronage among the signatories so as to reduce internecine conflict. But these formal agreements were often only reflections of less formal family alliances sealed by intermarriage within the elite—an elite that was less directly and actively involved in the commerce and industry of Holland as time went on.

Hence, one forms the general image of an originally bourgeois republic undergoing a process of aristocratization. But as H. F. K. van Nierop has shown us, the municipal oligarchies are only part of the story, even in urban and commercial Holland.[33] Though the Dutch Revolt clearly diminished the importance of the *ridderschap*'s one vote in the estates of Holland, it by no means eliminated the nobility of Holland as a social group or political force. To be sure, processes already at work under the Habsburgs transformed the knights of old into the regents of the republic, but through careful marriage and investment the nobility—or at least a segment of it—retained its separate political status and identity; and benefiting from several privileges accorded the first order of the estates, the *ridderschap* remained an important factor in provincial politics. Indeed, one is inclined to suggest that membership in the *ridderschap* brought with it better chances for an influential political career than membership in one of the municipal *vroedschappen*.

In Overijssel, these two alternative paths to political preferment and power were more closely matched than in Holland. In the formation of the republican regime, the once-dominant IJsselsteden retained their essential independence, but they lost their effective control of provincial politics. Within the estates, the requirement of consensus or unanimity in the most important matters of provincial and national policy (*punten van bezwaar*) effectively eliminated the possibility of majority decisions—that is, *overstemming* of the sort that had ensured the dominance of the cities under the *landsheer*. This naturally enhanced the position of the *ridderschap*, which had three votes in the estates as well as equal representation on each of its committees—not to mention an equal share of provincial patronage. Internally, the cities of Overijssel also saw the rise of marriage alliances and internal contracts to maintain unity, or at least to minimize internecine conflict within the oligar-

33. H. K. F. van Nierop, *Van ridders tot regenten* (The Hague, 1984).

chies.[34] By contrast with Holland, however, the *ridderschap* of Overijssel was not as narrowly defined: much to the nobles' chagrin, the cities, as members of the estates, voted on all admissions to the *ridderschap*, whereas relatively lax standards for admission had allowed for a broad membership and participation throughout the history of the republic. Yet here, too, it can be said that the knight of old was gradually transformed into the new republican regent.[35]

In Friesland, the perennial exception to Dutch rules, the formation of a republican oligarchy followed an entirely different pattern: on the one hand, the small cities of Friesland never developed the unitary independence of their counterparts in Holland and Overijssel; on the other, the nobility of Friesland enjoyed no corporate political status.[36] Though the eleven Frisian cities developed some of the oligarchic attributes found elsewhere—corporative election by cooptation, family alliances, and contracts to preserve harmony—they shared a single vote in the estates to which the council and the magistracy of each city sent its own representative in a curiously bifurcated way. Furthermore, these delegates were not bound by strict instructions, and consultation (*ruggespraak*) with their principals was not required as in the other provinces. All of this meant that the oligarchs of the Frisian cities were overshadowed by their co-sovereigns, the elites of the three rural quarters. For their part, however, the rural elite was defined and limited by the electoral system that was the foundation of political power in the countryside. Under this system, the owners of peasant freeholds not only chose (or nominated) village and district (*grietenij*) officials but each year elected two representatives (*volmachten*) to the provincial estates from each district. According to the instructions of 1581, one of the representatives was to be a nobleman, wherever possible; the other, a freeholder.

The broad-based complexity of this system of rural representation—there were upward of 10,000 votes in a population of approx-

34. H. Kronenburg, "In en om de Deventer magistraat, 1591–1795," *VMORG* 44 (1927).

35. See M. de Jong, Hzn., *Joan Derk van der Capellen* (Groningen–The Hague, 1921), p. 190ff. Van der Capellen is an example of an outsider seeking a political career; he could get into the *ridderschap* in Overijssel but not in his native Gelderland. After his admission, the *ridderschap* tightened its entrance requirements with the help of William V; see *Nieuwe Nederlandsche jaarboeken*, 1773, pp. 1223–1227. In 1787, there were a total of fifty-eight registered members of the *ridderschap*, although not all attended the meetings of the *landdag*; see *Naam-register van alle heren leden der regeering in de provintie van Overyssel . . . voor den jare 1787* (Zwolle, 1787).

36. Faber, *Drie eeuwen Friesland*, vol. 1, pp. 340–361; Grever, "Politics and Society;" C. J. Guibal, *Democratie en oligarchie in Friesland tijdens de Republiek* (Assen, 1934).

imately 100,000—gave rise to numerous disputes in the early years of
the republic, but following the intervention of the Generality in 1637
the franchise (*stemrecht*) was definitively attached to designated plots
of land that were specified in uniform registers drawn up in each of the
thirty *grietenijen* in 1640. Though the process may have begun earlier,
it is clear that after 1640 wealthy and influential families, both the old
courtly nobility and prominent roturiers, began to secure their positions of political prominence by systematically buying up enough of the
enfranchised real estate to ensure themselves majority votes in enough
of the approximately 340 villages that dotted the countryside to guarantee their control of the affairs and patronage of the *grietenijen*,
where each village had one vote regardless of size. Though the process
was necessarily slow and expensive, a fairly well defined office-holding
elite had, by 1698, come to control 38 percent of the total votes, which
through rational investment they could parlay into effective control of
seventeen of the province's thirty *grietenijen*. Thus, this peculiarly Frisian "regent" oligarchy managed to dominate both the district offices of
*grietman* (a lifetime appointment) and the annual elections of representatives to the estates, at which level many more political and administrative offices were distributed by carefully negotiated contracts and
schedules. For much of the seventeenth century, the Frisian nobility,
despite a steady decline in the number of noble families, continued to
maintain its prominent position within this elite, but in the course of
the eighteenth century they gradually lost ground to Frisian roturier
families of equal stature and significance.

## THE STADHOLDERS AND PROVINCIAL POLITICS

Such, then, was the political system Johan de Witt described in 1652
as a confederation of sovereign republics. It was a system that honored,
even nurtured, particularism as the sine qua non of republican self-government; it was also a political system in which Holland's commercial
interests could generally prevail as national policy under the leadership
and influence of a man like De Witt.[37] Following the grand assembly of
1651 and under the banner of True Freedom, local and regional oligarchies were "free" to reflect a diverse institutional and social heritage,

37. For De Witt's conduct of foreign policy, see Rowen, *John de Witt*, and J. C. Boogman, "The *Raison d'etat* politician Johan de Witt," *Low Countries History Yearbook* 9
(1978): 55–78.

while the politics of consensus prevented, or at least inhibited, the simple domination of one group or one set of interests over another. What is conspicuously absent from this idealized political equation, however, is the dynamic of international competition, dynasticism, and almost unending warfare. No sooner had the United Provinces ended their long war against Spain than they began a series of wars over the next six decades with England and France, among others. And however much politicians like De Witt might have wished it otherwise, international conflicts like these ensured that the princes of Orange would continue to be an integral part of Dutch political development. But if the Dutch were no exception to the general European rule that war making and state making go hand in hand, the impact of war on the development of the Dutch state was, once again, variable.

There was a time when the whole political history of the Dutch Republic after its peace with Spain in 1648 was seen as one grand struggle between two parties—the partisans, on the one hand, of such men as De Witt, the party of Holland, or of the "estates"; and the partisans, on the other, of De Witt's nemesis, William III, the party of the House of Orange.[38] But research on the local and provincial politics of Dutch elites in the past twenty-five years has clearly shown the older view from the center to be an oversimplification, if not a distortion, of a much more complex and interesting political reality. In particular, we now know that the political struggles involving the stadholders and the province of Holland did little to alter the basic patterns of republican politics as I have described them here: sovereign provinces ruled consensually by well-defined oligarchies continued to be the norm for Dutch republican politics.

In the formative years of the republic, the estates of Holland and their designated leaders were instrumental in the preservation and adaptation of the position of stadholder.[39] Initially, the estates of Holland used their own appointment or, more precisely, recognition of William of Orange as stadholder as a lever, first against Philip II and then later against the count of Anjou, whom the Estates General selected as a substitute sovereign. But following William's assassination in 1584, the

38. For a critique of the literature on parties, see De Bruin, "Gouden Eeuw," p. 92ff.; see also D. J. Roorda, *Partij en factie* (Groningen, 1960).

39. Fruin, *Staatsinstellingen*, pp. 218–227. For a useful appreciation of this unique office, see H. H. Rowen, "Neither Fish nor Fowl: The Stadholderate in the Dutch Republic," in *Political Ideas and Institutions in the Dutch Republic* (Los Angeles, 1985), pp. 3–31; see also H. H. Rowen, *The Princes of Orange: The Stadholders in the Dutch Republic* (Cambridge, 1988).

estates quickly appointed Maurice of Nassau as stadholder in order to preempt the earl of Leicester's bid for such an appointment. Following Leicester's departure in 1588, the Estates General, under Holland's guidance, began appointing stadholders in such provinces as Overijssel and Friesland as they were recaptured from the Spanish and integrated into full membership in the union. Not until 1620, when Friesland appointed Ernst Casimir, did other provinces begin to select their own stadholders. In these early days, however, the ill-defined position of stadholder paled in significance alongside the position of captain general of the republic's troops; it was as military leaders especially that William and Maurice excelled and established the notion that somehow the destiny of the Dutch Republic was tied to the House of Orange-Nassau.

That the duality of the prince's role—as stadholder and as captain general—was politically explosive became evident with Maurice's heavy-handed intervention in the religious politics of the republic during the truce with Spain (1609–1621). By contrast, his successor as stadholder in Holland, Frederick Hendrik, began to realize the potential of the position of stadholder to influence republican politics along lines very much parallel and alternative to that of the *raadpensionaris* of Holland. But it was William II's aborted coup d'etat in 1650 that convinced many a republican oligarch that the positions of stadholder and captain general should forever be separated: hence, the grand assembly's definitive reaffirmation in 1652 of the principle of provincial sovereignty and its attempt to give more control over the republic's army to the provincial estates by giving them direct responsibility for the troops under their "repartition." Though Holland's attempt to leave the position of stadholder unfilled and to separate the offices of stadholder and captain general for "eternity" was unsuccessful, it was clear that henceforth the basic condition for expansion of the stadholder's power was his ability to influence provincial politics in all their diversity.[40]

The basic ebb and flow of the stadholders' power and influence after 1650 was, of course, related to broader developments in international affairs and to the republic's fortunes in land warfare in particular. In the 1650s and 1660s, the republic proved itself capable of mobilizing for naval warfare with England, and following William III's death in 1702 it managed to outlast Louis XIV's final assault without a prince of Orange as military leader. But in both 1672 and 1747, land

40. Fruin, *Staatsinstellingen*, pp. 270–283.

invasions from France and her allies precipitated domestic crises that threw the republic back into the arms of ambitious captains general who combined their military roles with enhanced influence in domestic affairs. What is chiefly of interest here is how the larger shifts in the history of the Dutch stadholders—in 1672, 1702, and 1747—intersected with the diverse patterns of republican state making we have seen in Holland, Overijssel, and Friesland.[41]

Between 1650 and 1787 the province of Holland had nearly as many years of government without a stadholder as with one, and throughout this period the office of stadholder remained as ill defined as ever. It might well have been otherwise. In 1672, William III was swept into office by a wave of popular protest, which he and his supporters parlayed into the unprecedented declaration that the office be considered hereditary in the male line of the House of Orange. His dynastic ambitions were ruined, however, by his lack of either male or female offspring (though he had tried unsuccessfully before his death to have his young relative, Johan Willem Friso, recognized as his heir). Although it is often said that, after 1688, William III ruled like a stadholder in England and like a king in Holland, it is clear that he did nothing to change either the office of stadholder or the structure of provincial government in Holland. Like Maurice before him, he used the expedient of the *wetsverzetting* (temporary suspension of the law) in 1672 to install municipal governments more sympathetic to his policies, and thereafter he used (and sometimes abused) his limited prerogative of choosing municipal magistrates from double nomination lists to ensure that his ambitious foreign and military policies would prevail in the powerful estates of Holland. For the rest, however, William assumed no active or direct role in the internal politics of Holland or its constituent cities, and on his death his critical electoral prerogatives simply lapsed.

Heaving a collective sigh of relief, the regents of Holland simply returned after William's death in 1702 to the patterns of oligarchic and consensual politics that had obtained between 1650 and 1672. The many years of war making had taken an enormous political and financial toll, however, and living with the old ways proved to be more difficult than before.[42] In particular, the difficulty of arriving at a consensus on military policy within the union occasioned the calling of a

41. For what follows generally, see Fruin, *Staatsinstellingen*, pp. 284–362.
42. See J. Aalbers, "Holland's Financial Problems (1713–1733) and the Wars against Louis XIV," in *Britain and the Netherlands*, ed. A. C. Duke and C. A. Tamse (The Hague, 1977), pp. 79–93.

second grand assembly in 1716. During nine months of deliberation, the provinces agreed on a reduction in the size of the union's army, but they did nothing to reform the decision-making process as the advisory council of state had urged. Likewise, when *raadpensionaris* Simon van Slingelandt proposed to replace the traditional decision making by consensus within the estates of Holland with, in most cases, majority decision making, the old ways were defended and maintained. Though the political process was cumbersome and inefficient, it remained more acceptable to the political elite than the alternatives, which seemed to threaten domination in one form or another. At the same time, however, popular protest against the heavy tax burden occasioned by the wars against Louis XIV became a common feature of the urban political landscape.[43]

Toward the end of the War of the Austrian Succession, the republic proved unable to maintain its neutral position, and when French troops moved up from the south in 1747, William IV, the son of Johan Willem Friso, whom the estates had refused to appoint in 1702, was swept into power by another wave of popular protest in the cities of Holland—only this time the office of stadholder was declared hereditary in both the male and female lines.[44] Unlike 1672, however, the popular protests did not disappear once the stadholder had been reinstated. In places such as Amsterdam, Haarlem, and Rotterdam, radical demands for reform of the tax system and the urban civic guards presented William IV with an opportunity to change municipal and provincial politics in Holland. Fearful, however, of the persistence of the popular mobilization, William closed ranks with the regent oligarchy, contented himself with *wetsverzettingen* and the revival of the electoral prerogatives of his predecessors, and instituted only a limited reform of the hated tax farms. To be sure, the situation had been sufficiently altered that, following William IV's untimely death in 1751, regencies were provided for his young son until he could become stadholder in his own right as William V in 1766. Still, for the rest, Holland's regent oligarchy remained essentially intact, and the stadholder had to make do with such indirect political influence as the systematic use or abuse of his electoral prerogatives gave him in the eighteen voting cities and, by extension, in the provincial estates.

43. R. M. Dekker, *Holland in beroering, Oproeren in de 17de en 18de eeuw* (Baarn, 1982), pp. 28–38.

44. J. A. F. de Jongste, *Onrust aan het Spaarne: Haarlem in de jaren 1747–1751* (The Hague, 1984); P. Geyl, *Revolutiedagen te Amsterdam* (The Hague, 1936).

By contrast with Holland, Overijssel saw a significant increase in the powers and prerogatives of the stadholder, even though it had virtually the same experience with stadholderless government in 1650–1672 and 1702–1747. With the outbreak of war in 1672, Overijssel, along with Gelderland and Utrecht, was quickly and easily overrun by troops of the bishop of Munster, who was allied with France against the republic. Occupied without overt resistance by foreign troops until 1674, Overijssel was readmitted to the union in 1675 only on the condition that it, like Utrecht and Gelderland, accepted a new governmental regulation (*regeerings reglement*) designed by the stadholder, William III.[45] In addition to the right to approve the elections of all municipal regents, the stadholder was given the right of selection from double nominations for the most important political offices at the provincial level: members of the executive council, delegates to the Estates General, regional and district officials (*drosten* and *schouten*), and so on.[46] Thus, besides controlling access to municipal office, such as he did in Holland, the stadholder now also controlled political preferment, becoming thereby the patron of the provincial leadership. It is striking, then, that, although the stadholder had more influence in Overijssel in 1675 than he did in Holland in 1672, he did not fundamentally alter the structure of decision making and authority, except in one limited sense. The new regulation provided that, when consensus could not be found in the provincial estates, the stadholder, instead of a Generality commission, would function as mediator.

In practice, the governmental regulation gave the stadholder control of Overijssel's vote on military and foreign policy in the Estates General, which was William's primary interest, but it did little to alter the social composition of the patriciate. Rather, as in Holland, his patronage system only exacerbated the tendency toward factionalism in the elite. The result in Overijssel was a series of struggles for power between regent factions in several towns, large and small, after the prince's death in 1702. In Deventer the conflict even involved the inter-

45. Fruin, *Staatsinstellingen*, pp. 288–292. Many regents in Holland wished to treat the provinces that had capitulated as conquered territory, but William III's proposal for governmental regulations to curb existing abuses finally prevailed; see D. J. Roorda, "William III and the Utrecht 'Government-Regulation': Background, Events and Problems," *Low Countries History Yearbook* 12 (1979): 85–109.

46. Though the regulation stipulated that the stadholder was to make appointments from lists of nominations, the nominations were eventually dispensed with and the appointments were made directly by the prince; see M. de Jong, *Joan Derk van der Capellen: Staatkundig levensbeeld uit de wordingstijd van de moderne democratie* (Groningen–The Hague, 1921), p. 228ff.

vention of guild leaders—traditionally excluded from municipal office—who, in an "extraordinary election" in 1703, chose a new magistracy and appointed some of their number to the broader town council (*gezworen gemeente*).[47] Meanwhile, at the provincial level the reaction to the prince's death was equally strong: the governmental regulation was destroyed, the older patterns and mechanisms of decision making and political appointment were revived, and the provincial estates resolved to leave the position of stadholder unfilled. By contrast with Holland, then, the revival of the stadholdership in 1747 was almost uneventful in Overijssel. In the absence of popular mobilization demanding change, the regents of Overijssel held out as long as they could but eventually accepted what seemed inevitable: they reinstated the governmental regulation and appointed William IV hereditary stadholder as in Holland, but without an immediate shakeup in the oligarchy.

In Friesland, the history of the stadholders' role in provincial politics was entirely different.[48] From 1620 onward, Friesland had appointed its stadholders from the more fertile family of Nassau-Dietz, which descended from a brother of William I, and during the history of the republic there was no lapse in the office of stadholder.[49] Through successive marriages the families of Orange and Nassau remained allied, but it was not until Willem Karel Hendrik Friso (the Frisian stadholder since 1711) became William IV in Holland, Zeeland, Utrecht, and Overijssel in 1747 that all the Dutch provinces shared a single stadholder. In Friesland, then, the office of stadholder had a continuous existence, but it was not particularly powerful. The Frisian stadholders were never able to acquire the high military offices they aspired to in the union, and in Friesland their power was chiefly limited by the fact that they could not influence the election of representatives from the thirty *grietenijen* who constituted three of the four quarters in the provincial estates. Instead, their chief prerogatives included influence in the annual election of urban magistrates and the lifetime ap-

47. W. F. Wertheim and A. H. Wertheim-Gijse Weenink, *Burgers in verzet tegen regenten-heerschappij: Onrust in sticht en oversticht, 1703–1706* (Amsterdam, 1975); W. Th. Keune, "Gebeurtenissen rondom de verkiezingen van schepenen en raad en gezworen gemeente van Deventer in 1703," *VMORG* 81 (1966). See also A. H. Wertheim-Gijse Weenink, "Early-18th Century Uprisings in the Low Countries: Prelude to the Democratic Revolution," *History Workshop Journal* 15 (1983): 95–116.

48. H. Algra, "In de Republiek," in *Geschiedenis van Friesland* (Drachten, 1968), pp. 303–339.

49. See Table I in C. J. Guibal, *Johan Willem Friso en zijn tijd* (Amsterdam, 1938), pp. 8–9.

pointment of *grietmannen* and members of the provincial court from lists of nominations.

The outbreak of war on multiple fronts in 1672 brought not only the direct threat of foreign invasion to Friesland but, as in the cities of Holland, also a wave of popular protest. Under the leadership of some 150 Calvinist ministers, the protest movement especially challenged the power of the district officers, the *grietmannen*, demanding that they not be allowed to sit as delegates in the provincial estates. By the fall of 1672, the sovereignty of the province was claimed by two rival sessions of the provincial estates—one including *grietmannen* and the other not—but the opposing sides eventually agreed to arbitration of the dispute by a commission from the Estates General. The modest reforms that were finally agreed to in March 1673 came to nothing, however, and the regent oligarchy built around the *grietmannen* was ironically strengthened rather than broken by the experience. Meanwhile, during the crisis of 1672 the 15-year-old Hendrik Casimir II was confirmed as stadholder in his own right, and in 1675, following the example of Holland, Friesland made the office hereditary in the male line.

The stadholder's political significance changed dramatically, however, following the crisis of 1747.[50] On the one hand, the Frisian stadholders, in the past relatively isolated at their court in Leeuwarden and inferior to their counterparts in Holland, suddenly became important nationally, and both William IV and William V would henceforth be largely resident in The Hague. On the other hand, the stadholder's position within Friesland would be enhanced by another wave of popular protest. Shortly after the signing of the peace treaty in 1748, popular mobilization once again challenged the regent aristocracy, reviving the demands of 1672 but also attacking the tax system, as protesters were to do in Holland as well. In June 1748, some three hundred delegates from throughout the province met in Leeuwarden to present their demands to the estates. At the same time, the protesters developed plans for an annual popular assembly to monitor the work of the estates. But the prince, who was charged by the estates to draw up the necessary reforms in a new governmental regulation, intervened on behalf of the oligarchy as he did in Holland. He sent troops to counter the force of the popular mobilization, forbade the popular assemblies, and eventually issued a new regulation for provincial government that compromised the power of the *grietmannen* only by strengthening the

50. Guibal, *Democratie en oligarchie*, p. 138ff.

position of the nobility.[51] For his own part, the stadholder was especially concerned to reaffirm his political influence through the established system of political patronage. In the end, this was an outcome that satisfied virtually no one.

## PROVINCIAL HISTORIES AND NATIONAL REVOLUTION

Against the backdrop of centuries of distinctive development and decentralized self-government, the provincial histories of Holland, Overijssel, and Friesland can be said to have to converged in several important ways in the second half of the eighteenth century. For the first time, they had a common stadholder who was at the same time captain general and admiral general of the union. Though William IV and William V are often said to have had an unassailable position of virtually absolute power, the fact is that they were in no sense sovereigns within the republic; rather, they depended everywhere on the indirect influence of an elaborate patronage system. To be sure, the stadholders exploited the full potential of their patronage in this period by dispensing wherever possible with pro forma nominations and directly designating their choices for hundreds of important political offices.[52] Thus, in all three provinces, the stadholders could be said to be responsible for the oligarchic regime as it existed; in 1747–1748, they had in large measure determined the structure of the regime, and thereafter they designated, or at least had a hand in choosing, the bulk of its most important officials. How far from absolute the power of this patronage system was became abundantly clear in the 1780s.

Also, in all three provinces, the stadholder's patronage tended, as it had in Holland and Overijssel under William III, to exacerbate the factiousness of the regent oligarchies. Using indigenous "lieutenants" or "premiers" to represent their interests at the local and provincial level, the stadholders in effect divided the elite into *gunstelingen* (favorites or clients), who gained preferment and prestige, and the rest, who either never got anywhere or were punished for disloyal conduct by being

---

51. The new regulation abolished the old practice of allowing the *grietman*, whether noble or not, to sit in the estates in the place of a nobleman (each *grietenij* was to send one nobleman and one freeholder).

52. In the 1780s, the Patriots attacked these practices bitterly; see, for example, J. D. van der Capellen's famous and long-winded *Aan het volk van Nederland* (Ostend, 1781); see also De Wit, *Nederlandse revolutie*, p. 15ff.

removed from important offices. Factional divisions within the oligarchies were not unprecedented, but never before had they had such a clear focus that transcended both local and regional boundaries. How deep the divisions within the regent elite had become was revealed, once again, by the political crisis of the 1780s.

Finally, the history of these three provinces had shown that popular intervention in the world of aristocratic politics could have a dramatic impact on the course of political development. As Rudolf Dekker has shown, the province of Holland had a rich and fairly continuous history of popular protest; but especially in times of general crisis such as 1672 and 1747, when the elite was itself thoroughly divided, the disciplined and well-rehearsed crowds could decisively tip the political balance against those currently in office and bring a different faction to power.[53] Though violent popular protest was certainly not as common in Friesland, massive popular mobilizations in 1672 and 1747 were part of a popular political tradition that could be said to be at least as potent as that in Holland. Even in Overijssel, where popular insurrection never reached the proportions of either Holland or Friesland, the oligarchy was threatened enough by popular mobilization following William III's death in 1702 to issue stern warnings and to threaten immediate repression of dissent in the countryside, and the intervention of the guilds in Deventer changed the nature of local politics for years to come. In all cases, then, the ruling oligarchy was shown to be vulnerable to pressure for change from below.

All these developments were critical in the gradual unfolding of the Dutch revolution of the 1780s. During the 1770s, the William V's influence over foreign and domestic policy began to unravel as he pressed unsuccessfully for augmentation of the standing army and for military support of the English in their growing conflict with their North American colonies. Nevertheless, when, much to William's chagrin, the republic was dragged into the war on the side of the Americans, he was loudly blamed, as admiral general and captain general, for the disastrous course of the fourth Anglo-Dutch war (1780–1784).[54] The growing regent opposition to the stadholder was led not only by his traditional sparring partners in the urban oligarchies of Holland, such as pensionary Engelhart van Berkel of Amsterdam, but also by such men as Joan Derk van der Capellen, a member of the *ridderschap* in Over-

53. Dekker, *Holland in beroering*; see also Roorda, *Partij en factie*.
54. J. S. Bartstra, *Vlootherstel en legeraugmentatie, 1770–1780* (Assen, 1952).

ijssel, and C. L. van Beyma, a *grietenij* secretary and member of the rural regent elite in Friesland. Though these men represented very different political interests and could be privately contemptuous of one another, they publicly joined forces to oppose the alleged tyranny of the prince, whose patronage they certainly did not enjoy. Indeed, the remarkable breadth of regent opposition to William V is a backhanded compliment to William IV's success in changing the climate of Dutch politics (if not its structure) in the wake of the crisis of 1747.

Once the Anglo-Dutch war broke out, however, opposition to the stadholder exploded well beyond the exclusive circles of the regent oligarchy. In an unprecedented rush of political publications aimed at a surprisingly large reading public, common citizens everywhere were urged to mobilize for concerted political action. Beginning modestly in early 1782 with petitions asking for official recognition of the revolutionary United States of America, and accelerating with the creation of dozens of voluntary militias and citizens' corresponding and vigilance committees in 1783 and 1784, a broadly based popular Patriot movement pushed previously quiescent members of the regent oligarchy to join the chorus critical of the stadholder and his policies.[55] But if opposition to the influence of the stadholder were all the Patriot movement represented, there would likely have been no standoff in 1787; indeed there would have been, in a profound sense, no revolutionary conflict at all. The stadholder was, after all, not the sovereign of the Dutch Republic. What made the conflict between Patriots and Orangists revolutionary was the fact that the Patriots' popular movement, like its predecessors', was also directed against the ruling oligarchy.

Because the Patriots were also challenging the regent oligarchy, the distinctive political structure of the Dutch Republic ensured that the revolutionary conflict, fought out for the most part in sovereign provinces and independent municipalities, would be essentially diffuse and episodic. But it is also with regard to popular challenges of oligarchic rule that the legacy of Dutch provincial history, in general and in 1748 in particular, was most variable. We have already reviewed the different patterns of conflict in the provinces of Holland, Friesland, and Overijssel; it remains here to connect those patterns with the provincial histories we have just explored.

In the first place, it might be said that, although the Patriots had no Bastille to attack, the fragmentation of sovereignty at the heart of the

55. See Te Brake, "Popular Politics."

Dutch Republic actually worked to the advantage of the Patriots. In Holland and Overijssel, where municipal sovereignties to some degree compromised provincial sovereignties, the Patriots were provided with a generally manageable and conveniently incremental path to power. Though a long series of municipal revolutions might seem frustratingly slow and unheroic, this path to power had the enormous advantage of being relatively easy and generally bloodless.[56] Except in a city such as Amsterdam, where magistrates could usually count on the civic guard to repress civil disorders, municipal authorities were powerless to resist aggressive action by the Patriots' militias.[57] By contrast, in Friesland, where municipalities were less independent and provincial government more centralized, the Patriots clearly suffered from the lack of an equivalent or appropriate political space. Short of challenging the power of enfranchised landowners in the hundreds of villages that stood at the base of the electoral system, the Patriots had little choice but to challenge the power of the regent oligarchy at the provincial center by creating their own provincial estates—an alternative sovereign. As they did exactly that and at the same time assembled their militias in Franeker in the summer of 1787, it was not at all clear whether they could win the military confrontation that was shaping up. Yet it was abundantly clear to everyone that Patriot revolution in Friesland would not be easy or bloodless.

But structural legacies alone did not determine the varied patterns of Dutch political conflict in the 1780s. Divisions within the elite, while ubiquitous, were also variable in important ways. In Overijssel and Friesland, where the systematic use and abuse of the governmental regulations gave the stadholder extensive patronage and influence, his political impact was most divisive. In Overijssel, for example, the town councils of both the IJsselsteden and the numerous smaller towns, which had traditionally elected local magistrates, were clearly subordinated to the prince's lieutenants. Likewise, the magistrates of the IJsselsteden lost out to the prince's men in that they no longer controlled political preferment, even though they retained administrative patronage within their cities as before.[58] In Friesland, too, the Orangist premiers of the cities divided the urban oligarchies, while in the countryside the stadholders' abuse of the reforms of 1748—for example,

56. W. Ph. te Brake, "Violence in the Dutch Patriot Revolution," *Comparative Studies in Society and History* 30 (1988): 143–163.
57. On the question of repression, see Dekker, *Holland in beroering*, p. 95ff.
58. See Te Brake, *Regents and Rebels*.

appointing minors to political office in defiance of the governmental regulation—divided the office-holding elite as never before.[59] To be sure, the urban oligarchies of Holland were also factious and divided, but the stadholder's far more limited influence did not give rise to more fundamental political realignments as it did in Overijssel and Friesland. When the commercial interests of Holland were at stake, as they were in the fourth Anglo-Dutch war, opposition to the stadholder could be considered de rigueur for most of the regent elite. But, in Holland, opposition to the prince's foreign policy by no means implied a desire for more fundamental political change at home.[60]

These varied divisions within the regent oligarchies were important in that they offered variable opportunities for the alliance of disaffected factions of the elite with popular protest movements. But the history of popular political action had its own special legacies. In both Holland and Friesland, the history of collective action and popular protest was rich and dramatic, for in both 1672 and 1747 ordinary people had been decisive not only in changing the personnel of government but in transforming the conditions under which they governed. By contrast, the history of Overijssel seems placid and uneventful, especially in 1672 and 1747. Different lessons could be derived from these different histories. In Overijssel, it was possible to look all the way back to a mythical past when *het Volk* (the People) had exercised sovereign power through their sworn councils (*gezworen gemeente*); or, as the guildsmen of Deventer did, they could recall 1703 when *het Volk* had actually exercised their sovereignty through an "extraordinary election" of magistrates and sworn councillors.[61] But 1748 necessarily loomed large in Holland and Friesland. Reading history backward— that is, judging the *achtenveertigers* (the protesters of 1748 who had vaulted William IV into an unprecedented position of power) by the fruits of their labor—many Frisians and Hollanders were as fearful of *het grauw* (the undisciplined mob or rabble) as they were impressed by the political potential of *het Volk*.[62]

59. Van der Meulen, *Van Beijma*, pp. 13–54; see also J. de Boer, "Verhouding."
60. See Schama, *Patriots and Liberators*.
61. Te Brake, *Regents and Rebels*, p. 103.
62. I have explored the question of the Patriots' fear of "het grauw" in an unpublished paper given at the Universities of Amsterdam and Rotterdam in 1985 and the University of Michigan in 1986: "Rhetoric and Reality in the Patriot Revolution." The Americans, too, became suspicious of the politics of the crowd, but only after crowds had been instrumental in challenging British power in North America (and praised for doing so). See Gordon Wood, "A Note on Mobs in the American Revolution," *William and Mary Quarterly* 23 (1966): 635–642, and Gordon Wood, *The Creation of the American Republic, 1776–1787* (Chapel Hill, 1969). By contrast with the Americans, then, the Dutch Patriots' fear of the crowd, rooted in memories of 1748, seems almost preemptive. See also Colin Lucas, "The Crowd

The emergence of a viable revolutionary coalition including factions of the elite and an organized popular movement was, therefore, by no means a foregone conclusion in the 1780s. In Friesland there was enough resentment within the oligarchy for the provincial estates to toy with the idea of creating a universal militia as a countervailing force to the prince's standing army. But, once armed and organized, the popular movement proved not to be so easily controlled; its demands for reform quickly frightened the bulk of the elite back into reactionary and repressive legislation if not all the way into the arms of the stadholder. In Holland the creation of a revolutionary coalition was significantly retarded by a few well-publicized demonstrations of support for the prince in 1783 and 1784. These not-so-subtle reminders of 1748 served to give the formation of Patriot militias a reactionary, defensive quality and to ally the popular movement, for a time at least, with the traditionally anti-Orange but well-established elite.

It is not surprising, then, that Overijssel emerged as the Patriots' model for the successful formation of a viable revolutionary coalition. The disaffected segments of the elite gladly participated in the formation of Patriot militias as a weapon against the prince and his allies, and the popular movement's demands for constitutional reform (specifically, the destruction of the governmental regulation) promised mainly to rid the oligarchy of the hated "tyrant." When it came to devising new structures to replace the old, this coalition naturally began to discover its differences—but that is another story quite common to all revolutions.[63] Suffice it to say here that in Overijssel, precisely because of its distinctive history, the drive to institutionalize the idea of the sovereignty of the people—that is, to create a form of representative democracy in which dependence on the prince would be replaced by dependence on *het Volk*—came closest to being successful before outside intervention interrupted the process.

Thus, we come full circle: we return, in the end, to the intentions of the Patriots and their hopes for the future. Just as in judging revolutions primarily by their outcomes or the intentions of their leaders we are liable to miss much that is enduring and reflective of the past, so also in relating this diffuse and episodic revolution to the distinctive history of Dutch republican state making we are liable to downplay its

---

and Politics between *Ancien Régime* and Revolution in France," *Journal of Modern History* 60 (1988): 421–457.

63. On the political and social background of the disintegration of the Patriots' coalition, see Te Brake, *Regents and Rebels*.

newness, its anticipation of the future. "Representative democracy" and "sovereignty of the people"—these slogans of the Patriot revolution point us forward; these new political principles were, after all, finally realized in Dutch history under very different conditions than we have emphasized here, the circumstances of state centralization and constitutional monarchy.[64] Still, this analysis does suggest two general observations.

Historians have often suggested that the Dutch Patriots failed in 1787 in a larger sense than their defeat at the hands of Prussian troops: that they failed to project the political reforms that the feeble republic really needed; that they failed to understand that restoration of the glorious Dutch past was not realistic; in short, that they failed to overcome the legacy of the past.[65] Losers are particularly liable to historical second-guessing, of course, but there can be no doubt that a successful Patriot revolution would not have brought either state centralization or constitutional monarchy, at least not in the short run as an intentional consequence of their victory. In that sense, the Patriots did fail to anticipate the future. But that, in a deep and therefore nontautological sense, was hardly a revolution of which the Dutch were capable.

On the contrary, this analysis suggests that the Dutch Patriots were nearly successful precisely because of their history. They were able to mount the first major revolutionary challenge to Europe's old regime precisely because their fragmented sovereignties, their divided oligarchies, and their traditions of popular protest opened real, if variable, opportunities for the formation of a viable revolutionary coalition. Though it is not clear whether the Patriots would have been able to maintain and extend their revolution without a major civil war, the relatively bloodless revolution they got prior to foreign intervention might well be considered to be the revolution that the makers of a decentralized republican state deserved.

64. For the long, difficult history of the centralization and democratization of the Dutch state, see Schama, *Patriots and Liberators*, and C. H. E. de Wit, *De strijd tussen aristocratie en democratie in Nederland, 1780–1848* (Heerlen, 1965).

65. See, for example, Palmer, *Democratic Revolution*, vol. 1, pp. 364–370; E. H. Kossmann, "The Crisis of the Dutch State, 1780–1813: Nationalism, Federalism, Unitarism," in *Britain and the Netherlands*, vol. 4, ed. J. S. Bromley and E. H. Kossmann (The Hague, 1971), pp. 156–175; and I. Leonard Leeb, *The Ideological Origins of the Batavian Revolution* (The Hague, 1973).

# 4

# The Patriot Revolution: New Perspectives

## Nicolaas C. F. van Sas

O N and off, over the past two decades, the Dutch Patriot revolution of the 1780s has been the subject of fierce and occasionally even acrimonious historical debate.[1] The controversy was started with the publication in 1965 of C. H. E. de Wit's *De strijd tussen aristocratie en democratie in Nederland, 1780–1848*. In this book De Wit presented a challenging new interpretation of a crucial period in the history of the Netherlands: the years of the transition from the *ancien régime* of the republic, with its almost medieval political forms, to the unitary state and the "modern" political system of the nineteenth century. The *patriottentijd* of the 1780s was the first critical phase in this long period of transition.

The traditional historiography challenged by De Wit consisted broadly of two different schools of thought, one led by H. T. Colenbrander, the historian with whom scholarly research into Dutch political history of the late eighteenth century had started in the 1890s, the other more recent and embodied in the work of Pieter Geyl. In Colenbrander's eyes the activities of the Patriots and their Orangist opponents were simply a reflection of the struggle of the neighboring great powers to draw the Dutch Republic into their sphere of influence. In his view the Dutch by that time had sunk so deeply in comparison with

1. See E. O. G. Haitsma Mulier, "De Geschiedschrijving over de Patriottentijd en de Bataafse Tijd," in *Kantelend geschiedbeeld*, ed. W. W. Mijnhardt (Utrecht-Antwerpen, 1983), pp. 206–227

their golden seventeenth century that even their internal politics were being masterminded and manipulated by foreign powers. The English and French envoys in The Hague were the effective leaders of the Orangist and Patriot parties, respectively, handling the miserable Dutchmen as puppets on a string—a metaphor eagerly used by Colenbrander himself. This *international* interpretation of politics in the *Patriottentijd* went unchallenged for quite some time. It was in a sense self-perpetuating, for who would want to investigate this period, in which all elements that had made the Dutch great in their golden century seemed so palpably lacking? There were one or two historians who did, but the value of their work was not fully appreciated at the time.[2]

The first historian to offer a coherent alternative interpretation of the eighteenth-century Dutch revolution was Pieter Geyl in the 1940s. Geyl was then on the brink of becoming a figure of international renown, but in the narrow world of Dutch historiography he was still something of a muckraker. Interestingly enough, it was the German occupation of the Netherlands in the years 1940–1945 that provided him with his new insight into the Patriot movement.[3] Whereas, on the face of it, a straightforward historical analogy might seem appropriate, Geyl demonstrated that the two situations were really worlds apart. Far from showing up the self-styled Patriots as in fact unpatriotic collaborators, he offered a full-scale revaluation of the role of the Patriots in the 1780s and the Batavians in the 1790s. They had certainly not, Geyl argued, betrayed their country to the French in the same way the Dutch fascists of his own time were collaborating with the Germans. The essential difference was that the eighteenth-century Patriots, who were widely supported, were to all intents and purposes an authentically Dutch movement, whereas the N.S.B.ers, as the Dutch quislings were called, could not be considered part of the mainstream of Dutch politics. Geyl's revision of Dutch Patriotism had the double effect of denying the similarities between Patriots and N.S.B.ers—something these quislings prided themselves on—and refuting the disparaging puppet perspective of Colenbrander. Geyl's own interpretation is per-

---

2. Especially M. de Jong Hzn., *Joan Derk van der Capellen* (Groningen–The Hague, 1922), and J. S. Theissen, *Uit de voorgeschiedenis van het liberalisme in Nederland* (Groningen–The Hague, 1930).

3. P. Geyl, *Patriotten en N.S.B.ers: Een historische parallel* (Amsterdam, 1946). Geyl developed these views in *De Patriottenbeweging, 1780–1787* (Amsterdam, 1947) and subsequently in vols. 5 and 6 of his *Geschiedenis van de Nederlandse stam* (Amsterdam-Antwerp, 1962).

haps best called *nationalist*. He explained the activities of the Patriots as prompted by the need for national renewal, both economically and politically. On balance, he stressed nothing so much as their quintessential Dutchness.

In 1965, De Wit delivered his indictment against both Colenbrander and Geyl. Dismissing their international and nationalist interpretations, he presented a *social* interpretation of Dutch politics in the years 1780–1848. He contended that this period of transition was marked by a continuing struggle between aristocracy and democracy, that is, between members of the traditional ruling class, the regents, who were trying to keep the power to themselves, and emancipating burghers. Even when regents and burghers were cooperating, as they did during the *Patriottentijd*, this collaboration could only be a temporary alliance, for in reality they had no common interests whatever. The so-called Patriot regents were merely using burghers to add some muscle to their traditional battle with the stadholder. I do not enter into the merits of this particular argument; too much has been written about it already. Perhaps the main virtue of De Wit's book is that it has managed to keep alive a debate on Patriots and Batavians for over twenty years now. At the same time, it must be admitted that this discussion has not led to anything remotely like a new consensus, or even to an agreed set of problems on which it might be possible to differ. The chief criticism leveled against De Wit has been that his crudely drawn categories leave no room for a proper analysis of politics in what, by any definition, must be called a highly charged political atmosphere. In the end, he leaves us with a fairly static and simplistic picture in black and white of regents who are invariably in the wrong and burghers who always happen to be right.[4]

All said and done, it cannot be denied that a feeling of deadlock exists as to the interpretation of the eighteenth-century Dutch revolution. Even Simon Schama has not been able to break this deadlock with his *Patriots and Liberators: Revolution in the Netherlands 1780–1813* (1977), in spite of the new information and his many illuminating insights. His book is perhaps best seen as the ultimate synthesis of the three schools of interpretation I have outlined so far: the international, the nationalist, and the social. Captivated, I would suggest, by the richness of Dutch vernacular historiography, he has not been able

4. N. C. F. van Sas, "Geschiedenis als samenzwering," review article of C. H. E. de Wit, *Het ontstaan van het moderne Nederland (1780–1848) en zijn geschiedschrijving* (Oirsbeek, 1978), *Theoretische Geschiedenis* 7 (1980): 9–17.

to disentangle himself from its dilemmas and from the final impasse of this particular debate.[5]

The desire to continue the discussion on Patriots and Batavians on a different and more promising footing is now widely shared among Dutch historians. Though this does not mean we have to start again from scratch, it is certainly too early to try to develop a new overall interpretation of Dutch Patriotism. At least, I am not able to do so. I can, however, suggest some possibilities to break the present deadlock. It is worthwhile, I think, to begin by establishing links with the growing body of literature concerning the political developments of the late eighteenth century in various European countries. It may just be that our discussions have become somewhat parochial over the years, and that we have lost touch a little with international historiography. To give just an indication of the direction in which I am looking, I may refer to the work done on the French revolution by François Furet, Mona Ozouf, and Lynn Hunt; to the flourishing study of sociability in both France and Germany; to John Brewer's investigation of popular politics in England.

The interpretation I favor would be both political and cultural in emphasis, centering on the concept of "political culture" as defined (in a historically meaningful sense) by Keith Michael Baker to embrace the set of discourses and practices used by individuals and groups to express their competing claims in any given society. As Baker himself has demonstrated, this approach makes it possible to throw new light on a familiar problem in French historiography: the relationship between Enlightenment and revolution.[6] In a Dutch context, this connection has never been convincingly explored. The considerable advance, however, of Enlightenment studies in recent years (not least in the Netherlands) enables us to approach this old problem in a novel way. It seems to me a particularly liberating development that every country is now being allowed its own Enlightenment, with its own characteristics and pecu-

5. The contribution of foreign scholars to the historiography of the eighteenth-century Dutch revolution is reviewed in N. C. F. van Sas, "De Nederlandse revolutie van de achttiende eeuw," *Bijdragen en Mededelingen betreffende de Geschiedenis der Nederlanden* 100 (1985): 636–646.

6. For the definition of political culture, see the introduction to *The French Revolution and the Creation of Modern Political Culture*, vol. 1, *The Political Culture of the Old Regime*, ed. Keith Michael Baker (Oxford, 1987), pp. xii–xiii. For the relationship between Enlightenment and revolution, see Keith Michael Baker, "Enlightenment and Revolution in France: Old Problems, Renewed Approaches," *Journal of Modern History* 53 (1981): 281–303, and Keith Michael Baker, "On the Problem of the Ideological Origins of the French Revolution," in *Modern European Intellectual History: Reappraisals and New Perspectives*, ed. Dominick LaCapra and Steven L. Kaplan (Ithaca-London, 1982), pp. 197–219.

liarities, without having to conform to some French-inspired model.[7] Indeed, by treating both Enlightenment and revolution as truly multiple phenomena, an intriguing web of connections between them can be seen to emerge.

The first historian I mentioned was François Furet, the iconoclast and scourge of Marxist orthodoxy in the 1960s and 1970s, now himself a past master of revolutionary historiography. In his reflective and provocative *Penser la Révolution française* (1978) Furet offers an exciting new reading of the revolution, opening interesting venues of research and investing much older literature with new value and meaning. Furet puts the political dimension of the revolution in the forefront once again, a dimension perhaps still obvious to the man in the street but increasingly lost in the scholarly debate of the past decades. The revolutionary process as such takes center stage, from which it had long been ousted by the search for causes and conditions. Furet reestablishes the revolution as an *événement* in its own right and stresses that a completely new situation emerged as soon as it had actually broken out.

Rethinking the revolutionary process from a political and ideological point of view, Furet shows the critical importance of the manipulation and use of words. To understand the dynamics of revolutionary politics, he thinks it necessary to unravel its *circuit sémiotique*. In *Politics, Culture and Class in the French Revolution* (1984), Lynn Hunt offers an even more emphatically semiological interpretation of the revolution. Hunt too takes power as her central concern. She devotes considerable attention to political language, ritual, organization, participation, ideology, and propaganda. In her analysis, she tries to unravel the "values, expectations, and implicit rules that expressed and shaped collective intentions and actions," in other words, the political culture of the revolution. It is her contention that in many respects it was symbolic practices, the use of rhetoric and ritual, that called the new political class into existence. Rituals and symbols are not seen simply as metaphors of power; "they were the means and ends of power itself." Hunt explores the links between politics and culture more explicitly than Furet, for instance by tapping other sources than purely literary ones. Making full use of the imagery of revolution in prints and engravings, she can present the revolution as a truly semiological happen-

7. *The Enlightenment in National Context*, ed. R. Porter and M. Teich (Cambridge, 1981). On the Dutch Republic, see W. W. Mijnhardt, "De Nederlandse Verlichting in Europees perspectief," *Theoretische Geschiedenis* 10 (1983): 335–347.

ing. While firmly denying that politics can be treated separately from culture, Hunt considers "the institution of a dramatically new political culture" the most important consequence of the French revolution.[8]

Hunt sees the political discourse of the revolution as essentially rhetorical, "a means of persuasion, a way of reconstituting the social and political world."[9] Torrents of words were devoted to the revolutionaries' belief that they were creating a new nation. Subjects were transformed into citizens. Those formerly oppressed became proud republicans. The *ancien régime* was called into existence (only to be maligned and dismissed) to mark the creation of this new nation. Here Hunt develops one of the central insights of Furet's *Penser la Révolution française*. In a few crucial pages, though not perhaps the most lucid ones of the book, Furet argues that in the revolutionary situation power came to be seen as vacant, free, available for anyone to get hold of. In this vacuum the word became all important. Opinion took the place of power: "Speech was substituted for power as the only guarantee that power would belong only to the people."[10] Whereas *ancien régime* politics of power was marked (and marred) by secrecy, by contrast the word was public and transparent, that is, subject to monitoring by the people. A battle for the control of public opinion became the revolutionary equivalent of a struggle for power. What was essentially at stake was the right to speak for the nation. A successful claim in this respect took the place of a bid for power. Understanding public opinion therefore becomes crucial to understanding the revolution itself. Trying to explain what Keith Baker has called "the supremely political act of redefining the body politic" is what *Penser la Révolution française* is really about.[11]

This analysis offers interesting possibilities for comparative research into the various revolutions of the late eighteenth century. The battle for public opinion, the obsession with words (and indeed with the imagery of revolution), the redefinition of the political nation, all these elements do not belong exclusively to the French Revolution but are also to be found elsewhere. Notwithstanding important differences, a fruitful comparison can be made in my view between the dynamics of the Patriot revolution of the 1780s and the subsequent French Revolution. As in France, whatever the deeper causes, there was a sudden

8. Lynn Hunt, *Politics, Culture and Class in the French Revolution* (Berkeley, 1984), pp. 10, 13, 54, 15.
    9. Ibid., p. 24.
    10. François Furet, *Penser la Révolution française* (Paris, 1978), p. 71.
    11. Baker, *Ideological Origins*, p. 204.

change of climate that created a new, quite unexpected, "inedited" situation.[12] In a way, the sense of shock in the Dutch Republic in 1780 may have been even sharper than it was to be in France in 1789, for in the Netherlands it was war that started everything. Far from producing a feeling of national unity, the war crisis brought about a noisy and decidedly messy debate on the sad state of the republic and those responsible for it.

Let me recapitulate events briefly. Toward the end of 1780, England declared war on the United Provinces, the fourth Anglo-Dutch war, which began more than a century after the third had finished. In the meantime, both countries had been united by two alliances: the maritime one of 1674 and the defensive one of 1678. As a pretext for war, the English produced a treaty the city of Amsterdam was alleged to have concluded with the American rebels. The real English motivation, however, was that the Dutch Republic was on the verge of joining the League of Armed Neutrality, a pet project of Catherine of Russia aimed at boosting her own international prestige at the expense of Britain.[13] For the Dutch, joining this league would have meant distancing themselves from England, their "natural" ally. From the British point of view these ties may not have been of much practical value anymore, but the government clung to them firmly, to the point even of waging war, as it now turned out.

The outbreak of this war opened a pandora's box of political activity. The immediate consequences of the war were dramatic. Within weeks hundreds of Dutch merchant ships were seized. Many Dutch colonies were taken by the British. The last vestiges of great-power status were lost overnight and economic annihilation seemed imminent. The fleet that would have had to defend the interests of shipping and commerce proved to be in a very bad state. Years of endless bickering between the so-called land provinces and sea provinces of the republic whether to invest in the navy or the army had produced only the result that nothing at all had been done.[14] Criticism of the deplorable state of the Dutch fleet was not, however, directed against those responsible for dragging out this debate on military expenditure, but against the stadholder, William V of Orange, in his capacity of commander in chief of the armed forces. From the outset, the stadholder

12. See Furet, *Penser la Révolution française*, p. 39.
13. Isabel de Madariaga, *Britain, Russia and the Armed Neutrality of 1780* (New Haven, 1962).
14. J. S. Bartstra, Jr., *Vlootherstel en legeraugmentatie, 1770–1780* (Assen, 1952).

was victimized for something for which he was at most only partly responsible.

The effect of this vilification of the stadholder was a serious undermining of his prestige and a breakdown of authority at the center of the power structure of the republic. The war crisis was exploited by those who now called themselves Patriots—both regents and burghers—to erode the stadholder's position still further. In their opinion he had been usurping power at the expense of both the regent class and the people in general. The disastrous course of the war created a truly Machiavellian moment in the Dutch Republic. There was a characteristic dual threat to Dutch liberty: England the attacker from without and the stadholder the usurper from within. This situation was surely conducive to direct minds to reflect on the traditional values of Dutch liberty, which is exactly what the Patriots immediately started doing. They appropriated the voice of the nation and tried to capture public opinion with their newly forged language of Patriotism. They claimed the exclusive use of such terms as *patriot, vaderland*, and *vrijheid* ("liberty"). Doing so in the midst of a wartime crisis, they created a new phenomenon: a modern, aggressive nationalism, something at the time almost unprecedented. In this new nationalism the existing, rather loosely defined national consciousness of the Dutch was merged with a yearning for the traditional virtue of the seventeenth-century republic, which had been extolled for several decades in the highly popular spectatorial journals (literary periodicals modeled on the English *Spectator*). This new nationalism was accompanied by all those side effects that have since become only too familiar but were then experimental: glaring propaganda and the systematic vilification of the enemy without and within. This new nationalism was not, of course, a program for all Dutchmen alike. It was essentially a party-political program, the creed of the new political nation, self-appointed and trying to monopolize the voice of the republic. Because of its "natural" bond with Britain, the Orange party was in effect excluded from the nation.

Intimately linked with this charged notion of nationhood was an obsessive preoccupation with treason. Once again the comparison with the French Revolution comes to mind. Furet regards the idea of conspiracy as central to revolutionary ideology. It functions, so to speak, as the negative, the "anti-principle" of revolution.[15] The stadholder was an early victim of this obsession, his alleged *inactiviteit* as a military

15. Furet, *Penser la Révolution française*, pp. 78–79.

commander being considered conclusive proof of having sold his soul to Britain. In a cartoon captioned "Ecce Proditor," one of the prince's cronies, Van Goens, is being broken on the wheel, while William V stands weeping at the side.[16] The Patriot poet Jacobus Bellamy devoted two of his "Vaderlandsche gezangen" to the subject of treason.[17] The vocabulary of treason kept pace with the developing dynamics of revolution. In the spring of 1787, when many regents, feeling burghers breathing down their necks, wanted to make their peace with the stadholder, the discovery of such a "plot" in Amsterdam was made public in a broadsheet headed "Het Verraad Ontdekt" (Treason Discovered). This sparked off a purge of the city council in which nine councillors lost their seats. They lost their heads too, but in keeping with the nonviolent tradition of Dutch politics this happened only in a cartoon, which pictured these heads being carried off on a wheelbarrow to be dumped outside the gates of the Garden of Holland.[18]

As always in the history of modern nationalism, this new creed could flourish only because there were media to spread it. Perhaps the single most important political innovation of the *Patriottentijd* was the emergence, almost immediately, of a periodical political press.[19] Within weeks of the outbreak of the war, the first and most famous of these weeklies, *De Post van den Neder-Rhijn*, started publication. It was an instant success and its example was followed by dozens of other papers, *De Politieke Kruyer* being the second most important. This sudden explosion of political periodicals requires some explanation. According to the market-sensitive Leiden bookseller C. F. Koenig, it was the war that had made people eager to read.[20] This observation seems to be well founded. Judging only from the quantity of printed paper

16. Atlas van Stolk 4569. On the cartoons of the period, see Paul Knolle, *Comiecque tafereelen* (Amsterdam, 1983), and C. Veth, *Geschiedenis van de Nederlandsche caricatuur* (Leiden, 1921).

17. J. Bellamy, *Gedichten* (Haarlem, 1826), pp. 37, 73.

18. Atlas van Stolk 4719.

19. On the press of the *Patriottentijd*, see M. Schneider and J. Hemels, *De Nederlandse krant, 1618–1978*, 4th ed. (Baarn, 1979), pp. 85–104, and especially the numerous publications of W. P. Sautijn Kluit, listed by W. N. du Rieu in the *Levensberichten der maatschappij van Nederlandsche letterkunde* (Leiden, 1895). The points made in this article on the political press and the program of the Patriots are dealt with more fully in N. C. F. van Sas, "Opiniepers en politieke cultuur," in *Voor vaderland en vrijheid: De revolutie van de Patriotten*, ed. F. Grijzenhout, W. W. Mijnhardt, and N. C. F. van Sas (Amsterdam, 1987), pp. 97–130.

20. W. P. Sautijn Kluit, "De Post van den Neder-Rhijn," *Nijhoff's Bijdragen*, 2d series, 10 (1880): 293–385; W. P. Sautijn Kluit, "De Politieke Kruyer," *Nijhoff's Bijdragen*, 3d series, 1 (1882): 176–273; C. F. Koenig, *Koninklyke verdediging; en gedagten inzonderheid over het te hoog in prys stellen der boeken* (Leiden, 1784); W. P. Sautijn Kluit, "De politieke praatvaar en praatmoer, snapper en snapster," *De Nederlandsche Spectator* (1873): 268.

that has come to us, the war and subsequent politicization may well
have given reading a powerful impulse, especially by widening the
reading public. But the ground had already been well prepared; the
two best known Patriot weeklies, the *Post* and the *Kruyer*, imitated in
many respects the spectators that had been so popular over the past
decades.

These moralizing weeklies offered their readers a picture of natural
sociability, of social behavior in a civilized manner.[21] In many ways the
spectators were the voice of the Dutch Enlightenment, or at least of its
mainstream. They marked the cultural emancipation of the bourgeoisie
and they too enjoy a reputation of having taught the Dutch to read.[22]
Apparently the new political press wanted to take advantage of reading
habits already formed by the spectators. Many spectatorial forms remained the same in format, number of pages, price, and frequency of
publication. Indeed, the similarities went even further. The political
weeklies also borrowed some of the peculiarities that distinguished the
spectator as a literary genre. In these magazines, a cozy ritual was conducted to evoke an atmosphere of intimacy between the spectator figure and his friends on the one hand and the reading public on the
other. This communication was carried on mainly through letters published in the magazine and signed with some fictitious name. The great
majority of these letters to the spectator must have been fictitious
themselves, or so it is assumed. The *Post* and the *Kruyer* used this
formula quite cleverly. They too made letters to the editor their main
feature, and their letters were signed with the same sort of pseudonym
used in the spectators, such as Ignotus, Jan Overtuigd (John Convinced), and Pieter Nugter (Peter Sensible). We should not, however, be
taken in by this particular resemblance. Whereas in the spectators it
had been fictitious letters signed with fictitious names, similar pseud-
onyms were now being attached to letters that had nothing fictitious
about them.[23] Spectatorial forms were being exploited as a convenient

21. On the spectatorial ideal in general, see Wolfgang Martens, *Die Botschaft der
Tugend: Die Aufklärung im Spiegel der deutschen moralischen Wochenschriften* (Stuttgart,
1971). P. J. Buijnsters discusses Dutch spectators in several articles, collected in his *De
Nederlandse literatuur van de achtiende eeuw* (Utrecht, 1984); on the similarities and differences between the spectators and the political journals of the 1780s, see especially p. 72. See
also J. Stouten, *Verlichting in de letteren* (Leiden, 1984), pp. 52–54. J. Hartog summarizes
the contents of many Dutch spectators in *De spectatoriale geschriften van 1741–1800*, 2d,
enlarged ed. (Utrecht, 1890).
22. G. W. Huygens, *De Nederlandse auteur en zijn publiek* (Amsterdam, 1946), pp. 29–
46.
23. This same tactic had already been employed by the well-known economic spectator
*De Koopman* (The Merchant), which appeared from 1766 to 1776. It consisted of two-thirds

protection against ever-prying authorities. Using these forms had, however, still more important consequences for the new political press. By opening their columns to the readers, and by earnestly inviting their participation, these periodicals created a new political forum where no credentials were required apart from the ability to read and write.[24] Weeklies such as the *Post* and the *Kruyer* had in fact transferred the ritual of close intimacy between Mr. Spectator and his readers from the world of fiction to the real world, thus creating a powerful new means of communication.

In the contents of the political press, there was a clean break with the spectatorial tradition. Though very much given to opinionating, Mr. Spectator had generally refrained from venturing into the realm of politics. Advocating a world of social harmony, he had not challenged the existing social and political order. Of course, the moral lessons of the spectator may have had an indirect political effect, for instance, when the intemperate and luxurious lifestyle of members of the elite was taken to task. This moral message was spread not only in the spectators but also through prints and engravings. These caricatures satirized the antics of fashionable society, such as the wearing of crinolines or the highly volatile periwig fashion, which changed almost every night and became ever more grotesque.[25] Together with the criticism that the eighteenth-century Dutch had lost the pristine virtues that had accounted for the greatness of the seventeenth century, and that work-shy and spendthrift grandsons were running through the money their industrious grandfathers had amassed, this may have helped to undermine the prestige of the elite and to challenge the self-evident continuation of the existing social and political order. Whatever hidden meaning the spectators may have had, with the political press from 1781 onward we have no such interpretative problems. Here the message was clear and unambiguous. The reader was addressed as somebody who had a legitimate interest in politics—someone, in other words, regarded as a member of the political nation.

The role of the political press in the *Patriottentijd* did not stop at

---

readers' letters and one-third editorial matter. It was explicitly stated that no fictitious letters were published; H. Brugmans, "De Koopman: Mercurius als spectator," *Jaarboek der Vereeniging Amstelodamum* 10 (1913): 61–135

24. See Elizabeth L. Eisenstein, "On Revolution and the Printed Word," in *Revolution in History*, ed. R. Porter and M. Teich (Cambridge, 1986), p. 197.

25. See Veth, *Nederlandsche caricatuur*, pp. 157, 160. For the relationship between social and political caricature, see also Charles Press, "The Georgian Political Print and Democratic Institutions," *Comparative Studies in Society and History* 19 (1977): 216–238.

forming public opinion and voicing the feelings of the new political nation. In addition, the press became the chief integrating force of Patriotism. The fragmented political structure of the Dutch Republic made it almost a matter of course that Patriotism became a divided movement too, described once as "at bottom, a series of municipal revolutions."[26] The main Patriot periodicals, however, especially those distributed nationwide like the *Post* and *Kruyer*, were a vital link between these local movements. Besides, by giving pride of place to readers' letters, they went even farther in creating a nationwide community of feeling. More than any sort of formal organization, the press came to embody the cohesion in Dutch Patriotism. Each of the two main journals went about this in its own way, the *Post* by treating issues of national interest, the *Kruyer* by publishing many articles (or rather readers' letters) featuring local topics from all over the country. Sometimes this meant printing scandalous stories about misbehaving regents. This muckraking journalism rather tainted the later reputation of the *Kruyer*.[27] It should be recognized, however, that the accountability of local authorities was very much part of the Patriot program. Publishing these stories made the *Kruyer* no less a serious political journal.

Both the *Post* and *Kruyer* were enormously successful. This success is apparent both from public demand—with three thousand copies printed the *Post* approached the limits of what was technically possible at the time—and from public response. Both periodicals were flooded with readers' letters, and they continuously had to add pages or issue extra numbers. In the end, no less than 614 issues were published of the *Post*—set up as a weekly—in the 350 weeks of its existence between January 1781 and October 1787. The *Kruyer* managed 482 issued in five years' time.

From the start, it was the Patriot press that set the tone. The Patriots proved to be quite successful in winning the support of educated opinion. Orangist journals were reduced to reacting and refuting the claims and accusations of their opponents. The problem of the Orange party was not that it was in need of able publicists; it enjoyed the support of some of the best authors of the day, such as Elie Luzac and Rijklof Michaël van Goens. But all this proved of no avail. Luzac com-

26. Wayne Ph. te Brake, "Popular Politics and the Dutch Patriot Revolution," *Theory and Society* 14 (1985): 212.
27. For example, H. T. Colenbrander, *De Patriottentijd*, vol. 1 ( The Hague, 1897), p. 289; L. J. Rogier, *De Nederlandse pers van gisteren en heden* (Nijmegen-Utrecht, 1954), p. 7.

plained that the public did not want to be convinced; it only wished to have its prejudices confirmed.[28] The chief Orangist answer to the *Post*, the *Ouderwetse Nederlandsche Patriot*, though well written and elegantly produced, managed to sell only seven hundred copies. Still, despite this obvious lack of support, the Orangist press made an important contribution to political renewal in the Dutch Republic. By sharply accentuating the contrast with the Patriot press, it created a full-fledged alternative value system. The politicizing burgher now could choose between two such value systems, or ideologies, in which a particular reading and coloring of the past was coupled with a program of action for the future. This rise of ideologies, competing with each other for the favor of public opinion, is in itself an important facet of the new type of politics that was breaking through in the Western world in the late eighteenth century.

None of the other political periodicals of the 1780s could match the huge success of the *Post* or the *Kruyer*. Many of these weeklies were inspired in part by profit-seeking booksellers, who wanted a share of an apparently insatiable market. Market forces played a part not to be underestimated in the battle for public favor in the *Patriottentijd*. Politics in the 1780s was also very much a matter of business. Booksellers were out to make a profit and always on the lookout for a gap in the market. This, at least, was the opinion of Luzac, himself a bookseller by profession. He was clearly disappointed by the lack of interest in Orangist writings. Whereas in earlier times the civilizing influence of the printing press had been emphasized, now money seemed the only thing that mattered. Demand, taste, and fashion determined what was printed. One day it might be natural history or meditations on morals, now it happened to be politics. Being a present-day bookseller, Luzac grumbled, was not markedly different from being a merchant in chintz or damask.[29]

If commercial motives played an important part in deciding what was written and published, commercial success had an impact of its own. It made a publisher in a sense untouchable. Authorities who might want to ban a publication because of its subversive content could hardly do so in view of its unmistakable popularity. Success on the free market may well have offered the best guarantee against government repression. Working for the market also made authors inde-

28. E. Luzac, *Reinier vryaarts openhartige brieven*, 4 vols. (s.l., [1781–1784]), vol. 1, p. 7.

29. Ibid., vol. 2, p. 141.

pendent of the financial support of patrons and consequently of their possible political manipulations.[30]

Freedom of the press as a matter of principle was a major item of the Patriot program. The press in the Dutch Republic was, however, already very free in practice. Prosecutions had always been incidental; there was no systematic censorship. Though many authorities on various levels were empowered to take action against offensive publications, there was no coordinated central authority to make such action really effective. The fragmented political structure of the republic made it almost impossible to keep in check a volatile medium like the press. Once in print, it was no longer possible to withdraw a publication from circulation, or so the experience of two centuries seemed to prove. Everyone knew how to get around an injunction. When the sale of a certain newspaper or pamphlet was prohibited in one town, it was easily ordered by mail from elsewhere. But often this was not even necessary. It was quite normal for such banned publications to be made available just outside the city's jurisdiction. A citizen of Rotterdam had only to take the trouble of a pleasant fifteen minutes' walk to nearby Delfshaven to get hold of the forbidden.

Nevertheless, there were one or two notorious prosecutions of Patriot publications.[31] In 1782, the Orange party tried to provoke an action against the *Post*. Its publisher, Van Paddenburg, gave the local authorities in Utrecht (where the *Post* was printed) to understand that he would take his flourishing business (which gave work to eighteen people) elsewhere should any harm come to it. When the Orangist prosecutor pressed proceedings, the city's bench of aldermen cleared the *Post* of all charges, thus delivering a heavy blow to the Orange party nationwide. In 1785, the editor and publisher of the *Kruyer*, Hespe and Verlem, were taken into custody for some days and fined 3,000 guilders each. The paper itself kept coming out, however, and both men became instant martyrs of the Patriot cause. As soon as they were released, public celebrations were held all over the republic and Hespe and Verlem were made honorary members of many Patriot organizations. Editor Hespe even had a special visiting card printed, engraved with appropriate symbols like broken chains, which he delivered by carriage to all those who had paid him a visit in prison. In many places, collections were held to make up the heavy fine. In the

30. This should (at least partly) answer the point frequently made by C. H. E. de Wit about client relationships between regents and Grub Street hacks.

31. See Sautijn Kluit, "De Post van den Neder-Rhijn," and "De Politieke Kruyer."

end, this prosecution was painfully counterproductive. The prosecutors had succeeded only in putting themselves on trial by public opinion. The main consequence of their action was to undermine trust in the regents in general.

By starting legal procedures against the *Post* and the *Kruyer*, the tormented authorities openly showed how seriously they took these adversaries. They had clearly been caught unawares by the meteoric rise of the political press, which had in the shortest of times established itself as an impressive means of power. Meanwhile, there was a structural change in the use of the media for political purposes. During the whole period of the republic to this time, pamphlets had been the dominant political medium. These broadsheets, blue booklets, whatever they were called, had accompanied every political crises the republic had known. The highs and lows in the stream of pamphlets served as a barometer of the political climate. (Perhaps the republic was unique among European states in the virtually unrestricted use of this particular medium over more than two centuries. Other states had also known their bouts of intense pamphleteering, but these were often followed by reassertions of censorship.) In the *Patriottentijd*, however, the pamphlet lost its place as the main carrier of opinion to the political weeklies. This change was not immediately visible, and in a sense pamphlets in the 1780s even flourished as never before. If giving offense is the touchstone for a successful pamphlet, there certainly were some notorious ones published in these years. In his *Politiek vertoog over het waar sistema van de stad van Amsterdam* (Political Treatise on the True System of the City of Amsterdam, 1781), the Orangist Van Goens attacked Amsterdam as a perennial plague in the history of the republic. Even more sensational was *Aan het volk van Nederland* (To the People of the Netherlands, 1781), in which Joan Derk van der Capellen reviled every hint of Orangism in Dutch history.

If we turn away from individual pamphlets of great notoriety to look at numbers, the production of pamphlets in the 1780s was truly enormous. From 1778 onward, these numbers swelled noticeably, due to international tension. But in 1781, the first full year of the war with England, there was nothing less than an explosion of broadsheets. At the same time, however, the highest point had already been reached. During the following years the number of pamphlets appearing annually steadily declined (at least if we consider the collection of the Royal Library at The Hague as representative), whereas political conflict was ever increasing. It seems quite legitimate to conclude, therefore, that the great age of pamphlets was over. Mainly due to the spectatorial weeklies, the politicizing public appears to have become accustomed to regular supplies of fresh reading matter. This need could be satisfied by the periodical political press, but not by pamphlets that were by definition occasional writings. Precisely because of its periodicity, the political press could go on guiding and molding the public interest in politics, once that interest had been aroused in the first place. Instead of the incidental stimulus provided by pamphlets, there was the more continuous operation of the press. At a time when there was hardly any form of organized politics, this was an important innovation indeed.

It is quite impossible to do justice to the contents of the dozens of political periodicals and thousands of pamphlets that appeared in the 1780s. Still, it is not altogether unwarranted to deduce from this huge pile of paper something like a Patriot program. Patriots of different feathers were always seeking a common appearance. Their pretension to voice the feelings of the nation made this in a sense obligatory. As I have already indicated, trying to find the answer to the decline of the Dutch Republic in its various guises—economic decline, the deterioration of international standing, and, last but not least, moral decay— was the main inspiration of early Patriotism. *De Post van den Neder-Rhijn* wanted to suggest remedies "to prevent the certain destruction of the country"[32] and in so doing broke with the convention that politicizing was the monopoly of a small elite. Another influential periodical, the *Courier van Europa*, also explained its coming into existence "in an extremity, at the evening hour of our commonwealth," by the wish to take part in the crucial debate on the decline of the republic.[33]

The program evolving in the Patriot press, though at first rather disparate, gradually became more coherent. In this Patriot platform several planks may be distinguished. One bore on the international decline of the republic; in this sense Patriotism was a theory of national power.[34] Another referred to corrupt power relations within the country; in this sense Patriotism was a cry for constitutional safeguards. A third was concerned with the general decay of morals; in this final

32. *De Post van den Neder-Rhijn*, vol. 1, Preface.
33. *Courier van Europa*, no. 1 (5 Sept. 1783). The *Courier* did not use the spectatorial formula. It was a one-man paper, written by W. van Irhoven van Dam.
34. See E. H. Kossmann, "The Crisis of the Dutch State, 1780–1813: Nationalism, Federalism, Unitarism," in *Britain and the Netherlands*, vol. 4, ed. J. S. Bromley and E. H. Kossmann (The Hague, 1971), pp. 156–175. See also E. H. Kossmann, "Aan het volk van Nederland," in *Politieke theorie en geschiedenis* (Amsterdam, 1987).

sense the Patriot program can be seen as a call for moral rearmament. In the background was always the looming presence of the seventeenth-century past, pressing on eighteenth-century shoulders like a golden weight.

Having started in a rather negative way by criticizing the uncontrolled powers of the stadholder, the Patriots gradually formulated their constitutional demands in a more positive manner. They presented these demands as a plan for constitutional restoration, which meant purging from the gaudy variety of rights and privileges that made up the constitution of the republic all sorts of abuses that had crept in. This so-called restoration should not be taken too literally. The conventions of the time required that political demands be couched in good, or rather good-looking, historical terms. Though this may well have had a limiting effect on the free expression of political demands, on the other hand it is quite possible to discover innovative or even revolutionary designs behind such a front.

Regents and burghers were united in their demand to reduce the power of the stadholder to his original function as servant of the provincial estates. At the moment, he could influence decisively the composition of many town councils and consequently also the estates, which were supposed to be his masters. This created a vicious circle of power in which, in the final analysis, it seemed possible for the stadholder to supervise himself. The Patriots were not, however, content with eliminating power without responsibility only at the national level. This should also be done locally, in the town councils where regents ruled. Regents ought not behave like aristocrats—corrupt by definition—but should always be aware of the representative roles they were to play. The Patriots were advocates of a representative democracy. They were distinctly not aiming at government by the people outright. Even the most radical Patriot writers were quite convinced that such a thing could result only in chaos and anarchy.

The Patriot program, which had taken shape bit by bit in periodicals and pamphlets, was recapitulated in the mid-1780s in one or two central texts. Most important among these was the *Grondwettige herstelling van Nederlands staatswezen* (Constitutional Restoration of the Netherlands' Political System, 1784–1786), a two-volume political handbook written in a near scholarly fashion.[35] The authors began with

35. Page citations in the following discussion are to *Grondwettige herstelling van Nederlands staatswezen*, 2d ed., 2 vols. (Amsterdam, 1785–1786). E. J van Himbergen has analyzed its contents, concentrating on the constitutional aspects, in *Figuren en figuraties: Acht*

the apparently inevitable declaration that their book was "totally and solely intended . . . to lift the republic from its weak and ramshackle condition, and to raise it once more to the highest possible pinnacle of power and prestige" (vol. 1, p. iii). Defeatism must not be tolerated, however serious the present crisis. Those prophets of doom who argued on the basis of cyclical theories that the republic was past its prime and would only sink farther were not to be listened to. On the contrary, the present malaise should act as a stimulus for recovery (vol. 1, p. viii). It would be necessary to establish a well-regulated popular influence, and the state would have to be protected against attacks from without and tyranny from within. There was still time for a salutary restoration, without the need for "an overall recasting" (vol. 1, p. 14). Searching for the reasons of the present decline, the *Grondwettige herstelling* took the flowering of the seventeenth century as its point of reference. At that time, the blessings of personal and political freedom, tolerance, and equality before the law and the tax man had all worked together to create a great commonwealth. At present, however, other countries, having learned from experience, were quickly making up the arrears: "Because our wisdom has been relative, we are losing every day a little of what we owed to the folly of other nations, who are now becoming more enlightened." This diagnosis already contained the key for recovery: were the nation to be saved, it was an absolute necessity that "it should be enlightened ever more" (vol. 1, pp. 28–31).

According to the *Grondwettige herstelling*, the rights of the people were, naturally, inalienable. The power of the stadholder had to be curtailed, if only to prevent, as *De Post van den Neder-Rhijn* had already argued, the republic from becoming "a miserable little monarchy, soon to be eaten up by its petty monarchic court" (vol. 1, p. 101). Moreover, the influence of a court was supposed to deprave the morals of the regents. They would become estranged from "old Netherlands' simplicity" and would be plunged into luxury and extravagance. This in turn would foster hatred and malice between regents and burghers, and, even worse, inequality, "the pest of republics" (vol. 1, p. 107).

More interesting perhaps than the somewhat obligatory criticism of the stadholder was the way the regent aristocracy was weighed and

---

*opstellen aangeboden aan J. C. Boogman* (Groningen, 1979), pp. 27–39. See also, on the *Grondwettige herstelling* and on contemporary political theory in general, I. L. Leeb, *The Ideological Origins of the Batavian Revolution* (The Hague, 1973).

found wanting. The *Grondwettige herstelling* was sharply critical of what it called aristocratic conspiracies against the rights of the people, such as the infamous contracts of correspondence that ensured that the most important municipal offices were reserved for a small circle (vol. 2, p. 232). Family government was also strongly condemned. The *Grondwettige herstelling* presented its own version of the Good, the Bad, and the Ugly by outlining three different types of regent: the people's regent, the aristocratic regent, and the stadholderly regent. Stadholderly regents were in every respect little men. Flattering their betters and kicking their inferiors was the hallmark of these dependents of the court. The aristocratic regent was unbearably proud and a very dangerous creature indeed. Aristocrats saw the people as "just a common heap, only fit to endure their haughtiness, to obey their capriciousness, and to be an instrument for the furtherance of their particular interests." A people's regent, on the other hand, would only have reached his high position because he was a man of merit. He would always defend the interests of the nation as a whole and not just his own private interests (vol. 1, pp. 188–190).

The most intriguing aspect of the *Grondwettige herstelling* is perhaps its third part, which was in fact never published and of which only a brief outline of contents exists. This third part was to deal with the encouragement of sciences and arts, freedom of the press, religion and tolerance, economic recovery, and moral and physical education. The ambition of the Patriots to restore not only the constitution of the republic but also its morals is clearly demonstrated here. This intriguing volume was to have explained how to overcome decay with Enlightenment. Unfortunately, it never left the planning stage. We can only guess how the Patriots, after having successfully taken over the nation, would have attempted to appropriate the Enlightenment as well.

In the Patriot press, the *Grondwettige herstelling* was unanimously applauded as an impressive synthesis. A correspondent of the *Kruyer* knew of no other work "in which the whole Patriotic System is presented so perfectly, so well-reasoned and so convincingly." The appearance of this book had given the democratic party strength and solidity, it was said.[36] *De Post van den Neder-Rhijn* also warmly recommended it.[37] A more tersely worded version of the Patriot program was given in the so-called *Leids ontwerp* (Leiden Draft, 1785), or, as its full title

36. *De Politieke Kruyer*, vol. 5, pp. 203–206.
37. *De Post van den Neder-Rhijn*, vol. 7, p. 126.

reads, "Draft to Make the Republic through a Salutary Union of Interests of Regents and Burghers, Happy on the Inside, and Fearsome on the Outside."[38] The title is itself programmatic, referring to the main themes of Patriot thinking: national power, burgher participation, and moral rearmament.

In the *Leids ontwerp* the representative character of the system of government was worked out point by point. Regents should have no illusion that they were exercising power more or less in their own right, let alone that they could consider their offices private property. It was no longer sufficient to pay lip service to the majesty of the people; the influence of the people (that is, burghers of some means) had to be clearly spelled out. Governing bodies should not be dominated by a closed aristocracy; true union would have to be effected between the people and its representatives. This was the only way for the government to regain its authority and for prosperity to return. Burgher participation in local government might be realized at the yearly elections of municipal officeholders or when a vacancy occurred in the town council. Militias and guilds should be handed back the representative functions they were traditionally entitled to. The representative nature of the militia would be reinforced by having the militiamen elect their own officers. A permanent body of burgher commissioners was to be placed beside the town council to safeguard the rights of burghers. This body would be consulted, for instance, regarding decisions on new taxation, and it would supervise the management of public finance. Accountability, both financial and political, was a key concept in the purified political system the Patriots had in mind.

In the eyes of the Orange party, all this talk of ancient rights and burgher participation meant nothing but destruction and revolution. This view was put forward in propaganda aimed at the common people, but also at a more sophisticated level. One of the most able publicists fielded by the Orange party, the Leiden history professor Adriaan Kluit, was able to blend sound academic reasoning with a sharply polemical style. Kluit regarded the *Grondwettige herstelling* as a particularly dangerous piece of propaganda, mainly because of its seeming innocuousness. Far from indulging in inflammatory language, it presented its argument in a way almost certain to send its readers to sleep. Because Kluit saw many right-thinking people among his acquaintance

---

38. *Ontwerp om de republiek door eene heilzaame vereeniging der belangen van regent en burger, van binnen gelukkig en van buiten gedugt te maaken* (Leiden, 1785). Knuttel 21045.

falling for the Patriot case as it was presented here, he started a forceful counteroffensive. He duly recognized the important role played by the periodical press in recent years. He did not, however, share the Patriots' enthusiasm for the press as a mechanism to expose abuses and to inform the people about its rights. In his eyes the Patriot press—especially the three main periodicals, *De Post van den Neder-Rhijn, De Politieke Kruyer*, and the *Courier van Europa*—was almost solely responsible for the misery the Dutch Republic had gone through since 1781. Refusing to fall into the trap of a supposed "constitutional restoration," Kluit knew the Patriots were in reality aiming at something quite different: "novelties namely, that, however beautifully they might shine, however enchantingly they might be presented, did not stop them from being *dangerous* novelties."[39]

There was much more to Patriot tactics than the innovative use of the periodical press, however important that may have been. It was the combined use of various tactics, some old, some new, or old ones used in a novel way, that accounted for much of the impact of Patriot politics in the 1780s. A traditional means of applying pressure was collective petitioning. Van der Capellen warmly advocated this method because it had been in regular use since the days of princess-governess Anne.[40] In the 1780s, however, there was petitioning in the republic on a scale never seen before. People also started putting down their signatures—sometimes in the thousands—to qualify fellow citizens to speak in their name. Needless to say, these "qualified" burghers regarded themselves not as the mouthpieces of a particular interest group but of the citizenry as such. The same monopolizing mechanism that we have already seen at work nationally was now applied at a local level. The signing of petitions and acts of qualification often seems to have been restricted to people of some means (males only), demonstrating once again that it was not just everybody who was allowed a say in politics.

The typically eighteenth-century phenomenon of organized sociability was also put to political use in the 1780s. *De Post van den Neder-Rhijn* quite appropriately called the eighteenth century the "Age of Societies."[41] Only in recent years, however, has this phenomenon attracted widespread scholarly attention. In German historiography it

39. A. Kluit, *De souvereiniteit der staaten van Holland, verdedigd tegen de hedendaagsche leere der volks-regering* (1785), especially pp. 160–161. In 1788, Kluit published a new edition, enlarged with annotation applauding his foresight.

40. *Brieven van en aan Joan Derck van der Capellen van de Poll*, ed. W. H. de Beaufort (Utrecht, 1879), p. 425.

41. *De Post van den Neder-Rhijn*, vol. 1, p. 274.

has been argued with some emphasis that there is a crucial link between the concept of association (*Vereinsbildung*) and the development of modern bourgeois society, of which it is considered a distinctive feature and even a constitutive element.[42] In France, the concept of sociability has been approached from various angles, among others by Daniel Roche and Maurice Agulhon. François Furet, in his creative reading of the work of the half-forgotten historian-sociologist Augustin Cochin, has tried once more to make sense of the relationship between Enlightenment and revolution.[43] The *socialisation de la pensée* in the numerous societies of the prerevolutionary period could provide the "missing link," accounting for the dissemination of Enlightenment ideas and (unwittingly) preparing a climate for revolution. In England, the impact of association has recently been analyzed by John Brewer, who stresses the opportunities created by association and the accompanying fund raising to break the vertical bonds of eighteenth-century social dependency.[44]

It seems well worth the effort to look at the role played by sociability in general and political sociability in particular in bringing about the political transition in the Netherlands from the late eighteenth century onward. It would be quite wrong, however, to look only at sociability in its modern associative guise, as is often done in German literature, which overstresses the contrast between *Korporation* and *Assoziation*. At the start of the process of political modernization in the Netherlands in the 1780s, such old corporate structures as guilds and *markevergaderingen* sometimes played important parts.[45] Indeed, the nation was once defined by Van der Capellen as "burghers, guilds, militias."[46] Political sociability as such was very much a product of the

42. Th. Nipperdey, "Verein als soziale Struktur in Deutschland im späten 18. und frühen 19. Jahrhundert," in *Geschichtswissenschaft und Vereinswesen im 19, Jahrhundert* (Göttingen, 1972), pp. 1–44; Otto Dann, "Die Anfänge politischer Vereinsbildung in Deutschland," in *Soziale Bewegung und politische Verfassung*, ed. Ulrich Engelhardt a.o. (Stuttgart, 1976), pp. 197–232; Wolfgang Hardtwig, "Strukturmerkmale und Entwicklungstendenzen des Vereinswesens in Deutschland, 1789–1848," in *Vereinswesen und bürgerliche Gesellschaft in Deutschland*, ed. Otto Dann, *Historische Zeitschrift* 9 (1984): 11–50.

43. Furet, *Penser la Révolution française*, pp. 212–259.

44. John Brewer, "Commercialization and Politics," in Neil McKendrick, John Brewer, and J. H. Plumb, *The Birth of a Consumer Society* (London, 1982), pp. 197–262.

45. See Wayne Ph. te Brake, *Revolutionary Conflict in the Dutch Republic: the Patriot Crisis in Overijssel, 1780–1788* (unpublished thesis, University of Michigan, 1977); Wayne Ph. te Brake, "Revolution and the Rural Community in the Eastern Netherlands," in *Class Conflict and Collective Action*, ed. Louise A. Tilly and Charles Tilly (Beverley Hills, Calif., 1981), pp. 53–71; Te Brake, "Popular Politics and the Dutch Patriot Revolution." See also J. L. van Zanden, "De opkomst van een eigenerfde boerenklasse in Overijssel, 1750–1830," *A. A. G. Bijdragen* 24 (1984): 105–130.

46. *Brieven van Joan van der Capellen*, p. 518.

war. The atmosphere of crisis and the new nationalist feeling recalled the age-old idea that citizens, in order to be truly free, had to be able to defend themselves and their commonwealth without having to resort to (foreign) mercenaries. It was in a sense the ultimate test of their being true burghers. These martial feelings were soon translated into practical suggestions. In 1774, Van der Capellen published a Dutch translation of Andrew Fletcher's well-known pamphlet on militias. In his preface, Van der Capellen drew attention to Article VIII of the 1579 Union of Utrecht, which provided for the draft of all men between the ages of 18 and 60 for military service—an article that had never been carried out. (The Union of Utrecht, originally a defensive treaty against Philip II from the times of the Dutch Revolt, served as a kind of constitution for the Dutch Republic. Many of its provisions, especially those overstepping provincial boundaries, were a dead letter from the outset.) In 1782, the Friesland district of Oostergo proposed to revive this particular article. This proposition had the double advantage of being beautifully in line with the aforementioned classical ideal while at the same time having a perfect historical pedigree in Dutch terms, reaching back to the Union of Utrecht. This idea of a *levée en masse* attracted widespread attention, though once again it proved impossible to carry it out. Subsequently, however, the concept of an arms-bearing citizenry was brought to life in an urban setting. In many towns the initiative was taken to revive the old burgher militias (*schutterijen*), which had often become obsolete or almost nonexistent. It should be noted that these were attempts to revitalize a time-honored corporate structure with very much an *ancien régime* flavor to it. As I mentioned earlier, these *schutterijen* were seen not just as paramilitary organizations but also as representative institutions for their burgher members.

Apart from trying to revive the *schutterijen*, the Patriots often started new military societies of their own to be able to drill more freely and more frequently. Sometimes these *exercitiegenootschappen* were linked with existing *schutterijen*; sometimes they were truly independent *vrijcorpsen*. Again, such arms-bearing clubs were not merely paramilitary organizations but very much political pressure groups as well. They were always organized according to the modern associative principle, that is, on democratic lines. Members chose their own officers. The democratic organization of these *exercitiegenootschappen* and *vrijcorpsen* was clearly meant to serve as a model for the reconstruction of the *schutterijen*. Such reconstructions were, however, often thwarted by local authorities, who feared to lose their grip on the militia. Ideally, after a *schutterij* has been successfully reformed, a fusion might take place with the local *exercitiegenootschap*. In one or two cases this did in fact happen. Elsewhere, harmonious relations were maintained between the two. It was, however, also possible for a fierce antagonism to exist between a Patriot *vrijcorps* and the *schutterij*, especially when the latter was controlled by a non-Patriot town council.

It is easy to make fun of this "playing soldiers" of so many earnest burghers all over the republic, drilling as much as they could, parading their highly colorful (and costly) uniforms, and having their first experience of politics in the meantime. The scale of the civic militarism was nonetheless rather impressive. Arms bearing was now positively associated with the Patriot idea of citizenship. The best-selling Patriot treatise *De vrijheid* (Liberty) saw this as a matter of course. Indeed, the militia came to be regarded as a school for citizens to such an extent that the *Leids ontwerp* made serving in it a necessary precondition for holding public office. It should be noted that, in the Dutch context, arms bearing and active citizenship were not at all connected with the ownership of land, as they are in J. G. A. Pocock's Machiavellian paradigm.[47] Van der Capellen (who as an east Netherlands Patriot nobleman and a warm advocate of militias was ideally positioned to develop this connection) once likened the state, in a long, drawn-out, and distinctly unlanded metaphor, to a joint stock company with the people as participants.[48] There even seems to have once been an inverse association between land, arms, and citizenship. When the estates of Holland ordered the creation of a land militia in 1784, in view of the menacing behavior of Joseph II on the Belgian border, it met fierce resistance from the countryside. Many people living there did not at all appreciate this appeal to their civic feeling, especially when they were Orangists at heart and had their cows to take care of.[49]

Apart from these paramilitary organizations, many political societies were established in the 1780s. Often these were called reading societies, not from any desire to hide their real activities but because reading and subsequent discussion formed the core of activities.[50] To

47. J. G. A. Pocock, *The Machiavellian Moment* (Princeton, 1975); J. G. A. Pocock, *Virtue, Commerce and History* (Cambridge, 1985).

48. E. H. Kossmann, "Dutch Republicanism," in *L'Età dei Lumi: Studi Storici sul Settecento Europeo in Onore di Franco Venturi*, 2 vols. (Naples, 1985), vol. 1, pp. 455–486; reprinted in Kossmann, *Politieke theorie en geschiedenis*, pp. 211–233. See also the symposium in *Theoretische Geschiedenis* 9, no. 1 (1982).

49. Geyl, *Geschiedenis van de Nederlandse stam*, vol. 5, p. 1319.

50. On Dutch reading societies, see P. J. Buijnsters, "Lesegesellschaften in den Niederlanden," in *Lesegesellschaften und bürgerliche Emanzipation: Ein europäischer Vergleich*, ed. Otto Dann (Munich, 1975), pp. 143–158.

give just one example, let us follow a visitor to the *Vaderlandsche Societeit* in Leiden, established at the end of 1784. Entering a spacious room, he saw many people engaged in friendly conversation. Smartly dressed men of rank were mingling comfortably with others still wearing their aprons and apparently taking a short break from work for a heartening political conversation. The Patriot weeklies, the *Post* or the *Kruyer*, were passed from hand to hand and served as an agenda for discussion. Members (who had to belong to the city's *exercitiegenootschap*) paid 24 stuivers a year for these amenities. The rooms were open to them all day and in the evenings. The great benefit of a society like this one, in the eyes of our visitor, was that people from all walks of life could meet here in an informal, relaxed atmosphere. This made it a breeding ground for true, free burghers. Indeed, the idea of natural sociability, with its civilizing influence, is very much present in this account, published in the *Kruyer*.[51] The *Kruyer* itself warmly endorsed this happy tale from Leiden and called it an example for other places.

In the *Patriottentijd*, it may be argued, "an alternative structure of politics" was being developed in the Dutch Republic, to borrow the phrase John Brewer has applied to England at the time of Wilkes.[52] All layers of society (though not every individual) were drawn into politics. The mass of the people was active on both sides of the political spectrum. In Rotterdam, an Orangist crowd led by the notorious Kaat Mossel engaged in violent street action; in Utrecht, thousands of ordinary people pressured the council to accept Patriot policies by surrounding the town hall. Apart from this popular politics, there were all sorts of civic rituals, sometimes older customs given a new meaning. Large festive dinners, such as those traditionally held by guilds or militias, were organized to mark the cooperation of Patriot regents in Holland and the aristocrats of the eastern provinces, or to celebrate the alliance between the Dutch Republic and France.[53] Funerals were sometimes turned into full-scale political demonstrations, such as the burial in Utrecht in May 1787 of G. C. Visscher, who was killed in the battle of Vreeswijk (a victory of the Utrecht Patriots over Orangist regular troops). The most important among these civic rituals were elections and oath-taking ceremonies according to the new Patriot-inspired rules

51. *De Politieke Kruyer*, vol. 4, pp. 533–535.
52. John Brewer, *Party Ideology and Popular Politics at the Accession of George III* (Cambridge, 1976). See also John Brewer, "English Radicalism in the Age of George III," in *Three British Revolutions*, ed. J. G. A. Pocock (Princeton, 1980), pp. 323-367, and John Brewer, *The Common People and Politics, 1750–1790s* (Cambridge, 1986), in the series *The English Satirical Print, 1600–1832*.
53. See Frans Grijzenhout, "De Patriotse beeldenstorm," in *Voor vaderland en vrijheid*, ed. Grijzenhout, Mijnhardt, and van Sas, pp. 131–155.

and regulations. Again, Utrecht provided the most memorable example. In August 1786, amid much Patriot pomp, the local council was revolutionized and new councillors chosen. An extremely complex electoral ritual was performed to avoid undue influence on the outcome. To crown it all, an elegant Temple of Liberty was erected on the Neude, the main square of the town. This was the scene of solemn oath taking by day, and of illuminations and declamation by night.

The impact of politics in the 1780s was such that it penetrated many aspects of social life. Politics seemed to be almost everywhere. Musical life and the theater were much affected as was, in a most extraordinary way, material culture. All sorts of everyday objects were made into political symbols.[54] The distinguishing marks of both parties were painted on, printed on, or carved into a bewildering variety of things. The Orange party wanted to be recognized by the portraits of the stadholder and his wife or by the orange tree. The Patriots came to regard the keeshond as their main logo, though they also appropriated such allegorical symbols as the Maid of Liberty for their exclusive use. Moreover, to underline the historical roots of their anti-Orangist battle, they took full advantage of the great names of the so-called estates tradition in Dutch politics; Van Oldenbarnevelt, Grotius, and the De Witt brothers became the saints and martyrs of their image religion. Added to these personalities were such contemporary saints as Van der Capellen and the Amsterdam burgomaster Hooft.

Most political objects were not made with a particular didactic or propagandistic purpose in mind; rather, they were meant to symbolize solidarity and to rally the faithful. The politically active in the 1780s made no attempt to hide their feelings; they adorned themselves and their surroundings with party symbols. They wore ribbons and cockades in the appropriate color (black for the Patriots, yellow and orange for their opponents) or anything from a wide range of insignia, starting simply with the stadholder's head cut out of an Overijssel doit, to custom-made images in silver of Van der Capellen or Hooft. Political artifacts enlivened many aspects of daily life. There were politicized snuffboxes, tobacco boxes, knife handles, fans, needlecases, cake molds, and huge amounts of (mainly Orangist) ceramics, to give just a random selection. The exquisite and the banal were sometimes almost indistinguishable. Beautifully cut glassware might carry the image of a kees-

54. See, for example, the exhibition catalogues *De wekker van de Nederlandse natie* (Provinciaal Overijssels Museum, 1984); *Goosen Geurt Alberda van Dijksterhuis, 1766–1830* (Groninger Museum, 1981); *Oranje in de huiskamer* (Nederlands Openluchtmuseum, 1980). See also Serge Bianchi, *La Révolution culturelle de l'an II* (Paris, 1982).

hond pissing against an orange tree with the device "Honi soit qui mal y p . . ." Even an innocent pastime such as drinking a cup of tea could become a political manifestation, judging from the tea sets and sugar castors bearing party symbols that have been preserved. The production of all these artifacts was often—like the printing of political writings—a commercial venture. Many inventive businessmen must have doubled as political trendsetters. One of the first to see the possibilities of this political market was Josiah Wedgwood, the great Staffordshire potter, who was also a pioneer in marketing technique. In the Netherlands he exploited the market to the full by catering to both parties.[55] He supplied the Patriots with life size busts of their heroes, such as De Witt and Van Oldenbarnevelt, and the Orangists with lockets and scent bottles carrying the images of the family of the stadholder.[56]

In the autumn of 1787, the Patriot bulwark collapsed like a house of cards. Although they had been "playing soldiers" for several years now, the Patriots had no chance against the professional Prussian army. At the same time, the Orangist regime was propped up once again thanks only to foreign support. The restoration therefore was rather an artificial affair, as observant contemporaries could see for themselves. "The suppressed faction, though suppressed, exists," remarked that well-known connoisseur of the revolutionary process, Edmund Burke, in 1791; "under the ashes, the embers of the late commotions are still warm."[57] In spite of the final defeat, the consequences of what had been happening in the Dutch Republic since the outbreak of the war were not so easily undone. Between 1781 and 1787, a form of popular politics had been created in which participation was a key element. In Patriot politics it was both end and means. Many people from all ranks of society had joined in, either by drilling, petitioning, discussing, reading, or simply wearing the appropriate ribbon. In the meantime, the legitimacy and the credibility of the old order had been broken beyond repair. The new political nation that had been called to life, chiefly by the Patriot press, could hardly be spirited away just like that in 1787. Even 25000 Prussian soldiers could not rob the freedom-calling, abuse-shouting, and petition-making Patriots (to borrow some

55. Neil McKendrick, "Josiah Wedgwood and the Commercialization of the Potteries," in N. McKendrick, John Brewer, and J. H. Plumb, *The Birth of a Consumer Society* (London, 1982) pp. 100–145.

56. Exhibition catalogue *Wedgwood en Nederland in de 18de eeuw* (Princessehof Leeuwarden/Gemeentemuseum's Gravenhage, 1982).

57. Edmund Burke, *Thoughts on French Affairs*, in *The Works of the Right Hon. Edmund Burke*, vol. 1 (London, 1837), p. 571.

of Adriaan Kluit's qualifications) of the idea of belonging to that political nation.

The relatively mild nature of the Batavian revolution of 1795 (it is commonly called a "velvet" revolution) can be explained in large part by the revolutionary experience of the Dutch during the *Patriottentijd*. It was then that they took leave—though perhaps only semiconsciously —of their particular ancien régime. Antiaristocratic feeling often ran high in the 1780s, sounding indeed like a "language of class struggle without class."[58] Regents were frequently portrayed as corrupt aristocrats and incompetent profiteers. The tone of the burgher Patriots was often irreverent, subversive, and antiestablishment. They discarded the idea that politics was reserved in perpetuity for a self-appointed elite. In the 1780s, the Patriots laid a firm foundation for a new political culture on which they could build again from 1795 onward. In creating their own type of modern politics, the Patriots were not afraid to make the most of the traditions of the republic. It has often been held against them that they indiscriminately mixed old and new elements in their attempted reform. They were, however, quite clever at turning tradition to their own advantage, as they did for instance with the alleged representative nature of regent rule.

It will have become clear by now that, when I am pleading for a renewed political approach to the age of revolution, it is political history with a difference, concentrating on political culture and the invention of modern politics. This invention was, in my view, not an exclusively French affair. It was part and parcel of the complex of late eighteenth-century revolutions, the Dutch Patriot movement not being the least among them. I take issue therefore with Lynn Hunt when she writes of the "unexpected invention of revolutionary politics."[59] Several important aspects of the new political culture she discovers are only too familiar to (for instance) the student of Dutch revolutionary politics in the 1780s. Naturally, the French Revolution was by far the most momentous in the series of democratic revolutions recorded by R. R. Palmer. But by taking a bird's-eye view of political culture—instead of focusing on the sequence of events, as in traditional political history— and by looking at the vocabulary and the imagery of revolution and the evolving mechanism of modern politics, the French Revolution does not appear to be all that exceptional.

Turning finally to the main themes of this book—decline, Enlight-

58. Hunt, *Politics, Culture and Class*, p. 50.
59. Ibid., p. 3.

enment, and revolution—many questions remain unanswered. The whole concept of decline, for one, is beset with problems and ambiguities.[60] Looking at the moral side, the talk of luxury, corruption, and depravity was so commonplace at the time that we should be careful not to think that we are dealing with a specifically Dutch phenomenon. Is it possible, then, to draw a line somehow between the use of this classical topos and a special awareness of Dutch problems? Long ago we were warned not to take too literally the well-rehearsed story of eighteenth-century merchants losing touch with the world of their grandfathers and falling into a life of luxury and depravity.[61] Our main authorities for this sorry picture are the spectatorial weeklies and satirical prints. But these were very much in the business of criticizing and moralizing, and they are almost certain to have picked out the exceptions and the excesses. The contemporary observer could see this easily enough. Standing at a considerable distance in time, however, we run the risk of generalizing the exception and taking the caricature for the real thing. Where on the one hand luxury, splendor, and extravagance" were said to ruin the country,[62] the idea was also firmly disputed. Even the much maligned periwigs got some sort of defense when Adriaan Kluit argued that they, together with embroidery, costly liveries, and refreshments, were no less objects of trade and industry than grains, fish, or meat.[63]

Enlightenment may have been the patent medicine for corruption and decline. It was, however, not the exclusive privilege of the Patriots to be enlightened. The Enlightenment as such was very much a politically neutral phenomenon. The Patriots were undoubtedly children of the Enlightenment. But so were many Orangists. Van Goens, one of the most despised members of William V's circle, was at the same time a paragon of enlightened learning. Whereas the Patriot revolution was not a necessary consequence of the Enlightenment, it certainly cannot be explained without it. It needed, however, the sudden shock of war to make the link between Enlightenment and revolution, to bring about that "supremely political act of redefining the body politic" and to create Dutch Patriotism as a peculiar blend of moral righteousness, participatory politics, and aggressive nationalism.

60. See Reinhart Kosselleck and Paul Widmer, eds., *Niedergang: Studien zu einem geschichtlichen Thema* (Stuttgart, 1980).
61. Brugmans, "De Koopman," p. 108.
62. Ibid., p. 99.
63. A. Kluit, *Iets over den laatsten Engelschen oorlog met de republiek en over Nederlands koophandel, deszelfs bloei, verval, en middelen van herstel* (Amsterdam, 1794), p. 315.

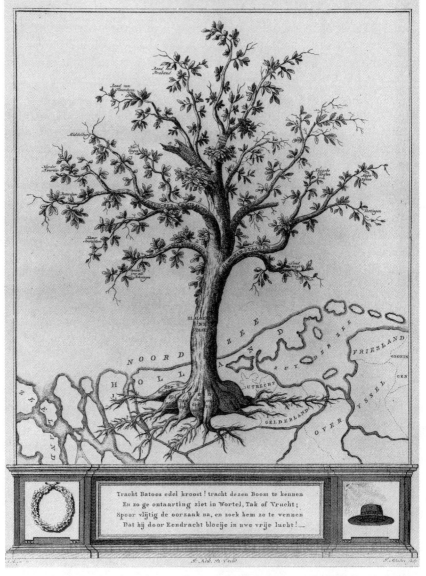

*Staat- en Regeering-kundigen boom.* The complicated constitution of the Dutch Republic is illustrated by a tree. The roots represent the towns and knights that together make up the provincial estates. The provinces are brought together in the trunk, which represents the Generality. The branches represent various institutions of the republic. The stadholder has been assigned a subordinate position. The caption admonishes the Dutch citizenry to guard against all violations of the original constitution. Engraving by J. Schultsz after A. Resinger (1786). Private Collection.

# THE
# DUTCH REPUBLICAN
# TRADITION

# 5

# Elie Luzac and Two Dutch Revolutions: The Evolution of Orangist Political Thought

## Wyger R. E. Velema

THERE was a time in the historiography of eighteenth-century Europe when the existence of a causal connection between the Enlightenment and revolution was considered to be almost self-evident. Conservatism was accordingly interpreted as an antirationalist and frequently deeply religious reaction against the onslaught of the combined perils of Enlightenment and revolution, or—which amounted to the same thing—against the birth of the modern world. Conservatism was traditionalism made conscious, a transformation brought about by the massive secular challenge to the status quo that the late eighteenth century witnessed.[1] In recent decades, however, we have been forced to modify our views, particularly in regard to the Protestant nations. First of all, it has become clear that various Protestant countries experienced what has been termed a conservative Enlightenment. The figure of the enlightened conservative has become a familiar one.[2] Second, the purely

Research for this chapter has been made possible by grants from the Johns Hopkins University and from the Netherlands Organization for the Advancement of Pure Research.

1. For example, K. Mannheim, "Conservative Thought," in *Karl Mannheim, Essays on Sociology and Social Psychology*, ed. P. Kecskemeti (London, 1953), pp. 74–164; K. Epstein, *The Genesis of German Conservatism* (Princeton, 1966).
2. For example, E. H. Kossmann, *Verlicht conservatisme: Over Elie Luzac* (Groningen, 1966); J. G. A. Pocock, "Clergy and Commerce: The Conservative Enlightenment in England," in *L'Età dei lumi: Studi storici sul settecento Europeo in onore di Franco Venturi*, 2 vols. (Naples, 1985), vol. 1, pp. 525–562; R. B. Sher, *Church and University in the Scottish Enlightenment: The Moderate Literati of Edinburgh* (Princeton, 1985).

modern and enlightened character of the late eighteenth-century challenge to the ancien régime has come to be doubted, and a link between late eighteenth-century radicalism and older varieties of republican thought has been established.[3] These two historiographic revisions have necessitated a reconsideration of the connections between the Enlightenment and revolution and have rendered the nature of eighteenth-century conservatism problematic. In effect, these revisions force us to rethink the whole development of late eighteenth-century political thought.

On the whole, these themes have had little impact on the study of Dutch political thought.[4] Indeed, the development of Dutch political thought in the second half of the eighteenth century has not been studied in depth at all.[5] The debate about the *Patriottentijd* seems to have come to a halt at a time that predates the revisions mentioned above. As we saw in the Introduction, it started with H. T. Colenbrander's vilification of the Patriots as puppets in foreign hands. Through various stages the debate arrived at C. H. E. de Wit's extremely Whiggish account in which the Patriots, seen as the Dutch exponents of R. R. Palmer's "age of the democratic revolution," appeared as the embodiment of modernity. Yet, despite this change of perspective, Patriot political thought—a handful of texts excepted—has largely remained unstudied. We are still ignorant about the exact nature of the Patriot challenge to the status quo.[6] We know even less about the attempts undertaken to defend the established regime. The only thorough book-length studies of late eighteenth-century conservatism are devoted to Gijsbert Karel van Hogendorp. The interest in Van Hogendorp, however, seems to owe more to his role in the early nineteenth-century founding of the Kingdom of the Netherlands and to his subsequent

3. F. Venturi, *Utopia and Reform in the Enlightenment* (Cambridge, 1971); J. G. A. Pocock, *The Machiavellian Moment: Florentine Political Thought and the Atlantic Republican Tradition* (Princeton, 1975); J. G. A. Pocock, *Virtue, Commerce, and History: Essays on Political Thought and History, Chiefly in the Eighteenth Century* (Cambridge, 1985).

4. But see Kossmann, *Verlicht conservatisme*; M. C. Jacob, *The Radical Enlightenment: Pantheists, Freemasons, and Republicans* (London, 1981); J. G. A. Pocock, "The Problem of Political Thought in the Eighteenth Century: Patriotism and Politeness," *Theoretische Geschiedenis* 9 (1982): 3–24.

5. There is one comprehensive study available: I. L. Leeb, *The Ideological Origins of the Batavian Revolution: History and Politics in the Dutch Republic, 1747–1800* (The Hague, 1973).

6. For a recent historiographic survey, see E. O. G. Haitsma Mulier, "De geschiedschrijving over de Patriottentijd en de Bataafse Tijd," in *Kantelend geschiedbeeld: Nederlandse historiografie sinds 1945*, ed. W. W. Mijnhardt (Utrecht-Antwerp, 1983), pp. 206–227.

place in the development of Dutch liberalism than to his contribution to the political thought of the late eighteenth century.[7]

In this chapter I focus on the political thought of the most prolific Orangist author of the second half of the eighteenth century, the Leiden jurist, publisher, and publicist Elie Luzac. In many ways Luzac was a central figure in the Dutch Enlightenment. In his long career as a writer he addressed every conceivable topic from epistemology to ethics and from natural law to political economy.[8] Here I concentrate on Luzac as a political pamphleteer and on his contribution to the late eighteenth-century debates on Dutch politics. Between the years 1754 and 1792 Luzac wrote more than ten thousand pages of political commentary, the bulk of which, published in the 1780s, dealt with the dangers of Patriotism. I first discuss the earliest manifestations of Luzac's Orangism and the ways he came to change these youthful views as the century progressed. Then, the two following sections address the dominant theme in Luzac's political writings, his negative assessment of the practice and principles of Patriotism. The last section provides a brief sketch of Luzac's attempts to formulate a political alternative to Patriotism.

## LUZAC, LOCKE, AND THE REVOLUTION OF 1747

In 1754, Luzac published his first important political pamphlet, *Het gedrag der Stadhouders-gezinden verdedigt* (The Conduct of the Stadholder's Party Defended). It was occasioned by the campaign against the former *Doelisten* leader Daniel Raap and intended to justify the restoration of the stadholderate in 1747.[9] The main theoretical argument Luzac used to support his case was the existence of a popular right of resistance to unjust authority. As his motto he took a quotation from the last paragraph of John Locke's *Second Treatise of Government*, in which it is stated that, when the supreme power is forfeited

7. For example, H. van der Hoeven, *Gijsbert Karel van Hogendorp: Conservatief of liberaal?* (Groningen, 1976).

8. The best brief introduction to Luzac's thought is Kossmann, *Verlicht conservatisme*.

9. *Het gedrag der stadhouders-gezinden, verdedigt door Mr. A. V. K. rechtsgeleerden* (s.l., 1754). The pamphlet was banned by the Amsterdam government on the grounds that it was contrary to that city's laws, seditious, and libelous. It was publicly burned in Amsterdam on 15 May 1754. In 1755, Luzac published a second and revised edition, more than twice as long as the first one. The most recent commentary is L. H. M. Wessels, "Jan Wagenaar's 'Remarques' (1754): A Reaction to Elie Luzac as a Pamphleteer. An Eighteenth-Century Confrontation in the Northern Low Countries," *Lias* 11 (1984): 19–82.

by miscarriages of those in authority, it then "reverts to the Society, and the People have a Right to act as Supreme, and continue the legislative in themselves, or erect a new Form, or under the old form place it in new hands, as they think good".[10]

Luzac adopted the following line of argument. The fundamental and God-given law, the foundation of all human duties, is the promotion of one's own and other people's well-being as much as is possible. From this law there arises a second rule, namely, that everyone should contribute as much as possible to the well-being of civil society. The promotion of the general well-being has been entrusted to governments, but it is inconceivable that this absolves the people from their duty to adhere to God's first law. If governments violate that law, resistance by the people as "original and rightful rulers of themselves" is entirely therefore justified. As Locke had done, Luzac assured the reader that such a situation would seldom occur. He then proceeded to show that stadholderless governments ruined the country, or, as he would put it in 1757, "destroy civil society," and that in 1747 the very survival of the republic had been at stake. The people had thus been entirely justified in restoring the stadholder to power.

Throughout the theoretical part of his argument, Luzac leaned heavily on Locke. His use of the *Second Treatise* was highly selective, and almost all quotations came from Chapter XIX, "Of the Dissolution of Government." Luzac did not speak of compacts or natural rights. He emphasized the fact that the people are normally, and rightly, excluded from the process of government. He stressed, especially in the second and enlarged edition of the *Gedrag*, the duty to obey established governments under normal circumstances. Yet, he did state that the people had restored the stadholder and had removed a number of regents. He also seemed to imply the existence of a residual popular sovereignty. And in his 1757 pamphlets, written against the work of the historian Wagenaar, he emphasized that all legitimate governments were based on consent.[11]

Apparently Luzac gave little thought to the possibility that this line of argument might conceivably be turned against the Orangists. There were, I suggest, two reasons for this myopia. In the first place, the historical association between brief and limited popular movements in times of crisis and the Orangist cause was firm. In the 1750s, it was

10. John Locke, *Two Treatises of Government*, 2d ed., P. Laslett (Cambridge, 1970), p. 446.

11. Elie Luzac, *De zugt van den Heere Raadpensionaris Johann de Witt, tot zyn vaderland en deszelfs vryheid, etc.* (Leiden, 1757), pp. 91–126; *Het oordeel over den Heere Raadpensionaris Johann de Witt, etc.* (Leiden, 1757), pp. 1–18.

hard to imagine that the people would ever independently formulate anti-Orangist demands or desire large-scale and permanent participation in politics.[12] Second, Luzac's right of resistance and theory of consent were completely aimed at what he perceived to be the absolutist tendencies of the regent aristocracy and were totally unconnected with "democratic tendencies."[13] Only in highly exceptional and desperate circumstances were the people allowed to act as a safeguard against repressive regent despotism. Luzac's argument, in other words, was intended specifically for a situation in which the only relevant political fact was the traditional opposition between the States party and the Orangist party.

But as the century progressed, it gradually became clear that the coalition between Orange and the people could no longer be taken for granted. It also became clear that elements from Luzac's argument could be used to attack all constituted authority. In his later writings Luzac, remarkably enough, never mentioned Locke again, except in a critical way. He also never referred to the *Gedrag* after the 1750s; but he kept quoting from all his other works. What had happened? The most likely hypothesis seems to be that the Orangist uses to which Locke had been put were no longer feasible from the 1770s onward. We know very little about the fate of Locke's political writing in the eighteenth-century Dutch Republic. Locke's work was widely available in French translation.[14] M. C. Jacob has shown that the *Second Treatise* was used both by establishment and radical Orangists in the 1740s and 1750s.[15] Luzac seems to fit that pattern. But we also know that later in the century Locke's writings served as a source of inspiration to various Patriots, such as Joan Derk van der Capellen and Pieter Paulus.[16] It is highly probable that in the Patriot writings Locke's political teachings were developed into a Lockean radicalism similar to and derived from the variety that surfaced in England from the 1760s on, a doctrine insisting on a continuous active political role of the sovereign people.[17]

12. On the weakness and lack of independence of eighteenth-century popular movements before the Patriot era, see J. Hovy, "Institutioneel onvermogen in de 18de eeuw," in *Algemene geschiedenis der Nederlanden*, 15 vols. (Haarlem, 1977–1983), vol. 9, pp. 136–138.

13. The phrase is, of course, Geyl's.

14. Laslett, ed. *Two Treatises*, p. 126.

15. M. C. Jacob, "In the Aftermath of Revolution: Rousset de Missy, Freemasonry, and Locke's Two Treatises of Government," in *L'Età dei Lumi*, vol. 1, pp. 487–521.

16. M. de Jong Hzn., *Joan Derk van der Capellen: Staatkundig levensbeeld uit de wordingstijd van de moderne democratie in Nederland* (Groningen-The Hague, 1921), p. 212; W. J. Goslinga, *De rechten van den mensch en burger: Een overzicht der Nederlandsche geschriften en verklaringen* (The Hague, 1936), p. 70. A thorough investigation of Locke's role in eighteenth-century Dutch political thought is urgently needed.

17. H. T. Dickinson, *Liberty and Property: Political Ideology in Eighteenth-Century Brit-*

The writers expounding this doctrine in England, such as Richard Price, Joseph Priestley, and Thomas Paine, were enormously popular in the Dutch Republic.[18] Luzac himself seems to have recognized this lineage when, in 1784, he made one of the characters in *Vryaarts brieven* mention Locke and Price in the same breath as pernicious influences on Dutch political thought.[19]

While Locke was thus being appropriated by the Patriots, Luzac's thought progressed in an altogether different direction, a development that can be discussed only briefly here. In the late 1750s, Luzac devoted his energies to annotating an edition of Montesquieu's *Esprit des lois* and in the mid-1760s to refuting the writings of Rousseau. Montesquieu he greatly admired, but Rousseau he judged to be no more than a dangerous primitivist whose doctrines of inalienable popular sovereignty and the general will smacked strongly of arbitrary rule and popular despotism. Throughout the 1760s, Luzac also worked on an edition of Christian Wolff's *Du Droit de la nature et des gens*; it was published in 1772. Luzac's notes contain sharp criticisms of such concepts as the state of nature, the original community of property, natural equality, and the original contract. In these notes Luzac tried to develop a deeply conservative version of natural law that stressed human natural inequality and dependence, the existence of a hierarchic cosmic and social harmony, and the slow historical growth of societies and states. Most of these themes were clearly foreign to the conceptual world of Locke and certainly to that of his late eighteenth-century heirs. In the 1770s, finally, Luzac turned to political economy and adopted the argument that only nonparticipatory forms of political organization were appropriate to highly developed commercial states.[20]

Against this background, Luzac, reacting to a profoundly altered

*ain* (London, 1977), pp. 197–199; I. Kramnick, "Republican Revisionism Revisited," *American Historical Review* 87 (1982): 629–664; J. G. A. Pocock, "The Varieties of Whiggism from Exclusion to Reform: A History of Ideology and Discourse," in Pocock, *Virtue, Commerce, and History*, pp. 256–264.

18. De Jong, *Van der Capellen*, pp. 211–225, 523–525; Goslinga, *Rechten van den mensch*, pp. 17–21.

19. Elie Luzac, *Reinier vryaarts openhartige brieven*, 4 vols., 12 pieces (s.l.,[1781–1784]), vol. 12, p. 341.

20. Both Luzac's natural law and his political economy need to be studied in national and international contexts. For a first attempt, see W. Velema, "The Rise and Fall of Morality: Elie Luzac on the History of the *Science des Moeurs*," *Theoretische Geschiedenis* 14 (1987): 143–156, and W. Velema, "Homo Mercator in Holland: Elie Luzac en het achttiende-eeuwse debat over de koophandel," *Bijdragen en Mededelingen betreffende de Geschiedenis der Nederlanden* 100 (1985): 427–444.

political scene, started to write and publish the steady stream of pamphlets that would last into the 1790s. It is in these political pamphlets that we encounter his changed and more guarded views on the revolution of 1747. For the sake of peace and quiet, it would be much better, he now pointed out, not to keep returning to the events of 1747 and to let bygones be bygones. But if discussion was deemed necessary, then at least the important questions should be asked: "Did the people have a right to revolt? Were they entitled to do the things they did during that revolt? Did disturbances occur that should not have happened and that went too far? These are questions I shall not decide." The only relevant questions were "whether the restoration of the stadholderly government, by whatever means it was brought about, has not been most salutary? And whether our present form of government, whatever its deficiencies may be, is not by far the best for our state?" Whether or not the events of 1747 had been completely legitimate, in short, they had brought about a most satisfactory situation and matters should be left at that. If the role of the people had to be brought in, however, this should only be done in the context of a right to self-defense in an emergency situation, a right that derived from the duty to self-preservation and certainly did not imply the existence of original or residual popular sovereignty. Finally, it was undeniable that, although there had been popular commotion in 1747 and 1748, the stadholder had been restored not by the people but by the then established regime.[21]

By limiting the discussion as much as possible to the happy factual consequences of the revolution, by emphatically divorcing the right of resistance from popular sovereignty of whatever variety, and by substituting the established government for the people as the main actor in 1747, Luzac tried to eliminate all potentially dangerous elements from his analysis of the revolution of 1747. About doctrines of consent, which he had wholeheartedly espoused in 1757, he now remarked that it might be asked "whether such systems, which are not derived from the nature of humankind as it exists, but from our arbitrary notions about the nature of humankind as it never has existed, are not more harmful than advantageous to learning."[22] Luzac's adoption of a new analysis of the revolution of 1747 was made urgent by and formed part

21. Luzac, *Vryaarts*, vol. 12, pp. 38–40, 58–59, 195–197; Luzac, *De vaderlandsche staatsbeschouwers, etc.*, 4 vols. (s.l., s.a.), vol. 3, pp. 198–199.
22. Luzac, *Vryaarts*, vol. 9, p. 114. On the preceding page, Luzac identifies Locke as the most extreme theorist of consent.

of his anti-Patriot polemic, as indeed the Patriots themselves scornfully pointed out.[23] I therefore now turn to Luzac's views on Patriotism.

## PATRIOTISM ASSESSED: PRACTICE

Many contemporary observers interpreted the first stirrings of Patriotism as just another episode in the familiar struggle between Orangists and *staatsgezinden*; this is precisely what Luzac did in the early 1780s. Yet, as the movement expanded, he was gradually forced to the conclusion that Patriotism was something without precedent in Dutch history. It was much more than a Catilinarian conspiracy of aristocratic regents. It would not stop at the removal of the stadholder but threatened every aspect of civilized life.

One of the most remarkable new phenomena of the Patriot era was the birth of the political press. For the first time in its history, the republic was flooded with vernacular political weeklies, replacing the political pamphlet as the primary means of communication. Newspapers such as *De Post van den Neder-Rhijn* and *De Politieke Kruyer* played a crucial role in the dissemination of Patriot views.[24] Luzac was well known for his defense of the freedom of the press. In 1749, after he had been persecuted for publishing La Mettrie's *L'homme machine*, he wrote the celebrated *Essai sur la liberté de produire ses sentimens*. But this essay, radical as it was, was primarily intended to defend the freedom of an elitist republic of letters against clerical interference and governmental repression. Even in those days Luzac did not deny the desirability of punishment for those who, blinded by their passions, abused their freedom with *termes immodérés* and *expressions indécentes*. He would always remain a "lover . . . of free thought and free speech," and he would keep defending the freedom to publish "such truths as belong to abstract learning."[25] But by the 1780s the problem, as he saw it, was no longer the defense of scholarly inquiry. The issue now was the defense of reputation or good name against the scan-

---

23. *Grondwettige herstelling van Nederlands staatswezen*, 2 vols. (Amsterdam, 1784–1786); vol. 1, pp. 71–72, opposes the *Gedrag* to *Vryaarts brieven*.

24. S. Schama, *Patriots and Liberators: Revolution in the Netherlands, 1780–1813* (New York, 1977), p. 80; N. C. F. van Sas, "Opiniepers en politieke cultuur," in *Voor vaderland en vrijheid: De revolutie van de Patriotten*, ed. F. Grijzenhout, W. W. Mijnhardt, and N. C. F. van Sas (Amsterdam, 1987), pp. 97–130. See also Chapter 4 of this volume.

25. Elie Luzac, *Essai sur la liberté de produire ses sentimens* (s.l., 1749), pp. 119–120; *Vryaarts*, vol. 1, p. 113; *Staatsbeschouwers*, vol. 2, p. 203.

dalous, libelous, and seditious filth that streamed from the Patriot presses. Liberty of the press had turned into license.

Luzac formulated two main objections to Patriot political writing. For one, there were clear limits to what should be written about politics. Affairs of state should be discussed only by writers of sufficient ability and knowledge, who should carefully abstain from publicly damaging the fatherland. Discussion of specific policies and persons was highly undesirable because it disturbed peace and unity, ruined the essential trust of the subjects in their rulers, inflamed the passions, and undermined the foundations of quiet sociability by sowing discord. Once the business of government was "drawn from the circle in which it should remain enclosed," however, it became everyone's duty to participate in the public debate and to combat dangerous opinions. This was precisely what the Patriot newspapers had brought about with their Athenian demagoguery. It was Luzac's first justification for his own voluminous political writings.[26]

Luzac's second objection was that the accusations brought against the stadholder and the Orangists in the Patriot press were completely unfounded. They were slanderous and libelous and as such contrary to Scripture, natural law, Dutch law, and common decency. Luzac insisted that reputation was as important as life and property. Defamation therefore belonged in the same category as murder and theft and should be punished accordingly. It was the government's duty to do this. But the government, dominated by anti-Orangist regents, refused to take its responsibility. The result, Luzac claimed, was that every individual gained the right and duty to engage in "self-defense in writing." This was his second and most important justification for his own political publications. When by the mid-1780s the anti-Orangist regents in turn became the target of radical Patriot attacks, Luzac could only conclude that they had themselves to blame for this unfortunate fate, for they had started and encouraged something they could now no longer control.[27]

Luzac followed a similar line of argument in condemning the Patriot campaigns of petition and assembly. The right to petition, he

26. Luzac, *Vryaarts*, vol. 7, pp. 3–6; *Staatsbeschouwers*, vol. 1, pp. 191–193; vol. 2, pp. 200–202. The comparison between Patriot newspaper writers and Athenian demagogues is in Elie Luzac, *De voor- en nadeelen van den invloed des volks op de regeering, etc.* 3 vols. (Leiden, 1788–1789), vol. 1, p. 102; and in Elie Luzac, *Lettres sur les dangers de changer la constitution primitive d'un gouvernement public, etc.* (London [Leiden], 1792), pp. 220–222.

27. Luzac, *Vryaarts*, vol. 5, pp. 41; vol. 7, pp. 30–52; *Staatsbeschouwers*, vol. 1, pp. 46–47; vol. 2, pp. 194–202, 247–248, 555–561.

stressed, was extremely useful and valuable. Citizens should always be allowed to present their government with specific grievances and even to form societies and appoint delegates for that purpose. Governments could not possibly promote the common good if they completely closed their ears to the voice of the population. But the Patriots were now perverting these simple truths by presenting their petitions as commands instead of requests. Equally, the Patriot societies and their delegates had no intention of voicing specific and limited grievances. Instead, the delegates were used for the purpose of overthrowing the established government and of seizing power.[28] The Patriots were enabled to bring things to this point by what Luzac considered to be the most abominable feature of their behavior, the formation of citizen militias.

In that most famous of all Patriot pamphlets, *Aan het volk van Nederland* (1781), Joan Derk van der Capellen had called the Dutch citizens to arms. In the following years, free corps of armed citizens, claiming a variety of roles, sprang up all over the country. Citizen armament became a veritable Patriot obsession.[29] Ideologically, theirs was a curious combination of elements of the classical republican tradition, the glorification of Batavian valor, and the belief in ancient Dutch liberties and privileges. Luzac thought these free corps superfluous, illegal, and anachronistic. Indeed, a close scrutiny of their behavior suggested that the members of the free corps aimed for nothing less than "the violent introduction of a North American form of government."[30]

External defense should be left in the hands of a professional army, and the maintenance of peace and quiet in the towns was the task of the *schutterijen*. It was undeniably true, Luzac admitted, that the institution of the urban guard had decayed over the centuries. This was unfortunate, for even in modern times it still had the useful function of promoting sociability and manliness. But the decay of the urban guard certainly did not warrant the formation of completely new militias. The history of Dutch medieval towns clearly showed that the guard had originally been established by the sovereign, or at least with his permission. The citizen militias, by contrast, had been organized independent

28. Luzac, *Voor- en nadeelen*, vol. 3, pp. 140–149. On the difference between legitimate and illegitimate petitioning, see also *Vryaarts*, vol. 12, pp. 230–240, 349–350; *Staatsbeschouwers*, vol. 2, pp. 423–431.

29. Schama, *Patriots and Liberators*, pp. 80–88; J. W. Schulte Nordholt, *The Dutch Republic and American Independence* (Chapel Hill-London, 1982), pp. 271–273; H. L. Zwitzer, "De militaire dimensie van de Patriottenbeweging," in *Voor vaderland en vrijheid*, ed. Grijzenhout, Mijnhardt, and Van Sas, pp. 33–39.

30. Luzac, *Staatsbeschouwers*, vol. 1, p. 326.

of all established authority and were therefore illegal. Dreams of a return to Batavian manners were preposterous. The Batavians, after all, could hardly be said to have lived in a civil society. Was it the Patriots' desire to turn the well-ordered Dutch Republic into "a monstrous assembly of people, with more resemblance to a band of savages than to a civilized nation"?[31]

The anachronistic character of the free corps became most evident, however, in the light of modern military and economic developments. The Patriot belief that imitation of classical republics was still feasible was simply pathetic: "These smartheads have heard about a Roman burgomaster who stepped from behind his plough to command an army, and therefrom conclude that they are capable of similar things." On the one hand, the introduction of permanent standing armies had made modern warfare so sophisticated and demanding an activity that only full-time professionals were fit for the task. Nothing could be more ridiculous than the thought that a band of armed citizens could equal or surpass the strength of a huge and well-disciplined modern army. On the other hand, the modern system of commerce, with its advanced and time-consuming specialization, had made the notion that all male citizens should engage in intensive military exercise utterly unrealistic. The actual behavior of the free corps—their intimidation of Orangist citizens and regents, their increasing impatience with regents altogether, and the growing shrillness and radicalism of their demands—convinced Luzac that he was dealing with "a conspiracy to destroy the legitimate and established government . . . and to exercise a violent tyranny over those who disagree with these aims."[32]

Licentious newspaper writing, seditious petitioning, and violent armed action were, then, the three most salient characteristics of the practice of Patriotism according to Luzac. He persisted in thinking that Patriotism had been initiated by anti-Orangist regents, but he had come to realize that their aristocratic desire to rule without a stadholder had rapidly been supplanted by a strong demand for popular influence on government. Luzac found it impossible to associate democratic Patriotism with one particular group in the republic. Patriots could be found among the intelligent and the stupid, among the literate and the illiterate, among rich and poor, among theologians and atheists.[33] What

31. Luzac, *Voor- en nadeelen*, vol. 3, pp. 174; *Staatsbeschouwers*, vol. 1, pp. 89–103; vol. 3, p. 191.

32. Luzac, *Vryaarts*, vol. 9, p. 25; *Voor- en nadeelen*, vol. 3, pp. 150–153; *Staatsbeschouwers*, vol. 1, p. 104.

33. Luzac, *Staatsbeschouwers*, vol. 2, p. 271.

finally united these people, other than pure wickedness and unfocused dissatisfaction, was their perverse political thought. It was therefore of the utmost urgency to expose the fallacies of Patriot doctrine.

## PATRIOTISM ASSESSED: DOCTRINE

Luzac sometimes had his doubts about the existence of a coherent body of Patriot political thought. Patriotism seemed to show a close resemblance to religious enthusiasm, a phenomenon abhorrent to Luzac, who favored a reasonable, calm, and sociable form of Protestant Christianity. Like religious enthusiasts, the Patriots had come to regard certain notions derived from their "seething imagination" as incontrovertible truths. This had made them incapable of listening to reasonable arguments. They had become totally divorced from the normal process of communication. Factual truths, rational proof, and elementary logic had lost their meaning for these modern zealots. Their fanaticism was so strong that, like their religious predecessors, they felt an urgent need to persecute anybody who dared to disagree with their mad ravings. It certainly was no coincidence, Luzac repeatedly remarked, that dissenters and especially Mennonites were so powerfully attracted to Patriotism.[34]

Patriot political language, moreover, seemed to be an incomprehensible "mixture of gibberish and humbug." Luzac was both a trained jurist and an admirer of the Wolffian mathematical method. One of the reasons he thought modern moral and political reasoning vastly superior to the ancient understanding of these topics was the modern sensitivity to the importance of unambiguous definition and rigorous logic. But the whole achievement of enlightened modern moralists since Grotius was now threatened by a return to ancient rhetoric. Luzac first discerned this tendency in the work of Rousseau. In his anti-Patriot polemic, he repeated many of his previous objections to Rousseau. The Patriots were incapable of logical or systematic reasoning, they abstained from defining their concepts, and they used terms with generally accepted meanings in highly idiosyncratic ways.[35]

Patriot vocabulary, Luzac thought, was a strange composite of meaningless battle cries such as "constitutional restoration," "ancient rights and privileges," "inalienable rights," and "popular influence on

34. Ibid., pp. 315, 332; *Vryaarts*, vol. 11, pp. 67–69, 86; vol. 12, pp. 31, 104, 185.
35. Luzac, *Staatsbeschouwers*, vol. 1, pp. 417, 421, 451–452; vol. 3, pp. 183.

government." He summarily dismissed the demand for constitutional restoration and a return to ancient rights and privileges. First, it was completely ridiculous to pick some arbitrary time in the country's past and then desire that things return to that time, ignoring subsequent developments, the progress of society and institutions, and all acquired rights. Second, and even worse, the historical foundation on which the Patriots based their demands was fictitious. They might proclaim the need for constitutional restoration, but what they were in fact bringing about was the total destruction of the established constitution under the pretense of restoring it to some imagined earlier state.[36]

Fortunately for the Patriots, Luzac sarcastically observed, they found it remarkably easy to switch from historical arguments to those derived from the state of nature when this happened to be convenient. Their talk about inalienable natural rights he judged to be dangerous, because it ignored the essential differences between a supposed state of nature and civil society. Nothing could be more subversive than to confront a well-ordered state with all kinds of random natural rights: "To dig up natural rights, to peddle them as truths, and to desire their enforcement regardless of the civil laws and regardless of a country's constitution and the patterns of its social life is, in our eyes, a sign of enormous foolishness." Only rights that directly flowed from natural moral duties could truly be called inalienable. Such rights, however, could not directly be related to specific forms of government, which depended on particular circumstances.[37]

Having thus pointed out what he thought to be the most obvious absurdities in Patriot rhetoric, Luzac concluded that the essence of Patriot doctrine was the demand for popular influence on government. The core of the Patriot case, according to Luzac, was the contention that the people originally were sovereign and always so remained. They might elect representatives, but these were no more than servants or mandatories of the people, always answerable to their principals. The crucial and related concepts to be discussed were therefore popular sovereignty, popular government or democracy, and representation. These themes dominated Luzac's analysis of Patriot political thought.

Original popular sovereignty, Luzac remarked, was no more than a hypothesis. Nowhere was there to be found any factual proof of its

---

36. Luzac, *Vryaarts*, vol. 9, pp. 22–24; *Staatsbeschouwers*, vol. 3, p. 178; *Voor- en nadeelen*, vol. 3, pp. 169–170.

37. Luzac, *Vryaarts*, vol. 12, pp. 340–341; *Staatsbeschouwers*, vol. 2, pp. 191, 205; vol. 3, pp. 260–261.

existence. But even if one agreed to make a purely juridical and hypothetical argument about the origins of sovereignty, it would soon be
clear that this was a most curious notion. The simplest definition of
sovereignty could be found in Grotius's *ius gubernandi civitatem*. It
was evident, so that definition went, that the people, in the sense of all
the inhabitants of a country, were incapable of ruling, since they lacked
means to produce the necessary unitary will. What they resembled
most was a swarm of flies. But if this was true, then it was also true
that sovereignty could not originally reside in the people, because a
right can never be vested in those who by their nature and essence are
incapable of exercising it. The most that could be said, then, was that
the people, once united in civil society, had the right to *create* a sovereign authority, without originally *being* sovereign themselves. The consequence of this line of argument, Luzac emphasized, was to make
nonsense of the claim that the people, after instituting a sovereign authority, could still make subsequent changes because they supposedly
had never completely transferred their original sovereignty.[38]

Judging by the amount of space he devoted to it, Luzac found the
analysis of the theoretical and practical merits of popular government
more to his taste than speculation about original popular sovereignty.
Democratic theory was by no means something new, Luzac observed,
not even in the Dutch Republic. Indeed, he maintained, the principled
democratic republicanism of the first stadholderless era, although ob-
jectionable, was considerably more intelligent and consistent than the
ambivalent ideas of the Patriots. It was, moreover, one of the important sources of Patriot thought. To refute democratic theory, Luzac
therefore concentrated on the arguments in favor of popular government to be found in Pieter de la Court's *Politieke weegschaal*.[39]

Popular government was natural, reasonable, and in itself just, De
la Court had claimed in the 1660s. He had explained this pronounce-
ment by way of rhetorical questions. "What can be more natural than
to live *by one's own judgement, order, and laws*? What can be more
reasonable than *to obey those one has chosen oneself*? What can be
more just *than to suffer mistakes and tolerate people that one can cor-*

38. Luzac, *Vryaarts*, vol. 12, pp. 106–123, 146–167, 186–204.

39. Pieter de la Court, *Consideratien van staat, ofte politieke weegschaal*, 4th ed. (Amsterdam, 1662). On De la Court, see E. H. Kossmann, *Politieke theorie in het zeventiende-
eeuwse Nederland* (Amsterdam, 1960), pp. 36–49; E. O. G. Haitsma Mulier, *The Myth of
Venice and Dutch Republican Thought in the Seventeenth Century* (Assen, 1980), pp. 120–
169.

*rect and punish?*"[40] To the first question Luzac answered that it was a regrettable error to think that living in a democracy meant obeying one's own judgment. Rousseau had made the same mistake. Nobody in civil society completely obeyed his or her own judgment, and a democracy implied obedience to the judgment of the majority of the people. Given individual differences and the fact that the best were always the minority, it was perverse to call this natural. To the second question Luzac replied that the reasonableness of obedience depended not on choosing one's own rulers but on the rulers' superior capacity. Since the people had limited ability to judge capacity, it was unreasonable to demand that they choose their own rulers. This same argument served to disprove De la Court's contention that merit was only sought after in popular governments. De la Court's last question Luzac treated as a poor joke. Is a disaster made less bad by causing it oneself?[41]

Luzac summarized his whole antidemocratic line of argument by vigorously contradicting De la Court's contention that the general good is promoted only in popular governments.[42] De la Court was mistaken in thinking that the general good coincided with the sum of individual goods. He moreover neglected the fact that no people, however much enlightened, can ever judge what constitutes the general good "because everybody is distracted too much by his *particular* affairs to worry about what is necessary for the *common good*." Apart from that, there were several more factors that made the people unfit to judge. To begin with, in most states it was impossible to bring the people together in an orderly fashion. Second, the people were fickle and generally more guided by their feelings and passions than by reason; as such they were easy prey for ambitious demagogues. Third, the people could easily be bought.[43] All these things, Luzac insisted, had been known for a long time. They could find confirmation in the study of the practice of ancient democracy.

To study the history of ancient Greece for antidemocratic purposes was a well-known conservative strategy in the late eighteenth century. In England, this tendency culminated in William Mitford's *History of Greece*, published between 1784 and 1810.[44] The German reviewer of

---

40. De la Court, *Politieke weegschaal*, p. 530.
41. Luzac, *Voor- en nadeelen*, vol. 1, pp. 45–49.
42. De la Court, *Politieke weegschaal*, pp. 530–531.
43. Luzac, *Voor- en nadeelen*, vol. 1, pp. 15–21.
44. F. M. Turner, *The Greek Heritage in Victorian Britain* (New Haven-London, 1981), pp. 189–204.

Luzac's *Lettres sur les dangers* remarked that it was a pity the author had not read all the latest German publications on the subject, for he would have found his antidemocratic conclusions confirmed and reinforced.[45] According to Luzac, most Greek states had been happy and prosperous monarchies at first, but they had for a variety of reasons subsequently degenerated into democracy and despotism.

One need not follow Luzac in his detailed discussion of the evolution of Greek government nor repeat all his harsh judgments on the people's capacity to act in politics. The single most important lesson Luzac derived from his study of Greek history, was that a real democracy, in the sense of political participation by all or most inhabitants of a state, had never existed and could never exist. All so-called democracies had in fact been aristocracies; criteria of sex, age, occupation, or property had always been used to limit the definition of what constituted the people. More important, the body of citizens defined as the people was incapable of acting by itself and therefore dependent on a few of its members. This meant that democracy could not be and had never been more than a struggle for power between various groups of ambitious and unscrupulous demagogues. The people were no more than "puppets in the hands of flattering orators." This power struggle invariably ended in lawless despotism by one or a few. Since the victors were not bound by any established order or limited by fundamental laws, and since they claimed to embody the ever-changing will of the people, they could perpetrate the bleakest crimes without punishment. Indeed, the justice of a Turkish sultan was a wonder of mildness compared to the total arbitrariness to be found in so-called democracies, Luzac remarked.[46]

The Patriots, unfortunately, failed to recognize that the same consequences would result from their attempts to introduce popular government in the Dutch Republic. Their claim that an increasing enlightenment would make the people capable of orderly political participation Luzac held up to ridicule. Were not the Athenians among the more enlightened people known in history, he asked them; yet look at the results of their introduction of democracy. He dismissed as equally irrelevant the Patriot argument that what they wanted was no more than popular government by representation. Popular government and representation were opposites, Luzac remarked, unless one made the repre-

45. *Göttingische Anzeigen von gelehrten Sachen*, April 15, 1793, pp. 607–608.
46. Luzac, *Vryaarts*, vol. 12, p. 201; *Voor- en nadeelen*, vol. 1, p. 22; *Lettres*, pp. 149, 151, 158, 220.

sentatives subservient instruments of the popular will. But, if that was the case, then representation would entail all the disadvantages of pure democracy.[47]

Another element in Luzac's battle against democratic Patriotism was his attempt to show that popular sovereignty and real representation had no basis whatsoever in the history of the Dutch state. Their introduction would mean the sudden and complete destruction of a regime that had gradually developed over the centuries. In his discussion of the pre-Revolt history of the Netherlands, Luzac made eager use of the findings of eighteenth-century Dutch historians and antiquarians from Frans van Mieris to Adriaan Kluit. These scholars had definitively exploded the Batavian myth or the belief that the assemblies of the estates had been sovereign from time immemorial.[48] Luzac remarked that very little could be said with certainty about pre-Frankish times. The fundamental fact about Dutch medieval history, he stressed, was that the counts had been sovereign. In their rule, they had always been assisted by a feudal nobility. Gradually, as the population expanded and economic life became more complex, the sovereigns had supplemented this nobility with deputies from the rising towns. Nobles and deputies from the towns together formed the assemblies of the provincial estates, representing the estates of the country. The burgomasters and city councils (*vroedschappen*), sending their deputies to the estates assemblies, represented the whole urban population. They did so, however, not because they had been elected by the urban inhabitants but because the sovereign count had so decided. The relationship between the urban population and its representatives could best be compared to that between a pupil and his guardian, appointed by a third party.[49]

The crucial significance of this pre-Revolt situation for later times was "that the representative nature of our constitution does not result from a popular election . . . but from ordinances formerly made by the counts and introduced to improve the stability of administration on all levels." For what had happened during the Revolt? The assemblies of the estates had taken over the count's sovereignty, without protest

47. Luzac, *Staatsbeschouwers*, vol. 2, p. 496; vol. 4, p. 101; *Voor- en nadeelen*, vol. 1, pp. 12, 18–25; vol. 2, pp. 21, 29–31.
48. I. Schöffer, "The Batavian Myth during the Sixteenth and Seventeenth Centuries," in *Britain and the Netherlands*, ed. J. S. Bromley and E. H. Kossmann, vol. 5 (The Hague, 1975), pp. 78–101; G. A. Boutelje, *Bijdrage tot de kennis van A. Kluit's opvattingen over onze oudere vaderlandsche geschiedenis* (Groningen–The Hague, 1920).
49. Luzac, *Vryaarts*, vol. 9, pp. 136–139; vol. 12, pp. 254–260, 265; *Staatsbeschouwers*, vol. 1, p. 69; vol. 2, pp. 348–349.

from the people and with their later consent as expressed in various oaths of allegiance to the constitution. The assemblies of the estates had acquired sovereignty in its sixteenth-century form, that is, considerably limited by earlier laws, ordinances, and privileges. Their sovereignty, moreover, was not exercised *jure proprio*, as the count's had been, but *vi administrationis*, because they had been representatives before they became sovereigns. A change of its location had therefore changed the nature of sovereignty during the Revolt. But the most important point was that nothing else had changed, and that this one identifiable change had nothing to do with either the exercise of popular sovereignty or a modification of the nature of representation. Since the sixteenth century, this new situation had not been fundamentally altered. According to Luzac, the Patriot desire for government by the active and continuous consent of the governed was therefore misplaced. Both popular sovereignty and real representation were deeply foreign to the historical development and present structure of the Dutch state.[50]

## THE DEFENSE OF THE ESTABLISHED ORDER

Luzac's thought has always been described as conservative, justifiably. But it should be stressed that he regarded the intellectual, socioeconomic, and political order of things he defended against Patriotism as essentially modern and enlightened. Intellectually, reasonable Christianity and an enlightened *science des moeurs* were recent triumphs over religious enthusiasm and ancient rhetorical moralism. On the socioeconomic plane, modern commercial society and its attendant prosperity were vastly preferable to earlier systems of conquest. Politically, the moderate Orangist regime, more firmly established since 1747 than ever before, was far superior to both ancient forms of democracy and seventeenth-century forms of absolutism. Patriotism, whether it took the form of a relapse into classical rhetoric, a quasireligious enthusiasm, Batavian primitivism, or the glorification of popular sovereignty

50. Luzac, *Staatsbeschouwers*, vol. 1, p. 429; vol. 2, pp. 349–351; vol. 4, pp. 337–338; *Vryaarts*, vol. 12, pp. 309–310; *Voor- en nadeelen*, vol. 3, pp. 193–196, 211. In order not to complicate matters further, I have here concentrated on the antidemocratic element in Luzac's historical argument and therefore on the towns. It should be noted, however, that I am simplifying his account of the Dutch Revolt and its consequences by leaving out of consideration the position of the nobility and the stadholder.

and democracy, Luzac could only regard as a regressive movement that threatened the essentials of modernity.

We have seen how in the 1780s Luzac turned against the Patriot desire for popular influence on government. In those same years, he explicitly modified his earlier Lockean statements on the themes of resistance and consent and his analysis of the revolution of 1747. It is abundantly clear, in short, that he came to reject everything that smacked of popular participation in politics. But did he formulate any positive doctrines, other than the ones implicit in his anti-Patriot arguments? At the most fundamental level the answer, I suggest, is that Luzac substituted the primacy of the social for the primacy of the political. This tendency is evident in both his preference for a certain type of state and his doctrine of historical utilitarianism. Throughout his work Luzac emphasized that happiness was the supreme human goal. It consisted of self-preservation and an agreeable life.[51] This agreeable life he explicitly defined in apolitical terms. He constantly referred to the happiness provided by "une vie réglée, douce, sociable" and to the "agréments de la vie sociale," and he opposed this to the turmoil and discord generated by widespread political participation and to the stifling social effects of lawless despotism.[52] The fact that happiness was primarily a social achievement meant that the state, although clearly defined, had an essentially limited function in Luzac's thought. It never appeared as the creator of happiness, as it did in German political discourse. Instead, it was there to provide the structure within which happiness could be achieved through a life of calm, uninterrupted, and ever-increasing commerce, in both the social and economic senses of the word. Between the two—sometimes overlapping—poles of democracy and despotism, a wide variety of political forms were acceptable. To fulfill its modest role, Luzac claimed, the state had only to be efficient and moderate.

Luzac was not blindly opposed to all reform. He repeatedly observed that states should constantly adapt themselves to changing circumstances. He felt no need to deny that the Patriots were right in some of the criticisms they leveled at the established regime in the republic, although they were utterly wrong in the proposed remedies. The first problem with the Dutch state, according to Luzac, was the

51. Elie Luzac, *Du droit naturel, civil, et politique, en forme d'entretiens*, 3 vols. (Amsterdam, 1802), vol. 1, p. 116.
52. Luzac, *Lettres*, pp. 46, 206.

enormous complexity of the decision-making process, a complexity frequently resulting in an inability to reach any decisions at all. The most authoritative commentary on this state of affairs had been written in the early eighteenth century by Simon van Slingelandt, an author whose work Luzac greatly admired. It was clear, Luzac remarked, "that the destruction of the count's authority has broken the unity of our state too much. As a result, the administration now runs over too many wheels: l'administration est devenue trop compliquée." The only person who potentially could cut through this tangle and increase efficiency was, of course, the stadholder. Any attempt to weaken his position was therefore disastrous.[53]

The second problem with the Dutch state was the incompetence, corruption, and number of its regents. The Patriots had been absolutely right in pointing this out, Luzac thought. But the Patriot suggestion that matters would improve by making the regents dependent instruments of the popular will he rejected, as we have seen. "Does it matter to a people by whom it is governed or how the regents are appointed, as long as it is governed well?" Democracy, in fact, was the direct opposite of efficient administration and contrary to the interests of the people. The aim should be an enlightened, professional, efficient, minimal administration. The professional administrators should be selected on the basis of merit and training, a training desperately in need of improvement by reforms of the academic curriculum. They should, moreover, be supervised and kept in their proper place by the stadholder. The conclusion, again, was that the stadholder was indispensable if the state was to be efficient. The most urgent political reform, therefore, was a strengthening of the position of the stadholder within the limits of the existing constitution.[54]

But Luzac's plea for more efficiency was intended only to make the Dutch state better at performing its essentially limited task of providing the inhabitants with external security and the possibility to lead "une

53. Luzac, *Vryaarts*, vol. 8, p. 116; vol. 10, pp. 84–99; *Voor- en nadeelen*, vol. 3, pp. 39, 125, 155; *Staatsbeschouwers*, vol. 1, pp. 284–290. On Van Slingelandt, see Leeb, *Ideological Origins*, pp. 40–57.

54. Luzac, *Voor- en nadeelen*, vol. 3, pp. 60–64, 169. On merit, see ibid., pp. 55, 59. On the deficiencies of the future regents' academic training, see, for example, *Vryaarts*, vol. 9, pp. 1–18, 41–55. That administrators should be supervised by the stadholder was a recurring theme in Luzac's writings from *Gedrag* (1754), pp. 43–49, to *Voor- en nadeelen*, vol. 3, pp. 229–254. Luzac's views on the specific merits of the stadholderate are discussed at greater length in W. Velema, "In Praise of the Stadholder: Elie Luzac and the Modernization of Orangism," in *Papers from the Second Interdisciplinary Conference on Netherlandic Studies*, ed. W. H. Fletcher (Lanham–New York–London, 1987), pp. 25–34.

vie aisée, douce, paisible et tranquille."[55] The crucial domestic precondition for the attainment of such a life was a reasonable civil liberty, which in turn depended on the limitation of the state's power. According to Luzac, the fundamental distinction to be made in judging political constitutions was that between arbitrary or absolute and limited or moderate government. This distinction firmly placed him in the mainstream of eighteenth-century constitutionalism and in the company of Montesquieu.[56] In the Dutch context, it allowed him to criticize the more specific demands of both *staatsgezinden* and Patriots as not only dangerous but also extremely parochial.

Fundamental laws, the separation of powers, and mixed government were the central components of Luzac's constitutionalism, in this order of importance. These three devices to contain arbitrary power were, by historical accident, all present in the Dutch Republic, he claimed.[57] It was a topos in Dutch political thought to describe the republic as a *regnum mixtum*, the form of government admired as ideal since antiquity.[58] Luzac, too, repeatedly did so, but he had growing doubts about the usefulness of this concept and about the whole classical typology of governmental forms on which it was based. Monarchy, aristocracy, and democracy were concepts so abstract and vague as to become almost meaningless. The claim that a combination of these three forms resulted in the best form of government thus meant very little. It lacked specificity, it could be applied to almost every existing government, and it offered no explanation of the practical working of such a polity.[59]

Much more helpful, Luzac thought, was the way Montesquieu had made the functional division of governmental powers central to the definition of moderate government. Montesquieu had pointed out that sovereignty could be divided into three types of power—legislative, executive, and judicial—according to the object on which it was exercised.[60] These terms were not new in themselves, but it had been Mon-

55. Luzac, *Lettres*, p. 209.
56. On Montesquieu's constitutionalism, see M. Richter, *The Political Theory of Montesquieu* (Cambridge, 1977), pp. 84–97.
57. On the importance of chance in the emergence of the republic's moderate government, see, for example, Luzac, *Hollands rijkdom*, 4 vols. (Leiden, 1780–1783), vol. 3, pp. 126, 325; *Voor- en nadeelen*, vol. 2, p. 2.
58. Kossmann, *Politieke theorie*, pp. 7–29; Leeb, *Ideological Origins*.
59. Luzac, *Voor- en nadeelen*, vol. 2, p. 9; *Lettres*, p. 313; *De l'Esprit des loix, . . . avec des remarques philosophiques d'un anonyme, etc.*, 4 vols. (Amsterdam-Leipzig, 1763), vol. 1, p. 303, note i; *Hollands rijkdom*, vol. 1, p. 326.
60. *Esprit des loix*, vol. 1, p. 258, note d.

tesquieu's seminal contribution to observe that the combination of these powers in the hands of one person or group of persons destroyed liberty. Having thus explained Montesquieu, Luzac proceeded to show that these three functions of sovereignty were indeed exercised by different bodies and persons in the Dutch Republic. The final, simplest, and most important mark of the moderate state was the limitation of sovereignty by fundamental laws. In the republic, the way sovereignty had been acquired by the estates' assemblies in the sixteenth century meant, as we have seen, that it was limited by earlier laws and privileges such as the *ius de non evocando*. Any suggestion that sovereignty in the Dutch Republic was not bound by fundamental laws and simply consisted of the *ius de Republica et ejus Civibus pro lubitu disponendi* Luzac firmly rejected. He accused both *staatsgezinden* and Patriots of adopting such unacceptable and despotic doctrines.[61]

Luzac's political norms, although clearly antiabsolutist and antidemocratic, were highly flexible. They could accommodate a large variety of governmental forms. In the late 1780s and early 1790s, under the impact of the international expansion of Patriotism, this flexibility became even more pronounced. Clearly inspired by Montesquieu's relativism and in some ways paralleling Edmund Burke, that most famous conservative defender of a modern ruling order, Luzac groped for a new discourse on politics. Its outer limits remained defined by the laws of nature, but its language was nonjuridical. It can perhaps best be described as a form of historical utilitarianism in which practical success, historical experience, and political prudence appeared as the central elements.[62]

The fundamental error of radical political reformers all over Europe, Luzac claimed, was to think that established political structures could be changed on the basis of simplistic maxims or an abstract *plan de construction politique*. A best form of government simply did not exist. Different circumstances demanded different political solutions. In the end, the only standard by which these solutions could be judged

61. Luzac, *Zugt*, p. 97; *Staatsbeschouwers*, vol. 1, pp. 329–337; vol. 2, pp. 546–547; *Voor- en nadeelen*, vol. 2, pp. 5–6; vol. 3, pp. 196–197.

62. On Burke as a modernist, see J. G. A. Pocock, "The Political Economy of Burke's Analysis of the French Revolution," in Pocock, *Virtue, Commerce, and History*, pp. 193–212. The term "historical utilitarianism" has been used to characterize Burke's political thought; see I. R. Christie, *Stress and Stability in Late Eighteenth-Century Britain: Reflections on the British Avoidance of Revolution* (Oxford, 1984), p. 165. For a recent discussion of the conservative uses of utilitarian argument, see T. P. Schofield, "Conservative Political Thought in Britain in Response to the French Revolution," *Historical Journal* 29 (1986): 605–611.

was their practical success: "You can dispute as much as you want about the forms of a government, trying to determine which is the best: in my opinion the best is incontestably the one that makes a state flourish, which gives its inhabitants an easy and comfortable life." Not their juridical origin or their conformity to some abstract standard should determine our judgment of political constitutions; the only relevant test was historical experience. The only acceptable standard was whether the life of the inhabitants had been prosperous, peaceful, and happy over a long period of time.[63]

States, of course, were not unchanging and inert structures. On the contrary, they kept changing and adapting themselves to circumstances and to the needs of the population. But these changes, Luzac emphasized, should always take place within the limits set by their original form, for a complex relationship existed between the form of the state and the life of the nation. This relationship grew more complex and consistent with historical development and should never be rudely disturbed. This was true for the stadholderly government in the Dutch Republic. But the same was true, for instance, for France. What could be more foolish than to confront these structures, raised over the centuries and reasonably successful in practice, with demands for sudden and complete change? It was a fatal mistake not to consider "if the measures which one believes useful and which seem to be so in theory are suitable for a nation, and if the character, genius and particular inclinations of a people can be fitted and adapted to them." The conclusion was clear. Prudence dictated not to risk the certain practical benefits of a reasonably successful established order, whatever its form, for the highly uncertain and probably disastrous results of radical political innovation.[64]

This was the position Luzac took in his last political pamphlet, published in 1792. It was, he emphasized, a tract about prudence, not about rights.[65] The question that remains is how Luzac integrated this historical utilitarianism with his doctrines of political right. It is a question we may never be able to answer, for the final synthesis of Luzac's thought, *Du droit naturel, civil, et politique*, was only partly published. The planned volumes on *droit politique* unfortunately never appeared.[66] We may be certain, however, that they would have contained nothing

63. Luzac, *Lettres*, pp. 32, 102; *Voor- en nadeelen*, vol. 2, pp. 32–33.
64. Luzac, *Lettres*, pp. 67–68, 91, 107–108; *Voor- en nadeelen*, vol. 2, p. 38.
65. Luzac, *Lettres*, pp. 2, 367.
66. The first three volumes were posthumously published in 1802. The manuscript of the remaining volumes seems to have been completed, but it is untraceable.

to further substantiate Kluit's and Tydeman's early nineteenth-century accusations that Luzac, "long before all Prices, Paynes, and Capellens," had extolled popular sovereignty.[67] These remarks referred to the 1754 *Gedrag der stadhouders-gezinden*. It had been Luzac's endeavor for the last decades of his life to make people forget the content of that unfortunate youthful statement.

67. H. W. Tydeman in *Briefwisseling van Bilderdijk*, vol. 1, p. 231, as quoted in P. Geyl, *Pennestrijd over staat en historie*, (Groningen, 1971), p. 255; A. Kluit, *Historie der Hollandsche staatsregering tot aan het jaar 1795*, 5 vols. (Amsterdam, 1802–1805), vol. 3, pp. 408–410.

# 6

## Constitution, History, and Natural Law: An Eighteenth-Century Political Debate in the Dutch Republic

### I. J. H. Worst

IN the last chapter of his *Observations upon the United Provinces of the Netherlands*, Sir William Temple, the English ambassador in The Hague in the age of grand pensionary Johan de Witt, contemplated rather prematurely the decline and fall of the Dutch Republic in the crisis of 1672. But throughout much of the rest of the book, Temple admirably put forward the highly ambiguous character of this extraordinary state. The Dutch Republic, Temple wrote,

> cannot properly be styled a commonwealth, but is rather a Confederacy of Seven Sovereign Provinces united together for their common and mutual defence, without any dependence one upon the other. But to discover the nature of their government from the first springs and motions, it must be taken yet into smaller pieces, by which it will appear, that each of these Provinces is likewise composed of many little States or Cities, which have several marks of Sovereign Power within themselves, and are not subject to the Sovereignty of their Province.[1]

Neither a commonwealth nor, in the full sense of the word, a confederacy, the republic consisted of semiautonomous towns and cities. In the next century, Montesquieu—who had visited the country in 1729 on

1. William Temple, *Observations upon the United Provinces of the Netherlands*, ed. G. N. Clark (Cambridge, 1932), p. 56.

his journey from Italy to England—was not altogether wrong when he described the republic as compounded of fifty independent city-states.[2] In this chapter, I consider how Dutch political thought confronted the problem of decline and the fading away of the republic as a European power of the first rank, given that the problem of decline was indissolubly connected with the political and institutional structure of Dutch society.

The fundamental fact about the political structure of the Dutch Republic is that the towns and cities, and more specifically the larger and wealthier ones of the province of Holland, served as the political centers of gravity. The cities and consequently the country as a whole were ruled by closed bodies of wealthy citizens. When these local aristocrats, or regents, were chosen as members of the governing bodies of their province and of the central committees and organs of the republic, they acted as the informal representatives of local interests. Central government, even in the feeble form it took, was used primarily for the protection of vested interests and local immunities and jurisdictions. At no time during the old regime were the authorities in the position of interfering with particularistic rights and liberties. The rulers of the Dutch Republic lacked the power to make decisions when conflicting views about the common interest struggled with each other. Ruling the country was possible only through careful persuasion and a constant seeking of consensus. Ironically, consensus was possible only in situations of extreme danger, when the common interest of all provinces was self-evident.

In the day-to-day business of politics, the republic was ruled most effectively when the province of Holland, or a determined and capable stadholder, imposed its view of the common interest on the rest of the provinces and other authorities. This was true, as far as it goes, for most of the seventeenth century. In the next century, it was altogether more and more impossible for either Holland or the stadholder to do what in the century before had often succeeded. The Dutch Republic as an independent state originated in a war against a foreign enemy. Purposeful political action and an accepted sense of direction on the part of large sections of the population more than compensated for the ad hoc character of the political institutions and governing practices. But after winning the war against Spain, the ruling elite grew satisfied with the existing situation. All their energy—and for all sorts of economic

2. Montesquieu, *De l'esprit des lois*, in *Oeuvres complètes*, 2 vols., ed. Roger Caillois (Paris, 1951), vol. 2, p. 370.

and financial reasons this energy was diminishing in the eighteenth century—was put into a conservative politics of neutralism and isolationism.

The authorities of the Dutch Republic thereby voluntarily abandoned the means of effectively directing the state. To overcome the strong forces of inertia in the machinery of the Dutch state, it would now be necessary to pursue a vigorous politics of intervention and to define politics as a purposeful and substantive activity. It is largely to the credit of eighteenth-century Dutch political thinkers that they addressed the task of giving an ideological answer to this crucial problem.

## JUSTICE VERSUS WILL

In analyzing this ideological development, we can perhaps start with the conceptions proposed by Keith Michael Baker in his brilliantly suggestive studies of French political thought in the eighteenth century.[3] Baker gives strong arguments for the existence of three different definitions of the body politic, which in France were originally united in the authority of the king but then gradually developed into rivalry. In the traditional discourse of *justice*, political power in the state was limited and established for the sake of protecting the constitution and the rights and liberties of the nation. In the discourse of *will*, the public order was defined not by justice and fundamental law but rather by liberty, choice, and participation. But a supreme political will could not acknowledge constitutional limitations in any form; on the contrary, the public order was made dependent on a succession of willful political actions. Finally, Baker distinguishes a third discourse, of *reason*, in which society is seen from the viewpoint of a rational and administrative vision of politics. The signal characteristic of the Dutch political debate was that arguments in support of a rational political order, inspired by the ideas of the Enlightenment, were advanced only after the possibility emerged of establishing a distinct political will within society.

By using these vocabularies, and especially those of justice and of

---

3. Keith Michael Baker, "A Script for a French Revolution: The Political Consciousness of the Abbé Mably," *Eighteenth-Century Studies* 14 (1980–1981): 235–263; Keith Michael Baker, "French Political Thought at the Accession of Louis XVI," *Journal of Modern History* 50 (1978): 179–303; Keith Michael Baker, "On the Problem of the Ideological Origins of the French Revolution," in *Modern Intellectual History*, ed. Dominick LaCapra and Steven L. Kaplan (Ithaca, 1982), pp. 197–219.

will, we can perhaps construct a model for generalizing about eighteenth-century Dutch political thought. Without doubt, the history of the Dutch Republic, and more specifically the sixteenth-century revolt of the Dutch against the Spanish king, furthered an almost exclusive use of a judicial vision of politics. The Dutch had to legitimate their resistance by referring to an ancient constitution and a set of fundamental laws. This resistance against a despotic and arbitrary will and the defense of the rights and liberties of the nation designated the new political authorities of the republic as the guardians of a near-sacred constituted order. The government and the administration were limited by an alarmingly large number of particularistic rights and liberties, but also by a legacy of profound distrust in every attempt to establish a political will within society. Traditional political opinions were expressed in terms of justice and the rule of law. Dutch history was held to be dominated by tradition, stability, and continuity; a historically constituted order prevented the exercise of an arbitrary political will.

The decline of the Dutch Republic, its economic stagnation and the notorious inability of the authorities to do anything at all, provoked criticism of the principles that were so long considered highly characteristic of Dutch political life. In the eighteenth century this criticism mounted gradually, in the end being tantamount to a fundamental redefinition of the principles that underlay the body politic. The effect of the criticism was, in one way or another, to establish for the first time in the history of Dutch political thought a political will without constitutional limitations. It is important to notice that this political debate took place in the context of the study of constitutional history. Progress toward formulating a political discourse of will was possible only when several long-accepted ideas about Dutch history were eliminated. When pushed to its logical consequences, the concept of a political will was of course hostile to every attempt to analyze political action in terms of fundamental law and a constituted order, of tradition and continuity. A crucial turning point in this political debate was the moment it was unambiguously acknowledged that the sixteenth-century revolt was in fact a violent expression of willful political activities.

## A FREE AND FRIENDLY STATE

During the so-called second stadholderless period (1702–1747), it was customary to formally forbid the grand pensionary of Holland to make or even propose any changes in the constitution.[4] The provincial estates of Holland went even farther. They ordered their functionary to warn them immediately if he became aware of any attempt to change or even amend the political status quo. Generally, this conservatism and intense fear of change is considered highly typical of the political thought in the Dutch Republic during a large part of the eighteenth century. In the first half of the century, there seems to have been only one exception to a rule of conservatism. Simon van Slingelandt (1664–1736) wrote several treatises about Dutch constitutional history, and, although the content of these treatises was more or less generally known, they were not published before 1784.[5] But Van Slingelandt's ideas went much too far.

Although he was generally acknowledged as a man of great capacities, Van Slingelandt was not elected grand pensionary until 1727. At that time his energies were limited by his advanced age and also by a clear instruction and a solemn oath to uphold the existing constitution. It is particularly in retrospect that we find Van Slingelandt's ideas interesting and important, if only because the conclusions he formulated at the beginning of the century became generally accepted by its last decades.

Van Slingelandt studied the history and constitution of the republic from a remarkably nonpartisan point of view. The historical and constitutional arguments he so fluently presented were not intended to commemorate the past or to idealize the superior wisdom of the founding fathers of the republic. Van Slingelandt had learned from history to appreciate and to accept change. He knew that history is studied as a succession of changes, and this fundamental fact was principally an argument in favor of a rational, realistic, and sober politics of constant adaptation. His treatises can be understood as an attempt to analyze the constitution with the objectivity and impartiality of a diplomat who was thoroughly trained in the principles of the "reason of state." According to Van Slingelandt, there was simply too much respect for the literal content of that supreme and fundamental law of the republic, the Union of Utrecht. His conclusion was that, forced by circumstances, the forefathers had failed to give this new state a strong executive power. Van Slingelandt made effective use of two different arguments. On the one hand, he used the classic argument in the rheto-

4. [J. Wagenaar], *Vaderlandsche historie*, 21 vols. (Amsterdam, 1749–1759), vol. 19, pp. 224–226; vol. 20, pp. 46–47.
5. Simon van Slingelandt, *Staatkundige geschriften*, 4 vols. (Amsterdam, 1784–1787).

ric of constitutionalism when he was defending a return to the just principles of an ancient constitution; on the other, he was increasingly critical of major parts of the political structure of the republic. He pretended to be surprised that this republic, which was so deficient in statecraft, had remained so wealthy for so long. He claimed that this was accidental, but that now the circumstances had drastically altered and it was obvious that simply maintaining the existing institutions was not enough.[6]

In the end, Van Slingelandt criticized every attempt to idealize the republic as a state in which true liberty had taken a definitive and unique form. There could be no question of anything like a free people and a free government if the power to make decisions did not exist: "It is a free people and a free government, where the power to make laws, to draft taxes, to make war and peace, and to change the established form of government, is in the hands of the people, or of the States which represent the people, and not where every member can bind the hands of the people or the States, and prevent the most useful and necessary resolutions."[7] With a cool and perceptive eye, Van Slingelandt had come to conclude that the republic needed the introduction of a distinctly modern concept of legislative sovereignty to escape the inertia so characteristic of Dutch politics during his lifetime.

There is a world of difference between this dynamic and activist vision of politics and the attempts to legitimize the rule of the aristocracy in the first part of the eighteenth century. How great this difference was can be apprehended by comparing the ideas of Van Slingelandt with the content of a book published anonymously in 1737. The *Verhandeling van de vryheid in den burgerstaet* (Treatise on Liberty in a Civil Society), written by a regent from Zeeland, Lieven de Beaufort (1675–1730), can be interpreted as a sign of the stability of the republic, since it was the sole attempt to provide a closed theoretical argument in defense of the ruling oligarchy.

The government of the Dutch Republic, according to De Beaufort, admirably combined democratic and aristocratic elements. This government of the provincial estates, to paraphrase him, was free of the usual defects and calamities of aristocracy and democracy. In it, besides the gentleness and moderation employed by the government, Freedom in all her parts and fullness excelled; Freedom so beautiful and splendid as one had never seen in other free states. The government was essen-

---

6. Van Slingelandt, *Geschriften*, vol. 1, pp. 47–48, 67–68, 203–204; vol. 2, pp. 13–14.
7. Ibid., vol. 1, p. xiv.

tially mild, pleasant, and salutary.[8] The republic was ruled by moderation and prudence. De Beaufort, moved by a deep and profound distrust of political power, saw the state as constantly threatened by human passion, ambition, and partisanship, and all this made it extremely dangerous to entrust the government and the welfare and prosperity of the nation to the single will of one or many persons.[9] Because political power in any form or extension did corrupt, in the best state the constitution or the legal order functioned as a guarantor of justice by constraining the government as well as the citizens. De Beaufort's fear of despotism was directed in the first place against the position of the stadholder. The free government he so lavishly praised was a government of the many in an attempt to prevent the use of arbitrary power by the one, in this case the stadholder.

It is revealing to compare De Beaufort's political ideas with earlier defenses of the aristocracy during the first stadholderless period (1650–1672). Although Spinoza and the brothers De la Court, for example, used the same antimonarchic sentiments to attack the position of the stadholder, their attitude toward politics was diametrically different. The outstanding characteristic of seventeenth-century political theory was the application of the modern concept of absolutist sovereignty.[10] But the core of De Beaufort's position was a polemical argument—in every respect inferior to that of his seventeenth-century predecessors—to rule out every possibility of establishing a strong political authority.

From a historical point of view, absolutism was a reaction against the threat of civil war. If this threat was not entirely hypothetical in the Dutch Republic in the middle of the seventeenth century, in the first half of the eighteenth century it was even less apparent. There is at least a possibility of reading De Beaufort as proof that the supremacy of the oligarchy was unquestionable: there was simply no need to equip their authority with full political power. De Beaufort's political and constitutional ideas reflected an important aspect of public opinion about the character of the Dutch Republic in the first half of the century. The Dutch were apparently largely satisfied with their own government, which preferred to act in a moderate and limited way and respected the rights and privileges of the nation. But there was also complacency.

8. L. F. de Beaufort, *Verhandeling van de vryheid in den burger-staet* (Leiden, 1737), pp. 123–124, 134.

9. Ibid., p. 22.

10. See E. H. Kossmann, *Politieke theorie in het zeventiende-eeuwse Nederland* (Amsterdam, 1960).

The republic was perhaps not perfect, but for many it was in every respect unique and without comparison. De Beaufort, in a poorly expressed argument whose drift is nevertheless clear, tried to give the citizens a political role next to the aristocracy. He attributed sovereignty to the people, but the provincial estates represented the entire body of the people. The political role of the people consisted in choosing the members of these councils. De Beaufort's concept of sovereignty was essentially the older one. He was recapitulating the position of sixteenth-century popular sovereignty in which sovereignty consists primarily of the power to protect the constitution and the legal order.

In comparing Van Slingelandt with De Beaufort, we detect two different political attitudes. The former diplomat and elected grand pensionary argued in favor of a dynamic political power with the explicit purpose of escaping the rigid limitations of the status quo. This point of view would lead to a modern concept of sovereignty, and in this Van Slingelandt belonged to the seventeenth-century tradition of Dutch political thought. He was entirely consistent when he attacked the rhetoric of liberty as the great obstacle to a definition of politics as a substantive activity. Against this ideology of sovereignty, De Beaufort used the argument of constitutionalism. Because this constitutionalism was a resistance theory, he described sovereignty in the most gloomy terms as a constant threat to liberty. But in this polemic against sovereignty and political power, which were always presented as ambition and despotism, no form of political action was in fact possible. De Beaufort was idealizing a political society without a political will. In his opinion, the Dutch Republic was a gift of God, not the result of deliberate and purposeful human intervention. Like the Jewish people, the Dutch were chosen, their liberty was the consequence of an act of providence, by a God who was the supreme legislator and the supreme judge.[11]

The language used to formulate judgments about the Dutch state indicates the popularity of a vocabulary of constitutionalism. It is remarkable to see the almost universal acclaim of the republic as a gentle, free, and friendly state with a mild, limited, and moderate government.[12] This vocabulary of political self-analysis did not differ between the first half of the century and the second—between describing a government without a stadholder and with one. We can safely assume that

11. De Beaufort, *Verhandeling*, pp. 147–148, 532, 540ff.
12. See, for example, [C. van Bynkershoek], *Vrymoedige bedenkingen over de vryheid* (Amsterdam, 1738), p. 79.; Wagenaar, *Historie*, vol. 1, p. 1; De Beaufort, *Verhandeling*, pp. 123–124, 134.

these generally accepted political perceptions seriously hindered the introduction of a political will within the body politic. So the question
remains. Was it possible within a constitutionalist political view to
come to a less passive and less defensive attitude toward political life in
general? The answer to this question generates important repercussions
for several widely and long accepted views about Dutch constitutional
history.

## THE CONSTITUTION UNDER ATTACK: HISTORY

No form of constitutionalism can survive if it avoids the question of
legitimacy. De Beaufort had given a more or less theological justification. But it was far more authoritative to use a historical justification
that interpreted the constitution as respectable and fundamental simply
because it had always been there.[13] Such an appeal had already been
used in the sixteenth century against the pretensions of the monarchy.
It was basically an attempt to protect the laws and privileges, the rights
and liberties of the nation, from any form of interference by a centralizing political power.

It was with the publication in 1610 of Hugo Grotius's *Liber de
antiquitate reipublicae Batavicae* that the ancient constitutionalism
took a definitive form. Grotius gave a version of a theory of ancient
liberty that was humanist in content and deeply influenced by the ideas
of François Hotman and Jean Bodin. According to Grotius, the Batavian Dutch people had possessed their own distinct political institutions for more than 1,700 years. The laws and customs of the nation
reflected the unique character of this renowned and civilized people.
Liberty was embedded and guarded in a constitution that consisted of
the whole body of law, custom, and usage, and of the institutions,
procedures, and regulations of the body politic. Holland was an ancient republic in which the representatives of the people held the power
to elect the count simply as a judge or military commander with limited
authority and on strict conditions. But after this classical golden age,
primitivism gained control. Dutch medieval history was a lamentable
story of usurpation and systematic abuse of power by the numerous
counts who ruled the country. Only at the end of the sixteenth century
did a tormented but patient Dutch people, in a heroic act of legitimate

13. For the following discussion, I am greatly indebted to J. G. A. Pocock, *The Ancient
Constitution and the Feudal Law*, 2d ed. (Cambridge, 1987).

resistance, at last dismiss count Philip II (the king of Spain) and thereby restore the Batavian constitution.

Grotius's elegant formulation of a Batavian myth became a constitutional argument. In the early seventeenth century, when the republic was divided by deep conflicts and many observers were doubtful about the destiny of the young and still precarious state, Batavianism did perhaps make a contribution to Dutch self-respect. In fact, references to the Batavians and an alleged Batavian past were used right until the end of the old regime. But, although the Batavian past figured as a polemical and rhetorical argument and appeared in literature and even in painting, it did not play an essential part in debates about the political and institutional structure of the republic. This is not altogether surprising. How could it be otherwise in a republic where nobody defended that logical counterpart of a Batavian constitutionalism, monarchic sovereignty? Moreover, the intellectual climate of the seventeenth century Dutch Republic was hostile to historical arguments in a political debate and generally in favor of a strictly rationalist political theory. It was regarded as a supreme sign of modernism to use the concept of absolutist sovereignty in search of the best and most rational state. There was strong discomfort with constitutionalism; many Dutch clearly realized the danger such a theory presented to any established political authority.

Batavian constitutionalism was not an attempt to make the past useful in political argumentation; rather, its effect was to accept the existing state without further discussion, and without historical research into crucial periods of the Middle Ages. On the contrary, the central theses of the Batavian argument—a constitution that had remained unchanged for more than 1,700 years and the sovereignty of the provincial estates—could only be maintained by accepting the skeptical and Pyrrhonist doubt about the value and utility of historical knowledge.[14] Because the Batavian historical argument was not the subject of an energetic ideological historical debate, there was no need to scrutinize and adapt its premises and interpretations.

All this changed in the eighteenth century, when historical and antiquarian thought became increasingly popular. The rising tide of empiricism supported historical criticism and the use of historical arguments. With growing confidence, the historians entered the political

---

14. This is eminently clear in two books: [P. de la Court], *Historie der gravelike regeering in Holland* (s.l., s.a.); [J. Uytenhage de Mist], *Begin, voortgang ende eind der vrye, ende der gewaande erfgravelyke bedieninge, in Holland ende West-Vriesland* (Amsterdam, 1683).

debate. Gerard van Loon (1683–1768) possessed the kind of historical erudition typical in the first half of the century. He was, before anything else, a collector and compiler, as his unreadable and badly organized volumes prove, but he drew important conclusions from his historical investigations. As a Roman Catholic, he had studied in the Southern Netherlands and perhaps there first became interested in the history of the Middle Ages and consequently of feudalism. But in the republic it was thought no longer necessary to discover feudalism. The jurists and the academic historians of the seventeenth century knew perfectly well what feudalism was all about.[15] It was to Van Loon's credit that he used the feudal interpretation as a criticism of the Batavian constitution.

In 1748, Van Loon published a small pamphlet that concisely stated the conclusions he normally buried in his undigestable volumes.[16] In this treatise, which because of its implicit criticism of aristocratic rule was fittingly dedicated to the newly elected stadholder William IV, Van Loon demolished the idea of the uninterrupted existence of a free, independent, and unchanged Batavian Dutch republic. He made good use of a few fundamental facts. According to him, there was no trace of any Batavians after the fall of the Roman empire, and there could be no doubt that the Franks had conquered Holland, which became a part of the Frankish and later of the German empire. In this feudal system, large segments of the population were unfree and in a state of vassalage. But the central part of his polemic was directed against the sovereignty of the estates of Holland. According to Van Loon, there was in medieval history only one sovereign: the count possessed sovereignty in the full sense of the word, without limitations and without restricting conditions.

The annihilatian of the Batavians, the conquest of Holland, feudalism, and the sovereignty of the count—all this changed several received notions about Dutch history. The most important consequence of these ideas was to break an imagined historical continuity. The Dutch Republic was not a renewed confirmation of an age-old constitution but a new state. Van Loon's careful and painstaking study of countless medieval chronicles and documents did in the end have the ironic effect of making medieval history of subordinate importance. After Van Loon,

---

15. H. Kampinga, *De opvattingen over onzer oudere vaderlandsche geschiedenis bij de Hollandsche historici der XVIe en XVIIe eeuw* (The Hague, 1917), pp. 120–134.

16. Gerard van Loon, *Historisch bewys, dat het graafschap van Holland altyd een leen des Duytschen Ryks geweest is* (Leiden, 1748).

medieval history was at its best prehistory, not unimportant but explored only for its striking differences with the republican age that followed. The implications of closely scrutinizing Dutch medieval history seemed clear. The relevant historical period from which precedents could be extracted was neither a mythical Batavian past nor the dark centuries of usurpation that followed; it was, rather, the years of struggle against the Spaniards, when the republic gradually formulated its institutions and political practices.

By accepting the fact that the difference between the medieval county and the republic was a difference in the location of sovereignty, and by accepting the transfer of sovereignty from the count to the provincial estates, Van Loon made the legitimation of the Dutch Revolt again an urgent problem. Batavian constitutionalism assumed that the sovereignty of the estates was lawful and legitimate only if it could be demonstrated that these ruling bodies had always possessed this power. Making the estates the legitimate sovereigns allowed the use of an always potentially dangerous resistance theory. When any count stepped outside the boundaries of his office, he could easily be removed. Historical criticism made an important contribution to a more realistic use of constitutional arguments, in that the period from which these arguments were extracted was now much shorter. Constitutional history was compressed to those crucial decades in the sixteenth century when the republic came into existence. But if constitutionalism was in a position to be more realistic and more practical, it was also more restricted, and it was forced to take into account a violent break in historical continuity.

For the most authoritative attempt to use constitutionalism in discussing politics and for an indication of the problems it now confronted, we turn to Adriaan Kluit (1735–1807). Considered the best Dutch historian of his age, Kluit had a profound knowledge of the history of Holland and was an expert judge of historical sources and documents. It could have been no surprise that in 1778 Kluit was appointed the first professor of Dutch history and antiquities at the University of Leiden. His lifelong objective was to use his historical knowledge to defend the republican constitution against growing criticism. It is possible to see Kluit's work as the last attempt to use a purely historical vocabulary, and in a sense he was a direct heir of Grotius's constitutionalism. But, when the evolving political debate made the ambiguities of his position clearer, he was forced to use all sorts of other arguments.

In his inaugural lecture of 1779, Kluit accepted the challenge of the feudal interpretation and tried to formulate a strategy for legitimizing the rebellion of the Dutch people. Without reservation Kluit followed Van Loon's view about the authority and the sovereignty of the count. From the German study of public law Kluit borrowed the concept of a *superioritas territorialis*, and he identified this power, without further discussion and certainly not entirely correctly, with pure, unconditional sovereignty. The counts of Holland were at the same time "supreme lords, judges, masters, administrators, and proprietors of these countries." But, because Kluit stayed in the mainstream of Dutch constitutionalism, he repeated once more the constitutionalist argument against sovereignty. In reality, the power of the medieval counts was barbaric and entirely incomprehensible to the free citizens of modern times in a free state like the Dutch Republic. Kluit's conclusion was, in any case, a profoundly historical one. Every age, he wrote, possessed its own unique laws and manners and its own distinct form of government. The difference between the medieval and the republican period was radical and fundamental; it was a difference between slavish submission and liberty. But in admitting this Kluit now faced the supreme question: Why study these medieval times if one cannot draw conclusions from one period to the other? He made it clear that he had no intention of doing that: "No one should think that I seek to draw any conclusion from that older and earlier situation of government under the counts for the present state of our republic." It seems that Kluit realized the limitations of a defense of the constitution from history alone. He was not only a historian but also a participant in a political debate, one knew that he needed to prove the legitimacy of the existing authorities.[17]

Kluit found himself in the difficult position of defending the sixteenth-century forefathers in their resistance to a sovereign prince and at the same time ruling out any possibility of resisting the present sovereign bodies, the provincial estates. In Batavian constitutionalism, the count held a weak position; he found himself constantly in need of deliberation and advice from the representative bodies, and for practically all his activities he needed approval and consent. Kluit and Van Loon had criticized this interpretation as simply wrong. In their opinion, the count possessed unlimited and undivided sovereignty. Kluit re-

17. Adriaan Kluit, *Inwydingsrede over het recht 't welk de Nederlanders gehad hebben, om hun wettigen vorst en heer Philips koning van Spanje af te zweren* (Leiden, 1779), pp. 23, 28–29, 186 note 82.

jected from the outset that well-known and much used argument in which Philip II had become a tyrant the moment he violated the laws and privileges of the nation, since the obligation of the people to obey the Spanish king was then automatically dissolved. Kluit used extensive quotations from Pufendorf to support the view that active resistance against a legitimate prince, even one who was harsh and unjust, was not allowed. Kluit acknowledged only one exceptional occasion in which it was acceptable to take up arms against a prince: "This is after all that general, that famous law of the Roman Rhetors, not prescribed to us, but innate, that when our life is exposed to danger, to violence, to murderous attack by an enemy, we are allowed to use, in a just way, all possible means of self-preservation." This is a remarkable passage. As a historian by vocation, Kluit constantly appealed to history and used historical arguments with a passionate concern, and he never tired of warning against the use of abstract principles. But when he had to legitimize the Dutch Revolt, his historical arguments fell short, and he considered it necessary to use at least one fundamental and abstract principle. When the existence of a whole nation was in danger and no escape was possible, this was a legitimate cause for declaring war on the oppressor. The Dutch had waged a just war against the Spanish king, about this Kluit had no doubt; but he had to explain in theoretical terms what permitted them to do so.[18]

What were the consequences of Kluit's analysis for the late eighteenth-century constitutional debate? First, the notion of a basically unchanged constitution that consisted of the whole body of law and custom, manners and usages, became untenable. Second, the crucial period of Dutch history was now the last part of the sixteenth century, when a new state arose out of a revolutionary situation. Constitutional arguments had to be extracted from this phase of Dutch history. The political institutions of the republic were not the outcome of a slow coral-like process of growth and adaptation and of age-old experience and wisdom, but of voluntary and rebellious action on the part of the nation as a whole. An appeal to history and antiquity as a mode of political discussion was only useful if it referred to these particular years. In this respect, Kluit found the position of Burke in English conservatism impossible to apply to the Dutch Republic. The Dutch revolution was not, like that in 1688 in England, an effort to reformulate a

---

18. Ibid., pp. 83–84, 105, 107–108, 120–121, 128–129, 158–159, 180–187.

body of ancient laws and liberties and to confirm an ancient constitution in which these laws and liberties were guaranteed.[19] Kluit's historical investigations acknowledged the fatal discontinuity of Dutch history, which compelled him to defend the right of resistance of the forefathers and consequently that act of political will in which a new government was formed.

Kluit was clearly in an awkward position, and it is easy to see the limitations of his historical defense of the constitution. To simplify a complicated argument, Kluit was in severe difficulty in answering two fundamental questions. First, if the sixteenth-century forefathers had the right to form a new government, why was the power to change a constitution absent in the eighteenth century? Kluit argued extensively to show the exceptional circumstances in which the formulation of a new constitution had taken place, but now the legitimacy of the existing authorities had to be defended according to a contractual theory. Because there was a transfer of sovereignty from the count to the provincial estates, Kluit could not avoid using the concept of a contract between these sovereign bodies and the people. But to admit the existence of this contract was to open the discussion about its content. As an ardent Orangist and energetic defender of the political status quo, Kluit, in the political debate of the 1780s, insistently argued against giving an exact definition of the content of this hypothetical contract. His defense against a second major argument of the opposition—that reforming the constitution was necessary because it had degenerated from its original principles—was weakened by his admission that a set of fundamental principles was embodied in a contract. The outstanding character of Kluit's constitutionalism was its ambivalence toward sovereignty. Constitutionalism in the republic before Kluit was hostile to any attempt to establish a political will within society. But the age of stability was gone. Kluit realized that a defense of the constitution needed some sort of political power. Although the republic was the outcome of an act of political will, the use of this power was restricted and in the end purely defensive. The constitution Kluit defended was again all that existed. What Kluit tried to do was to accept one unique and supreme sovereign act and to prevent any further attempt to separate a political will from society as a whole.

19. See J. G. A. Pocock, "Burke and the Ancient Constitution: A Problem in the History of Ideas," in J. G. A. Pocock, *Politics, Language and Time* (New York, 1973), pp. 202–203.

NATURAL LAW AND THE NECESSITY OF A
POLITICAL WILL

The effect of Van Loon's and Kluit's historical research was in a sense
purely negative. The historical period deemed relevant for a constitutional argument was very much abridged. It is not surprising that in the
1770s and 1780s the political debate centered more and more around
the Union of Utrecht of 1579 as a fundamental law on which the political life of the republic was built. In 1779, when Kluit delivered his
inaugural lecture, the bicentennial of this famous treaty was solemnly
celebrated. In academic lectures and popular pamphlets the Union of
Utrecht was praised as a perfect, wise, and prudent fundamental law.
Its content was studied with respect and admiration and even now and
then with deep emotion.[20] It is tempting to see this attitude as an indication that historical criticism and the acknowledgment of a historical
act of legislation gave rise to an interpretation of the Union and
thereby of the Dutch constitution as a fundamental law. What clearly
made this late eighteenth-century celebration of the Union interesting
was the fact that it was largely undertaken by jurists and professors of
public law. It was in the context of the study of public law that a new
understanding of the character of the constitution arose. Once this constitution had lost one of its essential characteristics—an antiquity of
more than 1,700 years—it was more difficult to formulate a defense of
the existing institutions and laws as a whole. It is possible to see the
growing number of studies, editions, and commentaries on the Union
as a different strategy for discussing politics, carried out by jurists
within the context of public law.[21]

In the republic after the middle of the eighteenth century, public
law came under greater scrutiny—scrutiny that combined a historical
investigation of all sorts of documents with the rational principles of
natural law. We can use Kluit to testify to the difference between the
traditional use of historical arguments intended to bolster the constitution and the arguments put forward in the new public law. In another
academic lecture, which was translated into Dutch in 1787, at the

20. See G. J. Schutte, "Van grondslag tot breidel der vrijheid: Opvattingen over de Unie
van Utrecht in het laatste kwart van de achttiende eeuw," in De Unie van Utrecht: Wording
en werking van een verbond en een verbondsacte, ed. S. Groenveld and H. L. Ph. Leeuwen-
berg (The Hague, 1979), pp. 199–225.
21. Pieter Paulus, Verklaring der Unie van Utrecht, 4 vols. (Utrecht, 1775–1777); L. P.
van de Spiegel, Ontwerpen van de Unie van Utrecht (Goes, 1778); Pieter Bondam, Redevoering over de Unie van Utrecht (Utrecht, 1779).

height of the political unrest, Kluit attacked not only the Patriots but also, although much more cautiously, his Leiden colleague and professor of public law, F. W. Pestel (1724–1805).[22] Kluit distinguished between two different methods of studying the state, the laws, and the constitution. In the philosophical view, state and society were considered hypothetically—how it could have been in an ideal state of perfection. The historical point of view was of course far less dangerous because it offered a realistic and moderate study of the actual situation and the constitution. Kluit criticized Pestel as being insufficiently aware of the danger of using abstract and rationalist principles in analyzing the body politic. He himself used natural law reluctantly, as an argument that justified the prevailing social order—as a support of the established institutions and as a body of fundamental values underlying the legal system.

Kluit was right, at least, in one sense. Pestel was the foremost representative of the new science of public law. He was born in Germany and went to Leiden in 1763. Like Kluit, Pestel was an Orangist; unlike Kluit, he was largely satisfied with his professorial position and did not participate directly in political debates. An eminent lecturer, he was held in high regard by generations of students. His books grew out of his lectures and reflected the content of public law as a university discipline. In 1773, Pestel published *Fundamenta jurisprudentae naturalis*, a success that was reissued four times and translated into French and Dutch.[23] After finishing this book in which he gave his version of an enlightened moral philosophy, Pestel devoted the rest of his academic career to the analysis of Dutch public law from a philosophical point of view. His *Commentarii de Republica Batava* (1782) was the first attempt to give a full and comprehensive description of the institutional and constitutional history of the Netherlands.[24]

This relatively new discipline of public law had been introduced in the universities of the republic, even before Pestel, by German jurists.[25] In the German empire, the study of public law had developed into a modern, enlightened, and pragmatic science of politics and legislation

22. Adriaan Kluit, *Over het misbruik van 't algemeen staatsrecht of de onheilen die uit deszelfs verkeerd gebruik voor alle burgerstaten te wachten zyn* (Leiden, 1784).

23. F. W. Pestel, *Fundamenta jurisprudentiae naturalis* (Leiden, 1773); reissued in 1774, 1777, 1788, and 1806. I have used the Dutch translation: *De gronden der natuurlyke rechtsgeleerdheid*, 2 vols. (Utrecht, 1783–1785).

24. F. W. Pestel, *Commentarii de Republica Batava* (Leiden, 1782); reissued in an extended but not completed edition in 1795. A German translation was published in 1784.

25. See S. J. Fockema Andreae, *Geschiedenis van de Nederlandsche wetenschap van de Nederlandsche rechtsgeschiedenis* (Amsterdam, 1950), pp. 48–64.

that combined basic principles of natural law and an empirical and historical study of law.[26] German public law was in chaos, without unity or principle, and desperately in need of rationalization.

The situation in the Dutch Republic was similar. There was some truth in designating the republic as a constitution and not as a state. The rights and liberties and the institutions that gave this constitution its distinct character were the products of history. Because this constitution was not granted but rather abstracted from a sovereign will, it was difficult to see it as a unity. In fact, there was no unity. The constitution was a collection or compilation of all that was available about the relations between the authorities and the citizens. In consequence, to study this constitution and public law was to give a description of all laws and liberties and all regulations and institutions. The public law of the republic was a collection of arrangements and procedures, a storehouse of facts without any order other than a strictly chronological one. It was the result of accumulation and growth, so full of contradiction that interpretation was a highly complex procedure. The protean character of the republic—was it a commonwealth, a confederacy of seven sovereign states, or a loose federation of fifty city-states?—prevented the domination of one distinct interpretation of this public law. The unique character of Dutch public law was that in administration and in the day-to-day political practice it functioned as a formidable obstacle to any use of public power.

To escape its startling complexities and to prevent arbitrary and conflicting interpretations, public law was in need of definition. Accordingly, Pestel used natural law in its eighteenth-century form as an enlightened moral philosophy. His *Fundamenta* was certainly not very original, but it was conveniently arranged and it had a clear line of argument. Starting from a few simple principles of moral philosophy, Pestel formulated important conclusions about jurisprudence, legislation, and politics. Like his predecessor in this discipline, Jean Barbeyrac, Pestel reasoned in an undogmatic, practical way. Pestel and Barbeyrac were both satisfied with the recent progress in this enlightened branch of thought, and both were relieved to live in an age when, they believed, humankind could at last know the firm and certain principles of its conduct. From this most useful of sciences, one could learn to act responsibly. The most fundamental principle of the science of morals was happiness as the supreme end of all human life. In this,

26. N. Hammerstein, *Jus und Historie: Ein Beitrag zur Geschichte des historischen Denkens an deutschen Universitäten im späten 17. und 18. Jahrhundert* (Göttingen, 1972).

Pestel was clearly influenced by the "science of felicity" as articulated by his compatriots Leibniz and Christian Wolff. From these famous German writers, Pestel learned that "all men by nature are invited to enjoy a happy life."[27] For him, this pursuit of happiness and perfectibility as a principle of fundamental importance in fact replaced the *socialitas* in the theories of classical natural law of Grotius and Pufendorf.

Of course only within society, in harmonious cooperation among all citizens, was happiness possible. Everyone knew instinctively that this individual happiness could not be separated from the happiness of all members of a society. The deeply felt desire to be happy invited one to be active, responsible, and reasonable. Happiness gave society and the state a peculiar character. The first task of every government was the protection of the life, liberty, and property of all its citizens precisely because there was a "natural connection" between the conservation of society and the happiness of the people.[28] The protection of fundamental values required the rule of law. Order, peace, and tranquility were the foundations of social life. But protection and maintenance of order were not enough. Society was a community of citizens who had solemnly made the decision, in close cooperation, to further their happiness and perfectibility.

Pestel's account of the science of morals led to one conclusion: legislation was the most important instrument in advancing happiness. To live in a society was to try to improve it by formulating new laws and by improving outdated laws and regulations. Legislation was an act of sovereignty, and Pestel was now in a position to give a clear definition of this public authority. There could be no doubt about the fact that the quality of politics and legislation was the decisive factor in making citizens happy. In the tradition of German natural law, Pestel made a sharp distinction between the public authorities and the rest of the citizenry. In the Dutch Republic there were actually two sorts of citizens: the regents, administrators, and officials in public functions of high and low rank enjoyed an altogether different status from normal citizens who acted only in their own interests.[29]

If these two different kinds of citizen acted in the right manner, they could arrive at two different kinds of happiness. Happiness for ordinary citizens was to benefit from "the abundant expediences soci-

27. Pestel, *Gronden*, vol. 1, p. 110; see also p. 226.
28. Ibid., vol. 2, pp. 137–138.
29. Ibid., vol. 2, p. 220; Pestel, *Commentarii*, pp. iv–v, 49–50.

ety provides, to live a safe and comfortable life."[30] But for the authorities, pleasure was connected with a sense of duty, a pleasure in serving the common good. Pestel defended the political role of the aristocracy but at the same time instructed them to be a managerial elite and to carry out enlightened legislation. Of course, to rule was not simply to order. Only if the public authorities acted in an effective and expert way was an increase of happiness possible, and this was the criterion of success: "The happiness of a nation is judged by the greatest number of happy citizens, and by the constancy of their hope that this happiness will last."[31] Legislation was the single most important task of the sovereign body. But to draft laws and ordinances was a matter of the science of natural jurisprudence. What made natural law of such crucial importance was that it could prevent conflicts within society by making a rigid and unquestionable distinction between right and wrong and between just and unjust acts. The universal precepts of natural law were a guide to every form of legislation.

But Pestel warned against too much self-confidence. The foremost qualities required in the process of making laws were prudential reasoning, experience, and observation. Legislation was a practical business. In Pestel's account, the theoretical and philosophical dimensions of natural law gradually disappeared, to leave a juristic and pragmatic view of the society in which this project of legislation took place. In his view, all sorts of factors influenced the achievement of happiness. It was dangerous to ignore the existing laws and institutions, manners and usages, of the nation. The analysis of the *status respublicae* was a precondition of any form of legislative activity that pretended to be both useful and effective. In a systematic way, Pestel moved from moral philosophy to jurisprudence, politics, and legislation. What made his version of a science of humankind interesting was not only that it could give the relatively simple and evident principles of social organization and moral conduct; perhaps even more important was the confidence it gave to an empirical study of society in all its aspects. This is not to deny the grave inner tensions between rationalist and empiricist arguments which gave this doctrine its peculiar character. But the metaphysical argument was more and more reduced to a few simple truths: happiness, perfectibility, and harmony functioned as the principles of social life. In an empiricist strategy, description was the alternative for the rationalist quest for essence and substance. When

30. Pestel, *Gronden*, vol. 2, pp. 225–226.
31. Ibid., vol. 2, p. 193.

Pestel in his *Commentarii* attempted to give this description of Dutch public law, he condensed the science of humankind into a few preliminary remarks and devoted the rest of the book to an extensive analysis of the possibilities and limitations for a project of enlightened legislation.

What Pestel practiced was statistics in its eighteenth-century form. His description of the Dutch Republic was comprehensive and exhaustive, but not in the unorderly and unselective way of the many-volumed compilations of the antiquarians and historians. His description of the history and the natural environment, of the citizens and their economic activities, colonies, churches, and universities, was an attempt to portray society as a device for advancing happiness. Every society was a product of history, and history was a summary of the attempts of many generations to further the cause of happiness by designing prudent institutions and sensible laws. Society, according to Pestel, was not only an alliance of citizens who inhabit a country at a particular moment. The will of past generations and of the forefathers was in a sense preserved and expressed in the institutional structure. This was one of the reasons the existing state deserved respect. Dutch society was constructed with supreme diligence and inventiveness by its own citizens. Dutch history was a heroic narrative of the lasting attempts, by means of effective laws and institutions, to conquer a hostile nature and to open the sources of happiness.[32]

The term "narrative," however, suggests far more than Pestel could offer in his *Commentarii*. Although the tendency of his argument is more or less clear, the form in which he delivered his message was not exactly successful. The history of Dutch public law and of its institutions was scattered throughout his voluminous book. Nevertheless, Pestel wrote history from a remarkably nonpartisan point of view. The republic was a highly respectable state in which the protection of life, liberty, and property was secured by the rule of law. The government acted in a moderate and limited way, respected the fundamental laws, and demonstrated a careful attitude in furthering the common interest of the nation.[33] But of fundamental importance was that this legal order was formulated by generations of citizens and constantly adapted to changing circumstances. And this gave the present generation the right, if not the obligation, to change the laws and the constitution.

The acceptance of change and its necessity dominated Pestel's ac-

32. Pestel, *Commentarii*, p. 174.
33. Ibid., pp. 67, 72–73.

count of the history of Dutch law. We read in his *Commentarii* how the customary law of primitive centuries, when manners and usages changed, was gradually replaced by more sophisticated systems of law. We read how the rise of cities and commerce was accompanied by new laws and new institutional devices. In an unorthodox way, Pestel stressed the advantages of the acts of codification and legislation and the introduction of Roman law by the centralizing monarchy of the Burgundian and Habsburg princes. But in Pestel's discussion of the law of the republic, the implication was, in many respects, that the republic was not yet finished. Even that celebrated fundamental law, the Union of Utrecht, was in an important sense a compromise. The rights and obligations of the seven allied provinces had to be deduced from this treaty, which was the subject of so much recent attention. But the dominating conclusion of these studies, and of Pestel's account, was more and more the inadequacy of the Union. Accepting the Union of Utrecht as the most important fundamental law had the ironic effect of proving its striking imperfections.[34] This was rather the same conclusion Van Slingelandt had reached at the beginning of the century. Political theory had been slow in following the practical advice Van Slingelandt had formulated decades earlier, although we should remember that his treatises were not published until 1784.

What the science of public law offered was the use of natural law as a fixed standard by which to regulate and interpret the laws of a country. The Dutch Republic needed interpretation and codification, and not the compilation of rights and laws. But interpretation and codification of law were activities of a political will and the attributes of sovereignty. The need to redefine the public order was in theory inescapable. Pestel's academic oeuvre offered the vision of a political society that consisted of citizens who realized their rights and obligations. The pursuit of happiness and the application of the precepts of natural law in a project of enlightened legislation were the legitimation of a magisterial elite, a ruling aristocracy, educated in public law, who could inspire the rest of the citizens with a public spirit and sense of obligation. Perhaps for the first time in the Dutch Republic, Pestel framed a "specifically political mode of thinking"; in Baker's definition, this was "a representation of the social field that emphasizes will, contingency, choice, participation."[35] Pestel's enlightened science of legislation was in the final

34. Ibid., pp. 76–77, 392–395.
35. Baker, "Script," p. 235.

analysis an exercise of reason: nature was the basis of a rational social order.

There is in the study of Dutch political thought a tendency to give the Batavian revolutionaries and their ideological predecessors, the Patriots, the credit for realizing for the first time that the exercise of a collective will and the use of reason in government and administration were necessary for reforming Dutch society, for remedying the process of decline and escaping the rigid limitations of the status quo. Although this broadly accepted opinion is not untrue, it is only part of the story. Several important participants in the political debate of the second half of the eighteenth century, even those who belonged to the Orangist party, were trying to redefine the public order. Discussing the constitution, investigating Dutch history, and using natural law contributed to a vision of politics as a willful and substantive activity. Finally but gradually the Dutch Republic developed from a constitution in which justice was embodied into a state in which the exercise of will was necessary. It was Edmund Burke, that most perceptive of political observers, who formulated the problem that now confronted all European states in a revolutionary age, including the Netherlands. I conclude by quoting him: "The moment Will is set above Reason and Justice in any community, a great question may arise in sober minds, in what part or portion of the community that dangerous dominion of Will may be the least Mischievously placed."[36] This question came to dominate the political history of almost every Western European country in the 1790s.

36. *The Correspondence of Edmund Burke*, 9 vols., ed. T. W. Copeland (Cambridge-Chicago, 1958–1970), vol. 6, p. 42.

# 7

# Between Humanism and Enlightenment: The Dutch Writing of History

## Eco O. G. Haitsma Mulier

THE history of Dutch historiography has yet to be written. We sorely miss an overall view of historical writing in the early modern Netherlands, particularly one that goes beyond the study of narrative works on Dutch history. For the early modern period and thus for the eighteenth century as well, when the study of history had not yet acquired what we now think of as scientific characteristics, my approach must be to consider what contemporaries thought to be the task of historians and how they ought to compose their works. It is also important to study the images historians created of the past, which reveal their methodological and ideological presuppositions, and not reproach them for inadequate research. Their concept of historiography did not require that the handling of documents be their first duty. History was still used mostly to justify the present, to demonstrate in a pragmatic way the validity and legality of the present situation. As such, it reflected the cultural ideas of its age. Appropriately, one of the pioneers of modern Dutch history, Jan Romein, warned against believing the words of historians who always had their own agendas.[1]

Eighteenth-century Dutch historiography, in the few cases in which it has been studied intensively, has had bad press: tedious, of no importance, nothing remarkable as compared with the great Dutch historians

---

1. See J. Romein, *Geschiedenis van de Noord-Nederlandsche geschiedschrijving in de Middeleeuwen: Bijdrage tot de beschavings-geschiedenis* (Haarlem, 1932), pp. xxiii–xxiv.

of the seventeenth century. The last point especially reflects an attitude that even in the eigthteenth century many expressed toward the century and its representatives. Yet the historical research undertaken then reveals many of the strains that troubled the period as a whole.

As the result of recent research, we are now able to discern what kind of historical works were written in the roughly hundred years that concern us.[2] We can now say, for example, that certain general trends from seventeenth-century historiography continued. Many works of church history were written, not only by all kinds of Protestants but also by Catholics who now expressed themselves more openly. Numerous too were the descriptions of cities and villages in which it was the custom to add to the traditional story of the past many particulars about institutions, buildings, and antiquities. Histories of the fatherland still came in profusion, especially those destined for the greater Calvinist public. Again and again, that part of the religious community emphasized the fact that the Dutch Republic had prospered and survived thanks only to the presence of its elected Reformed church.[3] In their histories the Calvinists and other religious groups forcefully expressed their own identity, although with more tolerance than in the previous century.

Many histories concentrated exclusively on single towns, a phenomenon that reflects the high degree of urbanization in the Dutch Republic and the jealousy with which the towns guarded their own interests. In the course of the eighteenth century, however, a growing identification with units such as provinces and the country as a whole can be discerned. More descriptions of provinces and even of the territory of the republic were published.[4]

The trend toward a national history was also visible in the traditional histories of the fatherland, in the many books written by the orthodox Reformed who identified their group and their prevailing church with the fatherland, and also in the highly successful work of the Amsterdam historian Jan Wagenaar. In the mid-eighteenth century, Wagenaar took up the tradition of the seventeenth and wrote a com-

2. This paragraph is based on E. Haitsma Mulier and G. A. C. van der Lem, *Repertorium van geschiedschrijvers in Nederland (1500–1800)* (The Hague, 1990).

3. For a general survey of this part of the historical production, see C. Huisman, *Neerlands Israël: Het natiebesef der traditioneel-gereformeerden in de achttiende eeuw* (Dordrecht, 1983).

4. For instance, in the *Hedendaagsche historie of tegenwoordige staat van alle volkeren.* This multivolume series, begun in the 1730s and completed at the end of the century, comprised descriptions of the Austrian Netherlands and of all provinces of the republic.

plete history of the republic in which he expanded the traditional hollandocentric view to include an interest in other parts of the republic.[5]

By contrast, the nearly complete disappearance of books dedicated to the history and curiosities of extra-European parts of the world is surprising. Only the first decades of the eighteenth century still produced some of these studies, which had been an important part of Dutch historical interest, especially in the second half of the seventeenth century. We do not know why this happened. Did international competition push the Dutch out of the market, or was it a question of the Dutch themselves getting more and more involved *in historicis* with the situation of their own country? Even in the seventeenth century, not many works of history concerned other countries in Europe. Contemporary events were often the direct impetus for these works. For instance, after 1685 and the revocation of the Edict of Nantes, Huguenots and their descendants in the Dutch Republic, long fascinated (when not horrified) by the power and expansion of France, wrote about Louis XIV and the impact of the European balance of power.[6] It looks as though the attention paid to the persecutions of coreligionists in other countries was a specifically Dutch phenomenon; the history of such places received a particularly thorough treatment.[7] Indeed, the writing of history was no independent scientific activity but remained closely intertwined with politics and rhetoric.

Although these genres had existed in the seventeenth century, a gradual change in the organization of their contents took place in the eighteenth century. Some new modes of the study of the past were introduced, including the encyclopedia, an adaptation of the new, historical dictionaries that appeared in the 1720s. Here historical subjects were intermingled with geographic and genealogical items. It is clear that the inspiration for these works came from Bayle's dictionary of 1697, and their appearance can be interpreted as a sign of the begin-

5. Wagenaar, considered by the Dutch as the central figure of their eighteenth-century historiography, is discussed in L. H. M. Wessels, "Jan Wagenaar (1709–1773): Bijdrage tot een herwaardering," in *Geschiedschrijving in Nederland: Studies over de historiografie van de Nieuwe Tijd*, 2 vols., ed. P. A. M. Geurts and A. E. M. Janssen (The Hague, 1981), vol. 1, pp. 117–140, and L. H. M. Wessels, "Jan Wagenaar's 'Remarques' (1754): A reaction to Elie Luzac as a Pamphleteer. An Eighteenth-Century Confrontation in the Northern Low Countries," *Lias* 11 (1984): 19–82.

6. For instance, H. P. de Limiers, J. Dumont, and J. Rousset de Missy. See the preliminary remarks in G. C. Gibbs, "Some Intellectual and Political Influences of the Huguenot Emigrés in the United Provinces, c. 1680–1730," *Bijdragen en Mededelingen betreffende de Geschiedenis der Nederlanden* 90 (1975): 255–287, especially 277ff.

7. This happened, for instance, in the works of D. Gerdes, F. A. Lampe, and J. F. Reitz. Each of these university professors was of German descent.

ning of the Enlightenment.[8] Another change was in biography. Not unknown in the seventeenth century, the *levensbeschrijving* of all variety
of people, especially in the second half of the next century, showed a
different interest in history. The encyclopedic and documentary trends
blended in the immensely popular collections of historical biographies,
for instance, in the enormous *Staatkundig woordenboek* of history, geography, genealogy, and politics of Johannes Kok, which went to the
press in the 1780s.[9]

The urge to document the past existed before the eighteenth century, and it emerged out of the traditional humanistic view of writing
history as a separate activity to be done by learned persons or antiquaries. Historiography meant maintaining a certain literary form in telling
the story. On the one hand, this attitude persisted; on the other, antiquarian subjects and observations slowly became included in narrative works of history where once this had been judged impossible.[10]
And research, *oudheidkunde*, boomed in the republic with the result
that numerous editions of old documents were published. This profusion of sources appearing in print did not mean, however, that the
technique of editing, apart from philological expertise, had become
more professional in our modern sense of the word. We must remember that patriotic pride often inspired the practice of collecting documents or including them in descriptions of cities. Many books were
initiated by magistrates and other persons in the government. But eru-
dites met difficulties in getting access to the archives. Regents as well as
church officials were anxious to withhold politically "dangerous" medieval documents. In a society in which history, law, and religion composed the foundation of the state, the contents of those archives could
have explosive implications, even more so when they were from the
recent past.[11]

8. For example, the enormous *Groot algemeen historisch, geographisch, genealogisch en
oordeelkundig woordenboek* ... , 10 vols. (Amsterdam, 1725–1733) begun by D. van Hoog-
straten and M. Brouërius van Nidek and completed by J. L. Schuer. This work did comprise,
as announced in its title, the most important items of the works by Bayle and Moréri.
9. Johannes Kok, *Vaderlandsch, geschied-, aardrijks-, geslacht-, en staatkundig woordenboek*, 38 vols. (Amsterdam, 1780–1799), presumably completed by J. Fokke after Kok's death
in 1788. Good examples of collections of biographies are the ten-volume *Levensbeschryving
van eenige voornaame meest Nederlandsche mannen en vrouwen* (Amsterdam-Harlingen,
1777–1783), and J. A. de Chalmot's unfinished *Biographisch woordenboek der Nederlanden* ... , 8 vols. (Amsterdam, 1798–1800).
10. See D. Hay, *Annalists and Historians: Western Historiography from the Eighth to the
Eighteenth Centuries* (London, 1977), p. 169ff.
11. See the excellent survey by J. Roelevink, "'Bewezen met authenticque stukken': Juri-
disch-oudheidkundige drijfveren tot het uitgeven van teksten op het terrein van de vaderlandse geschiedenis in de achttiende eeuw," in *Bron en publikatie: Voordrachten en opstellen*

*Oudheidkunde* in the republic thus was not a matter of institutions like the Royal Society of Antiquaries or the Académie des Inscriptions, let alone the House of Orange, promoting great enterprises in the field. Individuals, officials, or private persons collected more or less haphazardly the material for the edition they planned. Networks of antiquarians exchanged their documents and sometimes quarreled about who had been the first to make a discovery. Although they were collectors, they placed a high value on the usefulness and authenticity of the evidence supplied as proof of the story of the past. The increased precision in the edition of documents and narrative sources came from a few men. Influences of the newest techniques developed in Germany became evident only twenty years later in the works of the greatest medievalist of the century, Adriaan Kluit. But as we saw in Chapter 6, this learned man was also influenced in his work by political considerations.[12]

Let us consider more closely what contemporaries thought about the writing and purpose of history. At the universities, history was not taught as an independent discipline. The *antiquitates* and history were part of the curriculum of the faculties of arts, law, and theology; many of their professors also taught subjects such as Latin, Greek, and law. It is therefore not surprising to find that few historical works were composed at the universities. Moreover, the treatises on history written there show that the humanist legacy prevailed until the second half of the eighteenth century. For most historians at the universities, the past was a closed area about which the Bible and the authors from antiquity were absolute authorities.[13] History was the study of princes, magistrates, war, and battles (preferably written in Latin), which provided *exempla* of military experience, civil prudence, and virtue. Even in the

---

*over de ontsluiting van geschiedkundige bronnen, uitgegeven bij het 75-jarige bestaan van het Bureau der Rijkscommissie voor Vaderlandse Geschiedenis*, ed. K. Kooijmans (The Hague, 1985), pp. 78–99.

12. Kluit's conception of the study of medieval history has been studied by F. W. N. Hugenholtz, "Adriaan Kluit en het onderwijs in de mediaevistiek," *Geschiedschrijving in Nederland* 1: 143–162.

13. In this field, two studies by A. Th. van Deursen, *Leonardus Offerhaus: Professor historiarum Groninganus (1699–1779)* (Groningen-Djakarta, 1957), and *Jacobus de Rhoer: Een historicus op de drempel van de nieuwe tijd* (Groningen, 1970), are fundamental. The situation at the Dutch universities during the ancien régime is described in W. Th. M. Frijhoff, *La Société néerlandaise et ses gradués, 1575–1814: Une recherche sérielle sur le statut des intellectuels à partir des registres universitaires* (Amsterdam-Maarssen, 1981), and more specifically concerning the teaching of history in J. Roelevink, *Gedicteerd verleden: Het onderwijs in de algemene geschiedenis aan de universiteit te Utrecht, 1735–1839* (Amsterdam-Maarssen, 1986), with a summary in English.

1770s and 1780s we can discern this pattern of argument and the influence of antiquity in the resistance to the trend to study recent periods.[14]

Outside the universities, the situation was somewhat different. A man like Jean le Clerc, descendant of a Huguenot family who lived for nearly half a century in Amsterdam, and for that reason may be taken as participating in Dutch historiography, showed more contemporary influences in his ideas about the writing of history. More independent toward the ancients, he occupied a specific position in the so-called quarrel of the ancients and the moderns. His advice, given in the early part of the century, to write according to the new rules of literary classicism implied a nuanced resistance to the heritage of Tacitus and other ancient historians. In a discussion that showed the influence of skepticism, he also discussed the problems of writing contemporary history. He urged that the scope of history be enlarged beyond the old political historiography.

A closer view of Le Clerc's writings show that his purposes remained largely political, and that he paid much attention to the moral repercussions of human actions. In his Lockean and deistic universe, historiography must endorse the reign of tolerance over the peoples of the world, just as Grotius had conceived it.[15] No Dutch writer of history in the following years expressed himself in these high-blown concepts. Most Dutch historians remained, until well into the nineteenth century, deeply influenced by traditional religious ideas, sometimes clothed in physico-theological expressions. Nevertheless, the moralist and literary preoccupations of Le Clerc's ideal history and his attention to problems of research in the quest for truth, typical for this pre-Enlightenment *histoire raisonnée*, were repeated sixty years later.[16]

In 1758, Frans van Mieris, one of the most respected antiquarians of the country, published his treatise on how to write history (especially the history of the province of Holland). Van Mieris knew the works of such international authorities as Mabillon and Muratori, and although he stressed the importance of antiquarian research he went

14. See E. Haitsma Mulier, "'Hoofsche papegaaien' of 'redelyke schepsels': Geschiedschrijvers en politiek in de Republiek in de eerste helft van de achttiende eeuw," *Bijdragen en Mededelingen betreffende de Geschiedenis der Nederlanden* 102 (1987): 450–475.

15. Ibid., pp. 456–460. Le Clerc's expressed his ideas on historiography most clearly in *Parrhasiana*, 2 vols. (Amsterdam, 1699), vol. 1, pp. 130–223. See also A. Barnes, *Jean le Clerc (1657–1736) et la république des lettres* (Paris, 1938); this work does not, however, deal with Le Clerc's historiography.

16. See Ph. K. Leffler, "The 'histoire raisonnée', 1660–1720: A Pre-Enlightenment Genre," *Journal of the History of Ideas* 27 (1976): 219–240.

beyond it. Like his predecessors, he was preoccupied with the humanist topos of truth in history, a truth he tried to reach with prescriptions deduced from his own experience. And when he discussed the writing of history, he devoted much space to stylistic matters such as the use of speeches (one of the most important devices of seventeenth-century humanist historiography). Yet he condemned the otherwise admired Dutch historians of the seventeenth century, Hooft and Grotius, largely because of their rhetorical style. Van Mieris based all these observations on what he had read in Le Clerc and other writers from the first twenty years of the century; he followed the prescriptions of classicism but—typical of the later Dutch Enlightenment—tried to reconcile revelation with reason.[17]

Jan Wagenaar was of the same opinion when some years earlier he discussed his preparation of *Vaderlandsche historie*. A writer of history should be a rational being, he argued, who tries through the use of authentic documents to discover the motives of people from the past. Like Van Mieris and Le Clerc, Wagenaar looked for the "wheels" that made history move. He was also convinced that by explaining how things occurred the historian offered instruction to the young men who would someday govern the country. In contrast to Le Clerc, Wagenaar warned against judgments without foundations in the documents. It was better to avoid praise or blame and leave the verdict to the reader. History must not degenerate into a novel, he wrote, repeating what others had written before him. But, unlike Van Mieris, Wagenaar had little to say on stylistic matters. The subject of history was not princes and wars but the people, their customs, commerce, religion, and so on. This citizen of Amsterdam, the most important town in the province of Holland, made the explicit statement that only the history of the people was "our own history."[18]

---

17. It is significant, however, that Van Mieris took no notice of Le Clerc's Lockean ideal of the ultimate purpose of writing history; see E. Haitsma Mulier, "Frans van Mieris en de geschiedbeoefening in het achttiende-eeuwse Nederland," in *Geschiedenis, godsdienst, letterkunde: Opstellen aangeboden aan Dr S. B. J. Zilverberg ter gelegenheid van zijn afscheid van de Universiteit van Amsterdam*, ed. E. K. Grootes and J. den Haan (Uitgeest, 1988). The international position of Mabillon and Muratori is made clear by Hay, *Annalists and Historians*, pp. 161, 176ff. Even in 1819, the philosophical historian E. A. Borger discussed whether fictitious speeches ought to be included in historical works. The answer was negative; see his *Disputatio qua respondetur ad questionem a Societate Eruditorum Batava positam*. (Amsterdam, 1819).

18. For Wagenaar, see the literature cited in note 5 and C. Offringa, "Classicisme en verlichting: Wagenaar, Stijl en Van de Spiegel over de Middeleeuwen," in *Middeleeuwen: Tussen Erasmus en heden*, ed. H. B. Teunis and L. van Tongerloo (Amsterdam-Dieren, 1986), pp. 63–87.

Something was changing in the 1750s. The influence of French classicism with all its ambivalence about humanism is clear, and at the same time the move had been made in the direction of what we may call the historiography of the Enlightenment par excellence, philosophical history. It was only in the 1770s, however, that the first genuine philosophical history, significantly a national history, appeared in the Dutch Republic. From the modern point of view, this conception of historiography meant a retreat from the tendency to integrate the work of the antiquarian. The ideal was to broaden political history and to move into other aspects of history, for example, into comparisons of developments in different parts of the world. This approach also paid much attention to human motives in history. In contrast to the learned volumes then published, philosophical history was written without annotation, the story was meant to be readable and to appeal to many readers. This pragmatic approach soon became the accepted way to describe the past and became predominant in the Netherlands at least until the first decades of the nineteenth century.[19]

This episode in Dutch historiography displayed some special features. Aversion to Voltaire and his historical works was surprisingly general. This Frenchman who initiated a new kind of philosophical history was repudiated as an "infernal spirit" by the orthodox; for the others, whatever their beliefs, he had neglected factual accuracy in favor of a kind of novelistic history full of frivolities. The fate of Rousseau and his view of history was even worse: he was ignored.[20] The

19. On philosophical history, the work of E. Fueter, *Geschichte der neueren Historiographie* (Munich, 1911) is still valuable as a general survey. See also Hay, *Annalists and Historians*, p. 171, on Voltaire's historical work; but see also N. Johnson, "La Théorie et la pratique de l'historiographie dans la France du XVIIIème siècle: le cas du *Siècle de Louis XIV* de Voltaire," in *L'histoire au dix-huitième siècle: Colloque d' Aix-en-Provence 1,2,3, mai 1975* (Aix-en-Provence, 1980), pp. 253–269. A late example of philosophical historiography is Ph. W. van Heusde, *De school van Polybius of geschiedkunde voor de negentiende eeuw: Proeve eener geschiedenis des menschdoms en der menschheid* (Amsterdam, 1841). About this interesting figure, see J. Roelevink, "Historia Gentium: Ph. W. van Heusde and the Teaching of History at the University of Utrecht in the First Decade of the XIXth Century," *Lias* 13 (1986): 123–137.

20. Information on the Dutch situation is given in A. Th. van Deursen, "Wijsgerige geschiedschrijving in Nederland," in *Mythe en werkelijkheid: Drie eeuwen vaderlandse geschiedbeoefening (1600–1900)*, ed. J. A. L. Lancée (Utrecht, 1979), pp. 103–120, especially 108. For the orthodox opinion, see F. J. van Oldenburg, *Vaderlandsche brieven* (Kampen-Harderwijk, [1793]), p. 62. For other views, see P. Massuet's *Histoire des rois de Pologne*, 3 vols. (Amsterdam, 1733), vol. 1, pp. 7–7v., preface for an early remark on Voltaire's history of Charles XII; J. van Iperen, "Verhandelinge over de historie-kennis," in *Verhandelingen van het Bataviaasch genootschap der konsten en wetenschappen*, vol. 2 (1780), pp. 1–61; in the second edition of this work from 1784, pp. 22, he also condemned Hume for this reason; E. Luzac, *Lettres sur les dangers de changer la constitution* (London, 1792), p. 207; and L. P. van de Spiegel, in *Mr Laurens Pieter van de Spiegel en zijne tijdgenooten (1737–1800)*, vol.

works of Montesquieu, however, with their constitutional theories and ideas about the influence of climate on the laws and character of a people, were valued. Their popularity may be observed from the fact that in 1748 Van Mieris had already mentioned *Esprit des lois* and that the first philosophical historian, Simon Stijl, extensively discussed the theories of the great man.[21] Hume was controversial, but admiration was accorded the Scottish historian William Robertson, especially for his history of Charles V. In the opinion of a contemporary, this "everywhere famous and clever" man had produced work of such a "degree of perfection that presumably, in the coming centuries, it will hardly be possible to improve upon."[22]

How did this general agreement about historiography, even among political opponents in the struggle of the 1780s, come about? The explanation relies on the Dutch conception of philosophical history. Here I must reiterate that in the Dutch Enlightenment revelation and reason were combined, that is, Christianity was an integral part of the enlightened age. Providence, although relegated to the background in Dutch humanist historiography, still played its part behind the secondary natural causes. Thus, for orthodox and nonorthodox writers of history, Voltaire was too much of a freethinker. Robertson, a Presbyterian pastor, represented the ideal of tolerant, rational Christianity they preferred. Moreover, philosophical history was for them nearly exclusively identified with political history, which with the help of the study of the past aimed to discover the ideal circumstances, in particular the ideal constitution, for a commercial state in which citizens could live to-

---

4: *De toestand van Nederland en Europa (1788–1795)*, ed. G. W. Vreede (Middelburg, 1877), p. 530. Attitudes about Rousseau are made clear in W. Gobbers, *Jean-Jacques Rousseau in Holland: Een onderzoek naar de invloed van de mens en het werk (ca. 1760–ca. 1810)* (Gent, 1963); Gobbers mentions only the historian Kluit, p. 236. Even Cornelis Zillesen, a historian sympathetic to the new ideas, excused himself for the fact that some might think his ideas resembled those of Rousseau; see his *Wijsgeerig onderzoek wegens Neerlands opkomst, bloei en welvaard* (Amsterdam, 1796), p. 12.

21. For a preliminary survey of Montesquieu's reputation in the Dutch Republic, see S. J. Fockema Andreae, "Montesquieu en Nederland," *De Gids* 112 (1949): 76–183. See also Haitsma Mulier, "Frans van Mieris"; S. Stijl, *De opkomst en bloei der Vereenigde Nederlanden*, 2d ed. (Amsterdam-Harlingen, 1778), p. 25ff.; [J. Munniks], *Vaderlandsche historie, vervattende de geschiedenissen der Vereenigde Nederlanden*, 17 vols. (Amsterdam, 1781–1787), vol. 16, pp. xix, voorreden.

22. Quotation in Van Iperen, "Verhandelinge," pp. 31–32; see also E. Luzac, *Hollands rijkdom*, 4 vols. (Leiden, 1780–1783), vol. 4, p. 26ff., and W. R. E. Velema, "Homo mercator in Holland: Elie Luzac en het achttiende-eeuwse debat over de koophandel," *Bijdragen en Mededelingen betreffende de Geschiedenis der Nederlanden* 100 (1985): 427–444. Also J. H. Hering, *Aanhangsel tot de vaderlandsche historie van den heer Jan Wagenaar* (Amsterdam, 1780), p. 146, n. 10.

gether as civilized, prosperous beings. Better than all other sciences, history—and this was of the utmost importance to Dutch historians— would reveal the inner depths of the human heart. Humanity was now placed in a new dimension at the center of historiography with the purpose of furthering the progress of human destiny.[23]

But this understanding was not attainable by reason alone, as some asserted. Facts remained important for most Dutch philosophical historians, who wanted, as one said, to proceed experimentally. By putting the facts in a certain order, they were convinced, they would increase the knowledge of the past. In their theory, reasoning through ascertained facts must lead to a narration of what really happened in the past. Yet typical in this connection was the hesitation shown by some authors regarding ancient biblical history. Could one doubt what was written in Scripture when recent critics diverged from the version given there? Often the answer was negative.[24]

The emphasis in philosophical history was, however, largely on the human political condition; this was the study of the *prudentia civilis* of the man of state. Whatever the actual political position of the historian, most would have agreed that "philosophy, improved by humanity, sound politics combined with experience of men, gives princes and leaders of the people expedients . . . to consolidate the vacillating state."[25] In this kind of historical writing, the citizen yielded to the political leader in history. The writing of history, in this vision, entailed the use of the old in the service of the new.

This tension between old and new did at last appear in the universities as well. The opposition some offered philosophical history and the idea that one could lecture on contemporary history did not prevent the rise of what was called *statistiek*, the science of the state. The representatives of this new science were of the opinion that it was possible to consider the present situation and even to foresee the future of

23. See Luzac, *Hollands rijkdom*; Van Iperen, *Verhandelinge*, p. 20; Stijl, *De opkomst*, p. viii; C. Zillesen, *Onderzoek der oorzaaken van de opkomst, het verval en herstel der voornaamste oude en hedendaagsche volken*, 6 vols. (Utrecht, 1781–1784), vol. 1, p. 8ff. For a general discussion of the Dutch Enlightenment, see W. W. Mijnhardt, "De Nederlandse verlichting, een terreinverkenning," *Kleio* 19 (1978): 245–264.

24. Van Deursen, "Wijsgerige geschiedschrijving," pp. 105, 109; Zillesen, *Onderzoek*, vol. 1, dedication; Van Iperen, "Verhandelinge," pp. 20, 26. Van de Spiegel in Vreede, ed. *Mr Laurens Pieter van de Spiegel*, p. 533.

25. Quotation in C. Rogge, *Tafereel van de geschiedenis der jongste omwenteling in de Vereenigde Nederlanden* (Amsterdam, 1796), p. 6. For the humanist vision of history defended in the learned societies, see W. W. Mijnhardt, *Tot Heil van 't menschdom: Culturele genootschappen in Nederland, 1750–1815* (Amsterdam, 1987), pp. 207–211; see also Chapter 9 of this volume.

the state with the help of a thorough knowledge of the past. The problem was to get to the facts in an age when the authorities still preferred secrecy to open information. In Germany, where the science of the state originated, criticism by professors had led to conflict between these surely unrevolutionary men and the authorities. But in the Dutch Republic, the science of the state became an occupation of those who favored the House of Orange. From the 1780s, when this development began in a country torn apart by political contradictions, a man such as Kluit directed all his evidence about the past, present, and future toward the conclusion that the existing constitution and the stadholder had been and would remain the best for the republic.[26] Here again we see the connection between historiography and political reality that dominated in the Dutch Republic of the eighteenth century.

After having looked at the changing theory and ideal, we must consider in greater detail the practice and content of historiography. I have already emphasized that most historians focused on the history of the Dutch provinces. Traditional world history and church history continued to be written, but these were minor genres. The narrative of Dutch history occupied a prominent position in Dutch historical writing, and it seldom contained extensive meditations on the origin and development of civilization. Although there was a common view of the past with many shared values, history was the battleground on which disagreements over specific points continued to be fought.[27] In theory one professed to look for truth in history, but in practice everyone had a personal view of the past.

The republic and its constitution had been legitimized by historical argument. Thus, a new treatment of a situation in the past might engender dangerous consequences in the eyes of contemporaries. This situation occurred in the 1740s, when the Catholic antiquarian Gerard van Loon was furiously attacked for denouncing as nonsense the Batavian myth that postulated the independence of Holland from the time of the old Batavians and defined the count as a predecessor of the stadholder and a creation of the representatives of the notables. Van Loon's clear and well-documented evidence of a centuries-long feudal dependence on the Holy Roman Empire was swept aside by the argument that this opinion would imperil the republic and encourage for-

26. See A. Th. van Deursen, "Geschiedenis en toekomstverwachting: Het onderwijs in de statistiek aan de universiteiten in de achttiende eeuw," *Geschiedschrijving in Nederland* 2 (1971): 110–129, and Roelevink, "'Bewezen'."

27. I. L. Leeb, *The Ideological Origins of the Batavian Revolution: History and Politics in the Dutch Republic, 1747–1800* (The Hague, 1973), p. 5.

eign powers to attack. He was accused of freethinking and, because of his observation that the loosening of this tie came only with the revolt of the sixteenth century, even of resuscitating Catholic, pro-Spanish feelings.[28]

When Adriaan Kluit discussed the role of the stadholder more than thirty years later, his point of view was also determined by political circumstances. The fact that archival research showed that the count of Holland had held absolute power, which in the course of time devolved on the provincial estates, convinced him that demands from below for redress of the constitution and a reduction of the powers of the stadholder were not justified. For Kluit, it was not the prince of Orange who was to be feared but the citizens with their claims.[29]

There were many debates in which the positions of the great figures from the past were scrutinized. Did Prince Maurice, at the beginning of the seventeenth century, act on a political or a religious principle when he decided to attend the more rigorous contra-remonstrant church? An orthodox Reformed historian at the end of the next century affirmed the latter. A more moderate pastor and writer of history chose the former principle.[30] Did the office of stadholder present a danger to the republic by the continuous efforts it undertook to enlarge its powers? William II's years, cut short by his premature death in 1650 after he had tried to take Amsterdam by force, became a test case in historiography.

In 1757, during the war between France and England, the existence of a treaty with the latter country dating from 1678 threatened to involve the Dutch Republic. As a result, fierce conflict broke out about the political motives of grand pensionary Johan de Witt in the 1660s and 1670s. Although many accusations were gravely exaggerated, Jan Wagenaar, who by then had already acquired a great reputation as a historian, did not consider it beneath his dignity to involve himself— anonymously—in the affair for the sake of what he saw as historical

28. The Batavian myth is discussed in I. Schöffer, "The Batavian Myth during the Sixteenth and Seventeenth Centuries," in *Britain and the Netherlands*, vol. 5, ed. J. S. Bromley and E. H. Kossmann (The Hague, 1975), pp. 78–101. The myth was originally expounded in 1610 by Grotius, who emphasized the privileged position of the province of Holland and immediately met opposition from antiquaries in other provinces. See Leeb, *Origins*, p. 201, and Haitsma Mulier, "'Hoofsche papegaaien'," on eighteenth-century developments. For a more theoretical view, see J. G. A. Pocock, "The Origins of Study of the Past: A Comparative Approach," *Comparative Studies in Society and History* 4 (1961–1962): 209–246.

29. Leeb, *Origins*, pp. 198–203.

30. See Oldenburg, *Vaderlandsche brieven*, p. 35, who directs his wrath against the *Historie der waereld*, 9 vols. (Amsterdam, 1780–1788) by the more liberal pastor of Huguenot descent J. F. Martinet.

truth.[31] Nevertheless, the general purpose for which Wagenaar wrote his *Vaderlandsche historie* (1749–59) was to show how freedom in the Low Countries had been attacked and preserved through the centuries. He intended to explain these events accurately by using his sources objectively, and he was determined not to write a history of princes. In practice, however, the work was unmistakably constitutional, diplomatic, and political in character. Even in discussions of the position of the church, the use and abuse of temporal power became the essence of the matter. The people he described were magistrates, merchants, and middle-class citizens, not the masses he despised. Consequently, freedom meant civil freedom and independence from forces outside the country. But Wagenaar no longer accepted the Batavian myth. Although he tried to study the sources in a detached way, eventually he identified freedom with the untempered sovereignty of the provincial estates. The stadholder could only carry out his duties in close cooperation with the estates and within the bounds of the rightful privileges of the people. When Wagenaar arrived at the twentieth and last volume of his history, this strain became evident in his reticent description of what was nearly contemporary history—the last years of the 1740s and the restoration of the House of Orange.[32]

Twenty years later, freedom again stood in the center of a history of the Dutch Republic. The Frisian physician Simon Stijl produced an abridgement and adaptation of Wagenaar's work in his volume of 1774, which though permeated with the same quest for freedom and tolerance had a different spirit. Whereas for Wagenaar freedom was an idea with corporate overtones, Stijl conceived it more concretely as part of a dynamic system influenced by pressure from the outside. The philosophical historian did not bother with documentation. In his discourses, he preferred to show how peoples and individuals reasoned according to sound maxims. Blind passion could disturb this progress of humankind, but virtue would eventually answer the challenge. Stijl discussed the Dutch past with the firm conviction that the republic was the most happy commonwealth in the world. Like Montesquieu, he considered the relationship between its laws and morals, the extension of its territory and form of government, and the genius of its people. Still, his was mainly a work of political history in which the constitution avoided with its checks and balances the extremes of democracy

31. Leeb, *Origins*, p. 76ff.; Wessels, "Jan Wagenaar's," p. 41.
32. Leeb, *Origins*, p. 75ff.; Wessels, "Jan Wagenaar," especially p. 127; Offringa, "Classicisme en verlichting," p. 73.

and autocracy. The historical analysis of this system of government—with its hereditary stadholder, reasonable patrician elite, and people in all their tensions and cooperation—was to stimulate readers to understand the interests of the state and thereby to be conscious of their place in the universe created by God and their duties as citizens.[33]

Stijl also participated in the discussion of the second half of the century when he postulated the importance of commerce for the Dutch Republic and accused Great Britain of unfair rivalry. Thus he discussed the theme of his country's decline. These three topics appeared more prominently in historiography during the struggle of the 1780s and after the disappointment of the revolution of 1795. The feeling of decline gained force. In the first half of the century, complaints about the loss of moral strength in the republic were heard. These remarks could be traced mainly to the conviction that the orthodox interpretation of religion had been injured. Writers of history in particular deplored the fact that young people no longer knew the history of their own country; they explained this as the effect of too much attention to ancient history. They also complained about the preference in elite circles for French over Dutch.[34] In a plea for religious tolerance and for the general well-being of the community, Van Mieris expressed himself bitterly in 1758 about the moral decay of the fatherland in which vanity and lawlessness imperiled virtue in this "civilized and enlightened" age.[35]

The same observations reappeared when Stijl accused his compatriots of sensuality and uncritical admiration of everything foreign. They followed the French to a ridiculous degree in manners and customs; the young in particular were the victims of these evil results of good manners and followed deism without even knowing the principles of rational religion. For Stijl, real refinement remained the essence of society and the loveliest companion of virtue.[36] This complaint about luxury and the corrupting influence of everything French was later adapted by those who desired reorganization of the Dutch government. Orthodox Protestants coupled it with a dislike of the moral degradation of the French court of the ancien régime.[37]

33. Leeb, *Origins*, pp. 122–136; H. Smitskamp, "Simon Stijl als verlicht geschiedschrijver," in *Mythe en werkelijkheid*, ed. Lancée, pp. 86–102.
34. See Haitsma Mulier, "'Hoofsche papegaaien'," pp. 466–467.
35. See Haitsma Mulier, "Frans van Mieris." Leeb, *Origins*, p. 123, is mistaken when he states that Stijl was among the first to use the word "enlightened."
36. Stijl, *Opkomst*, pp. 284–290.
37. For complaints about luxury and the situation at the French court see, e.g., Zillesen, *Onderzoek oorzaaken*, vol. 6, p. 84ff., and *Wysgeerig onderzoek*, p. 46; Oldenburg, *Vaderlandsche brieven*, p. 50; Rogge, *Tafereel*, p. 5.

Decline was now more precisely identified with the difficult economic position of Dutch commerce. For decades Dutch historians had been convinced of the utmost importance of trade for the Dutch. In the last decades of the century, commerce and decline became the most important themes of historiography. Those in favor of the House of Orange, men such as Luzac and Kluit, tried to demonstrate the dangerous cunning of the French, who sought to undermine the sound economy and constitution of the republic. But those who favored reexamining the situation concentrated their historical writings on the problem of decline, which they associated also with the faulty politics of recent and especially current governments. For example, the Patriot author of a sequel to Wagenaar's history (published 1781–1787), although he dealt with the difficulties of the existing constitution, argued that it had to be preserved at all cost because its destruction would mean the end of Dutch commerce and prosperity. Only with the nomination of new regents and a close inspection of the constitution, including the stadholder, would the people regain confidence in the government and could the reign of an aristocracy be avoided. The glory of the stadholder was closely connected with the general well-being of the country and an independent functioning of the constitution. Like many of his partisans, the author extolled the role of France in helping the Dutch regain their old position, whereas Great Britain had only tried to embarrass the republic when it could.[38]

This tendency in the historiography to look at decline and Dutch positioning in the world is clearly illustrated in the work of Cornelis Zillesen, one of the few Dutch historical writers at the end of the century to try to relate Dutch history to human evolution. As a tax collector and member of the Economic Branch of the Holland Society of Sciences, Zillesen wrote books typical of the increasing interest of the middle-class members of that society in the causes of the economic stagnation of the Low Countries. No wonder he dedicated his six-volume *Onderzoek der oorzaaken van de opkomst, het verval en herstel der voornaamste oude en hedendaagsche volken* (Enquiry into the Causes of the Rise, Decline, and Recovery of the Most Important Ancient and Present-Day Nations, 1781–1784) to the directors of the Economic

38. For Luzac's remark on Wagenaar, see *Hollands rijkdom*, vol. 1, p. 147, and Velema, "Homo mercator," p. 442. For a discussion of the dangers to the new commercial society, see J. G. A. Pocock, *Virtue, Commerce and History* (Cambridge, 1985). For Kluit's position, see Van Deursen, "Geschiedenis en toekomstverwachting," pp. 124–125. The sequel to Wagenaar's history was written by J. Munniks, *Vaderlandsche historie*; see, e.g., vol. 4, p. 212; vol. 15, p. viii; and vol. 17, p. 126.

Branch. In spite of its title, after the first volume this work narrated only the history of the Low Countries. Zillesen was obsessed with the problem of decline. Thus, he put at the top of each page on Dutch history the words "rise" or "decline." Each chapter, subdivided into paragraphs as was fitting for a philosophical history, ended with a moral lesson. In his *Wijsgeerig onderzoek wegens Neerlands opkomst, bloei en welvaard* (Philosophical Enquiry into the Rise, Flourishing, and Prosperity of the Netherlands: The Later Decline and What Remedies for Redress Have Been Left in Government, Finance, Agriculture, Commerce, Navigation, Factories, and Industry), he examined the whole problem again, but this book was published in 1796 after the revolution he sympathized with. The call for a search for solutions to the problems of the country he had announced in his first work now materialized in practical proposals for constitutional and financial reforms.[39]

Zillesen blended old elements of historiography with new. For him, human beings stood in the center of history. After a childhood phase, when uncivilized peoples roamed the empty world and lived by hunting, humankind settled down in society, practiced agriculture, and grew cattle. The human spirit then experienced a process of enlightenment, and civilization developed step by step. But, at the same time, the desires at the origin of industry, art, and sciences increased. These desires were also the starting point of rivalry and conflict, as a result of self-interested impulses. Zillesen explored the working of the soul and declared himself to be inspired by the books of Charles Bonnet, the Genevan philosopher and foreign member of the Holland Society of Sciences. At the beginning, humans were free and could have reached a degree of perfection with the help of their natural God-given reason, together with the prescriptions of revelation. Unfortunately, all good things were liable to be used badly, as happened only too often in history. Internal factors such as manners and customs, geographic conditions, and the air and external factors such as commercial contacts and other relations with the outside world always influenced the changing fortune of commonwealths. These influences came together, like mechanical powers, in a force of one direction. It was an easy task for the philosophical historian to detect and demonstrate this direction in chains of events and, by this procedure, to illustrate the philosophical maxim that every nation struggled for a certain degree of freedom

39. J. Elias, *Bijdrage tot de kennis van de historiographie der Bataafsche Republiek* (Leiden, 1906), pp. 58–69, gives an analysis of Zillesen's sources.

and lost it again. Zillesen concluded that propertied man should live in a well-ordered civil society, where a government founded in virtue and following the principles of checks and balances would further the happiness of all.[40]

Zillesen's narrative often digressed to the war's hindrance of commerce. Great Britain he indicated especially as the author of such mischief. In an interesting analysis of Britain's corrupt government, Zillesen declared that the promulgation of the Navigation Act in 1652 was the cause of the decline of the Dutch Republic. On the whole, however, his historical works are permeated by a spirit of moderation. In his earlier history, the observations on the role of the House of Orange were balanced, and after the revolution his attitude toward the partisans of the old regime remained conciliatory. These reasonable and realistic statements form a remarkable contrast with his deeply felt moral and religious convictions. Decline was, in his opinion, primarily the result of moral factors together with the influence of warlike, wicked Albion. Where religion was no longer heeded, vice gained the upper hand and decay set in, a process visible in world history. His works contain observations clearly derived from enlightened ideas found elsewhere in Europe as well as Christian overtones reminiscent of the old humanist cyclical view of history.[41]

Dutch historiography in the eighteenth century reflected the hesitations of a nation experiencing a changing world. The internal and external situation of the republic found its expression in questions of which version of the past was the right one. We noted the rise of new directions in the methodology and writing of history, but we must go farther in our discussion. Why were influences like a new antiquarian method of reading documents or new thoughts about the writing of history nearly always met by incomprehension or a defensive attitude? Why, for instance, did Van Mieris know the work of Mabillon but fail to apply his method? Why did Stijl, when at last he adopted the princi-

40. Zillesen refers to Charles Bonnet, *Essai analytique sur les facultés de l'ame* (Copenhagen, 1760; repr. Hildesheim-New York, 1973), pp. xix–xx. On Bonnet's natural philosophy, see L. Anderson, "Charles Bonnet's Taxonomy and Chain of Being," *Journal of the History of Ideas* 37 (1976): 45–58. Bonnet's sometimes fantastic theories were popular in the Dutch Republic; see J. Marx, "Charles Bonnet en de biofilosofische stromingen in Nederland," *Documentatieblad Werkgroep Achttiende eeuw* 7 (1976): 47–68, especially 50ff.; Zillesen, *Onderzoek*, p. 11.

41. Zillesen, *Onderzoek*, Introduction and chap. 1; Zillesen, *Wysgeerig onderzoek*, Introduction and p. 45; Zillesen, *Geschiedenis der Vereenigde Nederlanden, nevens de voornaamste gebeurtenissen in Europa*, 6 vols. (The Hague, 1798–1802), vol. 1, p. 7; vol. 5, p. 315.

ples of philosophical history, write yet another history of his own country without doubting for a moment that it was Christian and happy? And why did the critical revision of early Roman history by Louis de Beaufort, a man admired and visited by Gibbon, generally receive a cold shoulder from the few Dutch writers who intruded in this field of study?[42] Why is it that the Dutch did not participate in international historical debates but instead followed their own direction? Why this exclusive preoccupation with the Dutch past and late reception of foreign influence followed by a subtle but decisive transformation?

Much research must still be done before we can answer these questions, but a suggestion may be given here. In a world dominated by great nations, where in the eyes of its citizens the voice of the Dutch Republic was no longer clearly heard, the study of the past offered a path to national identity.[43] The slow growth from an instinctive identification with town or province to a kind of awareness of the whole republic as a country in decline perhaps excluded immediate interest in developments elsewhere. Possibly the concern about decline and then revolution increased the appeal of the humanistic and religious traditions of history. As in much else, the Dutch historians of the eighteenth century were both of their age and yet separate from it. They labored with a distinctive history, with greatness followed by decline, and they sought to make sense of it.

42. L. de Beaufort, *Dissertation sur l'incertitude des cinq premiers siècles de l'histoire Romaine* (Utrecht, 1738), and *La règpublique Romaine*, 2 vols. (The Hague, 1766). See also H. J. Erasmus, *The Origins of Rome in Historiography from Petrarch to Perizonius* (Assen, 1962).

43. E. H. Kossmann, "The Crisis of the Dutch State, 1780–1813: Nationalism, Federalism, Unitarism," in *Britain and the Netherlands*, ed. J. S. Bromley and E. H. Kossmann (The Hague, 1971), pp. 156–175.

# 8

## The Dutch Republican Tradition

### J. G. A. Pocock

I have here undertaken the exacting task of commenting on the Dutch national tradition of political thought from a standpoint shaped by study of the English-language tradition. The difficulty attending any such comparative history is that one all too easily finds oneself talking about the absence in one tradition of what is to be found in another, and thus laying oneself open to the question whether there is any point in trying to explain why it is not to be found where it is absent. There are, however, times when this risk must be run.

The Dutch ancien régime was a republic; the English was a constitutional and parliamentary monarchy. The Dutch Patriots were therefore radical republicans, attacking a republican structure that could be conservatively defended; one might expect that the American revolutionaries, and any English or Scottish radicals who proved to be like them, were republicans in the simple sense that they were attacking a monarchy that answered for itself in monarchic terms. But things were by no means as simple as that. The Patriot attack was directed against both the old republic and what looked like its monarchic component, the House of Orange, which indeed emerged in the nineteenth century as a constitutional and parliamentary monarchy. By contrast, Anglo-American radicalism was aimed at the alliance of king and parliament. Much of what was "republican" in the latter political tradition had been formulated to explain, or to criticize, how this alliance worked. The political debates we find in the 1770s and 1780s shared concepts, language, and texts; but we have to reckon with some sharp differences between the two contexts in which they did so.

In both, the language of mixed government was employed and the work of Montesquieu was venerated; and much of what we call republicanism originates in using the language of mixed government in a special way. English republicanism, wherever we meet it, takes the existence of a central monarchy and a unitary realm for granted. Charles I's *Answer to the Nineteen Propositions of Parliament* in 1642, which inadvertently became the classic of English republican thinking, declared that sovereignty in the realm of England was lodged with three coordinate, but equal and separate, powers—king, lords, and commons; monarchy, aristocracy, and democracy; executive, judiciary, and legislature—whose function was to control and balance one another. There arose in reply a doctrine of strict monarchy, which held that sovereignty was lodged in the king alone, and a doctrine of strict republicanism, which held that a coordinate and balanced sovereignty could be better constructed without a king or house of lords. But between these extremes, Anglo-American republicanism was a dialogue about the separation of powers within a coordinate sovereignty. When it was put to revolutionary purposes in the American colonies, it led to the construction of a federal republic with separation of powers at the very core of its central government—as we are constantly being reminded.

To theorists in the Anglo-American tradition, and to many Dutch theorists too, the old republic seemed less a republic than a confederation, less a state than an alliance of states; and what makes Dutch political thought difficult for the Anglo-American student is, crudely, that the doctrine of sovereignty seems to have been applied on the behalf of the several and particular powers of provinces and cities, whereas the central and coordinating powers lack a clear theory of sovereignty and seem to have had no theory of monarchy at all. I am always looking for theory in which the princes of the House of Orange, or their servants and spokesmen, expound a view of political order as it appeared to them; but I never seem to find one, and perhaps I am asking the wrong question. As we commemorate 1787 as well as 1688, I wish someone would explain to me the sense of identity and the view of the world which must have been possessed by William III. He was prince of Orange; he was stadholder of many provinces and captain general of the Dutch Republic; he was the king of England and supreme governor of its church; he was king of Ireland and finally king of Scots. To know who he thought he was and what he thought he was doing would bring light into what I believe is something of a black hole in Dutch historiography. But perhaps I am asking for the impossible. We have heard of Orangists in 1747 who were radical populists, Orangists in 1787 who were conservative patricians, but not of Orangists who expounded a princely view of politics. Even those drastically conservative historians, such as Gerard van Loon or Adriaan Kluit, who dwelt on the feudal historiography of the counts of Holland, did so less to affirm a prerogative than to undermine claims made on the grounds of Batavian ancient liberty; it was like dwelling on the Norman conquest in the England of George II—except that the latter's prerogative was still more effective than it looked.

We have been hearing about a conflict between the old republic and a new, between the structure of privileged and self-representative oligarchies to which we apply the concept of an ancien régime and new patterns of civic and popular association often built around the formation of militias. *Aux armes, citoyens!*—the model of ancient Rome was much alleged when this call to arms sounded late in the century in France, Ireland, and America, as well as in the Netherlands. It did not go so far in England, where the militia was controlled by the regime, or in Scotland, where it was not instituted at all; but English historians anxious, in a fit of belated Europeanism, to insist that the Whig polity was an ancien régime too, rightly point out new patterns of association that took shape as patronage and clientage became less effective. Britain and the Netherlands are alike in that what was to emerge after ancien régime was a liberal parliamentary monarchy in a state more effectively centralized than before, but the English ancien régime was a parliamentary monarchy too. It seems to be a problem, in assessing the historical role of the Dutch Patriots, how far we are to regard them as French revolutionaries in the making—citizens sweeping away the ancien régime and substituting centralized rationality in the name of democratic sovereignty. Perhaps they would never have done that if the French had not imposed it on them; perhaps the English would never have done that (and did they do it?) if they had not had to fight the French for twenty years.

But if the old republic was a Venice or a confederation of Venices—republics as patrician oligarchies—the new republic envisaged by Van der Capellen and others in Patriot rhetoric was a Rome, unitary, public, and based on the armed virtue of active citizenship. There was, by the way, nothing unusual about including a natural aristocracy in such a republic. Here we encounter one of the basic tensions in eighteenth-century historical thought; and here we also encounter the problem of Enlightenment, that buzzword of our historiography which can mean so many things and to which we must be so careful before prefixing the definite article. As a reader of Montesquieu, Hume, Gibbon, and Adam Smith, I am especially aware of Enlightenment as a phenomenon in historical consciousness; the names I have mentioned are all those of authors concerned with the emergence of modern from ancient society, whether the ancient be characterized as classical, heathen, and republican, or—as was equally possible—medieval, Christian, feudal, and corporate. What further complicates our understanding is that eighteenth-century anciens régimes (as we call them), which could obviously be described as medieval, feudal, and privileged, could with equal force be described, defended, and attacked as modern, commercial, and enlightened; we never understand the argument if we do not understand that. It also follows that the Patriot or radical assertion of active citizenship in Roman terms can be characterized either as a forward movement toward the liberal state or a regressive movement back to the ancient republic; a lot of misunderstanding has arisen because historians do not or will not understand that either.

This is the point at which we find in Dutch historiography some traces at least of the creative tensions between ancient and modern that occur in Scotland, France, and England. Many of the chapters in this volume have alluded to these tensions. The central problem around which Adam Smith, for example, organized much of his vision of history was that ancient society was based on the possession of arms and land, modern on that of rights and increasingly movable property; and some of the essays here enquire how far this was an organizing principle in Enlightenment Dutch historiography. Or, Haitsma Mulier suggests in the previous chapter (if I am not overreading him) that the reality of life in an ancient commercial society had made this issue superfluous, and certainly one can find as far back as Pieter de la Court the conception that the very existence of the Dutch as a nation originated in the medieval revival of commerce. But I am not sure this was enough to take away all incentive to employ the ancient-modern antithesis I have just stated. I should like to interject at this point the name of Louis de Beaufort—no kin to Lieven—a Maastricht scholar whose De la republique Romaine was consulted by Gibbon. He may be described as a radically populist Montesquieuian, a warm defender of the Roman plebs and its tribunes, and a keen critic of the religion of the augurs as a tissue of Etruscan superstitions imposed by the Tarquins and the senators on the pure Celtic religion of nature taught by Numa Pompilius. Margaret Jacob may see in him the lineaments of masonic illuminism, and I should not be at all surprised; but he is also a defender—and this is rare—of Tiberius Gracchus and *lex agraria* aimed at preserving the Italian citizen-warrior-smallholder against the inroads of the great slave-worked *latifundia*. It was at least possible— we learn from Louis de Beaufort—for a Netherlands scholar to join the great enlightened historians in interpreting history as the decline of the ancient republic.

It is true that De Beaufort drew no connection between the ancient republic and the modern; but, at the risk I spoke of in the beginning of this essay, I suggest at this point that, if indeed nobody was interpreting Dutch history in terms of this movement, I should still find the fact surprising. In the midst of so much debate about the ancient freedom of the Batavians, it would be truly remarkable if nobody wrote about them as ancient Goths or Gauls, whose liberty was rooted in allodial tenure and then subverted, or not subverted, by the introduction of feudal dependencies. This issue was debated, almost literally from Pennsylvania to Transylvania, wherever the history of freedom was being discussed in the eighteenth century, and it would be a most remarkable circumstance if Dutch scholarship was an exception. Indeed, when I hear of Gerard van Loon, Elie Luzac, and Adriaan Kluit maintaining the feudal power of the count of Holland, the only question in my mind is whether the count is being said to have acquired his sovereignty as the chief of a barbarian warband conducting something like a Norman conquest—as would have been contended by Robert Brady or Thomas Carte in England—or as a Roman provincial governor inheriting his share of imperial authority, as would have been contended by Du Bos or Mably in France. The Dutch historians were attentive readers of Montesquieu, in whose later chapters the whole controversy is laid out; and if they did not apply such models to the early history of the Netherlands, the questions to be asked are, if not, why not? if not, what else? Here I do believe we are on well-trodden ground. The link between the Gothic and Roman worlds is formed by the presence in each of a free militia—typically but not necessarily of landowners; in the midst of so much debate about militia service as the manifestation of civic virtue, it would once again be remarkable if nobody raised the question about division of labor and asked with Adam Smith whether a militia could be formed in a population of tradesmen and artisans.

The Dutch, I think, had an answer of their own; what I need to know is whether they bothered to ask the question.

We have learned from Margaret Jacob, Nicholas Phillipson, and others to regard the Enlightenment as a complex and various business that comes in many forms. There is a civil Enlightenment that empties religion of some of its mysteries the better to reinforce social, political, and even clerical authority; and there is an illuminist Enlightenment in which the freedom of the spirit becomes the freedom of citizens to associate as they choose in the pursuit of truth and virtue. Both were well represented in the eighteenth-century Netherlands, though how far they were formed in the context of the old republic and how far in that of the republic of letters seems to be open to debate. But when it came to debating the structure of civil society, it is the former we expect to hear speaking in the tones of patrician conservatism, whether regent or Orangist, the latter we expect to hear in the voice of the radical Patriots. That Luzac accused Van der Capellen of enthusiasm can surprise no reader of the period. The civil or conservative Enlightenment of which I speak found two modes of expression that concern the theme of this book. One was the growth of polite societies, whose literature was disseminated by Joseph Addison in the spectatorial form so much more fascinating to enlightened Europe than it is to me. The other was the development of natural jurisprudence as a science of polite and sociable morality, and in this Utrecht and Groningen had leading parts to play. It seems to emerge from Worst's discussion in this volume that it was in the language of public law that German jurists sought to develop a coherent theory of the state. They were necessitated to do so because the German empire had become, in Pufendorf's famous phrase, a juristic monster; and it is not hard to imagine a jurist saying much the same of the Republic of the Netherlands. On its seaward side, the Dutch political tradition belongs to an Atlantic world of Anglo-American patriot commonwealthmen and French patriot revolutionaries; on its landward side, do we not move from a world of republics toward one of princes and caesars?

Monument for Jan van Nieuwenhuijzen, founder of the *Maatschappij tot Nut van 't Algemeen*. The *Nut* sought to end the processes of social and cultural decline by distributing enlightened knowledge among the lower classes. Engraving by S. Portman after J. Kuyper. Private Collection.

# THE DUTCH
# ENLIGHTENMENT

# 9

# The Dutch Enlightenment: Humanism, Nationalism, and Decline

## Wijnand W. Mijnhardt

THE process of reevaluating eighteenth-century Dutch economic and political history is now well under way. In these fields traditional stereotypes such as decay and decadence are now rarely employed, and few historians are prepared to argue that eighteenth-century economic or political decline were due to a catastrophic loss of stamina. Yet the field of eighteenth-century Dutch cultural history is still in its infancy. Here the shadows of the Golden Age of Rembrandt and Spinoza still loom, the more so because in intellectual history the concept of genius is even harder to defeat than, for example, in economic history. The study of the Dutch Enlightenment has also suffered from such a decline-focused perspective. A standard Dutch account of about fifteen years ago, comparing Dutch intellectual developments to those in France, chose to speak explicitly of the Netherlands *and* the Enlightenment, as if they were separate phenomena.[1]

Although recent historiography has paved the way for more national interpretations of the Enlightenment, interpretations less dominated by France, it seems that the Dutch phenomenon has hardly profited from the new perspective. In 1981, for instance, Simon Schama

---

1. H. H. Zwager, *Nederland en de Verlichting* (Bussum, 1972). Some more-balanced accounts have been offered since: P. J. Buijnsters, "Les Lumieres Hollandaises," *Studies on Voltaire and the Eighteenth Century* 77 (1972): 197–215; W. W. Mijnhardt, "De Nederlandse Verlichting: Een terreinverkenning," in *Figuren en figuraties: Acht opstellen aangeboden aan J.C. Boogman* (Groningen, 1979), pp. 1–25.

still qualified the Dutch Enlightenment as an unpromising subject. At the same time, however, he failed to link Dutch thought to the international Protestant Enlightenment or to account for the characteristically Dutch circumstances that determined the development of Dutch Enlightenment ideas.[2]

Because the history of the Dutch Enlightenment is intertwined with the problem of eighteenth-century Dutch cultural decline, we need to distinguish between decline as it actually happened, as an intersubjective phenomenon, and decline as perceived by contemporaries. A careful assessment of those cultural and intellectual circumstances that had been so vital in creating the Dutch Golden Age is also necessary. Finally, we need a delineation of Dutch cultural and intellectual developments, especially their relationship with the European Enlightenment. Only then will it be possible to establish the factors that determined the character of the Dutch Enlightenment and eventually that of Dutch cultural decline. All this of course constitutes an ambitious undertaking that cannot be executed within the scope of a single essay, the more so because the long-standing neglect of the period in many aspects leaves us with obsolete literature. In this chapter, I merely sketch the outlines of the Dutch Enlightenment. First, I discuss the relationship of Dutch Enlightenment thought to international intellectual developments; second, I assess specifically Dutch factors that gave the Dutch Enlightenment its indigenous coloring. Finally, I try to establish the relationship between the Dutch Enlightenment and the revolutions at the end of the eighteenth century.

## ENLIGHTENED BEFORE THE ENLIGHTENMENT?

At the end of the seventeenth century, Dutch intellectual circles encountered a large wave of learned immigrants. The religious policies of Louis XIV, culminating in the revocation of the Edict of Nantes in 1685, forced many Huguenots to take refuge in Protestant areas such as England, the Dutch Republic, and Brandenburg. The influx of large numbers of exiled intellectuals was no new phenomenon; between 1570 and 1630 a great many inhabitants of the Southern Netherlands

2. S. Schama, "The Enlightenment in the Netherlands," in *The Enlightenment in National Context*, ed. R. Porter and M. Teich (Cambridge, 1981); but see W. W. Mijnhardt, "De Nederlandse Verlichting in Europees perspectief," *Theoretische Geschiedenis* 10 (1983): 335–347.

also took refuge in the newly founded republic. But the cultural effects of the two waves were radically different. The immigrants from the Southern Netherlands played a decisive role in the formation of seventeenth-century Dutch culture. The post-1685 arrival of the Huguenots produced less-lasting effects.

The south, until about 1600 the cultural and intellectual center of the Low Countries, supplied not only numerous theologians and *predikanten* who proved essential to the Calvinization of the north but a host of scholars as well who put the educational system of the republic on a firm humanist footing.[3] The arrival of many printers and booksellers made the Dutch publishing industry Europe's greatest seller of Latin literature. Humanists and Calvinists together were responsible for the repute of Dutch universities. The international fame of Dutch editions of classical texts was based on humanist philological expertise, and the application of such methods to Calvinist biblical research resulted in the fine reputation of Dutch oriental studies.[4] Dutch seventeenth-century political theory drew heavily on both Calvinist and humanist traditions, and the writing of the Dutch language, strongly advocated by Dutch humanists, was according to principles derived from Latin literature. In summary, it may be said that Calvinism and especially humanism provided the dominant elements of seventeenth-century Dutch national cultural consciousness.[5]

The Dutch Republic undoubtedly profited from the arrival of the Huguenots as well. Due to the efforts of booksellers, scholars, and journalists such as De Lorme, Bayle, and Basnage de Beauval, the Dutch publishing industry developed new media such as the learned periodical and extended its grip on the European market, thus securing its position as a distributor of early Enlightenment ideas.[6] It should be noted, however, that, unlike their Southern Netherlands predecessors, Huguenot intellectuals used the republic above all as a sanctuary, an employer, or a printshop. They were hardly interested in the ideas cur-

3. J. Briels, *Zuidnederlanders in de Republiek, 1572–1630: Een demografische en cultuurhistorische studie* (St. Niklaas, 1985).

4. H. Lunsingh Scheurleer and G. H. H. Posthumus Meyers, eds., *Leyden University in the Seventeenth Century: An Exchange of Learning* (Leiden, 1975).

5. E. H. Kossmann, "The Development of Dutch Political Theory in the Seventeenth Century," in *Britain and the Netherlands*, vol. 1, ed. J. S. Bromley and E. H. Kossmann (London, 1960), pp. 91–110; E. H. Kossman, "The Dutch Case: A National or Regional Culture?" *Transactions of the Royal Historical Society*, 5th series, 29 (1979): 155–168.

6. See also G. C. Gibbs, "The Role of the Dutch Republic as the Intellectual Entrepot of Europe in the Seventeenth and Eighteenth Centuries," *Bijdragen en Mededelingen betreffende de Geschiedenis der Nederlanden* 86 (1971): 323–349.

rent in their adopted fatherland, nor were they keen on integration within Dutch society. They showed an international orientation instead and maintained intimate contacts with fellow refugees elsewhere in Europe, especially those in England. In addition, they entertained extended correspondences with acquaintances left behind in France or with congenial Jansenists who also suffered from religious persecution.[7] As a result, the Huguenot exiles together with other intellectual refugees constituted an international network that served the exchange of political and intellectual news.[8]

The Huguenots' main concern was the religious and political situation in France. The ensuing debates on the role of church, state, and tolerance—the key problems of the early Enlightenment—were entangled with discussions on the strategy and tactics of an eventual return to France. Some wanted to oppose absolutism and gallican Catholicism, and toward that end they tried to further the French Jansenist cause. Others supported by their writings the military actions of the great powers, intent on curtailing French hegemonic aspirations on the Continent. Still others were convinced that a mitigation of Louis XIV's religious policies would suffice for a safe return without a thorough reform of absolutism itself.[9] In this intellectual climate, more radical views on church and state could easily gain currency. Thus the international network of exiled intellectuals was responsible for the Continental dissemination of deist and republican ideas of English origin. English authors such as Toland, Collins, and Tindal, who propagated a naturalist concept of religion and formulated a radical republican ideal, could in this way serve as important sources of inspiration for the radical Enlightenment.[10]

It would seem, however, that to the majority of Dutch intellectuals such ideas bore little relevance. In their view, an acceptable though pragmatic compromise had been found for most of the problems that occupied these refugees. In the Dutch Republic, a large measure of religious tolerance was practiced; all citizens enjoyed protection under the

7. R. Shackleton, "Jansenism and the Enlightenment," *Studies on Voltaire* 57 (1968): 1385–1397.

8. E. S. de Beer, "The Huguenots and the Enlightenment," *Proceedings of the Huguenot Society of London* 21 (1965–1970): 179–195.

9. G. H. Dodge, *The Political Theory of Huguenots of the Dispersion* (London, 1949); P. J. W. van Malssen, *Louis XIV d'après les pamphlets repandus en Hollande* (Amsterdam, 1936).

10. F. Venturi, "The European Enlightenment," in F. Venturi, *Italy and the Enlightenment* (London, 1972), pp. 1–32. For a less orthodox approach, see M. C. Jacob, *The Radical Enlightenment: Pantheists, Freemasons and Republicans* (London, 1981).

law, and the enforcement of criminal justice was of a comparatively lenient nature. Furthermore, Dutch intellectuals were proud of their constitution. Although its loose federal structure precluded effective internal and foreign policies, its many built-in checks and balances ensured that absolute power and arbitrariness were never tolerated in the long term. In spite of the early abolition of all civic influence on the composition of the town councils—the core of the political organization of the republic—public opinion, well informed by a continuing flood of pamphlets, was a force government authorities had to reckon with. Finally, government policies in the republic, generally speaking, were aimed at the welfare of the country as a whole, while in adjoining absolutist states the interests of citizens were subordinated to the dynastic ambitions of monarchs.

The consequences of the republic's different social and political structure for contemporary political and religious debate have often been underestimated or misunderstood.[11] For instance, the well-known argument of the 1690s between Bayle and his fellow refugee Pierre Jurieu, both Rotterdam-based participants in this international network of exiles, at first sight seems to bear direct relevance to contemporary debates on internal Dutch political affairs. Jurieu's plea for popular sovereignty and his praise of William III's unabashed opposition to the godless French was well thought of in the orthodox Calvinist milieu, which traditionally had supplied many supporters of the House of Orange and its dynastic foreign policies. Bayle's moderate treatment of absolutism, resulting from his conviction that only the introduction of tolerance would prepare the ground for an eventual return to France, was acclaimed by those circles of regents who had always favored a pro-French or neutral stand in European politics. These superficial parallels, however, tend to obscure the fact that the arguments focused primarily on foreign policy and did not entail any fundamental discussion of changes in the political system of the Dutch Republic itself.[12]

The republic's complicated constitution also did not serve as a model for Huguenot theoreticians, who in fact often despised the

---

11. In his admirable survey of Huguenot influences in the United Provinces, Gibbs equally fails to distinguish between Dutch and Huguenot appraisals of contemporary debates; see G. C. Gibbs, "Some Intellectual and Political Influences of the Huguenot Emigrés in the United Provinces, c. 1680–1730," *Bijdragen en Mededelingen betreffende de Geschiedenis der Nederlanden* 90 (1975): 255–287.

12. F. R. J. Knetsch, "Pierre Jurieu: Theologian and Politician of the Dispersion," *Acta Historiae Neerlandicae* 5 (1971): 213–242; E. Labrousse, "Le Refuge hollandais: Bayle et Jurieu," *XVIIe Siecle* 76–77 (1967): 75–94.

Dutch for their pragmatic way of solving political and religious problems. Such reproaches were not completely unfounded. The sixteenth-
century rebels of the northern Netherlands had disposed of their lawful
king without making much use of the rich literature on theories of
resistance available in Europe. Moreover, the much-praised religious
tolerance of the seventeenth-century republic hardly received any theoretical justification. It was quite typical, therefore, for moderate Huguenots in the republic to adopt a completely different, even more
strict, but fully theoretically justified concept of tolerance.[13]

The lack of Dutch enthusiasm for much of the early Enlightenment
religious and political debate did not prevent the acceptance of other
early Enlightenment themes. From the beginning, Dutch humanism had
been open and eclectic. Moderate ideas that proved useful in contemporary Dutch debate were smoothly integrated; the introduction of
Cartesianism, for instance, stimulated the central Calvinist debate on
the relationship between human reason and divine revelation. Whereas
orthodox theologians such as the Utrecht professor Gisbert Voetius argued that original sin made reason insufficient as humankind's sole
guide, such liberal professors as H. Röell and S. van Til exploited Cartesianism to curtail the authority of revelation. A typical representative
of Dutch Calvinist Cartesianism was Balthasar Bekker, who in the
1690s denounced belief in witchcraft, comets, and the earthly role of
devils and launched a crusade against all types of pagan superstition
which in his view had contaminated Calvinist theology.[14] In these circles of liberal theologians, John Locke's ideas were equally acclaimed.
His *Letter on Toleration* had been conceived in close collaboration
with a Dutch friend, the Arminian professor of theology Philippus van
Limborch, and his *Essay Concerning Human Understanding*, written
during his exile in the republic, was well received because its principles
could be easily reconciled with Protestant theology as understood by
Dutch latitudinarians.[15]

Dutch scientists were among the first Continental disciples of New-

13. C. Berkvens-Stevelinck, "La Tolerance et l'héritage de Bayle en Hollande dans la
première moitié du XVIIIe siècle," *Lias* 5 (1978): 257–272.

14. W. P. C. Knuttel, *Balthasar Bekker, de bestrijder van het bijgeloof* (The Hague,
1906). See also M. C. Jacob, "The Crisis of the European Mind: Hazard Revisited," in
*Politics and Culture in Early Modern Europe: Essays in Honour of H. G. Koenigsberger*, ed.
Phyllis Mack and Margaret C. Jacob (Cambridge, 1987), pp. 251–272, especially 260–262.

15. C. L. Thijssen-Schoute, "De Nederlandse vriendenkring van John Locke," in C. L.
Thijssen-Schoute, *Uit de republiek der letteren* (The Hague, 1967), pp. 90–103; R. L. Colie,
*Light and Enlightenment: A Study of the Cambridge Platonists and the Dutch Arminians*
(Cambridge, 1957).

ton, just as they had been first in accepting the experimental component of Cartesian science.[16] Early Newtonians such as 's Gravesande,
Boerhaave, and Musschenbroek were not original scientists, yet their
writings and teachings made them the intermediaries between English
and Continental science. Like their English Newtonian friends, they
stressed the essential role of divine providence in explaining the universe and thus refuted the deist and materialist implications of Cartesian philosophy. The Boyle lectures, the English highlight of this reconciliation of science and religion, were translated into Dutch and soon
followed by original Dutch works. Bernard Nieuwentyt's *Het regt gebruik der wereltbeschouwingen ter overtuiginge van ongodisten en on-
gelovigen* (Amsterdam, 1715) laid foundations of Dutch physico-theology that proved extremely influential in advancing the latitudinarian
cause.[17]

This brand of science and religion was initially disseminated mainly
by intellectuals of dissenting origins, especially Mennonites, who in the
seventeenth-century Dutch Republic had been the most important sect
in what Chaunu has called "the Troisieme Reforme." They propagated
the idea that nature was dependent on an almighty and providential
Creator who was responsible for and the guarantor of a harmonious
universe. Within this group, the first popular scientific lectures were
organized under the directorship of Fahrenheit in Amsterdam in 1719.
At the Mennonite seminary of theology, founded in 1735, science was
included from the start. In this dissenting milieu, the Leibnizian concept of theodicy was equally acclaimed; from the 1730s on, such ideas
were strengthened by the spread of the writings of Christian Wolff,
Leibniz's pupil. In 1740, the Utrecht regents, curators of the local university, even considered his appointment to a professorship.

Quite apart from the mainstream of early Dutch Enlightenment
thought, the republic also saw small indigenous groups of more radical
authors. In the second half of the seventeenth century, the Dutch Cartesian Lodewijk Meyer had tried to discredit revelation, and the early
eighteenth-century poet Willem van Swaanenburg was much influenced

---

16. E. G. Ruestow, *Physics at Seventeenth and Eighteenth Century Leiden* (The Hague,
1973); K. van Berkel, "Universiteit en natuurwetenschap in de 17e eeuw, in het bijzonder in
de Republiek," in *Natuurwetenschappen van Renaissance tot Darwin,* ed. H. A. M. Snelders
and K. van Berkel (The Hague, 1981), pp. 107–130; C. de Pater, *Petrus van Musschenbroek
[1692–1761], een Newtoniaans natuuronderzoeker* (Leiden, 1979).

17. J. Bots, *Tussen Descartes en Darwin: Geloof en natuurwetenschap in de 18e eeuw in
Nederland* (Assen, 1972). An English translation titled *The Religious Philosopher, or, the
right use of contemplating the works of the Creator* appeared in 1718 (London).

by Bruno's hermetic writings. Spinoza also attracted a small band of devoted followers. Yet these Dutch radicals hardly influenced European debate, and they founded no viable Dutch radical tradition. A creative Dutch Spinozism, for example, did not emerge before the nineteenth century. Besides, deist and materialist ideas were fiercely attacked. For instance, Simon Tyssot de Patot, who suggested ideas that somewhat resembled those of Toland, was expelled from his chair at the Deventer Atheneaum.[18]

Yet the enthusiastic reception of much of early Enlightenment moderate thought did not reduce Dutch humanism to insignificance. In the universities, Calvinist Aristotelianism was still taught along with Cartesianism and Newtonianism. The new empirical method steadily gained more adherents and, however hesitantly, even came to be applied in classical and historical scholarship.[19] Nevertheless, Dutch intellectuals both in and out of the university were not inclined to discuss the usefulness of classical learning, which had been the pride of Dutch academic scholarship. The widely acclaimed inaugural lecture of the famous classical scholar Tiberius Hemsterhuis in 1747 bore the proud title "On the Study of the Classics as a Means toward the Improvement of Manners and the Practice of Virtue." Characteristically, in his lecture Hemsterhuis tried to reconcile classical learning with enlightened ideas.[20] It seems that the irrelevance of much early Enlightenment religious and political debate not only prevented an assault on the humanist tradition that constitued the core of Dutch national cultural consciousness but even made Dutch intellectuals less susceptible to new trends initiated elsewhere. As a consequence, the republic witnessed a completely different type of *querelle des anciens et modernes*.[21]

Little information is available about the audience for the Dutch synthesis of Calvinism, humanism, and Enlightenment. Very early,

---

18. See C. L. Thijssen-Schoute, "Lodewijk Meyer en diens verhouding tot Descartes en Spinoza," in *Uit de republiek der letteren*, pp. 173–194; *Een hel vol weelde: Teksten uit het werk van Willem van Swaanenburg (1679–1728)* (Assen-Maastricht, 1986); K. O. Meinsma, *Spinoza en zijn kring: Over Hollandsche vrijgeesten* (The Hague, 1896); A. Rosenberg, *Tyssot de Patot and his Work (1655–1738)* (The Hague, 1972); C. M. Geerars, "De vrijdenkerij in de journalistieke werken van J. Campo Weyerman," *Tijdschrift voor de Studie van de Verlichting* 3 (1975): 17–64.

19. J. G. Gerretzen, *Schola Hemsterhusiana* (Nijmegen, 1940).

20. For the extensive literature promoting the usefulness of the classics in the eighteenth-century republic, see A. J. van Duyvendijk, *De motivering van de klassieke vorming* (Groningen, 1955).

21. Th. Meijer, *Kritiek als herwaardering: Het levenswerk van Jacob Perizonius (1651–1715)* (Leiden, 1971); W. W. Mijnhardt, "Dutch Culture in the Age of William and Mary: Cosmopolitan or Provincial?" in *The Age of William and Mary*, ed. D. Hoak and M. Feingold (Berkeley, 1992).

however, it found an outlet in the *Boekzaal van Europe* (1692–1702), a Dutch imitation of the French learned periodical.[22] Its founder was Pieter Rabus, a Rotterdam Latin school teacher of Arminian origins. The journal may be characterized as a mirror of early Dutch Enlightenment thought: moderate, Newtonian, and averse to all radicalism in religious and political matters. It opposed Cartesianism, Spinozism, and resistance to government authority. Rabus was inspired by humanist and enlightened ideals alike. He edited some classical texts, and his plea for writing in the vernacular should therefore be interpreted in the Dutch humanist tradition. Typical was his neglect of Bayle's *Dictionnaire critique et historique*, also published in Rotterdam. Although Rabus was well acquainted with Bayle, he apparently could not endorse everything the Huguenot skeptic wrote. He even planned to publish an alternative Dutch dictionary adapted to Dutch intellectual needs. Rabus likewise devoted little space to the Bayle-Jurieu debate, which he viewed as irrelevant to his Dutch audience. Rabus's hero was Balthasar Bekker, whose crusade against superstition he heartily endorsed. Ultimately, *Boekzaal* was imitated by an extended sequence of learned periodicals instrumental in the dissemination of the Dutch variety of early European Enlightenment.

## ENLIGHTENMENT AND DECLINE

Intellectual culture in the Dutch Republic in the first decades of the eighteenth century may be characterized as janus-faced. On the one hand, it was a culture sponsored by the many refugees and exiles on Dutch soil. Its backing by the Dutch publishing industry made this culture one of the main bases and clearinghouses of the early European Enlightenment, moderate as well as radical. On the other hand, it constituted the Dutch version of the Enlightenment, favored by Dutch intellectuals and adapted to the religious, political, and intellectual values and traditions of the republic. Initially, moderate representatives of both cultures still had much in common, as can be shown from the latitudinarian milieus in such towns as Amsterdam and Rotterdam at the turn of the century. There Bayle and Rabus, Locke and Van Limborch often met, as did intermediary figures as well: Van Limborch's colleague and successor at the Remonstrant seminary, Jean le Clerc—humanist, moderate in the *querelle*, and secretary to the republic of let-

22. J. J. V. M. de Vet, *Pieter Rabus (1660–1702)* (Amsterdam, 1980).

ters—was an ideal figure of compromise acceptable to both cultures.[23] In the long term, however, the two intellectual worlds tended to grow apart, a process illustrated by the career of Justus van Effen.

Van Effen was a prolific journalist active in the French market. He edited periodicals such as *Le Misantrope, La Bagatelle,* and *Le Nouveau Spectateur Francois* and served on the board of the influential *Journal Littéraire* (1713–1722 and 1729–1736). Here he could meet the important Huguenot publisher Prosper Marchand and his fellow countryman, the mathematician 's Gravesande. Their contributions to French-language journals made both Van Effen and 's Gravesande instrumental in the dissemination of English science and literature to a Continental French-speaking audience.[24] About 1730, however, Van Effen began preparing his only Dutch literary project, the *Hollandsche Spectator,* which served as a model for the publication of a host of similar Dutch periodicals after 1747.

Historians have often asked why a successful journalist like Van Effen left the prestigious French market to devote his energies to the much less lofty undertaking of publishing a Dutch imitation of Addisonian spectatorial writing. It has been suggested that his scorn of early Dutch spectatoral literature incited him to produce a better example. I am convinced, however, that a solution to this problem lies elsewhere, for it is noteworthy that at the same time other Dutch authors turned their backs on the French market as well. This applies, for instance, to 's Gravesande, who in addition began to sign his letters as Willem instead of as Guillaume, which he had preferred up to then.[25] An analysis of the context and contents of Van Effen's *Hollandsche Spectator* supplies the explanation for this so-called national reaction.

The *Hollandsche Spectator* was characteristic of the moderate Dutch synthesis of humanism, Calvinism, and Enlightenment already popularized by Rabus's *Boekzaal.* Like Rabus, Van Effen advocated the use of the vernacular. He opened each issue with a classical quotation and derived his arguments from exempla and parallels from ancient history. On the other hand, Van Effen stressed the enlightened concept of the perfectability of humankind. Virtue was the result of the

---

23. H. Bots a.o., *De "Bibliothèque Universelle et Historique" (1686–1693): Een periodiek als trefpunt van geletterd Europa* (Amsterdam, 1981).

24. W. J. B. Pienaar, *English Influences in Dutch Literature and Justus van Effen as Intermediary* (Cambridge, 1929); J. L. Schorr, *Justus van Effen and the Enlightenment* (Michigan, 1981).

25. C. Berkvens-Stevelinck, "De Hugenoten," in *La France aux Pays Bas* (Vianen, 1985), pp. 38–40.

continuous testing of personal conduct by reason. Yet reason was not sufficient. Religion was indispensable because it served as the basis of all human morality. Van Effen's religious ideals derived not from orthodox sources but from latitudinarian theologians. Because humans were sociable animals, virtue could be reached only in society. Yet the principle of perfectability did not necessitate a restructuring of the social order, for humanity should try to find happiness in its God-given station in a static and harmonious universe.

The message of the *Hollandsche Spectator* was hardly original. It reveals striking resemblances to similar enlightened periodicals in England and Protestant Germany.[26] Van Effen, however, introduced a new and characteristically Dutch element which, typically enough, had been lacking in Rabus's *Boekzaal*: concern about the loss of Dutch prestige in international affairs. In my view, this anxiety explains why Van Effen began to feel uneasy about European culture on Dutch soil and decided to devote his energies to the strengthening of Dutch morale and morality.

Van Effen's uneasiness was not wholly unfounded. Although the republic had been one of the victors at the end of the War of the Spanish Succession (1713), the outcome was disastrous. The province of Holland, for example, responsible for almost 60 percent of the total financial burden of the Republic, after 1715 required about 70 percent of its yearly tax income for the redemption of debts and the payments of interest. Financial penury would strictly limit the republic's maneuvering space within international affairs in the future.

From the end of the seventeenth century, contemporaries had begun to see economic decline. The inability to compete with much more resourceful countries such as England and France forced the republic to retire to those markets in which it still could succeed, such as the money market. This change in economic structure meant less shipping and less industry, which entailed a slow polarization of the division of income. Beginning in industrial regions around Haarlem and Leiden, this polarization drove considerable numbers of the lower classes into poverty and pauperism and threatened the economic security of the middle classes.[27]

26. See E. A. Bloom and L. D. Bloom, *Joseph Addison's Sociable Animal* (Providence, 1971), and W. Martens, *Die Botschaft der Tugend: Die Aufklärung im Spiegel der deutschen Moralischen Wochenschriften* (Stuttgart, 1971).

27. See J. Aalbers, "Holland's Financial Problems (1713–1733) and the Wars against Louis XIV," in *Britain and the Netherlands*, vol. 6, ed. A. C. Duke and C. A. Tamse (The Hague, 1977), pp. 79–93; J. de Vries, *De economische achteruitgang der Republiek in de*

The *Hollandsche Spectator* should be seen as the interpreter of these feelings of anxiety. Van Effen tried to counter foreign reproaches, real or imagined, that the republic had lost international prestige. Each time, he reassured his fellow countrymen: "It is my conviction that our nation really merits esteem, even more than any other nation, even to the extent that, given the choice, I would be compelled by *reason* to choose being a Dutchman."[28] Van Effen's frequent use of the still rare word "Nederlander" suggests that the confrontation with international contempt was responsible for the concept slowly emerging in enlightened circles, that of a nation comprising all provinces. This prefigured the late eighteenth-century wounded Dutch nationalism.[29] The feelings of national confidence Van Effen tried to infuse into his audience drew inspiration from the glorious past of the republic. Time and again he presented worthy examples of Dutch sixteenth- and seventeenth-century bravery or of prestigious Dutch scholarly successes and exhorted his readers to follow the example of their fathers.

Van Effen perceived the cause of decline as moral. He therefore worried most about the Dutch imitation of the same French manners and morals he had been disseminating during an earlier phase of his career. He regarded the retirement from active business and trade—the logical consequence of the republic's change of economic structure—as the main symptom of this process of moral degeneration. Commerce being the backbone of Dutch prosperity and culture, he criticized the recent fashion among the regent elite of sending its sons to universities; it would be much better for the nation's welfare and the universities alike if the younger generation were taught the tricks of trade. By means of such and similar denunciations, Van Effen tried to reinvigorate the morals he saw as the guarantee of the continuing existence of the republic. His belief in the perfectability of humankind, which precluded any pessimism about the future, served as an incentive to continue spreading his enlightened moral philosophy.

The older historiography that imputed complacency and unjustified

---

*achttiende eeuw* (Leiden, 1968); and J. Hovy, *Het Voorstel van 1751 tot instelling van een beperkt vrijhavenstelsel in de Republiek (Propositie tot een gelimiteerd porto-franco)* (Groningen, 1966).

28. Justus van Effen, *De Hollandsche Spectator*, 4 vols. (Amsterdam, 1731–1735), vol. 1, p. 59.

29. E. H. Kossmann, "The Crisis of the Dutch State, 1780–1813: Nationalism, Federalism, Unitarism," in *Britain and the Netherlands*, vol. 4, ed. J. S. Bromley and E. H. Kossmann (The Hague, 1971), pp. 156–175.

contentment to Van Effen failed to appreciate the deep anxiety that underlay the *Hollandsche Spectator*. It equally failed to understand that Van Effen's denunciation of French manners as a cause of decline had been inspired by the apocalyptic atmosphere in the republic in the early 1730s. The discovery of pileworm, which was destroying the Dutch sea dikes, the revelation of extensive networks of homosexual activity, and heightened tensions between Catholics and Protestants all combined to build up this atmosphere, which strengthened Van Effen's moral diagnosis without impairing his underlying analysis of decline.[30]

Van Effen was neither the first nor the only author to recognize decline. Various Dutch regents, including the grand pensionary Simon van Slingelandt, had drawn up lengthy treatises devoted to isolated aspects of the issue.[31] Nor was decline a question that worried only the Dutch. In eighteenth-century European intellectual discourse, complaints about the corruption of morals were rather commonplace. People in a remote and rarely specified past were thought to have lived more virtuous and less corrupt lives. For the Dutch, however, such a past was not remote but very near, not imaginary but very real. Their image of seventeenth-century history revealed a nation that in a short lapse of time had reached an unsurpassed level of economic prosperity, political and social stability, and cultural greatness. Thus, for the Dutch, things had gone wrong recently. Van Effen was the first Dutch author to offer such Enlightenment-inspired concepts as progress and reason as antidotes against moral corruption. His belief in the salutary effects of commerce presented a coherent analysis of the problem of recent decline in which, however hesitantly, causes and remedies were assigned a logical place.[32]

## THE DUTCH ENLIGHTENMENT

The War of the Austrian Succession (1740–1748) exposed the Dutch Republic's inability to continue to fulfill its role as mediator on the European scene. The calamitous course of events that brought the re-

30. W. Zuydam, *Justus van Effen: Een bijdrage tot de kennis van zijn karakter en zijn denkbeelden* (Gouda, 1922); Gibbs, "Influences of the Huguenot Emigrés," p. 271.

31. See J. Aalbers, *De Republiek en de vrede van Europa* (Groningen, 1980), and Hovy, *Het Voorstel van 1751*, chap. 3.

32. For an extended discussion of the idea of progress in eighteenth-century Dutch thought, see E. H. Kossmann, *1787: The Collapse of the Patriot Movement and the Problem of Dutch Decline*, The Creighton Trust Lecture 1987 (London, 1988).

public to the brink of conquest by France culminated in a cry for reform and subsequently in revolution and the recall of the prince of
Orange. These developments produced an intensive debate on the
causes of economic and political decline which would continue until
the end of the century and in which the spectatorial press played an
influential role. After 1748, spectatorial periodicals became much more
popular. In the two decades before 1748, only seven original Dutch
titles had been produced, none of which was as successful as the *Hollandsche Spectator*. In the period 1748–1769, however, thirteen different periodicals were published and another twenty-six appeared in the
decade before 1780. These periodicals also succeeded in staying in
business for much longer periods. Because the publishing of spectatorial periodicals was a strictly commercial venture, it may be concluded that public interest in them was rapidly growing. Although little
is known about the authorship of these periodicals, journalists of dissenting origins seem to have taken the lead.[33]

Whereas in the *Hollandsche Spectator* of the 1730s the approach to
the problem of decline had been hesitant, the analysis of the issue in
the periodicals appearing after 1748 was much more direct. The influence of latitudinarian enlightened ethics had become more manifest as
well; the spectators preached the natural sociability of humankind. Yet
individual happiness was determined not by one's place in the social
pyramid but by a virtuous commitment to one's God-given duty in
society. The structure of society therefore was not to be violated, nor
was social mobility encouraged: "It is much better to be a happy porter
than a grumbling village vicar or a hungry barrister."[34] The spectators
deduced that moral decline would undermine virtue as the foundation
of society, and they atributed decline to the loss of the "civic virtue" of
the "old Dutchmen," a process that was especially pernicious for a
republic.

The spectatorial periodicals first criticized the regent elite. By their
retreat from trade, their imitation of French moral codes, and their
abominably poor knowledge of the ancient Dutch constitution and customary laws, they seemed to have lost their old Batavian virtues. But
the spectators began to detect moral decline in the upper middle classes
as well. They denounced their imitation of their social betters, their
praise of a leisured life, their sending their children to French, instead

---

33. On the spectatorial press in the Netherlands, see P. J. Buijnsters, *Nederlandse literatuur van de achttiende eeuw* (Utrecht, 1984).
34. *De Philosooph*, 4 vols. (Amsterdam, 1766–1769), no. 110 (1768).

of Dutch or Latin schools, and their contempt of the most virtuous activity possible—commerce and trade. The spectators glorified the merchant as the republican archetype. Because of commerce, "poverty had been averted, leisure with all its corrupting lusts banished, benevolence encouraged, common sense cultivated, superstition fought, scholarship promoted, the arts perfected and a society created, based on mutual obligations and necessities."[35]

It is one of Clio's ironies that Dutch historiography, convinced of the naturalistic character of spectatorial writing, has adopted this inaccurate contemporary diagnosis of decline, thus perpetuating two myths regarding eighteenth-century history for more than 150 years. The myth of moral degeneration as a cause of decline has been effectively dealt with by economic historians in the last few decades. But in many quarters the myth of the "frenchification" of eighteenth-century Dutch culture is still regarded as an empirical fact. If frenchification was a real feature of eighteenth-century Dutch culture, it should be interpreted as a European phenomenon and not just as a sign of Dutch cultural decline. In addition, we know little about the extent of the process except what spectatorial writing presented as so-called factual material.[36] It therefore seems much more fitting to interpret the charges of pernicious French influence as a sign of a new and wounded Dutch national feeling, which, unaware of the real causes of decline, was looking for comprehensible causes and workable remedies.

National consciousness as disseminated by the spectatorial press was directed toward the glorious past of the republic. Yet it was apolitical; it explicitly restricted itself to inspiring civic virtue, impartiality in political conflicts, and obedience to lawful governments. It also rejected constitutional changes: "The fabric of society in the United Provinces is so perfect that it fully protects the natural freedom and independence of its members. Furthermore, it supplies, more than any other civil society that we know of, opportunities to participate in public life."[37] Fully convinced of the faultless political preconditions the republic had been provided with and of the principle of human perfectibility, the spectatorial press was not disturbed by the gloomy diagnosis

35. *Ibid.*, no. 20 (1766).
36. On the limited circulation of French books and magazines as compared to their Dutch counterparts, see J. J. Kloek and W. W. Mijnhardt, "The Eighteenth-Century Revolution in Reading: A Myth?" in *Transactions of the Seventh International Congress on the Enlightenment*, 3 vols. (Oxford, 1989, *Studies on Voltaire and the Eighteenth Century*, 263–265), vol.2, pp. 645–651.
37. *De Nederlandsche Spectator* (Leiden, 1749–1760), no. 218 (1757).

it offered. If its audience would heed its weekly message, the republic would recover and soon be restored to its former glory and prestige.

Thus the problem of decline became one of the key issues of the Dutch Enlightenment. It is accepted practice now to interpret the Enlightenment as an attempt to solve contemporary religious and political problems. But the issues debated in the republic were completely different from those discussed elsewhere in Europe. Decline and Enlightenment together produced a new national consciousness, directed to the past, which fortified the intellectual traditions that had already decisively influenced the reception of early Enlightenment ideas. As a result, the debate on the moral causes and remedies of decline became intertwined with the issue of the relationship between reason and revelation. According to most Dutch authors, the recovery of virtue was impossible without the support of enlightened religion. Because of these fundamental constraints, intellectuals engaged in the development of Dutch moral philosophy, and in the study of human nature as one of its branches, were hardly receptive to the materialist Scottish version that saw virtue in the last resort only as a sort of propriety.[38] Consequently, the ideas of the radical French Enlightenment that were gaining currency after 1750 incited fierce opposition in the Netherlands.

The ensuing intellectual isolation of the republic within the European Enlightenment was only strengthened by the loss of its position as one of the centers of the European republic of letters. After 1750, the Dutch Republic served less often as a refuge for intellectuals driven from their own countries, not because of changes within the intellectual climate of the Republic itself but as the result of greater tolerance elsewhere. The severe drop in numbers of foreign students attending Dutch universities, which also has often been treated as a symptom of cultural decline, was caused mainly by the disappearance of the so-called *peregrinatio academica* and the founding of a greater number and variety of modern university facilities elsewhere in Europe. Dutch universities maintained their reputation as centers of classical and oriental scholarship, and the Leiden publishing firm Luchtmans continued to provide Europe with new Dutch editions of classical and oriental texts. Finally, the reduced position of the Republic as a European clearinghouse for French books and journals should be interpreted as the

38. N. T. Phillipson, "The Scottish Enlightenment," in *Enlightenment in National Context*, ed. Porter and Teich, p. 34.

result of the same sort of structural change that affected the republic's economy as a whole: the emergence of cheaper and more conveniently located production centers elsewhere.[39]

This growing isolation did not, however, imply that Dutch intellectuals no longer took interest in foreign intellectual developments. Many classics of the European Enlightenment, moderate as well as radical, were still published in the republic; such books could be found in many Dutch libraries and were reviewed in Dutch learned periodicals.[40] The favorable view such thinkers as Montesquieu and Adam Smith took of the republic was appreciated,[41] but their idealized pictures of Dutch conditions should be interpreted against the background of their own preoccupations with, for example, French politics or the Scottish economy. Their writings did not supply solutions to the problem of decline Dutch intellectuals were trying to cope with.[42] They showed a predilection for authors and themes that fit in the moderate Dutch synthesis of humanism and Enlightenment.

In the second half of the century, the German disciples of Wolff, Formey, Semler, and Michaelis were very much appreciated in the republic. These thinkers preached of a harmonious universe, led by an almighty Creator, in which a reasonable striving for one's self-interest was seen as the most suitable way to realize progress. The ideas of the Scottish commonsense philosophers, especially Thomas Reid and his pupil James Beattie, both of whom opposed Hume and Smith, were equally well thought of. German *Popularphilosophen* such as Nicolai, Mendelssohn, Abbt, and Gellert were reviewed with approval as well.[43]

39. W. Th. M. Frijhoff, *La Société Neérlandaise et ses gradués, 1575–1814* (Amsterdam, 1981); Gerritzen, *Schola Hemsterhusiana*; I. H. van Eeghen, *De Amsterdamse boekhandel,* 5 vols. (Amsterdam, 1960–1978); I. H. van Eeghen, "De uitgeverij Luchtmans en enkele andere uitgeverijen in de achttiende eeuw," *Documentatieblad Werkgroep Achttiende Eeuw* 34–35 (1977): 5–9.

40. W. Gobbers, *Jean Jacques Rousseau in Holland: Een onderzoek naar de invloed van de mens en het werk (ca. 1760–ca. 1810)* (Gent, 1963), pp. 68–78; Chr. Sepp, *Proeve eener pragmatische geschiedenis der theologie in Nederland van 1787 tot 1858* (Amsterdam, 1877), pp. 99–119.

41. S. J. Fockema Andreae, "Montesquieu en Nederland," *De Gids* 112 (1949): 176–183.

42. See the comments by Dirk Hoola van Nooten, translator of Smith's *Wealth of Nations: Naspeuringen over . . . den rijkdom der volkeren* (Amsterdam, 1796).

43. H. A. C. Spoelstra, *De invloed van de Duitsche letterkunde op de Nederlandsche in de tweede helft van de 18e eeuw* (Amsterdam, 1931); F. Sassen, *Geschiedenis van de wijsbegeerte* (Amsterdam, 1959), pp. 233–234, 248, 274–75. For a survey of Dutch intellectual presuppositions influencing the reception of English moral philosophy, see C. van Boheemen-Saaf, "The Reception of English Literature in Dutch Magazines, 1735–1785," in *The Role of Periodicals in the Eighteenth Century* (Leiden, 1984), pp. 7–17.

The central criterion for judging foreign philosophers seems to have been their position in the reason-revelation debate. Elie Luzac, for instance, translator of Montesquieu's *Esprit des lois* and publisher of La Mettrie's *l'Homme machine*, abhorred deism or even indifference in religious matters. Johan Lulofs, a Leiden professor who definitively established the primacy of reason over revelation in Dutch philosophical theorizing, took a similar view. Paulus van Hemert, the republic's most arduous propagandist of Kantian philosophy, deployed this system especially in his crusade against atheism, deism, and skepticism.[44] Dutch thinkers were not, however, primarily interested in fighting the philosophical assumptions underlying these radical ideas; they were mainly concerned with the supposed consequences. The spectatorial press took the same view: atheism and deism were a threat to society. Popular Dutch literary authors such as Betje Wolff and Rhijnvis Feith used their novels to support such ideas. Wolff, for example, abhorred Voltaire's *Candide*, which questioned the optimist Leibnizian world picture that served as the basis for Dutch faith in the future.[45] Dutch novelists and spectatorial periodicals alike did not limit their religious criticism to atheists and deists. Their attacks on orthodox Calvinists were even more ferocious, since the Calvinists, who believed that original sin made it impossible to achieve earthly virtue, constituted a much larger portion of the population than the religious radicals and therefore were seen as a more real threat to progress.

Although dissenters, especially those of Mennonite origin, remained important in the dissemination of the Dutch Enlightenment, gradually more *predikanten* and members of the official Reformed church came under the influence of enlightened latitudinarian ideas. Physico-theology, for instance, became immensely popular from the work of the Zutphen Reformed *predikant* J. F. Martinet. His *Katechismus der natuur* (4 vols, Amsterdam, 1777–1779), reprinted several times, was

---

44. E. H. Kossmann, "Enlightened Conservatism: The Case of Elie Luzac," *Acta Historiae Neerlandicae* 6 (1973): 67–82; F. Sassen, "Johan Lulofs (1711–1768) en de reformatorische Verlichting in de Nederlanden," *Mededelingen van de Koninklijke Nederlandse Akademie van Wetenschappen: afd. Letterkunde,* new series, 28, no. 7 (1965); W. W. Mijnhardt, "Veertig jaar cultuurbevordering: Teylers Stichting, 1778–1815," in *"Teyler, 1778–1978": Studies en bijdragen naar aanleiding van het tweede eeuwfeest* (Haarlem-Antwerpen, 1978), pp. 97–98.

45. H. C. M. Ghijsen, *Betje Wolff in verband met het geestelijk leven van haar tijd: Jeugd en huwelijksjaren* (Rotterdam, 1919), pp. 153–154. See also P. J. Buijnsters, *Betje Wolff en Aagje Deken* (The Hague, 1984); P. J. Buijnsters, *Tussen twee werelden: Rhijnvis Feith als de dichter van "het Graf"* (Assen, 1963); P. J. Buijnsters, *Hieronymus van Alphen (1746–1803)* (Assen, 1973).

responsible for the spread in reformed circles of the optimist Newtonian-Leibnizian synthesis. The universities, where the synthesis of humanism and Enlightenment had been steadily gaining currency, contributed to this process as well.[46]

Quite naturally, the introduction of enlightened ideas into the Calvinist milieu met with fierce opposition. Defenders of orthodox Calvinism, such as the Rotterdam *predikant* Petrus Hofstede, even founded their own periodicals to fight the *Vaderlandsche Letteroefeningen*, the advocate of moderate Dutch Enlightenment thought and a successor of Rabus's *Boekzaal.*[47] The short eruption of censorship in the 1760s, which attacked books by Voltaire and Rousseau, was also organized by these orthodox *predikanten.* In true Dutch fashion, the regents, tired of the continuous complaints of the *predikanten,* finally approved of suppression—without, however, wishing to enforce such measures.

The culmination of the orthodox Calvinist attack on the Dutch Enlightenment was the so-called Socratic war. The immediate cause of the conflict was the question posed by Marmontel's novel *Belisaire* (Amsterdam, 1768) whether Socrates was entitled to a place in heaven. At first sight, the debate may seem academic; but more was at stake. The orthodox party, similarly perplexed by decline, was looking for answers as well. To them, Enlightenment constituted the cause, and a return to the belief of the fathers, the remedy. The Socratic war showed the consequences of a reforming spirit turned toward the past, for to all concerned to understand the republic's decline the question of which aspects of the past should be stressed to make recovery a real possibility was acute. In the Socratic war, the choice between an orthodox and an enlightened view of virtue had presented itself. Soon, however, discussions concentrated on the issue of whether Latin or Dutch, humanism or Enlightenment, should guide the way; subsequently, the problem of which parts of the population should be included in the reforming process was discussed; next, the economic policies of the regent elite came under attack; and finally the debate concentrated on the so-called *Grondwettige herstelling* (Constitutional Restoration) of the republic. In all sorts of societies and academies founded after the

46. B. Paasman, *J. F. Martinet: Een Zutphens filosoof in de achttiende eeuw* (Zutphen, 1971); Bots, *Tussen Descartes en Darwin;* J. C. de Bruine, *Herman Venema, een Nederlands theoloog in de tijd der Verlichting* (Franeker, 1973); J. van den Berg, "Orthodoxy, Rationalism and the World in Eighteenth-Century Holland," in *Sanctity and Secularity: The Church and the World,* ed. D. Baker (Oxford, 1973), pp. 173–192.

47. J. P. de Bie, *Het leven en de werken van Petrus Hofstede* (Rotterdam, 1899).

War of the Austrian Succession, such problems were constantly debated.

## ENLIGHTENMENT AND SOCIABILITY

The emergence of Dutch philosophical societies should be interpreted as a result of the characteristically Dutch combination of Enlightenment and decline. Even learned societies of science, such as the Holland Society of Sciences (Haarlem, 1752), the Dutch counterparts of the Académie des Sciences or the Royal Society, had their origins in this phenomenon. The Zeeland Society of Sciences (Flushing, 1765), for example, chose as its motto the Latin *non sordent in undis,* which contained the double injunction "do not let them despise us" and "let us fight our backwardness." Yet, however similar their origins, the societies, ranging from learned academies to masonic lodges, reading associations, literary clubs, and improvement societies, often reached contradictory solutions to the problems of the republic.[48] Moreover, the nature of the discourse within these societies reveals the introspective constraints that decline, aroused national feelings, and the ensuing intellectual isolation within the European Enlightenment had imposed on Dutch thought.

The learned societies of science, such as the Zeeland and Holland societies, which recruited their members from all over the republic, enjoyed friendly protection from town and provincial governments.[49] All of them received provincial charters. The regents filled the very large boards of directors, and close relations were maintained with the Reformed church. This connection with authority, although a social asset, nonetheless impeded an open membership based on merit. Dissenters, particularly the intellectually prominent Mennonites, were hardly ever invited to join. Equally rare were representatives of industry. Members were recruited mainly from those groups that participated in the traditional Latin culture of the learned. To stimulate scholarly endeavor, these societies printed treatises by members and organized prize contests. Quite naturally, state interference left its mark on these activities

---

48. W. W. Mijnhardt, *Tot heil van 't menschdom: Culturele genootschappen in Nederland, 1750–1815* (Amsterdam, 1987).

49. Ibid.; see also J. Bierens de Haan, *De Hollandsche Maatschappij der Wetenschappen, 1752–1952* (Haarlem, 1952); J. G. de Bruijn, *Inventaris van de prijsvragen uitgeschreven door de Hollandsche Maatschappij der Wetenschappen te Haarlem, 1753–1917* (Haarlem, 1977).

as well. For instance, many of the prize contests were devoted to problems with which the regent directors had to cope in their capacity as town or provincial administrators or in their functions on the boards of the East India and West India companies. Furthermore, their prevailing attachment to the status quo was responsible for a tacit agreement among members to refrain from proposing controversial subjects.

Enlightenment ideas undoubtedly influenced these societies. Newton and Locke were admired as architects of the moderate Enlightenment, but, if Newton's ideas were generally accepted, Locke's encountered some resistance owing to their seeming conflict with the dogma of humanity's fallen state. A similar ambiguity reigned in the approach to enlightened theology. In the Holland Society, the decision to invite Priestley to become a member for his research in chemistry met with serious opposition because of his religious beliefs. In the Zeeland Society, where Petrus Hofstede was a prominent member, the writing of philosophical history was appreciated insofar as it stressed the importance of cultural and economic developments in the historical process. But when historians tried to exclude providence from historical explanation, inserting natural causes instead, the board discouraged such undertakings. In all these societies, the concept of usefulness was still quite undifferentiated. They saw no need to distinguish between sciences useful to the community and pursuits leading to personal improvement. Hence, the concept of usefulness covered all scholarship and science, from numismatics to applied physics, without any utilitarian bias.

Consequently, despite the familiarity with Enlightenment terminology, the learned societies of science showed distinct traces of another, older cultural pattern: Dutch humanism. These older attitudes seem to have lost none of their prestige in the societies, which in this respect resembled the Dutch educational system as represented by Latin schools and universities, the institutions that supplied most of these societies' members. Moreover, in the eighteenth century the universities came to be dominated completely by the regent class.[50] This does not mean that these societies failed to promote reform; they offered prize contests on topics ranging from educational improvements to proposals for commercial recovery. But through their judging of entries they showed that they were seldom prepared to endorse new, let alone radical, solutions. They favored remedies of a retrospective character.

50. Frijhoff, *La Société Neérlandaise et ses gradués.*

As decline became aggravated, the seventeenth century, with its emphasis on shipping and commerce, increasingly became the mythical yardstick of the ends economic reform should envisage. It was only natural that humanism (and in some quarters Calvinism as well), which had represented such a vital part of the cultural flowering of the Golden Age, became revitalized in the process. Because of their structure, laws, socially exclusive character, and activities, these learned societies of science embodied the compromise between Enlightenment influence and the restricted possibilities open to the elite within the Dutch ancien régime.

Besides these semiofficial societies, another type began to flourish as well. To this category belonged masonic lodges, literary societies, scientific societies, and reading associations, all with a strong local character. These may be seen as the result of the spectatorial message, for these periodicals had preached that only in voluntary association could men, and a few women, establish a basis for knowledge, virtue, and happiness.[51] Only in a society in which one felt at ease could one learn to control one's passions, to value consensus, to free oneself of prejudice and acquire virtue by means of the refining and useful sciences. Consequently, these societies' attitude toward official authority was completely different from that of the semiofficial learned societies of sciences. They did not need official recognition but rather sought confirmation from within. In the eyes of their members, the act of subscribing to the often minutely detailed statutes granted the society a much stronger basis than any government charter could supply.

In the 1750s and 1760s these societies were still limited in number and restricted mainly to the provinces of Holland and Zeeland and quite often were dominated by the regent class.[52] From the 1770s on, however, their numbers expanded and they appeared in the rural provinces as well. Although this growth applied equally to masonic lodges, literary societies, and scientific clubs, an extraordinary expansion was shown by reading associations. By the end of the century, about five hundred of these local societies had been founded. Their social composition changed accordingly and began to show a decidedly inclusive

---

51. Mijnhardt, *Tot heil van 't menschdom*, chap. 3; for comparable developments, see Phillipson, "The Scottish Enlightenment."

52. W. W. Mijnhardt, "Sociability in Walcheren, 1750–1815," *Tijdschrift voor de Studie van de Verlichting* 12 (1984): 289–320; P. J. Buijnsters, "Lesegesellschaften in den Niederlanden," in *Lesegesellschaften und bürgerliche Emanzipation: Ein europäischer Vergleich*, ed. O. Dann (Munich, 1981), pp. 143–158; H. Reitsma, "De beginjaren van Felix Meritis, 1777–1795," *Documentatieblad Werkgroep Achttiende Eeuw* 15 (1983): 101–139.

character, especially when compared to the semiofficial learned societies of science. The emphasis was on the middle classes that possessed no political power: the professional classes, well-to-do artisans, ministers, small merchants and rentiers. A remarkable feat was the entry of those without traditional education, many of whom were self-taught. Equally remarkable was the presence of dissenters, in numbers far exceeding their proportion of the Dutch population. They seem to have realized their cultural integration in the nation by means of these societies.

Closely connected to the growth in numbers, the character of the activities of the societies began to change as well.[53] This process may be illustrated by the changes within literary societies. In the 1750s and 1760s, these societies had devoted their attention almost exclusively to the application of humanist philological techniques to literary and historical texts in order to advance national literature and history. The literary societies of the 1770s and 1780s began to discuss the problem of decline and the role of civic virtue. Members came to realize that, for a recovery from decline moral education, and the spread of enlightened knowledge were essential and that literature could play an important role in this process. The resulting cultural nationalism caused a depreciation of Latin humanist culture. Quite often the societies presented themselves in their poetry as educators of their fellow citizens disclosing knowledge that had been hidden from the ancients. Thus humanism and Enlightenment, which until then had been cherished side by side and whose coexistence was still fundamental to the semiofficial societies of science, were now presented as opposites.

At the end of the 1770s, a third type of society came into being: improvement societies, the first of which was the *Oeconomische Tak* (Economic Branch), founded as a subsidiary of the Holland Society of Sciences in 1777 and intended to offer practical solutions to the aggravating economic decline experienced since the Seven Years' War.[54] The

53. W. W. Mijnhardt, "Het nut en de genootschapsbeweging," in *Om het algemeen volksgeluk: Twee eeuwen particulier initiatief*, ed. W. W. Mijnhardt and A. J. Wichers (Edam, 1984), pp. 189–220; C. B. L. Singeling, "De gezellige dichter: Over literaire genootschappen in de achttiende eeuw," *Literatuur* 3 (1986): 93–100; B. Thobokholt, *Het taal- en dichtlievend genootschap "Kunst wordt door arbeid verkreegen" te Leiden, 1766–1800* (Utrecht, 1983); J. J. Kloek, "Literatuur en landsbelang," in *Voor vaderland en vrijheid*, ed. F. Grijzenhout, W. W. Mijnhardt, and N. C. F. van Sas (Amsterdam, 1987), pp. 81–96.

54. J. Bierens de Haan, *Van Oeconomische Tak tot Nederlandsche Maatschappij van Nijverheid en Handel, 1777–1952* (Haarlem, 1952); H. F. J. M. van den Eerenbeemt, "Het huwelijk tussen filantropie en economie: Een Patriotse en Bataafse illusie," *Economisch en Sociaal-Historisch Jaarboek* 35 (1972): 28–64; Mijnhardt, *Tot heil van 't menschdom*, pp. 106–110.

*Oeconomische Tak* grew immediately. Within a year, it consisted of fifty-five departments all over the republic and counted more than three thousand members. Membership was composed of the urban elites and the politically powerless middle ranks, with each group offering its own solutions to the problems. Generally speaking, the regents, remembering the seventeenth century, were intent on promoting commerce, which they were convinced would initiate recovery. Most members with a middle-class background, appalled by the poverty and especially the moral degeneration of the lower strata of the population, pleaded for a policy of industrialization that would create the jobs to absorb the unemployed; the means most often suggested were the lowering of taxes and tariffs. As a result of these diametrically opposed views on the economic future, the *Oeconomische Tak* lost its appeal, the more so because its statutes prevented undertaking anything that was not approved by the provincial estates or the Estates General. Membership soon declined. In 1795, only a few hundred members and about ten departments remained.

The reading of enlightened literature, the activities of local societies, and disillusionment about the feasibility of active government policy as shown by the failure of the *Oeconomische Tak* taught those concerned with the welfare of the nation to take the initiative. In complete accordance with the moderate Dutch Enlightenment, they came to the conclusion that God's harmonious universe was made for happiness here and now. Toward this end, the existing order should be scrutinized in the light of reason and an enlightened reading of the moral prescriptions of the Bible. These intellectuals did not, however, want to change the structure of society itself, convinced as they were of its fundamentally static nature. The outcome was the *Maatschappij tot Nut van 't Algemeen* (Society for Public Welfare), the first society in the republic—more or less exclusively sponsored by the politically powerless middle class—to advocate public reform independently from the government.[55]

The character of this society's ideology was twofold. On the one hand, members were convinced that the spread of enlightened education would end lower-class ignorance and moral degeneration, at the same time providing these classes with the skills necessary for an economic recovery. Moreover, education and the ability to work would transform them into complete citizens, enabling them to occupy their

55. Mijnhardt, *Tot heil van 't menschdom*, pp. 259–295.

God-given place in society. The *Nut* explicitly blamed the semiofficial learned societies of science for failing to distinguish between sciences that were useful to the community and those that served only personal refinement. It did not question the value of the latter but declared that private enlightenment should be subordinated to the dissemination of useful knowledge as essential to a viable society. On the other hand, the *Nut* developed the new cultural concept that had been tentatively formulated by the literary societies into a full-blown ideology. Its cultural ideal was heavily dependent on Dutch Enlightenment thought, even to the extent of a complete repudiation of the humanist legacy. In various tracts—a debate that almost took the form of a delayed *querelle*—the society disputed the humanist claim that enlightenment of the people was not an appropriate means to recovery because it was contrary to the experience of the ancients. In the 1790s, an Utrecht member of the society launched a widely acclaimed attack on the humanist-inspired cultural ideal fostered by universities and the semiofficial societies of science alike, titled "On the Nature of the Enlightenment and its Consequences for Mankind, Civil Society, and the World."[56] The author blamed the limited circulation of enlightened philosophy in the republic on the overemphasis of classical learning in educated circles and the abominable practice of teaching in Latin in the universities. Such attitudes were deplorable because only through enlightenment could humankind reach a complete knowledge of the true character of God and nature. The tremendous progress in the arts and sciences came from such enlightenment alone, which should not be held in fetters. From the moment the whole nation was converted to enlightened precepts, the republic would recover and be feared again by its foes and respected by its friends.

The *Maatschappij tot Nut van 't Algemeen* opened its doors to all who subscribed to its Christian-inspired goals and paid a modest yearly contribution. The society not only wanted to include members from different social groups; it also wanted to appeal to the nation as a whole. Consequently, it operated on two levels. The national society, with its seat in Amsterdam, was responsible for the formulation of new initiatives for popular education. Local departments were to implement these initiatives, at the same time providing the cultural needs of their own members by means of regular lectures. Thus, a transitional model

---

56. G. van Bosvelt, *Over den aard en de natuur der Verlichting en derzelver gevolgen voor den mensch, den burgerstaat, en de gansche weereld* (Utrecht, 1792).

was created between the old and still strong local and provincial loyalties and the new sense of national unity. The impact of this new
cultural ideal may be measured by the society's popularity. After ten
years, membership had risen to more than 2,500 in more than twenty-
five departments. Shortly after 1800, membership passed the 10,000
mark.

## ENLIGHTENMENT AND REVOLUTION

It would be logical to expect that the local and improvement societies
would become politically active in the 1780s. But none of them developed political programs, nor did they put their views on the future of
the nation into something that could be called a political framework.
Moreover, they did not participate in the revolutionary events of the
1780s or 1790s. Almost all their statutes explicitly excluded politics
from their activities. The national board of the *Maatschappij tot Nut
van 't Algemeen*, for example, put heavy emphasis on the need to remain neutral in politics; its general secretary in 1786 still claimed that
neutrality in politics as well as in religion was absolutely necessary to
to convince the public of the rightness of its cause. The Utrecht ideo-
logue of the society who had attacked the Latin educational culture
refrained from politics as well. In his opinion, Truth and Enlightenment were synonymous, and thus he felt himself entitled to claim that
no false governmental policy or deceitful philosophy could ever stop
the progress of Enlightenment. Just as remarkable was the political
composition of these societies, which included Orangists as well as Patriots. Although the political dissension of the outside world occasionally entered these societies, politically inspired conflicts seldom
arose. More important still, the 1780s witnessed the emergence of large
numbers of purely political societies—modeled on the many local cultural and improvement societies already in existence—in which politically active citizens could discuss politics and policies, strategies and
tactics.

The Enlightenment was not the prerogative of the Patriots. Outstanding representatives of the Dutch Enlightenment such as Elie Luzac
and the Utrecht professor Rijklof Michaël van Goens served as key
defenders of the Orangist cause in the 1780s. Even Laurens Pieter van
de Spiegel, the last grand pensionary of the republic and squelcher of
the Patriot revolution, was an enlightened intellectual well acquainted

with current European debate. Dutch Enlightenment thought was eclectic and did not limit itself to political matters. Although a causal relationship between Enlightenment and the Patriot revolution cannot be established, the two movements had much in common. The political program of the Patriots, the Grondwettige herstelling, reveals a similar obsession with the glorious national past.[57] Consequently, it is no surprise that late eighteenth-century Dutch political thought was hardly influenced by the great political philosophers of the age. Montesquieu or Rousseau had but little to offer that was relevant to the Dutch situation, except for topoi about the natural equality of humankind or the inalienable rights of the people, and more congenial authors such as Locke, Price, and Priestley were often referred to.

The political significance of the Dutch Enlightenment was twofold. First, it stimulated the awakening of a political consciousness. Despite its continuous profession of political neutrality, the spectatorial press and the activities of philosophical societies explicitly served that function. Through their emphasis on the faultless nature of the Dutch constitution, blaming all decline on the frenchification of the regents' moral code, they systematically undermined the moral superiority of the regent class and its claim to rule. Second, both the spectatorial press and the philosophical societies ventured the idea that the pursuit of literature, arts, and sciences was an acceptable alternative to political participation; for those not participating in politics, cultivation of enlightened ideas and the spread of enlightened knowledge would provide an excellent means to restore the republic to its former greatness. In this way the responsibility for the welfare of the nation, which up to then had rested uniquely with the regent class, was brought within the reach of all self-supporting and well-cultured citizens.

Such ideas did not, however, necessarily imply political action. The final choice for Orangism or Patriotism, indifference or neutrality, was determined by many factors—such as local conditions, family relations, social positions, economic issues, and the political developments of the day. Still, the massive overhaul of Dutch political and social institutions during the Batavian period and the monarchy of William I would have been unthinkable without the extended reforms proposed in the Dutch Enlightenment.

57. E. J. van Himbergen, "Grondwettige Herstelling," in *Figuren en figuraties*, pp. 27–40.

# 10

# Radicalism in the Dutch Enlightenment

## Margaret C. Jacob

W E are frequently told by present-day historians that the Enlightenment in the Dutch Republic was a tame and pietistic affair,
largely devoid of deism, never mind Spinozism—in other words, still
deeply informed by a liberal Calvinism and humanism inherited from
the Reformation. We are told to expect, in the birthplace of Spinozism,
by the mid-eighteenth century only the physico-theology of Nieuwentyt
or Stinstra. We are told to expect, in the only Continental republic of
any consequence, little interest in the political writings of Locke, or
Montesquieu, or Burlamaqui, or Rousseau.

As a broad generalization, especially true for the provincial cities
and towns apart from Amsterdam, this conservative and pietistic Enlightenment, more Protestant than secular, was undoubtedly commonplace enough. But there was more to the Enlightenment in the Netherlands than liberal Protestantism. In 1760, an English merchant plying
his trade in Amsterdam wrote back to a friend the following account of
the profound discontent and seditious fraternizing about which he had
been told:

> their greatest grievance was to see their country enslaved by their
> own countrymen—by the very representatives who were chosen to
> protect their liberties and privileges. Why to procure the liberty to
> send over their just complaint to England a deputation of the richest
> merchants in Amsterdam danced attendance for three weeks at The

Hague before they could be heard . . . and yet Amsterdam alone pays fifty-eight out of one hundred of the whole public revenue. Nay they were so free to assure us that the principal people in Amsterdam formed an association to shake off every connection with the rest of the provinces and they did not doubt but it would soon come to this.[1]

From any perspective, what our English visitor recounted in 1760 must be described as radical, a fundamental discontent with the institutions of the old order in the republic, in particular with the estates and the stadholderate (hence the reference to The Hague), coupled with a willingness to talk openly about associations with rebellious tendencies, if not intentions.

The search for the radical Enlightenment in the Dutch Republic takes us by a devious and circuitous route from the Spinozism nurtured in the early years of the century to the discontent manifest in the revolution of 1747–1748 and again in the 1780s.[2] Could our visitor have been mistaken, or simply misled by coffeehouse boasting? Or was he glimpsing a radicalism common enough by the 1760s? Were these select Amsterdam circles of merchants and intellectuals, content for the most part to ply their trade, increasingly distressed by what they perceived as the weaknesses and failings in the political and economic order of the Dutch Republic? I am suggesting here that there were pockets of radicalism in the republic throughout the century, and it is my task in this chapter to locate at least a few of them.

To identify this radicalism, in both its philosophical and political forms, let us begin by stating what we mean by "radical" within the context of any Continental ancien régime. By the early eighteenth century in Europe, two new and potentially radical elements existed within the mental universe of the educated elites. The first, to which I return, was the new science and its attendant assumptions about application and the control of nature. The second is what I describe as a

1. Dr. Williams' Library, Wodrow-Kendrick correspondence, MS 24.157, f. 41, Utrecht, 6 August 1760; Samuel Kenrick to James Wodrow. Kenrick did not speak Dutch and talked to his hosts in French or through interpreters. In general, this is a fascinating correspondence, with mention of Hume and matters Scottish, descriptions of travel in the Low Countries, and in the 1790s (f. 173) a favorable reference to Mary Wollstonecraft's "Rights of Woman which will delight you and still more perhaps your daughters. She possesses the same original genius, undaunted intrepidity." I am grateful to John Creasey, the librarian of the collection, for his assistance.

2. On the survival of Spinozism in the republic, see Silvia Berti, "'La Vie et l'esprit de Spinosa' (1719) e la prima traduzione francese dell' 'Ethica'," *Rivista Storica Italiana* 98 (1986): pp. 5–46, and H. J. Siebrand, *Spinoza and the Netherlands* (Assen-Maastricht, 1988).

theoretically anchored republicanism. The English commonwealthmen are frequently cited as the most ideologically pure representatives of that originally Italian mode of political thought.[3] Yet, it cannot be forgotten that exiled English commonwealthmen, for example Algernon Sidney, spent their time in the Dutch Republic far from idly. They learned from its political theorists such as Grotius and, in the case of Sidney, incorporated Dutch and Huguenot ideas of government and liberty into their own thought.[4]

On the Continent, republicanism could encompass many and varied responses to the perceived corruption of the old order, of which monarchic absolutism and clerical hegemony were regarded as the most flagrant abuses. In this attenuated sense, Boulainvillier as well as Burlamaqui can be classified as advocates of alternative forms of political organization that would better suit some sort of republic than enforce the privileges of hegemonic regents, theocratic clergymen, or absolute monarchs. So too, as we now know, Locke's *Two Treatises* in its French translation could be recommended to citizens of the Dutch Republic. Indeed, Rousset de Missy's 1755 preface to a new edition of the French translation of Locke, published in Amsterdam, made precisely that recommendation. This 1755 edition, which became the most widely read edition of Locke in late eighteenth-century Europe, had been intended for publication in 1747. As leaders of the revolution that restored the stadholderate, Bentinck and Rousset thought it wise to recommend Locke as its justifier.

In eighteenth-century Europe, the ideological services Locke could be enlisted to perform might seem fairly obvious. The ideological serviceability of the new science was another, more complicated matter. Both Cartesianism and Newtonianism had been used at various moments in the seventeenth and eighteenth centuries to support established authority.[5] Yet, for differing reasons and circumstances both disturbed the traditional clergy, especially those entrenched in the Continental universities and dedicated to a scholastic reading of the natural order. In Utrecht in the 1650s, for instance, Voetius attacked Descartes from the pulpits of the city and warned the citizenry that in a purely mechanical universe, which he labeled atheist, the magistrates

---

3. J. G. A. Pocock, *The Machiavellian Moment: Florentine Political Thought and the Atlantic Republican Tradition* (Princeton, 1975).

4. Jonathan Scott, *Algernon Sidney and the English Republic, 1623–1677* (Cambridge, 1988), pp. 52–58.

5. See Margaret C. Jacob, *The Cultural Meaning of the Scientific Revolution* (New York, 1988), chaps. 2 and 3.

would renege on their charitable obligations to the populace at large. In the early manifestations of the Enlightenment in the Dutch Republic, those Calvinist clergy who championed the new science, such as Balthasar Bekker, did so in direct opposition to their clerical colleagues, dedicating their books to magistrates, lawyers, and doctors.[6] Both the Newtonian 's Gravesande and his successor to the chair of *natuurkunde* in Leiden, J. N. S. Allamand, were accused of Spinozism, although in neither case should the charge be seen as applicable. On the other hand, their contemporary, a teacher of mathematics and natural philosophy at Deventer, Tyssot de Patot, lost his position and descended into penury because the new science had indeed taken him down the slippery path to deism, if not Spinozism.[7]

But it might still be argued that by the mid-eighteenth century in the Netherlands both the new science and the republican tradition, of which Elie Luzac stands as an eloquent mid-century representative (see Chapter 5, this volume), had been safely domesticated, rendered pietistic to all but the most fundamental Calvinist, and harmless to all but the most backward and corrupt of regents. Yet, there is significant evidence to contradict that bland assessment of the Dutch Enlightenment, and that evidence comes from masonic and nonmasonic circles, predictably from Amsterdam. As Jeremy Popkin documents here (see Chapter 13), Amsterdam was one of the most literate places in Western Europe. It had nearly as many bookstores as Paris, a vastly larger city. Bookstores and publishers often put into the world texts that were subversive and about which they were immensely discrete. The radicalism of *les livres philosophiques* lay in their materialism as well as in their attack on established elites. I am suggesting here that beneath the surface of "acceptable" political thought and natural philosophy, especially in the larger cities of Western Europe, we can find evidence that other, more subversive ideas were wending their way into the minds of the literate. We should not rely only on what the booksellers advertised; we should also look for evidence of what was sold under the counter. In the heavily censored Austrian Netherlands, for example, the town of Namur—hardly a center of secular and Enlightened culture—supported twelve bookstores. In 1729–1730, the police raided

6. See Margaret C. Jacob, "The Crisis of the European Mind: Hazard Revisited," in *Politics and Culture in Early Modern Europe*, ed. Phyllis Mack and Margaret C. Jacob (Cambridge, 1987), pp. 251–271.

7. Margaret C. Jacob, *The Radical Enlightenment: Pantheists, Freemasons and Republicans* (London, 1981), pp. 186, 194–196.

all of them, confiscated "bad books," and for our convenience made a list of the subversive materials. We find on the list books about the English Revolution, Fontenelle on the plurality of worlds, works by Machiavelli, attacks on the corruption of the French court, and, not least, a goodly sampling of pornography.[8]

The police in Amsterdam possessed neither the interest nor the mandate to make such lists. We historians may regret their lack of zeal, but we should not go on from there to presume that, while a town such as Namur possessed a literary underground, Amsterdam was relegated to the status of a provincial backwater, a center solely for piety and physico-theology. It is safer to presume that readers could get just about any book they wanted in Amsterdam and possibly just about anywhere else. The caveat that Amsterdam is not the nation makes for an obvious truism; neither was Paris the nation in 1789. Yet, a great deal of important history unfolded in both places in the late 1780s, and we should not lose sight of our obligation to search for explanations and origins of a series of revolutionary upheavals which, from any perspective, ushered in the modern world as we know it.

Elsewhere I have presented evidence for the existence in the Netherlands during the first half of the eighteenth century of a radical tradition characterized by Spinozism—or pantheism, as Jean Rousset de Missy described his creed—and by a republicanism that led Rousset and some of his associates into revolutionary activity during the upheaval of 1747–1748.[9] His aggressive support for the democratically inclined and rebellious *Doelisten*, his subsequent arrest and exile, are well known to students of Dutch history. The fact that he was a leading freemason, in other words, that secular fraternizing was central to his life, adds more than simply mystery and intrigue to his story. It should also serve to unsettle any interpretation of the phenomenon of sociability that seeks at every turn to divorce it from political action or personal religiosity.[10]

8. Namur, Belgium, Archives de l'Etat; for listing of MSS, see F. Courtoy and C. Dourchamps-Lefevre, eds. *Archives du Conseil provincial de Namur*, vol. 1 (Brussels, 1986), p. 50; MS 122, 1718–1730, last bundle of which contains the lists made by the police. On the lists we find Rapin Thoyras's history of England and books listed simply as "Rebellion d'Angleterre; Chef d'oeurver [sic] d'un inconnu [by Sallengre], La femme docteur, ou la Theologie tombée en quenouille; les plaisirs et chagrins de l'Amour; Fontenelle, Entretien sur la pluralite des mondes; Biblio[thèque] raisonnée."

9. Margaret C. Jacob, *Radical Enlightenment*; for evidence of the continuity of that tradition into the nineteenth century, see Andreas Joannes Hanou, *Sluiers van Isis: Johannes Kinker als voorvechter van de Verlichting in de vrijmetselarij en andere Nederlandse genootschappen, 1790–1845*, vols. 1–2 (Deventer, 1988).

10. A good corrective to this tendency can also be found in the theoretical work of J.

There is more to be said about the phenomenon of secular fraternizing in Amsterdam during the second half of the eighteenth century.
Both in the masonic and nonmasonic forms, the literary and philosophical society, as well as the lodge, could serve as places where some men
(and a very few women) of reforming instincts and heretical proclivities, segregated from family, church, and sect, could organize themselves around mutually agreed on rules, or in the case of freemasonry
around constitutions and "household rules." They, as well as their
more orthodox colleagues, elected officers, made charitable donations,
or gave sermons on topics such as republican virtue or republican decadence, on the application of science to industry, as well as on the more
commonplace themes drawn from the humanistic tradition or the piety
of liberal Protestantism. The archives of secular associations such as
the philosophical societies *Concordia et Libertate* and *Felix Meritis* and
the masonic *La Bien Aimée*, the lodge Rousset de Missy nurtured into
the 1750s, attest to daily organizational practices that were both disciplined and democratic as well as to a tradition of enlightened oratory
mixing a variety of intellectual postures and strongly held convictions.
They provide evidence for the Dutch Enlightenment as it was lived;
they give context to the political and historical writings of Dutch reformers in the 1770s and 1780s. Indeed, those rich archives housed at
the Gemeente Archief in Amsterdam, and at the Grand Lodge in The
Hague, reveal the Dutch Enlightenment as it was spoken, by members,
or brothers, with a variety of intellectual interests and proclivities. Not
incidentally, from 1735 until well into the 1760s, masonic records
were kept in both French and Dutch, suggesting a degree of familiarity
with both languages on the part of most brothers. Here I purposefully
dwell on the radical elements found in those archives, not, I trust, to
distort our image of the Dutch Enlightenment, but rather to sharpen
our vision.

From the masonic archives we now know that the most widely cir-
culated edition of the French translation of Locke's *Two Treatises*,
done in 1755 and reprinted in 1780, 1783 (without the preface), and
1795, was the work of Rousset de Missy and his masonic brother and
Amsterdam-based publisher Johannes Schreuder. What is important
about that 1755 edition is the new preface and notes added by Rousset. These are in French, a language most members of the Dutch elite

Habermas, *The Structural Transformation of the Public Sphere* (Cambridge, Mass., 1989);
German text first published in 1962.

could read, if not speak. This point is important because it serves to correct a tendency among Enlightenment historians to treat all French texts published in the Dutch Republic (or anywhere else) during the eighteenth century as aimed simply at a French, or European-wide, audience. The new preface is quite specifically tied to the crisis of 1754–1755 in the Dutch Republic. In those years the fear of yet another French invasion led the regents to retreat from their obligation to their English allies and to opt for neutrality.[11]

In opposition to their neutrality, which Rousset believed threatened the safety of the republic, his preface argued that Locke's treatise must be seen in relation to the writings of Burlamaqui and that it placed sovereignty solely in the hands of the people. Locke's treatise (indeed, the French translation of 1691, and all subsequent editions of it, contained only the second treatise—hence the title, *Du gouvernement civil*) demonstrates "l'excellence de la Constitution Republiquaine telle que celle de notre État" ("the excellence of the republican constitution like that of our state"). But, Rousset warns, there are corrupt nobles in the republic akin to those found in Venice and Genoa. They would enslave the populace and deprive them of the freedom to exercise their will and of the right to self-preservation.[12] The message of the preface is clear enough: the cowardice of the regents can be opposed only by putting in place English principles of government (which so many European reformers incorrectly thought Locke to be describing); they stand as a model for the Dutch Republic.

This 1755 edition of Locke may also be said to have provided principles for another, more private, type of government. In these very years, as their letters reveal, Rousset and Schreuder were attempting to reconstitute their lodge, to establish what they called its legality. *La Bien Aimée* had been closed down by the authorities in 1749. Its archives tell us that "the *burgerlijke* unrest in 1748 had influenced our lodge. Some of our brothers were susceptible to it, others were offended by it and most were indignant about it."[13] The statement describes in microcosm the political sentiment in Amsterdam as a result

11. See Margaret C. Jacob, "In the Aftermath of Revolution: Rousset de Missy, Freemasonry, and Locke's *Two Treatises of Government*," in *L'Eta dei Lumi: Studi storici sul settecento europeo in onore di Franco Venturi*, 2 vols. (Naples, 1985), vol. 1, pp. 502–515.

12. L.C.R.D.M.A.D.P. [Rousset de Missy], ed., *Du Gouvernement Civil . . . augmentée de quelques Notes* (Amsterdam, 1755), pp. xv–xvii.

13. H. Rodermond, *De Vrijmetselaarloge 'La Bein Aimee,' Amsterdam, 1735–1985*, Maçonnieke Stichting Ritus en Tempelbouw, ISBN No. 90 9000 9973, 1985, p. 20, quoting from the manuscript correspondence of the lodge with another lodge.

of the *Doelistenbeweging*. This masonic microcosm was, however, sufficiently influenced by the radical movement, and one of its leaders, that the authorities turned against it. In 1754–1755, when Rousset and Schreuder quietly took up the task of reviving their lodge, they sought to impose greater discipline within, firmer adherence to its rules and constitution as well as to its officers and master. In Rousset's view the former lodge had been allowed to become too large—twenty-five, rather than the former ninety, members was now his ideal. He obsessively warned that the lodge not come under French influence, that it adhere firmly to English masonic practices and mores.[14] So, too, in his footnotes scattered throughout his edition of Locke, written precisely at this moment, Rousset uses masonic language to assure "the sons of Noah"—as masons often called themselves—that they possessed in their hearts an intuitive understanding of the necessity for a contract in order to assure their self-preservation as ordained "by the Master of Nature."[15]

Eighteenth-century private societies expressed many impulses, some in no sense political. Yet, even societies concerned with the fine arts, as well as with science, created an elaborate "contract" between the society and its members. By signing it they pledged their fraternity and loyalty and their dedication to work for the betterment of society.[16] Freemasonry, especially on the Continent, was particularly susceptible, however, to contemporary political concerns because of its emphasis on constitutions, rules, order, the election of officers, obedience to them, and, always, the moral improvement not only of society but also of each brother. Although there must have been many social clubs and gatherings in Amsterdam during the turbulent years at mid-century in which members kept their political interests and ideals separate from their sociability and conviviality, Rousset's lodge was not one of them.[17] It became politicized precisely, I suggest, because lodges could see themselves as idealized microcosms, reflective of, yet critical toward, the larger moral and political macrocosm. They were particularly sensitive

14. MSS *La Bien Aimée*, Grand Lodge of The Netherlands, The Hague, B.A. 5, December 10, 1754. Cited by kind permission of the lodge.

15. Rousset de Missy, *Du Gouvernement Civil*, p. 14n.

16. Gemeente Archief, the records of Felix Meritis, PA 59, no. l, ff. 13–17, "Certificatie en Contract."

17. For example, see "De Saturdagse Krans 1718–93: Een gezellige vereeniging van Amsterdamsche Regenten in de 18de eeuw," *Koninklijk Oudheidkundig genootschap Amsterdam* 77 (1934–1935): 66–79.

components in the web of a new civil society created under the suspicious eye of the old order.

But did that mindset continue into the 1780s and 1790s; do the traces of radicalism evident in *La Bien Aimée* continue into the 1790s? Certainly the impulse to see the masonic lodge as a political microcosm can be found in its contemporary historiography. Written in 1778, a manuscript history of Dutch freemasonry by a prominent and learned brother, Alexandre de Vignoles, who was also an officer for a time in the Grand Lodge of London, begins with these words: "The Royal Art of masonry must correctly be seen as the analogue to the spirit of sweetness and wisdom that lies at the base of the government of the Estates General of the United Provinces."[18] De Vignoles was not simply being metaphorical. In a letter he wrote to a rebellious lodge in Berlin, this one in his capacity as representative of the Grand Lodge in London, he recommended the Dutch system of masonic governance. He specifically explained that it had been modeled on the Estates General so as to offer each lodge a good measure of autonomy.[19] Such a government, a brother might well decide, should stay as it is, untroubled by *burgerlijke* demands for reform.

Yet, might not this son of Noah also ponder the political writings of Locke that his own brothers exhorted him to embrace, or discuss those principles with foreign visitors also restive about the abuses of the old order? We shall never hear the conversations that occurred, for instance in 1774, among the brothers in *La Bien Aimée*. The French visitor in that year was Jean Paul Marat. Did they discuss his political and journalistic writings, or his scientific interests? We shall never know. What we do know, however, is that those conversations occurred in the very rooms where the *Doelisten* of 1748 had first met. In

18. Quoted from MSS of Frère de Vignoles, The Grand Lodge of The Netherlands, unnumbered folder; the text here quoted is entitled "G.L.N. des Etats Generaux des Provinces Unies."

19. MS Kloss 190.E.47, The Grand Lodge of The Netherlands, "Quant à l'indépendance que vous reclaméz, jamais la société n'a admis d'esclavage, et le vouloir introduire, ce serait détruire son essence. Notre Gouvernment ne sera connu, qu'autant qu'on y verra l'heureux mélange, qui se trouve dans celui de Hollande. Les Etats Generaux composés des Députés de chaque Province forment le tribunal souverain de la Nation. Ceux de chaque Province en Particulier, quoique subordinés, n'en sont ni moins souverains, ni moins indépendans; et la Jurisdiction des Villes jouit, sous ces derniers de toute souverainité sur leurs territoires. Cette sage république avoit, j'ay osé le dire dans la G.L. de 1756, pris dans l'Administration de la société la forme, qu'elle à donnér à la sienne. Jaloux de leur liberté, tous les Etats, qui devaient le composer, voulurent assurer leur indépendance, mais ils sentirent en même tems, que sous un point d'union, qui tint toutes les parties ensemble, le [word left out] qu'ils formaient de tant d'états divers, serait si peu ferme, qu'il remproit bientôt."

1760, *La Bien Aimée* chose to move its headquarters to the "kloveniers of Oude Doelen," the hotel on Kloveniersburgwal from which the *Doelisten* had derived their name. In 1787, one of the lodge's brothers and its devoted orator, the prominent Patriot, Jacobus Adrianus Crajenschot, fled the country, only to return in 1795 and lend his support to the Batavian revolution.[20]

There is an eerie silence in the lodge's minutes in 1790 and 1791. By 1792, to the south, the French Revolution had taken a radical and Jacobin turn. At first, very little of those events seems to filter into the proceedings of the lodge—a myopia that other historians have noted also in the Dutch-language press, as opposed to the French-language press in the republic of the time.[21] Instead, the concern in the lodge is with virtue, which "if we would all exercise . . . [we would] avert much of the slander that the blind world maliciously spreads about us."[22] Again in late 1793 the ancient Romans are invoked, as are the ancient Egyptian priests. The Roman feast mentioned is that of the god Saturn.[23] Only two years later will Saturn once again be celebrated; those minutes contain the key to the allusion. For these Dutch brothers, it is a celebration of the banishment of "the tyrant Tarquin and his damnable wife Tullia." We may speculate that the celebration of virtual tyrannicide in late 1793 could not fail to have noticed, with approval, the execution in that year of the French king, Louis XVI, and his wife, Marie Antoinette. It may also signal a willingness to banish the stadholder.

The invasion by the French army in January 1795 was accompanied by the proclamation of its friendship for the Dutch people. That friendship, as the archives now reveal, extended to the membership of *La Bien Aimée*. In late February 1795, "before the opening of the lodge [meeting] our master wished the assembled fraternity happiness with the so long desired revolution in events in our beloved fatherland, through which now Freedom, Equality, and Fraternity is the motto of our days, and [which] moreover gives the fraternity knowledge that

20. Rodermond, *Vrijmetselaarsloge La Bien Aimée*, pp. 38, 50–61. For a discussion of the many societies in Amsterdam in the 1780s, see H. Reitsma, "Genootschappen in Amsterdam en de revolutie van 1787," in Th. S. M. van der Zee et al., *1787: De Nederlandse revolutie?* (Amsterdam, 1988), pp. 146–165.

21. A point made in Simon Schama, *Patriots and Liberators: Revolution in the Netherlands 1780–1813* (New York, 1977), p. 141. On the French-language press, see Jeremy Popkin, *Revolutionary News: The Press in France, 1789–1799* (Durham, N.C., 1990), with some attention to the *Gazette de Leyde*.

22. MSS *La Bien Aimée*, MS 41, f. 32 (1793).

23. Ibid. f. 39.

henceforth all titles will be abolished among us. The fraternal visitors, among them also brothers, who crushed and expelled our former rulers, . . . shall be most heartily welcomed." At the ensuing banquet the brothers and their French "liberators" sang "La Marseillaise." In addition, the lodge immediately and self-consciously altered its ceremonies to reflect the new fraternity and equality, and in particular to treat the brother-servants as more truly equal. At the same ceremony they welcomed back brothers who "had fled the country because of the advocacy of the people's rights." On Christmas day of the same year they celebrated "these commemorable times of Freedom, Equality, and Fraternity when all external, silly distinctions of honor should be destroyed and abolished."[24] What extraordinary scenes these would have been to Rousset (d. 1762), Huguenot refugee, pantheist and republican, violent opponent of French absolutism. Did he in some sense prepare his fraternal descendants, both Dutch and French, for those celebrations? I think we must now say that he did.

If, however, we were to confine our search for radicalism to the splendid archives of Amsterdam freemasonry, we might slip into conspiratorial traps set for us by such antirevolutionary mythmakers as the abbé Barruel and the host of propagandists who flourished in the postrevolutionary reaction. What the records of the lodge in Amsterdam show is quite simply the capacity for the new sociability of the eighteenth century to express vastly different political ideals and aspirations. Other impulses, more commercial and intellectual than fraternal, were also at work in the republic from at least mid-century, and these too possessed radical tendencies. Once again, the private societies permitted their articulation amid a variety of discourses.

During the revolution of 1747–1748, *Doelisten* propaganda aimed against the regents was strident in its condemnation of the corruption and apathy now attributed to the ruling elite. Some of that radical literature specifically condemned the absence of "arts and sciences" as well as the decline in trade and manufacturing that had beset the republic.[25] These charges linking intellectual innovation to industrial and commercial success, appearing as early as they do, are of particular

---

24. Ibid., f. 60. The records of the lodge MS 41, dated 1795, describe the alteration in ceremony in order to express this new equality. MS 41:10, December 25 and February 11, 1795.

25. Anon. *Aanspraak gedaan aan de Goede Burgeren, die tot Welzyn van stad en land, op den 9 Augustus 1748, op den Cloveniers Doelen vergadert zyn geweest* (Amsterdam, 1748), p. 1.

interest to the historian in search of the cultural origins of industrialization, both in Britain and on the Continent.

The highly mechanistic and materialist approach to the origins of industrialization once characteristic of the new economic history is now giving way to a more complex analysis, one that permits social and cultural factors to be added to the equation. For instance, we can identify among such early British industrialists as Josiah Wedgwood and the philosophical circle around Erasmus Darwin in Derby a specific interest in mechanically applied science intended for industry. We can find a similarly industrial perspective in Birmingham in the scientific liberalism of Joseph Priestley.[26] All were politically radical. But what, you may well ask, has this got to do with Dutch science; more precisely, what has it got to do with Dutch radicalism?

From its very inception the new mechanical science, as I have already noted, possessed the power to dislodge those segments within the lay and clerical elite who refused to accept either its supposed veracity or, by the second half of the eighteenth century, its applicability to manufacturing and industry. British engineers and industrialists of the 1760s and beyond—John Smeaton, Wedgwood, James Watt, and the Strutts of Derbyshire—saw themselves as "gentlemen of science" and reformers as much as they were businessmen and small capitalists. They self-consciously identified themselves with enlightened reform and approached parliamentary maneuvering on behalf of their interests, oftentimes in bills for canal construction, as political struggles against reactionary lords and bishops.

If we look to scientific circles in the Dutch Republic during the latter decades of the century, a similar ideological pattern, although set against very different circumstances, is also evident. In general it is true that established scientific bodies such as the *Hollandsche Maatschappij der Wetenschappen* in Haarlem were, not unlike the Royal Society of London, politically conservative bodies that set their fortunes with those of the oligarchic elite. Just as the Royal Society in the 1780s sought to exclude followers of Joseph Priestley from their ranks— Priestley himself having much earlier been admitted—so too at least one member of the *Hollandsche Maatschappij* sought unsuccessfully in

26. See Jacob, *Cultural Meaning*, chap. 5; Isaac Kramnick, "Eighteenth-Century Science and Radical Social Theory: The Case of Joseph Priestley's Scientific Liberalism," *Journal of British Studies* 25, no. 1 (1986): 1–30; and I. Kramnick, *Republicanism and Bourgeois Radicalism* (Ithaca, 1990).

1787 to forbid Priestley himself from membership in its ranks, supposedly for his religious beliefs.[27] The Haarlem society also had very little that was complimentary to say about the writings of Locke or Rousseau. Significantly, in May 1787 it finally posed a prize question on the state of manufacturing and industry in the republic.[28] In general, its proceedings are filled with pieties drawn from the physico-theology of English and Dutch Newtonians. Yet, even many members of the Haarlem society supported the revolution, although its leader, Martinus van Marum, did not.[29]

Once again, however, if we turn to scientific circles in Amsterdam a very different and more radical picture emerges. The literary and philosophical society *Concordia et Libertate* took shape in 1748. One of its most active members and first secretary was Rousset's masonic friend and publisher of Locke, Johannes Schreuder. In 1748, the society met in the same building as the *Doelisten*. In the 1770s and beyond, Benjamin Bosma was one of the society's members. He too was more than simply a scientific lecturer and mechanical applicator; he was also an aggressive critic of what he perceived as Dutch backwardness in matters scientific and industrial (see Chapter 15, this volume). His critique of scientific education was predictably tied to his belief that decadence and corruption beset the republic. Only in Amsterdam, he argued, could be found merchants who truly worked, or a school where science could be properly learned.[30]

At the meetings of *Concordia et Libertate*, Bosma labored the theme of reform and renewal.[31] He may have had a quite sympathetic audience. His brothers, as members sometimes called themselves, had a strong interest in science and the state of Dutch commerce; they were also by the 1780s aggressive nationalists. They watched events in the

27. *Hollandsche Maatschappij* MSS (Haarlem, 1781–1794), ff. 1421–1422; and see R. J. Forbes, ed. *Martinus van Marum: Life and Work*, vol. 1 (Haarlem, 1969), p. 34.

28. On discussions in political theory, see J. A. Bierens de Haan, *De Hollandsche Maatschappij der Wetenschappen, 1752–1952* (Haarlem, 1952), vol. 5 (1760), pp. 460–469, 530, and vol. 9, pp. 80–82 against *Emile* (1765); on the prize essay, see *Hollandsche Maatschappij* MSS, f. 1427. See also J. G. de Bruijn, *Inventaris van de Prijsvragen uitgeschreven door de Hollandsche Maatschappij der Wetenschappen, 1753–1917* (Groningen, 1977), p. 65. The Amsterdam branch of the *Nut* was much more practical in its orientation; see Gemeente Archief, Amsterdam, Archief 1e en 2e departement Nut.

29. Forbes, ed., *Martinus van Marum*.

30. Gemeente-Archief, Amsterdam, MSS *Concordia et Libertate*, P.A. 9, no. 1, "Resolutie Boek . . . 1748, 24 October tot 25 February 1750"; ibid., P.A. 9, no. 2, notes for 28 January 1777, n.f. See also Benjamin Bosma, *Redenvoering over de natuurkunde* (Amsterdam, 1762), pp. 6–8.

31. Gemeente Archief, P.A. 9, no. 2, 20 January 1778; see minutes in general for 1776–1777.

American colonies and wondered if "America would achieve her independence and freedom" from England.[32] They also spoke often about
"the fatherland" and the "laws and freedom of the Batavians."[33] Their
discourse was both nationalist and republican, in a classical sense.
They made reference to Machiavelli; they spoke incessantly about the
ancient Romans, their history and revolutions.[34] In religious matters
their voices were more mixed, and more pious. One of the members
piously opposed "the Christian religion of a *burgerlyke* society against
Rousseau"; but another presented a Dutch translation of D'Alembert's
preliminary discourse attached to the first edition of Diderot's great
*Encyclopedie* (1751).[35] By 1788, the writings of Montesquieu were being discussed for what they might reveal about the "grandeur and decadence of the Romans."[36] We can hear the radical undertones in a conversation that echoed many voices, all of them troubled, many of them
discontent.

One of the remedies offered by Bosma and others was practical
science, available to merchants who would know what to do with it. In
praising the scientific education found in Amsterdam, Bosma probably
referred to the Athenaeum and to *Felix Meritis*, where the Newtonian
J. H. van Swinden, among others, lectured on topics in astronomy, as
well as on the steam engine. Van Swinden's support for the Batavian
revolution is well known, as is his active membership in the literary
and philosophical society *Felix Meritis*. H. A. M. Snelders has already
pointed to the significant number of its scientific members who became
patriots and revolutionaries.[37] As W. W. Mijnhardt notes in Chapter 9,
many of the new the societies of the 1780s took this practical turn;
they were also frequently composed of Patriots.

The correspondence between James Watt, the inventor of the steam
engine, and J. van Liender, the foremost importer of the engine into the
Dutch Republic, makes explicit the link between industrial culture
there· and political radicalism. Van Liender was an ardent Patriot

32. Ibid., P.A. 9, no. 1, 24 October, 1780.
33. Ibid., 14 January 1783.
34. Ibid., for example, 29 October 1782. On 24 March 1783, the topic was "der groote
omwenteling van zaaken welke Rome ten tyde van Julius Caesar ondergaan heeft." In 1787,
for example, we find on 26 January a discourse given in "verdeediging van Machiavel" (defense of Machiavelli); on 27 February on the Roman "mayor" Fabricius; on 6 April 1790 on
Machiavelli and freedom.
35. Ibid., 28 March.
36. Ibid., 8 January 1788.
37. H. A. M. Snelders "Het Departement van natuurkunde van de Maatschappij van
verdiensten Felix Meritis in het eerste kwart van zijn bestaan," *Documentatieblad Werkgroep
Achttiende Eeuw* 15 (1983): 197–214; see also Jacob, *Cultural Meaning*, chap. 6.

throughout the 1780s as well as a supporter of the French Revolution throughout the 1790s. Having lived for some months in Watt's home, Van Liender felt that he could write freely about his political values, and his letters leave little doubt that Watt, at least until the autumn of 1792, and his son until well after then, shared those values.

Van Liender understood his own efforts to improve Dutch science to be part of his dedication as a Patriot and a nationalist. In October 1787 he believed that the republic had "suffered a revolution, the like of which never was recorded in any history." He meant the invasion; bitterly he commented, "the foreign tyrant . . . overturns all." Although he could not leave the country at that moment, Van Liender intended to leave and he vowed to Watt that "I shall first loosen every commercial connection." Transformation in commerce and industry and reform of the polity were linked in Van Liender's mind. He believed that Watt's engine represented a magnificent advance and he was fully conversant with its technology. Indeed, he had personally arranged for the engine's Dutch patent. Significantly, he also believed that the steam engine's introduction into the republic was a Patriot project blocked by Orangist opponents. He wrote to Watt in 1788 "that were public circumstances in another turn, than they now are, the Steam Engine would undoubtedly take footing in this Country; but by being a work of Patriots it is quite condemned and abhorred."

Van Liender and other Patriot industrialists gave their support to the revolutions of the 1780s and 1790s in part because they resonated with the values needed for industrial progress and enlightenment. As he put it to Watt, "How is it not to be lamented, that rulers of the Several States will not condescend to accommodate themselves more to the feelings of an enlightened age we live in, which will not suffer the tyrannical mode, in which those rulers dispose of men's liberty and property."[38] This was a vision that Van Liender's radical friends in Birmingham understood and approved.

Just as in Britain during the latter decades of the century, the link also existed in the Dutch Republic between political radicalism and what we may describe as an industrial vision. Van Swinden urged his fellow countrymen to follow the specific example set by Wedgwood and his kind, but he did so in a social and economic context hostile to industrialization. Indeed, if we listen to the voices of the radical and

38. Birmingham Reference Library, MSS of the firm of Boulton and Watt, Box 36, letters of 19 October 1787; February 12, 1788; 21 October 1793. Van Liender is writing in English from Rotterdam and then from his country house near Amsterdam.

scientifically inclined critics of the old order in the republic we hear another way to describe that illusive phenomenon of decline. They tell us that the old elite had lost its interest in new ideas, that scientific education and technology in the republic had fallen behind where once it had been innovative.

In a certain sense they were right. The Dutch universities had been the first anywhere on the Continent to accept Cartesianism and then Newtonianism. Its French-language press in the early decades of the century, not least the *Journal littéraire* published by 's Gravesande, among others, had disseminated Newtonian science throughout French-speaking Europe. In 1723, a correspondent from Surinam wrote playfully to Prosper Marchand, also an editor of the *Journal* and a close friend of Rousset, that he would abjure his Cartesianism if Marchand would abjure his Newtonianism.[39] Yet, by the mid-eighteenth century scientific education in the Netherlands had failed to take a populist direction that would have brought it out of the universities and into the commonplace knowledge of the literate classes. As C. A. Davids has shown, Dutch proficiency in applied mechanics for navigation remained strong throughout the century.[40] What is not significantly evident is scientific education with an industrial focus. As Van Liender warned Watt, who was about to demonstrate one of his engines to the Batavian Society, "Give as much explanation as possible and a great deal more even as you did to that Batavian Society's Engine because everyone there shall understand so little of the matter."[41]

The transition from commercial to industrial capitalism was a protracted and complex process in the Netherlands. As early as 1748, Hendrik van Gimnig, one of the radical leaders of the *Doelisten*, advocated the application of science to the problems of industry.[42] But as De Jongste shows, Van Gimnig's proposals were not taken up in his lifetime. Within certain philosophical circles we can discern by the 1770s a vision of the necessity of applied mechanics intended for industrial production. What I am suggesting here is a correlation between that industrial vision, born in part out of an understanding of mechanical science, and an attraction to Patriot causes and rhetoric.

39. University Library, Leiden, Marchand MS 2, 15 September 1723, Jac. de Roubain to P. Marchand.

40. C. A. Davids, *Zeewezen en wetenschap: De wetenschap en de ontwikkeling van de navigatietechniek in Nederland tussen 1585 en 1815* (Amsterdam, 1986).

41. Birmingham Reference Library, Box 36, 21 October 1790.

42. National Archives, The Hague, Stadhouderlijke secretarie, 579. First called to my attention by Jan de Jongste in Chapter 2 of this volume.

There is irony in this observation. The impulses of this generation of late Enlightenment progressives were, had they been effected, far more radical in their implications for the organization of society than either they or their contemporaries could ever have imagined. They look toward industrial society. By the end of the century, the coupling of radical republicanism, some might call it Jacobinism, with an interest in applied mechanics brings us back to those elements in the culture of early modern Europe that look toward modernity. Emphasizing the conservative character of the old order in the Dutch Republic tells a story that is only partially correct. To explain the secular modernity of contemporary Dutch society, historians of the late twentieth century must either postulate a dramatic rupture occurring sometime after 1800, or they must take another look at the eighteenth century. My task in this chapter has been to do just that.

# I I

# The Fiction of (National) Identity: Literature and Ideology in the Dutch Republic

## Christine van Boheemen-Saaf

In their angry letter to the guild of booksellers and publishers of October 1788, the mayors of Haarlem argue that "the recently ended troubles . . . had, to no small degree, been instigated and augmented by the books, pamphlets, and prints published during that unfortunate period."[1] In this chapter, I examine the Dutch novel in relation to the indictment of the Haarlem mayors. Among the books intended to foment trouble can we include the novel? What was the relationship between the eighteenth-century Dutch novel and the political and cultural developments of the period? The Haarlem mayors implied that all kinds of publications caused the political upheavals of 1787. But the facts prove that the literary text was surprisingly reticent and uninvolved in overtly political matters.

With the exception of an occasional dramatic performance such as the notorious *Burgerbloed* in Haarlem, where the character of a drunk named Willem suggested to the populace reference to another Willem, or with the writings of a Gerrit Paape or Pieter 't Hoen—better known to historians than to students of Dutch literature—contemporary political events had no connection with literary history. They left no direct reflection in the literary *discours*. At first, this may seem surprising. After all, is it not precisely the function of the novel to portray contem-

---

1. R. Daalder, "Haarlem en de democratische revolutie," in *Haerlem Jaarboek 1975* (Haarlem, 1976), p. 183.

porary life? It grows even more surprising when we consider how closely some writers of fiction were themselves actively involved in politics. I am not thinking merely of Wolff and Deken, who fled to France in 1788, or of Adriaan Loosjes, notable Patriot. There are less well known figures who prove even more interesting: J. H. Baron des Villates, who had held public office in Amsterdam, was imprisoned in the Gevangenpoort in 1789 for the attempt to raise a French army against William V. He spent his years in confinement writing romantic fiction without any allusion to contemporary politics. On the other side of the political fence was J. E. De Witte van Haemstede, fellow prisoner and eventually friend of Des Villates, sentenced in 1784 for the attempt to deliver Schouwen and Duiveland into English hands. The literary product of his confinement, *Henriëtte van Grandpré*, likewise fails to express political opinions, nor does it present characters who do.

With regard to the absence of political involvement in *Sara Burgerhart*, W. van den Berg has suggested that serious eighteenth-century Dutch literature celebrated the private and domestic sphere of life.[2] Indeed, what makes the Dutch novel thematically interesting in a comparatist perspective is that it generates its plots, not from the romantic suspense of the boy-gets-girl story, but from the idealization of the normal incidents of married life. Thus, both *Sara Burgerhart* and *Maurits Lijnslager* offer long and, to my knowledge, at that time, unique descriptions of the process of childbearing and labor. Beyond this interest in the propagation of domesticity, which does not hold for Des Villates or De Witte, for instance, there may have been an unwritten convention that forbade novels and moral-didactic tales to refer to matters of political dispute and public controversy. At least, a footnote to one of Adriaan Loosjes's "zedelijke verhalen," which breaks that convention, seems to suggest as much. In *Cornelia van der Horst*, the author apologizes for his plot, which alludes to the events of 1787, and defends himself against the possible charge that his writing stimulates faction and party spirit by citing French and German precedent. He continues: "But perhaps the wounds are too fresh, to touch the tender scars— though I would consider it meritorious work were a moral author to try and quench the flame of party spirit, at least, when it is burning without any possible use."[3] Since Loosjes is known not only as the

2. W. van den Berg, "Sara Burgerhart en haar derde stem," *Documentatieblad Werkgroep Achttiende Eeuw* 13 (1981): 151–208.
3. Adriaan Loosjes, *Zedelijke verhaalen* (Haarlem, 1804), pp. 192–194.

father of the Dutch historical novel but also as one of Haarlem's most active Patriots, contributor to the *Post van den Neder-Rhijn*, commemorator of such events as the American Declaration of Independence or the victory at the Doggersbank in verse, this metapoetic statement seems especially significant. What I address in this essay is the reason for the fictional disregard of contemporary political debate.

What my examples of disregard ultimately bring home is that our expectations of what fiction should do are determined by late nineteenth-century notions of mimetic realism. As I have argued elsewhere, eighteenth-century fiction should be regarded in terms of contemporary categorizations and expectations.[4] Fortunately, Ysbrand van Hamelsveld, enlightened Patriot, provides us at the end of his *Kort begrip der algemeene geschiedenis . . . der wereld* (Short Synopsis of the General History of the World) with a list of the cultural achievements of his own age, subdivided under different rubrics. Under "literature" he lists only poetry. It is under *menschkunde* (knowledge of human nature) that we find prose fiction. Here Van Hamelsveld, unusually promiscuous in his mingling of genres and nationalities, lists the names of Fielding and Richardson (but no Dutch novelists), Steele, Van Effen, and Shaftesbury. All these he frames in relation to Pope, through a citation to the *Essay on Man*.[5]

This grouping of spectatorial essays, the English novel, and moral philosophy under the common denominator *menschkunde* was apparently customary in the Netherlands. Thus, Adriaan Loosjes ends his award-winning *Verhandeling over de menschkunde* (Treatise on the Knowledge of Human Nature) of June 1786 with the declaration that "the human heart, well studied, is the true source of satisfaction." And he reminds his reader that "Homer, Theocritus and Sophocles, the masters of contemporary poets, had original insight into the human heart." What interests me here, again, is Loosjes's own annotation. As in *Cornelia van der Horst*, there is one extraordinarily long note—almost an essay—in which Loosjes comments that "he had almost added the name of Richardson, that *divine* genius . . . [because] his novels, the *Clarissa* and *Grandison*, are academies of *menschkunde*." Yet, he goes on,

4. Christine van Boheemen-Saaf, "The Reception of English Literature in Dutch Magazines: 1735–1785," in *The Role of Periodicals in the Eighteenth Century* (Leiden, 1984) pp. 7–17.

5. Ysbrand van Hamelsveld, *Kort begrip der algemeene geschiedenis van de schepping der wereld af, tot het einde der achttiende eeuw* (Amsterdam, 1802), p. 646.

we dared not recommend novels as one of the means of acquiring knowledge of human nature, since they serve that purpose only so rarely; in this respect our country may be congratulated with the *Sara Burgerhart* and *Willem Leevend*. Also for the same reason, we have left out the systems of the metaphysicians—these, on the whole, are better fit to promote the misjudgment of man than to enlighten his true nature and that of his fellow men.

The whole treatise concludes with a citation to Brooke; not the least of Loosjes's prize award were subscriptions to the *Hollandsche Spectator* and the *Philanthrope*—spectatorial magazines that advocated the moral philosophy that was the subject of Loosjes's treatise.[6]

The significance of Loosjes's footnote is not primarily that it classifies the novel with spectatorial literature—as I do here. Nor is it the fact that Richardson is singled out as a model. Most important, it seems to me, is the fact that here fiction is regarded as a form of moral philosophy that intends to propagate and exemplify a specific conception of the nature and identity of humankind: human beings as unchanging essence, neither perfect nor fully depraved, but as perfect as one ought to be—beings suited to place and rank in the creation, as Pope argued in his *Essay*. Moral fiction, then, brings into practice Pope's injunction that the proper study of mankind is man. In short, the authors and genres named earlier stood for and revealed a vision of the nature and identity of human beings which was at once universal (it could include both Socrates and Richardson) and heretical by strict Calvinist notions of human depravity.

It may now be easier to understand why the Dutch novel did not present a lifelike picture of the events of 1787. After all, the political event was no more than an individual incident, whereas fiction aspired to represent the general and universal qualities of virtuous human nature; contemporary revolutions were only of interest insofar as they illustrated a general moral point.[7] In fact, to the modern reader some eighteenth-century novels appear catechisms of moral philosophy or ideal human behavior rather than stories; and as such, they were, at least in part, intended. Richardson himself "digested" the "Moral and Instructive Sentiments, Cautions, Aphorisms, Reflections and Observa-

6. Adriaan Loosjes, *Verhandeling over de menschkunde* (Haarlem, 1786).
7. The titlepage of *Clarissa* carries the motto "Humanos mores nosse volenti / Sufficit una domus" ["If one wishes to know human behavior, one house suffices"]. In other words, the domestic emphasis in many eighteenth-century Dutch novels may also be regarded in the light of the economy provided by purposeful generalization.

tions, contained in the History of Clarissa, as [were] presumed to be of General Use and Service" under "proper heads" such as virtue, friendship, advice to women, providence, and prudence. This list, some eighty pages long, was appended to a later edition of the novel. Eventually, the author compiled a similar catechism from all three of his novels.

From this perspective, it is not so surprising to note that the translation, distribution, imitation, and emulation of English novels was in the Netherlands dominated by what the character Willem Leevend called the "tolerant churches," that is, the Mennonites and the Arminians, or Remonstrants. These groups traditionally shared an interest in practical Christianity, moral philosophy rather than dogmatic adherence to system, as well as a firm belief in humanity's inherent fitness for correction and improvement by education. Excluded from public office after the Synod of Dordt, they may have (not unlike the English dissenters after 1660) turned to writing, to the indirect, mediated communication of texts as an office to serve and educate the public as well as a means to divulge their antitrinitarian views about human nature. Although few in number, the Dutch dissenters were well represented among writers as well as among the Patriots. Thus, of Haarlem's 20,927 inhabitants in 1791, 12,109 were Reformed, 1,140 Mennonite, 67 Remonstrant, 6,239 Roman Catholic, 1,032 Lutheran, 114 Jewish, and 225 without denomination.[8] These proportions are virtually reversed when we look at the list of names involved in the transmission and production of moral philosophy: editors of spectatorial magazines, translators of Fielding and Richardson as well as many other philosophical, religious, or fictional works in English. Eventually, their activities led to the beginnings of a native tradition of serious prose fiction.

Of these men and women, the Mennonite minister Johannes Stinstra, who corresponded with Richardson about the translation of *Clarissa*, urging him to make a list of moral sentiments just as he himself used examples from *Pamela* to catechize his parishioners, may be the best known, but the list of names is long and prestigious.[9] Historically,

---

8. Municipal Archive, Haarlem 101 E 16. See *12 Opstellen over Haarlem e.o. in de Franse Tijd, 1780–1813* (Haarlem, 1983), p. 57.

9. Adriaan Verwer, son of the famous linguist, ought to be mentioned. Verwer contributed to Van Effen's *Hollandsche Spectator* (after berating him for his unfair treatment of the Mennonites). He wrote Van Effen's biography and contributed to the *Philanthrope*. He translated many works of serious English fiction, including *Amelia*. Stinstra tried to interest him in translating Richardson's *Sir Charles Grandison*. Other figures are Cornelis van Engelen, edi-

the connection between the Dutch dissenters and English moral philosophy began with an interest in English theology. From the days when the liberal theologian Jean le Clerc—advocate of the ideas of Locke—taught at the Remonstrant seminary (where Mennonites were also educated until 1735), an interest in literature was added to that in theology. His successor, J. J. Wetstein, continued this example; and it was his student and successor, A. A. van der Meersch, who in turn held a central position in the distribution of English texts around 1787. Van der Meersch had English correspondents (including William Warburton, Bishop of Gloucester—friend and critic of Richardson and Pope), edited the *Denker*, and contributed to numerous other spectatorial magazines.

Perhaps the implicit historical subtext of all this interest in moral philosophy was what Warburton, in a letter to Van der Meersch, referred to, with aversion, as the persecuting spirit of Calvinism. He went on to say that "the Ministers of the Calvinistical Church of Holland do not, nor are ever likely to abate their *intolerant* principles, yet in this enlightened Age (for which it is principally indebted to your Heroes) it is hoped, your Magistrates will no longer add terror to their *brutum fulmen*. Go on, Reverend Sir in supporting the Truth."[10] Thus the *Philanthrope* and the *Rhapsodist* were accused of heresy and unorthodoxy, just as the charge of Socinianism (anti-Trinitarianism) was an almost predictable event. Petrus Hofstede and Johannes Barueth, the self-proclaimed defenders of orthodoxy, openly declared war on the spectators. Hofstede founded his own magazine, and Barueth went as far as publishing a work titled "Literary Letters in Defense of the Dogma of the Ministers of the Reformed Church against the Secret Attacks in the Essays of the *Denker*."[11]

It may be useful here to consider what was new, "revolutionary,"

---

tor of the *Spectatoriaale Schouwburg* and contributor to the *Philanthrope*; Martin Schagen, Mennonite minister and man of letters who translated Hervey; Frans de Haes, poet, son of Joan de Haes, and cousin to Lucretia van Merken. De Haes signed his contributions to the *Philanthrope* "A." for Anglicanus. Of course, Cornelis and Pieter Loosjes, who started the *Vaderlandsche Letteroefeningen*, should not be forgotten; they made an important contribution to contemporary literary taste. The publishers Houttuin and Van Tongerlo, who over several years brought out three of the most prestigious spectators, need mention. Finally, the literary society *Laus Deo* and the publisher Meyer published a new translation of the Psalms to be sung in Remonstrant churches and agitated for a truly national literature in the vernacular.

10. Letter in archive of the Remonstrant seminary; Leiden University Library, RS 162, 4 April 1771.

11. J. Hartog, *De spectatoriale geschriften van 1741–1800* (Utrecht, 1890).

or anti-Calvinistic in this kind of writing. Jay Fliegelman argues that Locke's ideas about education and Hutcheson's emphasis on affective sociability combined in the works of Richardson to propagate a revision of the notion of authority that facilitated America's rejection of the father figure. Instead of the traditional, inherited, dogmatic, and literalist patriarchal concept of authority, *Pamela* and *Clarissa* presented a more egalitarian version in which the relationship between father and child is based on reasonable respect for human potential and characterized by affection.[12] No longer inherent in the institutional relation, authority grew conditional on moral quality and affection. Indeed, what was new about *Pamela* and *Clarissa* was not that they dramatized conflict with authority or defended individual autonomy— after all, drama and before that Greek romance had highlighted the conflict between generations. Strikingly original in Richardson was that he made sexual *virtue* the condition of authority and its educational ideal. It was an "invention" that provoked Diderot to an emphatic "Eloge" and Rousseau to a slightly perverse imitation in "La nouvelle Héloise." Thus Clarissa, who does not wish to marry the candidate her father singles out with the intention to elevate family rank, is partly forced, partly tricked into leaving her father's house. Increasingly isolated, socially outcast, raped, and ill, she nevertheless grows in the novel to the stature and reputation of a secular saint who commands authority, love, and respect from all who know her through the exemplary virtue of her character. Even Belford, and Lovelace, the aristocratic rake, finally become subject to Clarissa's moral perspective. While outcast from her father's house, Clarissa gathers around her a new affectionate group, a new family based on the voluntary ties of moral respect and friendship rather than the predestined and given one of blood relationship.

Thus Pope's moral philosophical premises that human beings can achieve the perfection of virtue appropriate to their place in creation was the rationale for a revisionist notion of authority and power. If we consider the rhetorical form, the model of communication of Richardson's fiction, it appears that the epistolary genre itself enacts this substitutive movement of revision. The author does not dictate to his readers; opinions are placed in contrasting dialogue in the shape of familiar letters. If the story dramatizes how, by means of the medium

12. Jay Fliegelman, *Prodigals and Pilgrims: The American Revolution against Patriarchal Authority, 1750–1800* (Cambridge, 1982).

of writing, Clarissa's confinement to the immediate and physical limitation to the actual is broken and a new community based on moral affinity and rational choice may be formed, that is also what the generic form of the novel itself intends and accomplishes with regard to its readership. Owing to the success of his fiction, Richardson himself became a moral authority, a "divine genius," whose wisdom was equal to that of Solomon in, for instance, the *Denker*.

If we look back to the novel's precursor—and, in the Netherlands, partner—the spectatorial magazine, we recognize a similar configuration of rhetoric, revisionist authority, and the new notion of human identity. Sending and receiving "letters" which in turn are printed and broadcast, the author creates a network of readers, an artificial family, addressed as friends. One of the striking aspects of the essays of Addison and Steele (in the famous and original *Spectator*) is that their authority is dialectical, based on example and exchange—the mutual response between writer and reader, and the intimate tone of familiarity. It does not inhere in the institution of authorship itself but is earned through greater insight and confirmed and affirmed by the readers' freely given response.

Seen in the Western European context, the Dutch Republic was slow in successfully imitating Richardson's example, while, perhaps paradoxically, it was exceptionally tenacious and prolific in the production of spectatorial magazines. The *Hollandsche Pamela* of 1754, which unites William III and Zoetje Gerbrands in a common aversion to the custom of dueling, completely misses the dialectical Richardsonian point. It celebrates the workings of divine providence, and, as P. J. Buijnsters argues, this early novel affirms aristocratic norms.[13] It was not until 1782, with Wolff and Deken's *Sara Burgerhart*, conventionally regarded as the first Dutch novel worthy of that name, that Richardson's form and ideas were transplanted to Dutch soil. Perhaps the slowness of assimilation was due to Calvinist aversion to Richardson's dramatization of human relationships, which gave human beings more freedom and greater perfection than Calvinist dogmas of predestination and original sin allowed. Egbert Buys, at any rate, in a long essay in the 1780s on the perils of mimetic writing, concludes after a perverse misreading of Richardson's novel that "*Clarissa* proves that no amount of suffering can justify the breach of moral duty, and

13. P. J. Buijnsters, ed., introduction to *Historie van Mejuffrouw Sara Burgerhart* (The Hague, 1980), p. 20.

that the obedience which children owe their parents is . . . inevitable."
With regard to Fielding's *Amelia*—another attempt to paint the portrait of fully virtuous and admirable human nature—Buys's almost sa-
distic suggestion is that "the many accidents that befall [the heroine],
serve as examples to warn others against marrying without their parents' consent."[14]

Whether the subtext of the rise of the novel in the Dutch Republic
was indeed the debate on the nature of human identity is difficult to
establish, since the media that printed book reviews were dominated by
the dissenters. We can only sense profound disagreement over the nature of human identity from a few texts: the antagonism between Egbert Buys and the *Vaderlandsche Letteroefeningen*, or the marked difference in opinion on one and the same text between that periodical
and the *Nederlandsche Bibliotheek*, which harped on the "imaginary
wisdom of this world" and the "deleterious products of luxurious
imagination," or the insufficient emphasis on "man's natural depravity
and the need for the Grace of the Holy Spirit."[15]

Although it was not until *Sara Burgerhart* that the Richardsonian
example took Dutch root, it is interesting to note that one of Wolff's
earliest efforts in the genre of the familiar letter was a satiric attack on
the authors of the *Nederlandsche Bibliotheek* in defense of Nozeman
(protagonist in the Socratic war) titled *Brieven van Cornelia Paulina
Dortsma*.[16] To the historian it may be interesting to add that one of its
points of ridicule is the accusation that the dissenters were enemies of
the House of Orange.

Wolff and Deken's debt to Richardson has been questioned recently. This seems unnecessary to me, since Richardson's characters
served as models for personal conduct. A poem for the wedding of a
personal friend in 1774 ends with a comparison of the "excellent"
groom to "Charles Grandison"; and from all Wolff's writings ema-
nates the suggestion that Richardson's characters were a realized
(*aanschouwelijk*) example of virtue. It was, moreover, Wolff and Deken's stated intention to adapt Richardson's glorious image of human
beings to Dutch cirumstances. The history of Sara Burgerhart demonstrates how a young woman attains moral authority and perfection

14. Egbert Buys, "Van de uitwerksels van *Romannen*, op de gemoederen der jeugd," *De
Hollandsche Wijsgeer* 4:107–116.

15. *Nederlandsche Bibliotheek*, vol. 8, pt. 1, pp. 441–447, 556–561.

16. Betje Wolff, *Brieven van Cornelia Paulina Dortsma . . . geschreven aan haar nicht
Scriblera te Utrecht* (Hoorn, 1776).

through insight and correction. What is significant, though, is that Wolff and Deken's Dutch imitation—let alone that of their epigones—reduces the dialogical complexity of *Clarissa* to an almost straightforward moral philosophical (*menschkundig*) essay. *Sara Burgerhart* (and *Willem Leevend* to an even greater extent) are lacking in narrative impulse. It is not surprising that the *Brieven van Abraham Blankaart*, one of their later works of fiction, should be a compilation of disquisitions on points of practical Christianity and social behavior which reverts to the model of the spectatorial essay.

What remains evident, though, is that their work clearly embodies egalitarian ideas. Sara Burgerhart flees the dogmatic authority of a blood relative to gather around her a new family of friends united by notions of tolerance. Wolff and Deken's fiction glorifies marriage and domesticity, not as institution, but because marriage offers the opportunity to select the most intimate friend and to create a circle of elective affinity—*wahlverwandtschaft*. Authority in these novels derives not from institutional power but from freely given moral consent. Characters such as the widow Spilgoed, Christina de Vrij, or Abraham Blankaart become the central moral focus and arbiters of their world through realized example. Finally, the relation between authority figures and their subjects is marked by the dialogical give and take Wolff and Deken call "friendship"—the ideal relation between parents and children is that of friends. As the letters between Sara and her friend Anna, or between Willem and Lotje, show, friendship entails the moral duty to guide and correct: "See here . . . what my friendship commands me to put down?" (*Willem Leevend*) marks the spirit of many a moralistic passage in these novels. Indeed, the example of moral virtue makes obedience a pleasure. Willem Leevend states, with regard to Mrs. Helder, one of Wolff and Deken's paragons of female virtue, "It is a delight to be punished by such a woman; what must it be to receive her approval." The authoritarian parent, on the other hand, is shown as a boorish, dogmatic, and finally foolish simpleton who brooks no argument and insists on a categorical difference between parent and child that prohibits comparison and criticism. Thus, Van Oldenburg addresses the mature Willem Leevend: "How now, infant, do you compare yourself to me?"

Again, important in this phenomenon of serious fiction is the fact that the ideal of friendship and education through moral example is not only staged as narrative. The form enacts its ideal of gentle persuasion. It places different opinions on matters of religion and conduct in

prismatic reflection through different spokespersons and correspondents. It leaves conclusions about right and wrong to the reader. Nowhere is dogmatic truth prescribed or asserted; the reader is trusted to
draw his or her own conclusions. No wonder then that *Willem Leevend* especially, which presents a wide range of opinions on the nature
of human beings and their relationship to their Maker, should have
raised such virulent opposition. The most malicious reaction came
from an anonymous orthodox Reformed minister and Orangist who
accused it of the heresy of Socinianism. Lotje Roulin's expectations of
heaven are ridiculed by the suggestion that in her heaven surely "the
Sodomite Socrates is . . . President."[17]

What is the use of this literary-historical discussion for our understanding of the revolution of 1787? Perhaps little in a factual way;
after all, the debate about literature articulated itself as a religious debate, not a political matter. Taking a longer perspective, however, it
may help to affirm some of the conclusions to which historians have
already come; religious opinion was political, since the dissenters were
excluded from public office. It is not accidental, then, that the dissenters predominated in both literary and anti-Orangist circles. Nor
does it seem irrelevant that the form in which Patriot sentiment expressed itself, its model of conviction and authority, was the spectatorial essay. Both the *Politieke Kruyer* and the *Post van den Neder-
Rhijn* offered themselves as guides whose greater wisdom, deriving
from better insight and information, was available for their reading
public. Thus, the authors of the *Post* argue, in their own defense, in the
preface to *Pleydoye in de zaak van de Post van den Neder-Rhijn* (Utrecht,
1785), that they "have made the greatest effort to bring home to the
ignorant Dutchmen their true interest; to make them see, what they
had been, what they are now; to expose their hidden enemies who
intend their downfall, and to paint those in dark, though true colors."
They demonstrate, moreover, their aversion to dogmatic authority by
incorporating queries and criticism from the public in their pages, and
in using the dialogue as a didactic form. Perhaps most significant is the
authors' expressed desire for the friendship of their honored correspondents.

I also find the positions taken by the proponents of the Dutch novel
significant on another level. They suggest that the revolution of 1787
was, in the final analysis, a rebellion not against the institution of polit-

17. P. J. Buijnsters, *Betje Wolff en Aagje Deken* (The Hague, 1984), p. 227.

ical authority but against its lack of moral example and conviction. It was a matter of *menschkunde*, moral philosophy, and it hinged, for the proponents of the novel, on the question of the identity and nature of the Dutch. The purpose of much Patriot writing was to elevate, to correct the follies and vices of contemporary manners which, as they saw it, imperiled the time-honored national identity. Just as Sara Burgerhart had to learn, through friendly admonishment and hard experience, that pleasure and entertainment imperiled her prospects and identity, just so, the Dutch republic might come to see its own true interest.

I began this chapter with a reference to Adriaan Loosjes; I should like to end it with him, too. In him, political commitment and literary practise fused—even more clearly perhaps than in the case of Wolff and Deken, whose only notable successor he was before the 1830s. His *Historie van Mejuffrouw Susanna Bronkhorst* of 1806 is a straightforward *Clarissa* imitation. More representative of his intentions, however, are the countless stories, dramatic sketches, and novels that portray an ideal Dutch character: frugal, charitable, sociable, courageous, disinterested, and tolerant in religion. Loosjes intended the fictional recreation of the Dutch past to remind his compatriots of their true identity, of what they could become again if they would give up their luxurious and sensual habits. To the twentieth-century reader, this image of solid moral Dutch identity is primarily a fictional construct. But to Loosjes and his contemporaries it was real; in fact, the fiction of identity supported the political debate. I have argued that in the Netherlands fiction owed its viability, its seeming natural reality, to that paradoxical vision of human nature and identity perhaps best argued and illustrated in Pope's *Essay on Man*, which had received actuality and truth (*aanschouwelijkheid*) in Richardson's *Clarissa*. In this sense could late eighteenth-century revolutionaries like John Adams say, "the people . . . are Clarissa."[18]

18. Fliegelman, *Prodigals and Pilgrims*, p. 89, citing Adams's letter to William Cunningham of 15 March 1804.

# 12

# Literary Sociability in the Netherlands, 1750–1840

## W. van den Berg

JUST as the flowering of arts and sciences is desirable and pleasant for every reasonable human being, so it is certain that these can nowhere be more advanced than by the founding of societies."—thus wrote a member of the literary society *Dulces ante Omnia Musae* from Utrecht in 1761.[1] Six years later, Jacob Lutkeman, a member of the Amsterdam society *Diligentiae Omnia*, spoke to the same effect in an essay with the telling title *Verhandeling over het nut der genootschappen ter bevordering van kunsten en wetenschappen* (Discourse on the Use of Societies for the Advancement of Arts and Sciences): "It is an undeniable truth, confirmed by reason and experience, that in practicing all useful arts and fine sciences, . . . daily contact and friendship with such people as are, with us, fellow practitioners of the same art or science . . . contributes not a little to excellent progress toward our intended goal."[2] Both society members touched on a keystone of the ideology of eighteenth-century sociability: progress in arts and sciences can be expected only from joint efforts. Approximately 70 years later, Jacob Geel denounced this topos of sociability by stating that "most societies, being instructive, that is, *teaching* bodies, have really served their time. They are burned-out craters, where Tom, Dick, and Harry,

---

1. *Maendelyksche By-dragen ter opbouw van Neer-land's Tael- en Dichtkunde*, vol. 34 (Utrecht, 1761), p. 181.
2. See the records of *Diligentiae Omnia* in the Royal Library, The Hague, cat. no. KA 180.

young and old, can sit at ease and without danger." And, he wickedly added, "though I would not wish, for that matter, that they were demolished and leveled with the ground: they are physically useful and teach how to climb."[3] The initial unlimited optimism that members could push one another to the top of the "Aenion Mount" had disappeared. The Helicon metaphor gave way to that of an extinct volcano.

Only recently has there been a revival of interest in the private societies and sociability of the eighteenth century. Literary historians have now become interested in the entire communication system in which literature is produced, distributed, and consumed. The focus on the literary scene as a whole has led to the discovery of literary sociability as an attractive object of study. Study of sociability in general, as initiated particularly by W. W. Mijnhardt, has also had a stimulating effect.[4]

There is a persistent misunderstanding that literary sociability in the Netherlands was a specifically eighteenth-century phenomenon. In contrast to the condemnation by Geel quoted earlier, I here try to show that literary sociability continued to play an important, albeit changed, role even after 1800. A confrontation of eighteenth- and nineteenth-century forms of literary sociability can help to identify essential differences. In the process, this comparison should also throw into sharper relief the distinctive characteristics of eighteenth-century sociability.

We possess an extremely useful inventory of literary societies for the years 1748–1800, including a list of publications and an account of the prize contests and prize entries that have been published.[5] Furthermore, we have a detailed description of two major literary societies as well as a handful of pilot studies.[6] On this basis, it is possible to

---

3. Jacob Geel, *Onderzoek en phantasie* (Leiden, 1838), pp. 56–57.

4. Of his many publications on societies, I mention here only, "Het Nederlandse genootschap in de achttiende en vroege negentiende eeuw," *De Negentiende Eeuw* 7 (1983): 76–101, and *Tot heil van 't menschdom: Culturele genootschappen in Nederland, 1750–1815* (Amsterdam, 1987). See also Chapter 9, this volume.

5. J. J. Kloek et al., "Literaire genootschappen, 1748–1800," *Documentatieblad Werkgroep Achttiende Eeuw* 15 (1983): 21–89. For a recent supplement, see C. B. F. Singeling, "Literaire genootschappen, 1748–1800: Aanvullingen en correcties," *Documentatieblad Werkgroep Achttiende Eeuw* 18 (1986): 65–74.

6. H.A. Höweler, "Uit de geschiedenis van het Haagsche dichtgenootschap *Kunstliefde spaart geen vlijt, 1772–1818*," *Tijdschrift voor Nederlandsche taal- en letterkunde* 56 (1937): 97–184; B. Thobokholt, *Het taal- en dichtlievend genootschap Kunst wordt door arbeid verkreegen te Leiden, 1766–1800* (Utrecht, 1983). Pilot studies include Kees Singeling, "De gezellige dichter: Over literaire genootschappen in de achttiende eeuw," *Literatuur* 3 (1986): 93–100; C. B. F. Singeling, "De lidmaatschappen van Ahasverus van den Berg of Nederlandse literaire genootschappelijkheid, 1750–1800, in vogelvlucht," *Documentatieblad Werkgroep Achttiende eeuw* 19 (1987): 31–46; W. van den Berg, "Het literaire genootschapsleven in de eerste helft van de negentiende eeuw," *De Negentiende Eeuw* 7 (1983):

make several observations. The concept of sociability has two definitions, which can be described as strict and broad. Those using the strict
definition speak about a society only if institutionalization and regulation of procedures through principles or laws can be demonstrated. For
those using a broader definition, a society qualifies with less formaliza-
tion: a date of foundation, a seat, a name or motto, membership, a
certain regularity in meeting suffice. Although there are examples of
extremely small societies with strict regulations, it seems likely that a
more explicit form of organization is required when a society is larger.
Since I want to include very small societies, I use the broad definition
of the term. I consider societies "literary" in the comprehensive eight-
eenth- and early nineteenth-century meaning of poetry and eloquence,
thus including linguistics, the knowledge of antiquity, and history.

Following Singeling, I confine myself to those societies that actively
dealt with literature, that is, societies in which the writing of poetry or
speeches was central or in which members were expected to express
themselves reflectively about literature in essays, critical notes, or theoretical dissertations.[7] I exclude passive societies in which acquisition
and collective reading of literature was the pivotal occupation, the so-
called reading societies. These societies, often with a highly formalized
structure, played a significant part in literary sociability, and their
number increased rapidly in the second half of the eighteenth century.
A provisional estimate is over three hundred reading societies in the
Dutch Republic in the eighteenth century and over eight hundred in the
nineteenth.[8] This category of society is useful for, among other things,
examining the reading public and reading preferences, be it that records have been handed down in scanty measure only. My distinction
between an active literary society and a purely passive reading society
is somewhat artificial; both the eighteenth and the nineteenth centuries
show examples of active societies that developed from reading societies.

Nineteenth-century commentators such as De Vries and Siewertsz
van Reesema placed the heyday of sociability in the first half of the

146–178; W. van den Berg, "Sociabiliteit, genootschappelijkheid en de orale cultus," in *Historische letterkunde*, ed. M. Spies (Groningen, 1984), pp. 151–170.

7. Singeling, "De gezellige dichter."

8. P. J. Buijnsters, "Nederlandse leesgezelschappen uit de 18e eeuw," in his *Nederlandse
literatuur van de achttiende eeuw* (Utrecht, 1984), pp. 183–198. For an exploration of the
nineteenth century, see Peter van Zonneveld, "Het leesgezelschap *Miscens Utile Dulci* te
Leiden in de periode 1830–1840," in *Nederlandse literatuur van de negentiende eeuw*, ed. W.
van den Berg and Peter van Zonneveld (Utrecht, 1986), pp. 92–102.

eighteenth century. They relied on the authority of Lublink de Jonge, who stated that more than thirty literary societies were founded between 1680 and 1715. Te Winkel was the first to deflate this view. As the aforementioned inventory confirms, the boom of literary societies must be situated in the second half of the eighteenth century, with a notable concentration in the 1770s and 1780s.[9] At a rough estimate, we are dealing with approximately forty societies in which about two thousand members were involved and produced something like 160 smaller and larger collections of poetry. There are great differences in lifespan among these societies. Some faded away after a few years, whereas others lasted for decades. Some started and ended with only a few members, whereas others grew rapidly and boasted of more than 150 members during peak years. The societies concentrated mainly in the provinces of Holland and Utrecht, and within these mainly in Amsterdam, Leiden, Rotterdam, The Hague, and Utrecht. The rest were in the smaller surrounding towns such as Haarlem, Schiedam, Dordrecht, and Gouda. Outside this circle they rarely occurred; exceptional examples were in Groningen and Vlissingen. The approximate number of forty societies mentioned here is based on preserved records, publications, and mentions in literary-historical sources.

The question is, however, whether there were not many more small societies, which operated in such privacy that they can no longer be traced. This supposition is prompted by, among other things, the accidental discovery of several such societies. I give two examples. In a "Ontwerp van een lijst van Amsterdamsche genootschappen en ver-eenigingen in de 18e eeuw" (Design for a List of Amsterdam Societies and Associations in the Eighteenth Century), one will search fruitlessly for a small society called *Tot Leerzaam Vermaak* (For Instructive Pleasure), which, incidentally, did not confine itself to literature.[10] This society, founded in 1774, consisted of five people. Even those who work with the strict definition of a society cannot deny that name to this

9. J. de Vries, "Antwoord op de vraag: Welke zijn de vorderingen, Welke is de veragtering der Nederduitsche dichtkunde, gedurende de achttiende eeuw, in vergelijking met vroegere tijdperken," *Werken der Bataafsche Maatschappij*, vol. 5 (Amsterdam, 1809); W. Siewertsz van Reesema, "Redevoering over dicht- en letterkundige genootschappen in ons vaderland," *Nieuwe werken der Hollandsche maatschappij van fraaije kunsten en wetenschappen* (Leiden, 1850), p. 17; J. Lublink de Jonge, "Over het vergelijken van de oude en de hedendaagsche dichters," *Algemeen magazijn van wetenschap, konst en smaak*, vol. 1, no. 2 (1785), p. 867; J. te Winkel, *De ontwikkelingsgang der Nederlandsche letterkunde*, vol. 5 (Haarlem, 1924), pp. 516–537.

10. W. R. Veder, "Ontwerp van een lijst van Amsterdamsche genootschappen en ver-eenigingen in de 18e eeuw," *Amstelodamum* 2 (1903): 123–138.

small society; at its first meeting, sixteen laws were laid down. Members read books together, were obliged to submit essays, kept to a regular schedule of meetings, and worked with an ingenious system of fines. Since no works of the society were published, nor prize contests organized, this small society with a largely Mennonite character, of which no fewer than 248 meetings were minuted and which was active at least until 1800, would never have been known to us were it not for the book historian I. H. van Eeghen, who discovered the records in the inheritance of a relative.[11] My second example concerns the small *Kunst en Vriendschap* (Art and Friendship), founded by Willem de Clercq and some friends in 1813 and defunct after six years. Short-lived and with a small membership, this group was a society in only the weakest sense. During meetings, held every two or three weeks, the members proposed poetic themes to each other, to be worked into a poem, which was then the subject of lengthy discussion. It was only when M. H. Schenkeveld was searching through the De Clercq records that she came across the society's documents.[12] It seems likely that these lucky finds are representative of a large group of silent societies, the traces of which have not been discovered, or have been erased, or never existed.

Uncertainty also persists with regard to the lifespan of certain societies. This is not a problem for the large literary societies, of which, in addition to publications, correspondence and extensive minutes have often been handed down. But what about the small society, whose archive was not preserved and whose communal activities are indicated by only one modest volume? Was it silently active for years before risking publication, and did it expire after that effort, or did it continue for years in seclusion? The picture of the extent of the cult of literary societies presented here is also slightly distorted in that only societies with the pursuit of literature as their main goal are taken into account. In both the eighteenth and nineteenth centuries, however, there were general cultural societies with programs that included, for example, music, drawing, and physics, in addition to literature. The aforementioned inventory lists fifteen such societies that gave a more marginal position to literature. But even if one considers only the approximately forty purely literary societies, there is such diversity that a further typology is desirable. Singeling proposed to distinguish between critical-

11. I. H. van Eeghen, "Het genootschap *Tot leerzaam vermaak*," *Amstelodamum* 47 (1960): 8–16.

12. M. H. Schenkeveld, *Willem de Clercq en de literatuur* (Groningen, 1962), pp. 8–9.

reflective and creative societies. It is, however, difficult to draw a hard and fast line between these two; the first group consists of societies in which the writing of poetry also received attention, and in creative societies theoretical aspects were not completely neglected in later years. A few excepted, critical-reflective societies preceded creative ones. They originated in academic or related circles, carried Latin mottoes, and recruited their members from students and professors.

Leiden's *Linguaque Animoque Fideles*, founded in 1757, and Utrecht's *Dulces ante Omnia Musae*, dating from 1759, are good representatives of such societies.[13] Their aim was the advancement of the Dutch language, national history, and literature, subjects that suffered at universities for the lack of chairs. The laws of the Utrecht society *Dulces* which have been preserved reveal an ambitious program every week. Each member of the company of six had to gather some twenty passages from contemporary and older literature which could be regarded as ornaments of poetry or which were linguistically relevant. Apart from that, there was an obligation to hand in an essay or poem, and members took turns reading a self-composed or translated speech, written in a lofty, ornamental style and conforming to several linguistic rules laid down by such authorities as Ten Kate and Huydecoper. Subsequently, fellow members criticized the written contributions. Time allowing, the members read books on linguistics together, extracting criteria for the evaluation of their own products.

Similar activities took place in Leiden. Moreover, through so-called external membership, members attended both societies. In some cases, the results of the exertions of these societies were published in a periodical with the telling title *Bijdragen tot opbouw van de vaderlandsche letterkunde* (Contributions to the Improvement of the Dutch Language)—thus acquainting a larger public with the ideas of these small, private student clubs. But, according to the Leiden merchant Van Lelyveld, "in order to make good progress in the reformation and cultivation of Dutch taste and literature," the matter had to be taken up on a larger scale. What he had in mind was a national society comparable to the *Académie Française*. In letters to Van Goens he repeatedly advanced his ideas. There were "a great many people . . . with certain natural talents, which will remain hidden if they are not encouraged." What was needed were a few people capable of leading the way by

13. For these societies, see J. Wille, *De literator R. M. van Goens en zijn kring* (Zutphen, 1937), and Singeling, "De gezellige dichter."

"rousing those naturally talented persons from their sleep, helping them to think, to work," and then the "reformation" of Dutch literature would occur.[14] With the foundation of the *Maatschappij der Nederlandsche Letterkunde* (Society for Dutch Literature) in 1766, Van Lelyveld saw his dream come true. This supralocal association, which still exists, brought together and expanded the activities of the small critical-reflective societies. By means of prize contests and the publication of a series of "Works" containing literary and linguistic essays, members tried to raise the level of the study of Dutch language and literature.[15]

Creative societies, or what could be called poetry clubs, differed from critical-reflective societies in having a more diverse membership and different types of activities. The tone was no longer set by students from academic circles but by the well-to-do bourgeoisie from urban communities: church ministers, lawyers, officers, medical doctors, notaries, booksellers, and successful merchants. We can deduce this from the membership lists of the larger creative societies. If we are to believe Lucas Pater, in the Amsterdam society *Diligentiae Omnia* not only young and old but also high and low in society were united by ties of friendship, although one can hardly suppose those distinctions ever to have been very significant.[16] Owing to illiteracy, the lower social milieus stood no chance of membership. The membership of Jacob van Dijk, explicitly mentioned as "formerly working in dredging," seems rather an exception than the rule in literary societies. The same holds true for women. Their role in societies, in the nineteenth century as well, remained marginal: an occasional honorary membership, or an award if a woman bested her male fellow poets in prize contests.

The activities in creative societies were geared toward the produc-

14. *Brieven aan R. M. van Goens*, vol. 1 (Utrecht, 1884), pp. 155–156. The child prodigy Rijklof Michaël van Goens—appointed professor of Greek, rhetoric, and history at the early age of eighteen—took up Van Lelyveld's proposal in his *Bedenkingen van den philosophe sans fard* (Considerations of the philosophe sans fard, 1766) and plead for the establishment of an artistic society modeled after the Italian *Academia della Crusca* or the French *Académie Française* in order to put a stop to the decline of Dutch literature. In his view, a society for national literature and letters might have a stimulating effect, if it could pride itself on the active support of "distinguished people": "Fortunate he among us who shall follow in the footsteps of Louis XIV: happy those who shall be our Richelieus!" (p. 466).

15. For this association, see F. K. H. Kossmann, *Opkomst en voortgang van de Maatschappij der Nederlandse letterkunde te Leiden* (Leiden, 1966), as well as *Gedenkboek bij het 200-jarig bestaan van de Maatschappij der Nederlandse letterkunde te Leiden* (Leiden, 1966).

16. Lucas Pater, *Redevoering over het nut der vriendschap ter bevordering van kunsten en wetenschappen* in the Municipal Record Office [Gemeente-archief] Amsterdam, Inv. no. S. 953.102.

tion of poetry. What counted was the acquisition of more poetic skills, resulting in a collection of poetry published by the society if the quality permitted it, and not the improvement of Dutch literature through the study of language and literature. Underlying this attitude was a notion of literature with normative traits, which suited well the ideal of sociability and legitimized collective poetic effort. After all, the contemporary classicist concept of literature articulated specific rules and laws by which actual poems could be tested. Appealing to the rules, it was possible to discuss the relative merits of a poem and to suggest corrections. Though it was not denied that poets were born, it was thought that rough genius needed polishing. "Practice makes perfect" was the device of an epoch in which the flawless line of poetry was held in esteem as an artistic ideal. Lucas Pater voiced the general opinion in referring to "a century like this, in which the purity of poetry, the correctness of language are required so strongly that a poem, though it be powerful, to the point, and composed according to the required rules, loses much of its splendor should one or two of these requirements have been infringed upon." The "instructive gatherings and friendly conversations with literary friends" may, according to the same spokesman, "help us to improve, and will show us failings which we failed to notice through oversight."[17] Polishing and admonishing, members helped each other along the way, or rather—in a pet metaphor of literary sociability—upward, up the slope of steep Mount Helicon. Reaching the top was a privilege reserved for inspired poets; but this did not mean that lesser talents should refrain from trying. The literary society offered the average or mediocre, but diligent, talent an opportunity to advance in the hierarchy of poets. This optimistic confidence is even reflected in their mottoes and devices: *Kunst Wordt door Arbeid Verkreegen* (Art is Won by Labor), *Kunstliefde Spaart Geen Vlijt* (Love of Art Spares No Diligence), *Door Oefening werd Veel Verkreegen* (Much has been achieved by Exercise). To what extent versifying was considered a collective enterprise is evident from the manner of presentation of the poems in the volumes published by the societies: the names of the makers are not listed, or the initials suffice.

To do justice to the diversity of creative societies, a further typology is desirable. In this, I follow the division made by Bonn and Scharp at the turn of the eighteenth century.[18] In their classification, it is crucial

17. Ibid.
18. Andreas Bonn, "Antwoord op de vraag: Welke schikkingen kunnen 'er, door de gezamenlijke geleerde Maatschappijen in ons Vaderland gemaakt worden," in *Verhandelingen*

whether a society sought the limelight or not. I divide the creative societies into more "closed" and more "open" societies, not supposing the dividing line to be clear-cut but assuming a continuum from more closed to more open. Accordingly, society is of the closed kind when mutual encouragement, refinement, or exercise were considered sufficient. Self-expression and recognition of qualities in the intimate circle sufficed. Seclusion from the outer world was cultivated by this attitude; work was done behind closed doors. The histories of the larger societies almost always mention an initial phase in which the society functioned as a closed association.

A closed character and small membership often coincided, but not always. Some small clubs published modest collections of poetry, and some sizable associations, such as the nineteenth-century V.W. and the Dordrecht society *Diversa sed Una*, eschewed publicity.[19] Nor can it be argued that closed associations always had an informal organizational structure. Some closed societies, such as W. de Clercq's *Kunst en Vriendschap*, had detailed codes of behavior from the very start. Sometimes members of closed societies took initiatives within their own circle that were a vital part of an open society, such as the organization of prize contests or the awarding of prize medals; this was true, for instance, in Amsterdam's V.W. More or less open societies aimed at publicity, often quite modest, in the form of a small volume of poetry with the name of the society. Their openness increased when, following the example of the large scientific societies, they organized prize contests and advertised in local and national newspapers, recruited distant members, acquired large premises, and convened annual meetings.

The urge for externalization in the more open societies makes it easier for us to reconstruct their procedures, activities, and organizational structures. It is not without reason that we know most about the four urban societies from Rotterdam, Amsterdam, Leiden, and The Hague, which published books of poetry and organized prize contests. Even if records are virtually nonexistent, as with the Rotterdam society *Studium Scientiarum Genitrix* (founded in 1773) and the *Amsteldamsche Dicht- en Letteroefenend Genootschap. Wij Streeven naar Volmaaktheid* (Amsterdam Society for Poetry and Literature. We Strive

---

*uitgegeven door het Zeeuwsch genootschap der wetenschappen te Vlissingen*, vol. 14 (Middelburg, 1790); J. Scharp, *Inwijdingsredevoering: Zijnde eene verhandeling over de letterkundige maatschappijen in het algemeen, en dit genootschap in het bijzonder* (Rotterdam, 1807).
    19. For these societies, see W. van den Berg, "Het literaire genootschapsleven."

for Perfection) (founded in 1783), it is possible to gain reasonable insight from the way these societies presented their publications. It was common to introduce collections of poetry with a reasonably detailed account of the society's foundation, activities, and membership, complete with lists of members. This form of self-promotion was probably introduced in 1773 by the society *Kunstliefde Spaart geen Vlijt* from The Hague, and other larger societies imitated it. The introductory discourse functioned to announce a society to the public as an association of a certain importance; one turns oneself inside out in an attempt to impress people.

Detailed accounts were given by the *Kunstliefde* of how the social, artistic, and financial prestige of the society had been secured by a sophisticated differentiation among members. Highest on the list was the category of members crucial for the social standing of the society: government officials, such as grand pensionaries (Steyn, Van de Spiegel, even Schimmelpenninck later on), the mayor, and aldermen of The Hague, with the protection of King William I as a supreme triumph in 1814, were included as protectors or patrons. Thanks to these connections, the Mauritshuis was available for board meetings and the annual meetings of the society. The protectors, usually four or five in number, were exempt from writing poetry, although they were involved pro forma in the judgment of prize verse. Artistic status was procured by the society through recruiting so-called extraordinary honorary members, poets of high reputation, the "brilliantly shining stars that decorate the pinnacles of the sacred Temple of Poetry," as the preface has it.[20] They, too, played a purely ornamental part, although an occasional contribution to add luster to a society publication was highly appreciated. A third and also the most sizable category of members, the contributing members, recruited from wealthy devotees of the arts, had to secure the financial well-being of the society by paying a considerable annual fee. In return, this group, consisting of almost a hundred people during peak years, was exempted from writing verse and admitted to annual meetings. The raison d'être of the society, the creation of poetry, was limited to a relatively small group, no more than twelve at first, of the extraordinary members.

The *Kunstliefde* also cared about *nachwuchs*, a special category of members was made up of "striplings," children with outstanding poetic talent. Guided by one of the board members, they were led step by

---

20. *Proeven van poëtische mengelstoffen* (Leiden, 1773), XXI–XXII.

step up the slopes of Mount Helicon, to be promoted to the ranks of extraordinary members after showing convincing proof of ability. Such an ingenious membership system required a great deal of organizational attention and talent. This was the task of the ordinary or board members—at first five "admirers and writers of Dutch poetry," senior members who had founded the society.[21] This was the most powerful group in the society; they selected the members in other categories, wrote poetry themselves, organized the prize contests, and had final say in the judgment of the entries.

Other large urban societies modeled themselves on the *Kunstliefde* in their procedures and organizational structure. By the middle of the 1780s, such large societies in Amsterdam, Rotterdam, and Leiden, with memberships between 100 and 170 persons, left the other societies far behind. It should be remembered, however, that only one-quarter to one-third of the members were actively engaged in collective poetic practice. The rest were decorations or sponsors. That the striving for publicity was determined partly by concern for the prestige of one's hometown is clear from the preface of the first publication of the Rotterdam society *Studium Scientiarum Genitrix*:

Maybe we would never have taken this step, if the laudable societies founded in neighboring towns had not encouraged us to follow their example in our endeavors too to present ourselves to the public. We were sorry to see that our hometown, art-breeding Rotterdam, formerly the seat of the Muses, . . . was now so poorly blessed with honest makers of divine poetry that it was well-nigh impossible to discover some trace of well-organized linguistic or literary societies or meetings.[22]

A final word about poetic output: here too, we note great uniformity in presentation and content. The collections usually begin with a section of religious verse, followed by moral-didactic verse and poems on various subjects, and conclude with the prize winning poems. The poems are not the product of an expressive conception of the art, but of a pragmatic notion of poetry that tends to emphasize the *utile* over the *dulce*. As the preface of a volume of poems by the society *Oefening Kweekt Kennis* (Practice Fosters Knowledge) tells us, didactic moral

---

21. Ibid., VI.
22. *Dichtoeffeningen van het kunstlievende genootschap, onder de spreuk Studium scientiarum genitrix*, 2d ed. (Dordrecht, 1789), VI–VII.

lessons and truths are less effective when presented in the form of discursive prose than in metrical lines. It is not surprising that almost all such poems are strongly moralistic and burst their seams with instructive examples. Though negligible as poetry, they deserve more attention than they had received hitherto, for they reveal much about contemporary notions of the true poet, the influence of the arts on society, the best education for the young, the ideal marriage, the outstanding citizen, philanthropy, the freedom of the printing press, the mark of the true Christian, and many other matters. They form an instructive source regarding the civilizing ideal subscribed to by the average citizen.

At the end of the eighteenth century, these societies declined rapidly. Most disappeared unnoticed; the larger societies managed to save themselves by merging. How can we explain this decline? Let me hazard two explanations.

In the first place, changes in the conception of literature seem to be responsible. Under the influence of the German cult of poetic genius, poetry was seen in a different light: individuality and originality were valued highly. This attitude can be seen, for instance, in Van Alphen's *Verhandeling over het aangeboorne in de poëzij* (Essay on the Innate Qualities of Poetry) of 1782, and it is significant that Van Alphen explicitly mentions societies toward the end of his long dissertation. In his opinion, one should write poetry only if gifted with an innate, natural talent. He wonders if "that large number of societies for poetry, which increased so much in a few years' time in this country, is not more disadvantageous than advantageous to our literature." Such highly esteemed poets as Bellamy and Bilderdijk, who initially suscribed to the ideology of sociability and had won fame through the societies, later dissociated themselves from the society culture in the name of true poetry. Bilderdijk's famous *De kunst der poëzij* (The Art of Poetry) of 1809 is not only an avowal of a romantic idea of poetry but also an unusually sharp settling of accounts with the "chattering quacking of ducks," of "deluded poets" for whom "hobbyism" equalled poetry.[23] This new idea of literature deflated the belief in a collective training in poetry and thus reduced the claims of the literary societies. Literary sociability therefore assumed a different shape in the nineteenth century.

23. H. van Alphen, *Digtlcundige Verhanclelingen* (Utrecht, 1782); W. Bilderdijk *Winterbloemen*, vol. 1 (Haarlem, 1811).

The decline of literary sociability in the last decade of the eighteenth century also seems to be related to the turbulent political situation. Complete neutrality in religious and political matters may be the cornerstone of the ideology of sociability, but there are signs that this neutrality could not be maintained completely. The *Kunstliefde* from The Hague, for instance, was known to sympathize with the Orangist cause. In 1789, it organized a prize contest with the theme of the planned marriage between the daughter of stadholder William V and Charles-George of Brunswijk-Wolfenbüttel. Two years later, the marriage vows of William V and Wilhelmina of Prussia also occasioned a prize contest. Rev. van Spaan, founder and for years a highly esteemed president of *Kunstliefde*, was nevertheless turned out in 1787 when it became clear that his sympathies had changed from Orangist to Patriot. An indication of the political leanings of The Hague and Rotterdam societies can be found in a letter of 1798 by the secretary of *Studium*, in which he terminated all contacts with *Kunstliefde* because this society suppressed the principles of liberty "during the slavery under the House of Orange" by the "illegal removal of a great many worthy Dutch poets, members of our society, after the vile triumph of the Prussian hirelings."[24] In the Leiden society *Kunst Wordt door Arbeid Verkreegen* (Art Is Won by Labor), Patriot tendencies grew stronger over the years. In 1778 and 1781, the stadholder still received the publications of the society, but not afterward. Well-known Patriots such as Wibo Fijnje, Gerrit Paape, Jan de Kruyff, Pieter Vreede, Cornelis van Hoogeveen, Jr., and Cornelis Heyligert were among the most active members of this society. Around 1783, political controversies also began to appear within the society:

The time and circumstances we are now beginning to experience, the diversity of political sympathies, ruling the republic for some time now, had begun to manifest themselves in this our society too; the general meeting this year did not have the generosity and cordiality that used to be characteristic of the meetings of fellow artists. The board therefore decided that it would be better not to finish this meeting with the usual meal, to avoid unpleasant situations, arising from disagreement about political issues.[25]

24. Höweler, "Het Haagsche dichtgenootschap," p. 168.
25. For this and the following minutes from this Leiden society, see Thobokholt, *Het taal- en dichtlievend genootschap*, pp. 19–23.

If one is to believe this reporter, political controversies within the society never led to a real conflict. Before this could happen, the Orangists had already left: "Never did any political quarrel arise between the two parties within our walls; those who differed in opinion from the majority of the fellow artists took their leave, others simply did not show up. They were no great loss." The society did, however, lose one of its most laureled poets, Willem Bilderdijk, in 1785. Toward 1787, society life was paralyzed by political events: "There was a dead silence in the monthly meetings from the start, the chairs were almost all empty, members looked at each other gloomily, as if they had a premonition: the lyre was out of tune because of the tumult of battle; no cheerful songs were heard." The restoration of the republic "in its former state" had disastrous consequences for the Leiden society: "Almost forty members were forced to leave the country or had to resign from their honorary posts and were deprived of their livelihood," among them a leading poet, Rhijnvis Feith. Recovery was remarkably quick, however. Two years later, membership was back to its former level and rose to an absolute peak in 1791. Ironically enough, this society did not really decline until after the institution of the Batavian Republic. Then members had other things on their minds: seats in the national assembly (Van Hamelsveld, Vreede, Kantelaer, Van Maanen, and B. Bosch) or in the executive government (Fijnje and Vreede). This was the reason in 1796 for moving the monthly meetings to Saturdays, in order to "enjoy the presence of several members for whom, staying in The Hague now, it would be impossible to attend in the middle of the week." This change would be of no avail. The last sign of life of *Kunst Wordt door Arbeid Verkreegen* as an independent society is a printed letter of 17 July 1797, which sums up the causes of the decline:

> Since the time and circumstances and the important events of the two most recent years have had such a considerable influence on the state and activities of almost all literary societies in our country, certainly nobody will be surprised that this influence made itself felt particularly in this society, as most of its members, in some office or other, have been called to their duty in the general government and have thus been bestowed lavishly with busy jobs, especially now. Naturally, this caused arrears in domestic affairs, a spirit of listless slowness, even with the most active members, a standstill in all practice of art, and, as a necessary result of all this, everywhere badly attended, nonproductive, or languishing meetings.

The same letter mentions a "most important proposal" "to merge this society with two of its sisters into one Society for Literature and Poetry." It was a successful attempt to survive; three years later, three of the four most important eighteenth-century literary societies, from Leiden, Amsterdam, and Rotterdam, amalgamated as the *Bataafsche Maatschappij van Taal- en Dichtkunde* (Batavian Society for Language and Literature), renamed the *Hollandsche Maatschappij van Fraaije Kunsten en Wetenschappen* (Holland Society for Liberal Arts and Sciences) in 1806. *Kunstliefde* from The Hague remained independent until 1818. It looks as if literary societies, despite a certain political color, were not centers of political activity; indeed, political agitation paralyzed their internal functioning. There were other matters to attend to than the collective writing of poetry. In the case of the private societies, the revolution had rendered the Enlightenment obsolete.

The new sociability of the nineteenth century emphasized solo performance and monologue and asked for applause rather than critical objections from the audience. The poem, the lecture, and the essay were no longer subjects of discussion but finished products, not needing refinement by the society; on the contrary, they bore witness to the artistry, eloquence, and expertise of the maker.[26] This new ritual seems indicative of an acceptance of the changing views on poetry in the societies: the true poet creates alone, without the help of others, and self-consciously presents his or her unique qualities to the public. In a literary society there was room for the talented as well as for those who admired talent, for those who were active and those who were passive. The first laws of the *Hollandsche Maatschappij* already mentioned both "practitioners" and "lovers" of Dutch language and literature as having the same status. The secretary of the general meeting of 1811 phrased this equality in the following way:

> A society for liberal arts and sciences certainly does not . . . require actual cooperation of *all its* members to flourish internally and to spread culture and enlightenment; those who look for this flourishing involving all members are completely off the track. On the contrary, dear Sirs! This is not a beehive in which each member, driven by instinct, by an external power, *must* contribute to its maintenance; it is an assembly of people with the same purpose, some of whom are actually productive because of their superior talents, learning, and

26. For the ritual of these nineteenth-century societies, see. W. van den Berg, "Het literaire genootschapsleven."

intelligence, whereas others promote the cause by listening, educating themselves, refining their taste, and discussing these issues with others.[27]

Each member might have a part to play, but this need not always be the same. Those who were once content with the part of audience could learn so much from it that they would have a greater chance of playing a more active part.

The shift from eighteenth-century societies to the nineteenth-century institutions for recitation and discourse gave new vitality to literary sociability, but not for long. Relinquishing the principle of collective writing of poetry meant removing one of the cornerstones of the ideology of sociability. The division of the society's members into those who were "actually productive" and the "lovers" would not itself hinder the advancement of Dutch literature, as long as both groups were willing to subscribe to the intended goal. A few decades later, however, society members preferred amusement over instruction; and to keep their customers satisfied, societies complied. "It may be that the founders aimed at something higher with the literary reform some time ago," Veder stated in 1848, but nowadays it was only "innocent, not unpleasant distractions for the daily affairs" that keep up the societies.[28]

The new formula of sociability met with criticism rather than approval. In the *Gids* (Guide) of 1843, for instance, Potgieter sneered at the "wretched hobby of our time, our country, to give lectures—deliver speeches—to discourse," and he mocked the "gentlemen in dress coat, who stand behind a lectern continuously and who, if they speak popularly, very popularly, are applauded most popularly."[29] More than ten years earlier, in the bosom of the *Hollandsche Maatschappij*, in a speech on "the duties of the audience," Geel had demonstrated in a

27. Minutes of the general meeting of 14 September 1811, in University Library, Amsterdam, record no. II C 17. See also the following statements in the laws of the society. Chap. 1, par. 1: "The aim of this society is to promote the improvement and practice of the Dutch language and literature." Chap. 1, par. 2: "This [society] consists of practitioners and lovers of Dutch language and literature, who intend to promote the aims of the society, each in accordance with his own capacities, and to present the fruits of their linguistic or literary endeavors to each other in the said meetings."

28. Aart Veder, "Gedachtenis-rede aan Mr. A. Siewertsz van Reesema," in *Nieuwe werken der Hollandsche maatschappij van fraaije kunsten en wetenschappen* (Leiden, 1850), p. 6.

29. *De Gids* 7 (1843), Boekbeoordelingen, p. 225.

bantering fashion how much speaker and listener had grown apart in the common practice of the societies.[30]

Around 1840, the new formula had to a large extent worn off. In the preceding seventy years there had been a great deal of tinkering with the formula of sociability: a change from small to large, from closed to open, from local to supralocal, from collective poetic production to a role division of performer and audience. Notwithstanding all these attempts at evolution, the literary societies did not manage to survive. The *Hollandsche Maatschappij* may have lingered until 1900, when the only surviving department of Amsterdam decided to close for lack of interest; but from its crater, to use Geel's caustic comparison of the literary societies with extinct volcanoes, hardly any smoke had ascended after the 1840s.

30. Geel gave this speech in the meeting of 13 April 1831 of the Leiden department of the *Maatschappij*; in 1838, it was published in his *Onderzoek en phantasie*.

*Hercules and Omphale*. Painting by Nicolas-Jean Delin (1786). Municipal Museum *de Lakenhal*, Leiden, the Netherlands.

# DUTCH CULTURE IN
# ITS SOCIAL SETTING

# 13

# Print Culture in the Netherlands
# on the Eve of the Revolution

## Jeremy D. Popkin

"I T has been said a hundred times . . . that our people love to read,"
the Dutch book-trade historian A. C. Kruseman wrote a century ago.[1]
There is no doubt that the Dutch provinces of the eighteenth century
were, in comparison with most other areas of Europe, an area of relatively high literacy, where a substantial percentage of the population
participated in print culture. This literacy permitted the remarkable
growth of the political press during the *Patriottentijd*, making the
Netherlands the only Continental country where such a phenomenon
occurred prior to the outbreak of the French Revolution. It is thus
natural to hypothesize that the extensive print culture of the Netherlands was one of the main factors favoring the growth of Dutch political radicalism, and that the events of the 1780s provide additional support for Elizabeth Eisenstein's conclusion, based on evidence from
England, the American colonies, and France, that "it would seem unwise to discount the power of pens—at least when they are harnessed
to the power of the press."[2] I argue here, however, that, although the
extensive network of publishers, booksellers, newspapers, and reading
rooms in the United Provinces was one of the preconditions for the
political unrest in the country beginning in the 1780s, the print culture

1. A. C. Kruseman, *De Fransche wetten op de Hollandsche drukpers van 1806 tot 1814*
(Amsterdam, 1889), p. 247.
2. Elizabeth Eisenstein, "On Revolution and the Printed Word," in *Revolution and History*, ed. Roy Porter and Mikulas Teich (Cambridge, 1980), p. 201.

of the period did not necessarily favor the triumph of new political ideas.

The necessary precondition for the spread of print culture in the Netherlands was the spread of literacy. The figures Simon Hart has provided on the percentage of immigrants to Amsterdam able to sign their own names in the marriage registers of the seventeenth and eighteenth centuries indicate that adult male literacy had risen gradually since 1600 and that the levels achieved in the period 1776–1800 were equal to those of the most advanced French provinces and the western regions of Germany. In a pattern familiar throughout western Europe, female literacy lagged considerably behind that of men, but in the period 1776–1800 it was over 60 percent in twenty of the twenty-three communities for which Hart provides data.[3]

Those late eighteenth-century Netherlanders who could read had

Map 1  Booksellers in the Netherlands, 1778

3. Simon Hart, *Geschrift en getal* (Dordrecht, 1976), pp. 78–79. Hart's figures may somewhat overstate the true degree of literacy in the country in the revolutionary era, since immigrants to Amsterdam tended to come from the more literate elements of the provincial population; A. M. van der Woude, "De alfabetisering," in *Algemene geschiedenis der*

relatively extensive access to books and other printed materials. A manuscript survey, or *naamlijst*, of booksellers compiled in 1778 records 295 booksellers, to which can be added an additional eight enterprises listed in the French *Almanach de la librairie* but not included in the manuscript list.[4] The data from the *naamlijst* give a clear indication of the geographic distribution of the Netherlands book trade on the eve of the Patriot movement (Map 1). Altogether, at least forty-one Dutch cities had a bookstore of some sort. Every province had at least one such establishment, but there were great differences in the density of the bookselling network from region to region. As one would expect, the territory of the future Randstad (the western provinces) was far better supplied than the rest of the country. Indeed, there was no other region of Europe as thickly blanketed with bookstores as the province of Holland. Amsterdam alone had 121, more than a third of the total in the republic and almost as many as Paris at the same period (129). There were an additional 70 in The Hague, Leiden, and Rotterdam, and 34 in the smaller cities of the province, leaving only 68 for the rest of the country, of which 20 were in Utrecht alone.

---

*Nederlanden*, vol. 7 (Haarlem, 1980), p. 262. For literacy levels in France in 1786–1790, see the map in François Furet and Jacques Ozouf, *Lire et écrire* (Paris, 1977), vol. 1, p. 60, derived from data gathered in the famous Maggiolo survey. It would be desirable to have studies on the Netherlands comparable to Jean Quéniart's magnificent *Culture et société urbaines dans la France de l'Ouest au XVIIIe siècle* (Paris, 1978). On western Germany, see Etienne François, "Die Volksbildung am Mittelrhein im ausgehenden 18. Jahrhundert," *Jahrbuch für westdeutsche Landesgeschichte* 3 (1977): 277–304, and Wilhelm Norden, "Die Alphabetisierung der oldenburgischen Küstenmarsch im 17. und 18. Jahrhundert," in *Regionalgeschichte: Probleme und Beispiele*, ed. E. Hinrichs and W. Norden (Hildesheim, 1980), pp. 103–164.

4. The origin and purpose of this *Alphabetische naamlijst der boekverkoopers, met hunne woonplaatsen, in de zeven provincien*, is unknown; the Dutch book-trade historian Isabel van Eeghen speculates that it may be an index to one publisher's commercial correspondence, but it could also be an initiative stimulated by the publication in 1778 of the first printed guide to European booksellers, Perrin's *Almanach de la librairie*. The *naamlijst* is now in the collection of Vereeniging ter Bevordering van de Belangen des Boekhandels, Amsterdam University Library. For Van Eeghen's reference to it, see her *De Amsterdamse boekhandel, 1680–1725* (Amsterdam, 1963–1978), vol. 5, pt. 1, p. 22. This source gives a somewhat larger total for Dutch book-trade enterprises than A. M. Ledeboer, *Alfabetische lijst der boekdrukkers, boekverkoopers en uitgevers in Noord-Nederland* (Utrecht, 1876), which identifies 274 enterprises active in 1778.

On the *Almanach de la librairie*, see Giles Barber, "Pendred Abroad, a View of the Late Eighteenth-Century Book Trade in Europe," in *Studies in the Book Trade in Honour of Graham Pollard* (Oxford, 1975), pp. 231–277. This was the first published almanac or guide to European booksellers. Its successors are discussed in Jeremy Popkin, "The Book Trades in Western Europe during the Revolutionary Era," *Papers of the Bibliographical Society of America* 78 (1984): 407–409. There had been an earlier booksellers' almanac in the Netherlands itself: *Almanach der boekverkoopers, drukkers, en binders* (The Hague, 1761), but it did not include a list of booksellers.

The inland provinces were poorly served; the *naamlijst* indicates only three cities with bookstores in the province of Overijssel and three in Gelderland. Zeeland and Friesland were somewhat better off, and there were booksellers in several towns in the northern region of Holland, the Noordkwartier, where literacy is known to have been higher than in the districts south of Amsterdam. The absence of local bookstores did not mean that the population had no access to books; publishers advertised extensively in the newspapers, of which the Netherlands had a considerable number, and the small size of the country coupled with its excellent transportation system doubtless enabled most residents to acquire books if they wanted them. Nor did it mean that the proportion of illiterates was higher than average; literacy in the land provinces of Overijssel and Gelderland was comparable to or even slightly higher than in Holland itself. But the data on booksellers do suggest a sort of Dutch equivalent of the famous "Maggiolo line" dividing northern and southern France, separating areas of relatively high access to printed materials, primarily the province of Holland, from areas with fewer printers and bookstores.[5]

Data on booksellers from a slightly later period indicate the impact the Patriot troubles and the French Revolution had on the distribution network for printed materials. After the Napoleonic annexation of the Kingdom of Holland to France in 1810, the French authorities undertook a comprehensive survey of all book-trade establishments in the Dutch provinces as a preliminary to applying the stringent French

*Table 13.1* Booksellers in the Napoleonic empire, 1810–1811

| | No. of cities with booksellers | No. of booksellers | Average no. of booksellers per dept. |
|---|---|---|---|
| France (86 depts.) | 413 | 1,585 | 18.4 |
| Belgium (9 depts.) | 52 | 202 | 22.4 |
| Germany (9 depts.) | 125 | 166 | 18.4 |
| Neth. (8 depts.) | 74 | 582 | 72.4 |
| Italy (16 depts.) | 62 | 219 | 13.7 |
| Switz. (2 depts.) | 3 | 11 | 5.5 |
| (130) | 729 | 2,765 | 21.3 |

5. It is possible, of course, that the *naamlijst* exaggerates the density of booksellers in the province of Holland because its compiler knew that region better. But the geographic distribution of the Dutch booksellers recorded in the international *Almanach de la librairie* of 1778 is very similar to that indicated by the *naamlijst*.

book-trade regulations (see Table 13.1 and Map 2).⁶ Since we do not know how the 1778 *naamlijst* was compiled, it is not clear how comparable the data from these two sources are. The data from 1810 certainly show a much more extensive network of booksellers. The number of cities with registered booksellers in 1810 was seventy-one, thirty more than there had been a generation earlier. The former province of Holland continued to have more bookstores than the rest of the country; Amsterdam alone contained 281, a figure larger than that for any other city in the Napoleonic empire except Paris (435). But the most marked change reflected in the 1810 data is the spread of bookselling in the eastern land provinces. Instead of three cities with booksellers, the department of Bouches d'Iyssel (essentially modern Overijssel) now had seven; Iyssel-Superieur (modern Gelderland) had gone from three cities to six, and Groningen from one to seven.

The differences between the 1810 data and that from 1778 reflect

*Map 2* Booksellers in the Netherlands, 1810–11

6. These data are derived from a manuscript register, "Etat general des libraires, bouquinistes, relieurs, cabinets de lecture et colporteurs," in Archives nationales (Paris), série F 18, carton 25. For a critical discussion of this document, see Popkin, "Book Trades," p. 406.

two factors: the 1810 list, carried out by the efficient French administration, was undoubtedly more thorough and may include small enterprises the compiler of the *naamlijst* ignored, and there may have been real growth in the number of book-trade enterprises over the thirty years since 1778. The 1810 data do demonstrate, however, that by the end of the revolutionary and Napoleonic period the Dutch bookselling network had ramified to cover the entire country. A subsequent almanac of booksellers from 1828 shows that these gains were permanent; even though the total number of bookstores had declined from 582 in 1810 to 342 by 1828, the number of cities with a bookstore had grown from seventy-one to seventy-three, so that the population's access to print culture had been maintained.[7] It is clear, then, that in the course of the revolutionary era even those regions that may have been relatively deprived of bookstores as late as 1778 came to have them. The period between 1778 and 1810 was the period during which the entire Dutch population came within easy reach of books and newspapers.

The French survey of 1810, although it is later than the period we are most interested in, is also valuable because it allows comparison of the bookselling networks of the different regions incorporated in the Napoleonic empire at the time of its greatest expansion. This comparison dramatizes the high level of development of the Dutch book trade at the beginning of the nineteenth century, and it is not unreasonable to project these findings back into the late eighteenth century. Table 13.1 shows that there were 72.4 booksellers per department in the eight Dutch departments, as compared to 21.3 per department in the empire as a whole. Even if one omits the department of the Zuyderzee, which contained Amsterdam, the remaining seven Dutch departments averaged 43.0 booksellers, more than twice the imperial average. The large number of bookshops was not simply a function of a dense population; in fact, the eight Dutch departments had the lowest average population of any region in the empire. Nor was it the result of stagnation in the book trades elsewhere in the empire; in France, the number of booksellers had risen from 932 in 1778 to 1,585 in 1810.[8]

It is undoubtedly true that many of these Dutch bookshops were modest affairs; observers had commented that the Netherlands had a plethora of marginal book-trade enterprises and few establishments that could compare with the great Parisian publishing houses of the

7. Data from *Naamlijst der boekhandelaren van het Koninkrijk der Nederlanden, voor 1828* (Rotterdam, 1828).
8. Popkin, "Book Trades," p. 415.

epoch. J. Grabner, a German army officer who had been in the Dutch service during the 1780s and whose *Briefe über die vereinigte Nieder-lände* is one of the most detailed descriptions of the country from this period, observed that "every bookbinder who sells catechisms and primers joins the booksellers' guild, even though his main profit comes from the sale of paper, quills and sealing wax. . . . All the streets in the cities are full of bookshops."[9] Even so, there is no question that the ratio of bookstores to population in the Netherlands as a whole was extraordinarily high, and that in the heavily urbanized province of Holland the products of the printing press were more accessible to the population than anywhere else in Europe except the great capitals of Paris and London. It is worth noting, however, that this bookselling network remained an urban phenomenon in the Netherlands, as it did in France. By contrast, the German data for the period show a distinctive pattern of book distributors located in rural communities smaller than those reached by the book-trade networks in any other country of the period.[10] It may well be that the rural population in western Germany had more access to printed material than the countryfolk of the Netherlands.

Booksellers' newspaper advertisements provide strong evidence that many of these enterprises were in fact active in disseminating printed works, and they also give some indication of what sort of reading material had the widest market. It was standard practice for such ads to list the booksellers in various Dutch cities who had agreed to stock the advertised work. An analysis of fourteen such ads, dating from the late 1770s to the mid-1780s, provides a list of 159 different bookstores in forty-one cities, the same number of cities indicated in the 1778 *naamlijst* (see Table 13.2 for list of advertised works). If the number of bookstores stocking a particular title can be interpreted as a rough measure of the expected size of the reading public for that work, non-political titles of general interest published in Dutch had the greatest audience, which is hardly surprising. Fifty-two booksellers in thirty-three cities stocked the most popular work, a marriage manual, and the biography of a celebrated astrologer had 39 distributors in twenty-seven cities. What is more surprising is that three of the next four longest lists of distributors were for French-language works: a condensed

9. J. Grabner, *Briefe über der vereinigten Niederlände* (Gotha, 1792), pp. 410–411.

10. Popkin, "Book Trades," p. 433; Reinhard Wittmann, "Das Buchgewerbe im Königreich Württemberg 1809," *Buchhandelsgeschichte* 2/5, no. 31 (11 April 1980): B257–B263.

Table 13.2 Titles Advertised in the Dutch press, 1777–1785

| Title | No. of cities | No. of booksellers |
|---|---|---|
| Handboek voor alle mannen en vrouwen en huwbaare jongelingen, of natuurkundige beschouwing van den man en de vrouw in den huuwelyksen staat | 33 | 52 |
| Egte en gedenkwaardige levensbeschrying van den alom beroemden doctor en astrologist Ludeman | 27 | 39 |
| Plaat, book-auction catalogue | 25 | 31 |
| Linguet, Annales politiques | 21 | 45 |
| Journal de poche, ou calendrier interessant | 19 | 29 |
| Esprit des encyclopédistes françois | 18 | 46 |
| Redenvoering aan de gewapende burgery in Nederland (Patriot pamphlet) | 14 | 21 |
| Portrait of William V | 13 | 24 |
| Politique hollandois | 13 | 17 |
| Het is beter half gekeerd als geheel gedwaald (Orangist pamphlet) | 8 | 18 |
| Werken van G. van Loon | 8 | 14 |
| Booklet about Danish bonds | 7 | 12 |
| Works of J. Gazola | 6 | 8 |
| Vrymoedige bedenkingen over de zogenaamde antidotaale speelvaarders (Orangist pamphlet) | 4 | 13 |

Sources: Hollandsche Historische Courant; 's Gravenhaagse Courant; Annales Politiques (Hague edition); Courrier de l'Europe; Leydse Courant; Politique hollandois.

version of the French *Encyclopédie*, the journalist Linguet's *Annales politiques*, and an almanac. As Margaret Jacob notes, the prosperous and educated Dutch burgers who were literate in French evidently made up a significant sector of the country's book market; indeed, more than a quarter of the booksellers listed in this sample of advertisements appeared only in the announcements of French-language works.

Even at the height of the Patriot period, only a minority of booksellers advertised the fact that they distributed partisan political literature. Twenty-one booksellers in fourteen cities stocked a Patriot pamphlet, and an engraved portrait of William V could be purchased from 24 sellers in thirteen cities, the same number of communities in which one could find the French-language Patriot journal *Politique hollandois*. Two Orangist pamphlets had even smaller lists of distributors, and the Patriot "archivist" Dumont-Pigalle listed only 19 "principal distributors of pro-stadholder literature" in twelve cities.[11] Political pamphlets and journals reached readers by other channels, too, but it is

11. Note in Algemeen Rijksarchief, Dumont-Pigalle papers, carton AAA, The Hague.

significant that the commercial bookselling network seems to have continued to distribute primarily nonpolitical texts. Finally, my sample includes lists for three works evidently directed at small, specialized audiences: two scholarly works intended for academics were advertised by 14 and 8 booksellers, and a booklet on investment opportunities listed only 12 distributors.

Even this small sample of booksellers' ads reveals the diversity of the late eighteenth-century Dutch book market. Decentralized, it was not dominated by a few large firms, and different booksellers in the same city evidently sought different clienteles, since analysis of which vendors appear on which lists shows that each vendor had a distinct profile. The number of booksellers engaged in marketing works in French is worthy of note and underlines the importance of the small but well-heeled stratum of genuinely bilingual readers. Finally, one can see that the Dutch book trade was not dominated by political ephemera, even during the *patriottentijd*.

As in most of Europe, Dutch readers had access to books not only through bookstores but also through reading societies and libraries. Voluntary groups whose members met to discuss common readings were numerous in the Netherlands; a subscription list for one book published in 1782 includes at least 68 of them.[12] These groups often had some particular purpose in mind, whether religious, political, or aiming at self-improvement. They ranged in size from small informal circles of friends to major establishments like the *Grand Société* in The Hague, whose two hundred members were mostly aristocrats and members of the diplomatic corps who came to read the foreign newspapers.[13] There were also commercial *lees-bibliotheeken* where readers could rent books they could not afford to buy. There had been such an establishment in The Hague since 1751. The French survey of 1810 identified 49 in twenty-one cities. At that time, Amsterdam alone supported 18 of these commercial lending libraries, more than any other city in the Napoleonic empire except Paris. Common as these institutions for collective reading were in the Netherlands, however, it is worth noting that they were even more widespread in the German-speaking world. The Dutch average of 6.1 *cabinets de lecture* per department was significantly lower than the average of 10.1 in the nine

---

12. P. J. Buijnsters, "Lesegesellschaften in den Niederlanden," in *Lesegesellschaften und bürgerliche Emanzipation*, ed. Otto Dann (Munich, 1981), p. 145.

13. K. G. Küttner, *Beyträge zur Kenntniss vorzüglich des gegenwärtigen Zustandes von Frankreich und Holland* (Leipzig, 1792), p. 310.

German-speaking departments, and the German establishments often existed in small rural towns, whereas the Dutch ones were limited to the larger cities. Thus, the Dutch department of Ems Occidental (Groningen) had four *cabinets de lecture* in 1810, all but one in Groningen, but the neighboring German department of Ems Oriental (Ostfriesland) had eleven, scattered among six cities.

Having established that the Netherlands had a dense network of booksellers, we naturally want to ask next what sorts of materials they offered for sale, and who their customers were. One fact is clear: by the time of the Patriot troubles, the Dutch publishers and booksellers were no longer heavily involved in the export of reading material to other countries. From at least the middle of the eighteenth century, the lucrative business of publishing French-language works for sale in France had shifted from the Netherlands to publishers in Germany, the Belgian provinces, Switzerland, and Avignon.[14] The celebrated journals of Bayle, Le Clerc, and Rousset de Missy had ceased publication, and the ubiquitous *gazettes de Hollande* that made up the European continent's high-level political press were being imitated in other countries. Jean Sgard's statistics on French-language periodicals published outside France show the situation for this branch of print culture with stark clarity: the number of such publications located in the United Provinces reached a high of thirty in the decade of the 1740s but fell to eight in 1780. In 1740, the number of French-language periodicals based in the Netherlands exceeded the total of those published in Belgium, Germany, England, and Switzerland combined; by the 1780s, Belgium, Germany, and England each housed more French-language journals than the Netherlands, and Switzerland had just as many.[15]

To make up for the loss of their foreign markets, the surviving Dutch publishers followed a pattern common to many areas of the Dutch economy in the eighteenth century: they turned to more intensive cultivation of their home market. The number of books in Dutch published each year was approximately two hundred in the late eighteenth century, a very respectable figure considering the small size of the potential market.[16] Many, perhaps most, of the actual books published

14. Van Eeghen, *Amsterdamse boekhandel*, vol. 5, pt. 1, pp. 97–100. On French-language publishing outside France, see the contributions to Roger Chartier et al., eds., *Histoire de l'edition française*, vol. 2 (Paris, 1984).

15. Jean Sgard, "Journale und Journalisten im Zeitalter der Aufklärung," in *Sozialgeschichte der Aufklärung in Frankreich*, ed. H. U. Gumbrecht, R. Reichardt, and T. Schleich (Munich, 1981), p. 32.

16. Van Eeghen, *Amsterdamse boekhandel*, vol. 5, pt. 1, p. 93; Yves Dubosq, *Le Livre française et son commerce en Hollande de 1750 à 1780* (Amsterdam, 1925), p. 41. Grabner, *Briefe*, p. 401; his estimate is in line with figures provided in Kruseman, *Fransche wetten*, pp.

during this period were translations from other languages, generally English, French, and German; Betje Wolff and Aagje Deken's polemic against the vogue of translations in the preface to their *Historie van Mejuffrouw Sara Burgerhart* is well known. Dutch readers had access to the full range of European thought in the age of the Enlightenment, although there is general agreement that all but a handful shunned the more radical tendencies of that movement. Foreign visitors sometimes lamented that Dutch booksellers preferred to stock translations of "lamentable novels" from their home countries rather than works on philosophy and politics.[17]

But Dutch publishers offered a wide variety of other materials for sale besides books. As W. P. C. Knuttel's famous catalog demonstrates, the revolutionary era saw an inundation of pamphlets. Verse making was a national pastime; Grabner claimed that even among the lower classes it was common to find "people who can make a perfectly decent verse," and many of these efforts found their way into print. A recent study of ephemeral literature concerning the controversial Patriot leader Joan Derk van der Capellen identified 93 published poems about him.[18] The republic's complex political structure generated an immense amount of publishing as well: the stout volumes of the *Nieuwe Nederlandsche jaarboeken*, an annual collection of resolutions and documents emanating from the various town councils and provincial assemblies of the country, testify to the volume of print that public affairs generated even in "normal" times. Long before the beginning of the Patriot troubles, all the major cities in Holland and some in other provinces had newspapers, which combined political news, mostly foreign, with commercial information and advertising. The most successful, such as the *Amsterdamsche Courant* and the *Oprechte Haarlemsche Courant*, had press runs of 4,000 to 6,000 or more, which put

244–45, which indicate that for the period 1790–1831 there were an average of 160 titles printed per year. During the relatively calm period of 1806–1809, the average number of titles per year reached almost 240.

17. H. H. Zwager, *Nederland en de Verlichting*, 2d ed., (Haarlem, 1980); W. W. Mijnhardt, "De geschiedschrijving over de ideeëngeschiedenis van de 17e- en 18-eeuwse Republiek," in *Kantelend geschiedbeeld: Nederlandse historiografie sinds 1945*, ed. W. W. Mijnhardt (Utrecht, 1983), pp. 162–205; Simon Schama, "The Enlightenment in the Netherlands," in *The Enlightenment in National Context*, ed. Roy Porter and Mikuláš Teich (Cambridge, 1981), pp. 54–71; Georg Friedrich Rebmann, *Holland und Frankreich in Briefen* (Berlin, 1981), p. 30.

18. Grabner, *Briefe*, p. 397; G. T. Hartong, "Joan Derk, bejubeld en beschimpt," in *De wekker van de Nederlandse natie: Joan Derk van der Capellen, 1741–1784*, ed. E. A. van Dijk, J. Trijsburg, W. F. Wertheim, and A. H. Wertheim-Gijse Weenink (Zwolle, 1984), p. 63.

them ahead of the most successful London newspapers of the era. The huge subsidies some of these papers paid to the town governments that licensed them prove that they were flourishing enterprises. Even in the period of Orangist reaction after 1787, these papers were able to provide Dutch readers with a broad range of political information, including details about the French Revolution. The domestic market thus provided Dutch printers with ample material to keep their presses occupied and offered booksellers a wide variety of items to tempt their customers.[19]

One of the peculiarities of print culture in the United Provinces then, as now, was the extensive public for books and periodicals in languages other than Dutch. Rather than exporting French-language materials, the Netherlands by the 1780s was importing them from elsewhere. An advertisement for a selection of the most radical philosophical articles from the *Encyclopédie*, published in London in 1779, listed 45 Dutch booksellers in eighteen cities who were willing to take orders; a similar advertisement for the French émigré journalist Linguet's *Annales politiques*, an edition of which was published in The Hague, also listed 45 Dutch booksellers, this time covering twenty-one cities. There was a market for such French-language items in Germany as well, but it does not seem to have been as extensive: the prospectus for Linguet's *Annales* listed only 17 north German distributors in thirteen cities.[20] English and German literature had some audience in the Netherlands as well, but neither seems to have approached French in popularity.

The Netherlands thus enjoyed a rich and diversified print culture. Not only was literacy quite high, but the literate population enjoyed

19. For an overview of the Dutch press, see Maarten Schneider and Joan Hemels, *De Nederlandse krant, 1618–1978*, 4th ed. (Baarn, 1979). The nineteenth-century Dutch press historian W. P. Sautijn Kluit collected a great deal of documentary information about the eighteenth-century papers, to which modern scholarship has not yet added very much. On the success of Dutch papers, see I. H. van Eeghen, "De Amsterdamse Courant in de achttiende eeuw," *Jaarboek Amstelodamum* 44 (1950): 45, and D. H. Couvée, "The Administration of the 'Oprechte Haarlemse Courant,' 1738–42," *Gazette* 4 (1958): 94. The Dutch-language *Leidsche Courant* paid that city 8,375 guilders per year under a privilege granted in 1772; W. P. Sautijn Kluit, "De Hollandsche Leidsche Courant," in *Mededelingen gedaan in de vergaderingen van de Maatschappij der Nederlandsche Letterkunde te Leiden* (1870–1871), pp. 59. See also J. W. Berkelbach van der Sprenkel, "De Fransche revolutie in de contemporaine Hollandsche couranten," *De Gids* (1939): 323–357; Jeremy Popkin, "La 'Déclaration des Droits de l'Homme' aux Pays-Bas," *Annales historiques de la Révolution française*, no. 265 (1986): 307–310.

20. Prospectus for *Esprit des encyclopédistes françois* in *Courrier de l'Europe*, 29 July 1779; prospectus for Linguet's *Annales* tipped in between pp. 214 and 215, vol. 3, of copy in Niedersächsisches Staats- und Universitätsbibliothek Göttingen.

relatively easy access to printed materials. And there is ample evidence that Dutch men and women used these opportunities. Contemporary prints frequently depict scenes of reading. A cartoon of Patriots gathering in a tavern shows a man reading aloud from a Dutch gazette; a print of a party picnicking outdoors shows men and women scanning a newspaper.[21] Grabner reported that all classes read the newspapers regularly, and that one could hardly participate in public conversation unless one kept up with the news. He was impressed with the number of woman poets, who were necessarily readers as well, and he asserted that "one often finds respectable collections of books in the homes of the better-off farmers."[22] There are frequent references to reading in the most celebrated Dutch novel of the period, Wolff and Deken's *Sara Burgerhart*. When the heroine flees her overbearing aunt, she takes a room in a boarding house and praises the proprietress because "she reads a good deal, in various languages," and the same fact testifies in favor of the other young lady in the house. When her friends fear that she may be abusing her new-found freedom from adult supervision, Sara assures them that she still reads regularly and, indeed, reads aloud to the other boarders. To be sure, there is reading and there is reading: another of the boarders is a snob who asserts that she will have nothing to do with literature in Dutch. She reads "philosophical" works in French and later collaborates with the villain who tries to kidnap the heroine.[23] In general, however, the novel, perhaps overoptimistically, depicts reading as an everyday activity among both sexes and all levels of society.

Although the Netherlands had a largely literate population and a highly developed network of publishers and booksellers, it lacked a real intellectual class capable of seeing print media as a means of transforming their society. To a surprising extent, the country failed to produce either philosophes or hack writers like those whose lives Robert Darnton has chronicled in France.[24] Even Germany was quite different in this regard, as Grabner noted. "The Dutch writers have a much less enviable lot than the Germans," he reported. "The deepest thinker will

---

21. Print of "Corps de Garde Patriottique Hollandaise en 1786," reproduced in Van Dijk et al., eds., *Wekker van de Nederlandse natie*, p. 116; picnic print from the collection of Dr. Martin Welke, Deutsches Zeitungsmuseum, Meersburg, West Germany.

22. Grabner, *Briefe*, pp. 285, 390, 397.

23. Betje Wolff and Aagje Deken, *De historie van Mejuffrouw Sara Burgerhart* (Utrecht, 1984), pp. 35, 74, 151.

24. Robert Darnton, *The Literary Underground of the Old Regime* (Cambridge, Mass, 1982).

not earn the least office for his writings, and if he didn't have so many other ways to make money, he could die of starvation, regardless of his talent." Grabner put this down, not only to the small size of the poten-tial reading audience, but to the absence of a genuine academic culture such as had developed in the Germany of his day. He noted with sur-prise that Dutch university professors were not expected to publish—he might have added that, when they did, they often continued to do so in Latin, thereby cutting themselves off from most of their potential audience—and he deplored the lack of periodicals devoted to learned criticism: "The Dutch press does not have a hundredth of the stimulus to activity that criticism gives to the German."[25]

In the Netherlands, even intellectual figures of considerable impor-tance such as Elie Luzac had to earn their living from other occupa-tions—in his case, from publishing and bookselling.[26] This meant, on the one hand, that the barriers to getting into print were not high; the pamphleteers of the Patriot period and the versifiers of the late eight-eenth century included numerous merchants, women, and other writers from social backgrounds that would have precluded literary activity in France or Germany. On the other hand, the absence of a professional literary class condemned Dutch print culture to a certain provinciality. The situation had changed completely since the seventeenth century, when the country had had an intellectual elite as distinguished as any in Europe, but one whose audience was the international republic of letters. The late eighteenth-century Netherlands had a much more dem-ocratic print culture, and one much closer to the level of ordinary edu-cated citizens; but, by the same token, it was a print culture dependent on amateurs, and its products reflected this.[27] The key roles such out-siders as the Jew Isaac da Pinto on the Orangist side and the French emigré journalists Antoine Cerisier and François Bernard among the Patriots played in political journalism are suggestive of the lack of ap-peal that paid scribbling had for the ordinary educated Dutch. Bernard was even hired to edit a Dutch-language Patriot newspaper, the *Ba-tavier*, although he could neither read nor write the language.[28]

To be sure, there were both skilled writers and political leaders who

25. Grabner, *Briefe*, pp. 401–404.

26. On Elie Luzac, see Jacques Marx, "Elie Luzac et la pensée éclairée," *Documen-tatieblad Werkgroep Achttiende Eeuw* (June 1971): 74–105, and Chapter 5 of this volume.

27. See similar conclusions about the state of Dutch poetry and literature in Chapter 12 of this volume.

28. Jeremy Popkin, "François Bernard," *Dictionnaire des Journalistes*, suppl. 4 (1985): 5–7.

understood the value of printed propaganda. Joan Derk van der Capellen first came into conflict with his fellow members of the estates of Overijssel when he defied custom by publishing one of his speeches to that assembly, and he virtually shaped the main debate between traditional "Patriot regents" and their more radical challengers with his anonymously published pamphlet, *Aan het volk van Nederland*.[29] All sides during the Patriot period understood that permitting regular printed publication of the debates in the town councils that ultimately governed the country was the issue that would determine whether Van der Capellen's suggestion that the public be allowed to influence the proceedings of those traditional bodies would be put into effect; it was precisely over that issue that Johan Luzac, the publisher of the *Gazette de Leyde*, which carried such accounts of the debates in the British Parliament and the French Parlement of Paris, broke with the more radical Patriots in his native Leiden.[30]

The *Patriottentijd* was marked by the development of an extensive popular political press; the Netherlands thus became the first Continental country to generate such journals. All parties in the *Patriottentijd* availed themselves of the press, the Orangists no less than the Patriots. All recognized that printed literature offered a means of organizing popular support for their cause, and all adopted basically similar strategies for appealing to it. Contemporary foreign observers were struck by this phenomenon, although usually in a negative sense. The Dutch correspondent of the *Politische Journal*, the most important German newsmagazine of the day, reported as early as 1781 that "we are overwhelmed with a flood of publications, each more disgusting and reckless than the other, and they achieve their intended effect only too well. They stir up the crowd, mislead them, and fill them with prejudices, hatred, and enthusiasm."[31]

The political press of the Patriot period still cries out for a thorough study, particularly one that would permit a comparison with the papers that emerged in France after 1789. One can say that the Dutch revolu-

29. Murk de Jong Henrikszoon, *Joan Derk van der Capellen* (Groningen–The Hague, 1921), pp. 204–205; Simon Schama, *Patriots and Liberators* (New York, 1977), p. 64.

30. [Pieter Vreede], *Eerkrans voor den steller van het rapport omtrend de Leydsche propositie van geheimhouding, den hooggeleerden Heer. Mr. Jan Luzac, Grieksch hoogleeraar te Leyden* (N.p, 4 February 1786), 14n, 24n. Luzac's opponents accused him of betraying his own principles by refusing to allow the same publicity for the Leiden *Vroedschap*'s debates that his paper provided for the proceedings of similar bodies abroad.

31. *Politische Journal*, October 1781, p. 298. The German press in general was strongly hostile to the Patriot movement.

tionary press differed considerably from the later French revolutionary papers, above all in tone. The Dutch papers tended to be folksy, down-to-earth, and extremely long-winded. Typical was the opening number of the most celebrated of the Orangist journals, the *Ouderwetse Nederlandsche Patriot*, in the form of a purported dialogue between the author and his nephew. The author depicted himself as conversing in his armchair, smoking a pipe, but he had little in common with that ferocious French pipe smoker of a few years later, the Père Duchêne. The fictitious *ouderwetse* Patriot soon had to defend himself against the charge that he took the country's political problems too light-heartedly. "Our greatest misfortune, in the midst of all our external disasters, is that we are too *serious*," he replied.[32] This was not a remark that any French revolutionary journalist would have made. Whereas most French revolutionary papers adopted an exalted declamatory tone, the Dutch editors put their messages in the mouths of fictional peasants and ordinary townspeople, like the rustics who are depicted discussing the latest issues of other political journals in the *Politieke Snapster* of 1786, one of whom concludes, "See, Janne, how each one of them calls the others liars: for that matter, see how often they declare themselves liars!"[33]

The political journalists of the French Revolution sometimes resorted to this kind of pamphleteering, too, but aside from Hébert's *Père Duchêne*, it rarely succeeded. The differences between the *Père Duchêne* and the Dutch pamphlet journals are significant, however. Hébert was a journalist of genius who kept his pamphlets succinct and used pseudo-popular language to make clear, simple points, often designed to motivate his readers to do something specific. His Dutch predecessors, on the other hand, while seeing the value of writing for a broad audience, were less concerned to mobilize their readers for immediate action. They could allow themselves an unrestrained verbosity, which their audience did not seem to have held against them. The rhetoric for political discourse in the Netherlands was thus quite different from that which developed a few years later in France. The serious Dutch political newspapers of the Patriot period also gave themselves over to endless discussions of trivia and to mind-numbing repetition. So, too, for the political proclamations of the competing parties. The *Leids ontwerp* of 1785, the clearest statement of the more radical Pa-

32. *Ouderwetse Nederlandsche Patriot*, no. 3 (1 September 1781), p. 39.
33. *Politieke Snapster*, no. 83 (10 July 1786). This was one of the numerous pamphlet-journals published during the Patriot period.

triots' program, has many analogies of content with the French Declaration of the Rights of Man. Like the French declaration, it defined freedom as "an inalienable right," asserted that citizens were only required to obey "laws, that they themselves have consented to, in person or through their representatives," and demanded freedom of the press. But this list of revolutionary principles was embedded in a text that occupies some sixty pages of small type. The document was hardly suited to the propagandistic uses for which the French declaration, with its seventeen concise articles, was employed.[34] The same holds for the Patriots' fullest statement of their program, the never-completed *Grondwettige herstelling*, which filled two good-sized volumes and was intended to be even longer. Even the most creative of the Dutch journalists and pamphleteers never felt the need to invent a rhetorical style suited to the urgency of genuinely revolutionary politics.[35]

Consequently, if one wants to study the individuals who really shaped and directed the print culture of the Netherlands during this period, one would do better to look at publishers than at authors. As the publisher Pierre Gosse, Jr., of The Hague told a correspondent in 1770, "Nowadays it is necessary to follow the taste of the century, the taste of the public, in one's enterprises. MM. the *scavans* [sic] are often fooled, [but] a successful bookseller judges the public's desires better than a *scavant* can." In political affairs, the printers and distributors of literature were more important than its authors, as the Patriot activist Dumont-Pigalle recognized when he compiled his list of booksellers who distributed Orangist propaganda. Even the most prominent journalists in the Netherlands were firmly under the thumb of their publishers, as Cerisier discovered in 1780 when the Utrecht publisher Wild had him imprisoned to keep him from relocating to Amsterdam without finishing a manuscript he had been engaged to write.[36]

34. "Ontwerp, om de Republyk door eene heilzaame vereeniging der belangen van Regent en Burger, van binnen gelukkig, en van buiten geducht te maaken. Volgens besluit der Provinciaale Vergadering van de gewapende Corpsen in Holland, den 4 October 1785 binnen Leyden geopend, ter kennisse der gezamenlyke Leden en verdere Ingezetenen der Provincie gebracht." Printed in Anon., *Verzameling van placaaten, resolutien en andere authenthyke stukken enz. betr. de gewigtige gebeurtnissen, in de maand Sept. 1787 en vervolgens in de Vereenigde Nederlanden* (Campen, 1789–1794), vol. 50, pp. 185–244. This 50-volume compilation of documents is ample testimony to the place of the printed word in the Dutch revolution.

35. For a discussion of the development of styles of journalistic rhetoric in France, see Jeremy Popkin, "The Pre-Revolutionary Origins of Revolutionary Political Journalism," in *The French Revolution and the Creation of Modern Political Culture*, ed. Keith Baker (Oxford, 1987), pp. 203–223.

36. Pierre Gosse, Jr., to Société Typographique de Neuchâtel (STN), 2 October 1770, in

The manifold activities of Pierre Gosse, Jr., and of his son Pierre Frédéric Gosse, the pro-Orangist publishers and booksellers of The Hague, demonstrate the great impact dynamic members of the book trades could exercise in Dutch society. After the death of M. M. Rey, the Gosses were certainly the last important publishers of French-language materials in the Netherlands, although the actual printing of their works was often done in other countries and in association with publishing houses such as De Felice's in Yverdon. But this publishing activity was only one aspect of the Gosses' activities. They also published both the French and Dutch gazettes in The Hague. The former was a minor enterprise, but the triweekly *'s Gravenhaagse Courant* was the main newspaper devoted to the Orangist cause—as opposed to the numerous Orangist pamphlet-journals of the 1780s—and its extensive advertising not only made the Gosses rich but gave them a perfect outlet for advertising the numerous French and Dutch works they published.[37] Pierre Frédéric Gosse seems to have run the paper himself, without an editor: his correspondence shows him giving orders and instructions even to such well-known contributors as the Orangist polemicist Le Francq van Berkhey. Gosse also published the most effective Orangist pamphlet-journal, the *Ouderwetse Nederlandse Patriot*, until he fell out with its other backers over his opposition to orthodox Calvinism.[38] Finally, as the head of an extensive enterprise, Gosse could call on his numerous printshop workers as shock troops during the Patriot troubles of the 1780s. He was widely considered the principal instigator of the St. Nicholas Day riot in The Hague in 1782, in which

---

STN Archives, Bibliothèque Publique et Universitaire de Neuchâtel, Ms. 1159, ff. 135–138. Dumont-Pigalle, "Principaux libraires qui débitent les Pamphlets Stadhouderiens," in Algemeen Rijksarchief, Dumont-Pigalle Archive, vol. AAA. On Cerisier, see J. Mandrillon to John Adams, letter of 20 December 1780, in Adams Papers microfilm, r. 353, The Hague.

37. On the Gosses, see E. F. Kossmann, *De boekhandel te 's Gravenhage* (The Hague, 1937), pp. 150–158. The Gosses had a long-standing arrangement whereby they had the right to act as the STN's sole distributor in the Netherlands, Belgium, and England for any work they were interested in; P. F. Gosse to STN, 24 March 1775, in STN Archives, BPU, Neuchâtel, Ms. 1159, ff. 183–184. P. F. Gosse's list of his own French-language publications in 1779 and 1780 shows that he had put out thirty-three titles, but twelve of these were printed in Yverdon, five in London, and others in cities as far away as Berlin and Bern; P. F. Gosse to STN, 11 May 1781, in STN Archives, BPU, Neuchâtel, Ms. 1159, ff. 257–258. The Gosses obtained privileges for the two Hague gazettes in 1770; W. P. Sautijn Kluit, *De 's Gravenhaagsche Courant* (Leiden, 1875), p. 59.

38. C. H. E. de Wit, *De Nederlandse revolutie van de achttiende eeuw, 1780–1787* (Oirsbeek, 1974), pp. 30–31. Pierre Frédéric Gosse was a leading proponent of the Swedenborgian sect; P. F. Gosse, *Portefeuille d'un ancien typographe* (The Hague, 1824), pp. 2–3. Gosse's letters to Le Francq van Berkhey are in the Gemeente Archief, The Hague, sig. Am 121.

his employees played a leading role.[39] It would be hard to think of a writer or journalist of the revolutionary period who had as much influence on the Dutch life of his day as Pierre Frédéric Gosse, who may never have penned more than a few sentences of his own for publication but who knew how to exploit the power of the printed word in so many different ways.

The political turmoil of the period beginning in 1780 thus took place in a society in which the printed word offered a ready means of addressing a large segment of the population. Publishers and writers with axes to grind were willing and able to use this means to further their causes. They took advantage of the fact that the Netherlands was "modern" in comparison with other European countries of the late eighteenth century because of the population's high degree of access to printed materials, and that its print culture was "democratic" in that the ability to get one's words into print was not limited to professional intellectuals wielding linguistic skills denied to the rest of the population. Because reading was already a fairly widespread habit, however, the flood of political literature in the 1780s was not as much a novelty as was the sudden outpouring of political journalism in France in 1789. And the press of the Patriot period spoke in a familiar idiom even when it presented new political concepts; the Dutch Patriots, unlike the French revolutionaries, did not seem to think that they needed a new language to suit their new order. They did not evolve a new journalistic style calculated to rush their readers into new forms of action. The diffuseness and verbosity of Dutch political polemics were more suited to the leisurely, indecisive character of the events from 1781 to 1787. The role of print in Dutch culture during the revolutionary era suggests the ironic conclusion that the modern-seeming aspects of Dutch print culture actually worked against the sudden growth of a genuinely revolutionary political culture in the Patriot period.

39. Dumont-Pigalle Archive, vol. QQ, note of 17 March 1786.

# 14

# The Dutch Enlightenment and the Creation of Popular Culture

## Willem Th. M. Frijhoff

ACCORDING to a firmly established historiographic tradition, reason and revelation are the two key words of the Dutch Enlightenment. Thus, we have Simon Schama's definition of Dutch Enlightenment as "encyclopedism without polemic; reform without scepticism."[1] Yet such a definition is not entirely complete. It emphasizes formal characteristics and runs the risk of neglecting profoundly ethical and indeed religious aspects. In the 1790s, at the time of the Batavian Republic, the ethical and religious scope of the Dutch Enlightenment was closely bound up with the aspirations of the Dutch middle and upper-middle classes. Protestant ministers and Catholic priests, headmasters of grammar schools and university teachers, lawyers and physicians, gazetteers and other cultivated professionals formed the core of the intellectual elite that criticized the dominant values of the Dutch ancien régime and drafted the outlines of new social arrangements. The

1. S. Schama, "The Enlightenment in the Netherlands," in *The Enlightenment in National Context*, ed. R. Porter and M. Teich (Cambridge, 1981), p. 70. On the Dutch Enlightenment, see H. H. Zwager, *Nederland en de Verlichting* (Bussum, 1972); P. J. Buijnsters, "Les Lumières hollandaises," *Studies on Voltaire and the Eighteenth Century* 77 (1972): 179–215; H. Bots and J. de Vet, "Les Provinces-Unies et les Lumières," *Dix-Huitième Siècle*, no. 10 (1978): 101–122; W. W. Mijnhardt, "De Nederlandse Verlichting: Een terreinverkenning," in *Figuren en figuraties. Acht opstellen aangeboden aan J. C. Boogman* (Groningen, 1979), pp. 1–25; G. J. Schutte and O. W. Dubois, "Rede en gezuiverde godsdienst: De Spectator 'De Denker' als spiegel van de Christelijke Verlichting," *Radix* 11 (1985): 14–22; L. H. M. Wessels, "Tussen ratio en revelatio: De Nederlandse Verlichting beoordeeld," in *De periferie in het centrum, opstellen door collegae aangeboden aan M. G. Spiertz*, ed. P. J. A. N. Rietbergen (Nijmegen, 1986), pp. 135–161.

social and cultural roots of these groups of spokesmen,[2] whose main representatives found each other from 1784 onward in the *Maatschappij tot Nut van 't Algemeen* (Society for Public Welfare)[3] gave the Dutch Enlightenment in the revolutionary era three main characteristics: (1) a basic acceptance of the society of orders, which had to remain the framework for a redistribution of social and cultural responsibilities, no longer along the lines of birth or rank, but according to merit; (2) the creation and diffusion of a strongly negative image of both the aristocracy (including the urban patriciate) and the poor; and (3) the conviction that a rational religion, respectful of a well-ordered society, would be the best transmission channel for enlightened virtue and the most convenient legitimation of the new societal order.

In the tradition of London's spectatorial journalism, inaugurated in Holland by the gazetteer Justus van Effen, such writers as the publisher and gazetteer Elie Luzac (himself the son of a French refugee), the physician Simon Stijl, and the minister and theologian Ysbrand van Hamelsveld blamed the rich for having forgotten the ancient Batavian virtues and for following the luxurious, depraved, and indeed ridiculous lifestyle of the French court aristocracy. Equally, the poor incurred reproach for still living in the savage, childish age of civilization. Hence the enlightened ideologies of the middle class, whether Patriot or Oran-

---

2. For the link between social aspirations and cultural developments, see the indications given by J. W. Oerlemans, "Carrièrisme en cultuur," *Hollands Maandblad*, no. 427/428 (1983): 41–50, and J. W. Oerlemans, *Sociale ongelijkheid als cultuurhistorisch thema*, Inaugural lecture, Erasmus University, Rotterdam, 1986 (Groningen, 1987).

3. See W. W. Mijnhardt and A. J. Wichers, *Om het algemeen volksgeluk: Twee eeuwen particulier initiatief, 1784–1984* (Edam, 1984). In an undated report to Louis Napoleon, king of Holland (1806–1810), the board of the *Nut* defined its scope as follows: "But: Elle se propose de travailler à l'avancement de la vertu et des bonnes moeurs conformément aux principes fondamentaux du christianisme parmi les classes moins cultivées. Objet de ses travaux. Les objets des travaux de la Société sont: I. les adultes. II. la génération naissante.

I. Elle travaille pour les adultes en leur fournissant des livres qui réunissant l'utile à l'agréable tendent à leur donner des idées nettes de leurs devoirs, des notions claires de la nature, des arts et des sciences qui influent sur le bonheur des classes moins éclairées et moins favorisées de la fortune. . . . II. Elle s'occupe de la génération naissante, en introduisant un mode d'enseignement plus analogue à la vraie marche du développement des facultés intellectuelles: en enseignant aux instituteurs la manière d'inculquer, déjà de bonne heure, à la jeunesse les principes des vertus sociales: et en fournissant des livres élémentaires à l'usage des écoles. . . . Borne de ses travaux. Pour devenir d'autant plus utile aux classes moins cultivées, la Société a renoncé absolument à tout ce qui peut porter une empreinte scientifique: elle s'efforce à faire germer les vrais principes du christianisme, sans en toucher les dogmes; elle veut vaincre les préjugés; mais elle ne protège aucun système; elle veut former de bons citoyens, mais elle n'entre en aucune discussion sur des matières politiques, et s'attache uniquement à démontrer que le bonheur d'un Etat est fondé sur la vertu des individus qui le composent." Paris, Archives Nationales, AF IV 1816, pièce 12.

gist, agreed on the need to regenerate Dutch society by focusing on a historical standard of national virtues, legitimated by religion in its enlightened form, that is, void of all superstition. To realize a nation-directed kind of responsible virtue, it was necessary to restrain the internationalizing tendency of the rich while educating the poor out of their uncivilized, prenational savagery of mind and manners.

The Dutch Enlightenment generated a two-pronged educational approach. A negative strategy opposed "depraved French taste," marked, it was claimed, by a luxurious, effeminate, and immoral way of life. French society was depicted as being imbued with an idle sense of honor, not the sound search for profit that was presumed to have been one of the major virtues of the ancient Dutch natives.[4] The positive strategy was a "civilizing offensive" toward the lower classes, which were considered to be living in an almost animal-like condition. As Van Hamelsveld put it, "entirely destitute of any skills, completely thoughtless and unconscious of their origin, duties, and destiny, ignorant of God and his commandments, a considerable part of these unfortunates live only for the passions; their human shape is the unique feature that distinguishes them from the brutes of creation. Their amusements are excessive, their behavior is savage."[5]

In a study about the notion of "the people," G. Bollème has shown that in eighteenth-century France the approach to "popular culture" in the anthropological sense of the word—that is, the lifestyle of the lower classes—leaned heavily on very old connotations of the term, most of which users of the word were normally unaware of.[6] From ancient times, "the people" were imagined to possess certain stereo-

---

4. C. J. Nieuwenhuys, *Proeve eener geneeskundige plaatsbeschrijving der stad Amsterdam*, vol. 1 (Amsterdam, 1816), pp. 222–234. E. Luzac, *Hollands rijkdom*, vol. 4 (Leiden, 1783), pp. 272–273; see also W. Frijhoff, "Modèles éducatifs et circulation des hommes: Les ambiguïtés du second Refuge," in *The Revocation of the Edict of Nantes and the Dutch Republic: International Congress of the Tricentennial, Leyde 1–3 April 1985* (Amsterdam-Maarssen, 1986), pp. 72–74; W. Frijhoff, "l'Usage du français en Hollande, XVIIe–XIXe siècles: Propositions pour une modèle d'interprétation," *Etudes du Linguistique Appliquée* 78 (1990): 17–26.

5. Y. van Hamelsveld, *De zedelijke toestand der Nederlandsche natie op het einde der 18e eeuw* (Amsterdam, 1791), pp. 117–146. I am indebted to J. Lenders, whose Ph.D. thesis "De burger en de volksschool" (Nijmegen, 1988) includes a fine compilation of enlightened Dutch utterances about the lower classes. For the notion of "civilizing offensive," related to the theoretical perspectives of Norbert Elias, see B. Kruithof, "De deugdzame natie: Het burgerlijke beschavingsoffensief van de Maatschappij tot Nut van 't Algemeen tussen 1784 en 1860," *Symposion Tijdschrift voor Maatschappijwetenschap* 1 (1980): 22–37; A. Mitzman, "Het beschavingsoffensief: mentaliteit, cultuur en psyche," *Sociologisch Tijdschrift* 13 (1986): 179–222; A. Pouw, "'Waare verlichting' van de vrouw: Vrouwen en gezin binnen het burgerlijk beschavingsideaal van de Maatschappij tot Nut van 't Algemeen, 1784–ca. 1840," *Comenius*, no. 23 (1986): 292–317.

6. G. Bollème, *Le peuple par écrit* (Paris, 1986), pp. 22–37.

typical features: uncontrolled strength, vital force, endless noise, gathering crowds, inconstant and passionate behavior, but also spontaneity and creativeness. Out of these stereotypes, came the ambiguous attitude of the enlightened middle classes toward their "people": the need to restrain and control the preindustrial crowd for the benefit of a well-ordered society clashed with the desire to use the unspoiled qualities and virtues of the uncivilized for the regeneration of the whole nation.

Such a semantic analysis of the Dutch term for the "people" does not yet exist for the northern Netherlands, but the basic lines of its linguistic evolution do not seem very different from French usage. As early as the Middle Ages, the Middle Dutch word *volc* (*populus*) acquired two different meanings: it indicated either the whole body of a city, region, or country (*gens, natio*) or the (socially speaking) lesser part of it (*plebs, vulgus* [*in populo*]; in Dutch '*t gemeyn* or, later, '*t grauw*).[7] A closer look at contemporary accounts of seventeenth- and early eighteenth-century disturbances in Holland reveals the primacy of the second meaning under the pen of the middle-class eyewitnesses: *volk* or *volkje* indicates the uneducated and even riotous mob, as opposed to the hard-headed *burgerij* (the citizens) and the ruling classes.[8] Significantly, Anthoni van der Helm, one of the few witnesses of lower, artisan origin, did not use the word *volk* at all but referred only to the citizenship as a whole. Nevertheless, several decades later the nobleman Joan Derk van der Capellen addressed his famous pamphlet *Aan het volk van Nederland* to the whole of the people of the Netherlands, excluding, however implicitly, the unbridled mob, which both the Orangists and the Patriots feared.

The ambiguity of the notion of "the people" accounts for two divergent approaches to "popular culture" on the part of eighteenth-century elites and for a twofold form of "popular politics." Both approaches introduced a new element: they acknowledged the autonomous existence of the "people" as a particular, socially relevant category with a definite place and even task in the history of humankind and related it to the equally new concept of "nation," imprisoned in a unitary state.[9] Both approaches "discovered" the people as an *object* of

7. E. Verwijs and J. Verdam, *Middelnederlandsch woordenboek*, vol. 9 (The Hague, 1929), pp. 842–845, s.v. 'Volc'.

8. See the documents edited by R. M. Dekker, *Oproeren in Holland gezien door tijdgenoten: Ooggetuigeverslagen van oproeren in de provincie Holland ten tijde van de Republiek (1690–1750)* (Assen, 1979).

9. Compare the following statement taken from a booklet about the rights of man and citizen, probably issued on behalf of the *Nut* in 1795: "Remember, children, true liberty is obedience to the Law, founded upon welfare of the people"; *De regten van den mensch en*

cultural or historical interest, set apart either in space or in time, and both made them the *subject* of historical action, each in its own manner.[10] Each approach can be seen in an author who might be considered typical of the first generation of ethnologists—or, better, of proto-ethnologists—able to look at the cultural practices and beliefs of the people in their own country with an observer's eye, from a distant point of view.

The first approach, embedded in the mainstream of enlightened encyclopedism, constructed a typical people in the dimension of time. In contrast to the vices of the rich and mighty, it demonstrated how the virtues of the ancient Batavian "nation" still persisted in that part of the people that had not yet been spoiled by corrupting influences from outside. Its main representative in the eighteenth century was a physician and, after 1773, reader in natural history at Leiden University, Johannes Le Francq van Berkhey (1729–1813). In spite of his aristocratic name, Le Francq was the son of a Leiden woolen draper and the grandson of an art dealer who gave him a broad education including classical and modern languages, drawing, and commercial studies. This encyclopedic education endowed him with the habit of observation, and his family's fortune enabled him to travel around the country. These two advantages enabled him to write the comprehensive *Natuurlyke historie van Holland* (Natural History of Holland, 1769–1778; French trans. 1781). This opus magnum may qualify him as the founding father of Dutch cultural anthropology.[11]

After describing the geography and geology of the province of Holland—which is the only one he dealt with—Le Francq offered a systematic description of the Dutch people and their life. First, following a

---

*burger, en de pligten daaruit voortvloeijende, voor de vaderlandsche jeugd* (Leiden, 1795), p. 27.

10. For a comparable evolution in Germany, see H. Moser, "Volk, Volksgeist, Volkskultur: Die Auffassungen J. G. Herders in heutiger Sicht," *Zeitschrift für Volkskunde* 53 (1956–1957): 127–140. The *vulgus* meaning of the term led Herder to the concept of "Volkssitte," but he made a clear distinction between the creative *vulgus* and the destructive mob. For bibliographic indications of the invention of "popular culture," see W. Frijhoff, "Literatuurwijzer," in *Religieuze volkscultuur: De spanning tussen de voorgeschreven orde en de geleefde praktijk,* ed. G. Rooijakkers and Th. van der Zee (Nijmegen, 1986), pp. 137–171. On the concept itself, see W. Frijhoff "Popular Culture, a Useful Notion?" in *Alledaagsleven: Vrije tijd en cultuur,* vol. 2, ed. E. Meijer (Tilburg, 1987), pp. 581–587.

11. J. J. Voskuil, "Geschiedenis van de volkskunde in Nederland: Portret van een dicipline," *Volkskundig Bulletin* 10 (1984): 53–55, whose analysis I follow. On Le Francq van Berkhey, see P. J. Meertens, "Joannes le Francq van Berkhey, ein Holländischer Volkskundler aus der Zeit der Aufklärung," in *In Memoriam Antonio Jorge Dias,* vol. 2 (Lisbon, 1974), pp. 309–317.

long tradition in Dutch historiography going back to Grotius (1610) and his predecessors, he identified the Dutch with the descendants of the Batavians mentioned by the Roman writer Tacitus.[12] He derived the current Dutch mentality from the state of mind, qualities, and virtues of the ancient Batavians. In the direct continuity between the two, he found a normative implication: real Dutch manners were similar to those of the Batavian people. Hence, in describing the lifestyle of the people of Holland, Le Francq paid particular attention to what he called its *volkseigen* aspects, that is, those aspects "typical of the people as such," the concept of "people" being employed here in a broad sense.[13] His book dealt extensively with four topics: the physical condition, dress, attitudes of mind, and temper of the Dutch inhabitants. Moved by a scholar's curiosity and rather detached interest, Le Francq described the morals, manners, and passions of the Dutch, the rituals of their life cycle, and the conditions of their education.[14]

A most interesting part of Le Francq's study is not just the utterly careful description, which is still delightful to read, but the cultural differences suggested for various groups of Dutch inhabitants. His explanation was essentially historical. On the borders of the province of Holland and in the Dutch cities, the original inhabitants had in the course of history mingled with immigrants and foreigners whose divergent customs and mentality spoiled the natives. Consequently, Batavian and indeed Dutch virtue in its most pure and original form might be found in the rural areas in the heart of the province of Holland, surrounded by the circle of corrupted cities and towns. Le Francq's rather sober and realistic description did not aim at a huge project of popular education. The material prosperity and the relatively high level of cultural achievements of the countryside of the province of Holland in his time contrasted strongly with the miserable physical, material, and cultural condition of the urban poor.[15] Nor did the enlightened stereotype of the good, unspoiled peasant imply a considerable effort of rural education.

12. See I. Schöffer, "The Batavian Myth during the Sixteenth and Seventeenth Centuries," in *Britain and the Netherlands*, vol. 5, ed. J. S. Bromley and E. H. Kossmann (The Hague, 1975), pp. 78–101; H. Kampinga, *De opvattingen over onze oudere vaderlandsche geschiedenis bij de Hollandsche historici der XVIe en XVIIe eeuw* (The Hague, 1917).

13. J. le Francq van Berkhey, *Natuurlyke historie van Holland*, 6 vols. (Amsterdam, 1769–1778), part. 3, vol. 4 (1776), pp. 413–414, 775. As far as I know, this term first occurs in the work of Le Francq, who seems to have coined it.

14. Ibid., vol. 5, pp. 1286–1326.

15. See L. F. van Loo, "De armenzorg in de noordelijke Nederlanden, 1770–1854," in *Algemene geschiedenis der Nederlanden*, vol. 11 (Bussum, 1981), pp. 417–435.

To be sure, Le Francq was not the first to describe features of Dutch popular life. Beginning with such scholars as Erasmus (in his *Laus stultitiae* and *Colloquia*) and other humanist opponents of superstition, a long chain of predecessors had analyzed selected aspects of popular beliefs and practices.[16] One of the most interesting of these was the Calvinist minister and physician Johannes Picardt (1600–1670). His antiquarian work about the Drenthe territory—where he was appointed—discloses a historical method that tries to establish a meaningful relation between the results of the author's personal observations, his discussions with members of his flock and other inhabitants of his region, and his learned culture, based on his readings in classical and biblical antiquity.[17]

But there are some fundamental differences between the early modern tradition of erudite polyhistorism on the one side and enlightened encyclopedism on the other.[18] In a spirit of *curiositas*, of criticism of the unusual and extraordinary, the polyhistorians picked up odd features of local popular life—fairy tales, uncommon rituals, or the existence of unexplained objects or artifacts such as the *monticuli* in the flat Dutch landscape noted by Picardt—and tried to make some sense of them. They combined bits of learned culture, almost haphazardly and in any case at a local level, or at best they sought to establish formal or verbal analogies between old and new names or ancient and recent customs. What was new with enlightened encyclopedism was its focus on a *traditio*, its regional and ethnic fixation, and, within these limits, its distinctly universal pretensions. Le Francq did not describe particular customs of the popular classes, either strange or familar; he described the people as a whole, through its customs, no matter how strange or fa-

16. See, for example, H. Trümpy, "Theorie und Praxis des volkstümlichen Erzählens bei Erasmus von Rotterdam," *Fabula* 20 (1979): 239–248; R. van Nahl, *Zauberglaube und Hexenwahn im Gebiet von Rhein und Maas: Spätmittelalterlicher Volksglaube im Werk Johan Weyers (1515–1588)* (Bonn, 1983); Chr. Daxelmüller, *Disputationes curiosae: Zum 'volkskundlichen' Polyhistorismus an den Universitäten des 17. und 18. Jahrhunderts* (Würzburg, 1979). In Holland, a famous and influential work was the compilation of food customs by C. van Alkemade and P. van der Schelling, *Nederlands displegtigheden*, 3 vols. (Rotterdam, 1732–1735).

17. J. Picardt, *Korte beschryvinge van eenige vergetene en verborgene Antiquiteiten der Provintie en Landen gelegen tusschen de Noord-Zee, de Yssel, Emse en Lippe* (Amsterdam, 1660). See also W. Frijhoff, *Cultuur, mentaliteit: Illusies van elites?* (Nijmegen, 1984), pp. 24–25.

18. On learned polyhistorism in the Netherlands, see J. Roelevink, *Gedicteerd verleden: Het onderwijs in de algemene geschiedenis aan de universiteit te Utrecht, 1735–1839* (Amsterdam-Maarssen, 1986).

miliar they might be.[19] Phenomena ascribed formerly to the transcendent world were now reintegrated into the ordinary, immanent world and interpreted as mere disorder, a disturbance of the normal order that could be reestablished. Among the people, in their uniqueness, he distinguished between groups or sectors of inhabitants according to which of them had remained more or less true to the ancient universe of beliefs and practices. In doing so, he delimited areas for possible intervention by less neutral observers, who did not subdivide the Dutch cultural universe into a succession of historical layers or sediments. Instead, they employed a synchronic and spatial dichotomy: the contemporary culture of the rural "people" against that of the urban civilized elites.

In a certain sense, Le Francq looked at the people from within, as a participant observer. The people he discovered were fundamentally his own; his historical discourse about them served merely to define degrees of group loyalty to the common national identity. His warning was directed toward those who went beyond the continuity and solidarity of the people as a whole, who marched quicker than the natural rhythm of evolution of the commonwealth, the natural rhythm of an idealized countryside. That is why his description of Dutch culture was included in his natural history, the two terms of the title being of equal importance.

The other approach to the "people" by Dutch Enlightenment observers deliberately operated from without. It applied a radically different discourse to the observed reality, and it may be linked with another type of natural history, the one David Hume proclaimed in the middle of the eighteenth century. In his *Natural History of Religion*, Hume drew a sharp line between the religious experience of the intellectual elite and that of the "vulgar." Human beings, he insisted, are not natural monotheists who, through sin (therefore historically), have lost their original simplicity of vision. On the contrary, theism depends on achieving a coherent and rational view of the universe from which the enlightened mind might then deduce the existence of a supreme being. The history of humankind is not a simple history of decline from an

---

19. For the general trend of this evolution, see H. Bausinger, "Aufklärung und Aberglaube," *Deutsche Vierteljahrsschrift für Literaturwissenschaft und Geistesgeschichte* 37 (1963): 345–362; K. D. Sievers, "Aberglaube in der Sicht der protestantischen Orthodoxie und der Aufklärung: Entwicklungsgeschichtliche Betrachtungen," *Kieler Blätter zur Volkskunde* 13 (1981): 27–54.

original monotheism; it is marked by a constant tension between theistic and polytheistic ways of thinking. "It is remarkable," Hume noted, "that the principles of religion have had a flux and reflux in the human mind, and that men have a natural tendency to rise from idolatry to theism and to sink again from theism to idolatry."[20] So the diachronic approach of Le Francq was replaced by a synchronic explanation which, for the benefit of the whole commonwealth, authorized a cultural and religious policy from the educated toward the uneducated. It inaugurated what Henry May has called the "didactic" phase of the Enlightenment.

In itself, this was not a new attitude. Several decades of research in religious history have taught us that both the Protestant Reformation and the Catholic (Counter-)Reformation had a similar goal: the creation of a new community of Christians, whose common mark and spiritual warrant was knowledge about their faith.[21] Anthropologically, the difference between the churches was not a greater or lesser tendency to superstition or to purity of faith but mainly a divergence of cultural tools used for attaining an identical scope. Puritan religion aimed at minimizing the semantic field of reality in order to achieve an almost naturally compelling movement toward God, whereas Catholic religion in its baroque alternative tried to maximize the universe of meaningful signs and symbols in order to pervade the whole society with God's theatrical ubiquity.

Both extremes were present in Dutch eighteenth-century society, although the Catholic alternative had to keep quiet within the gilt walls of richly decorated semiclandestine churches. As for the Puritan temptation, during the later seventeenth and the eighteenth centuries it permeated Dutch Calvinist mentality and imperceptibly changed its attitude toward the material aspects of life and religion, which it tried to remove from the field of perception. The monotheistic need for abstraction, as recorded by Hume, legitimated this long purifying effort, until in the beginning of the nineteenth century all the Protestant churches were turned into pure, whitewashed spaces, where the only relevant semantic feature was abstraction. We hear an unmistakable

20. D. Hume, "The Natural History of Religion," in *Essays, Moral, Political and Literary*, vol. 2 (London, 1875), p. 334sq.; quoted in P. Brown, *Society and the Holy in Late Antiquity* (New York, 1982), pp. 8–9.

21. This "acculturation" thesis of popular religion has been eloquently discussed and defended by J. Delumeau and R. Muchembled. Rather critical words have been uttered by J. Wirth, "Against the Acculturation Thesis," in *Religion and Society in Early Modern Europe, 1500–1800*, ed. K. von Greierz (London, 1984), pp. 66–78, followed by other scholars.

echo of this great design in the sermon preached at the Zeeland town of Veere in 1772 by the Reverend Josua van Iperen, at the occasion of the bicentennial of the Reformation: "Oh! what a metamorphosis! Wherever we go, wherever we turn, we find no images, no altars, nothing whatever that might give occasion for superstition. Everything tastes of the original Apostolic simplicity."[22]

This traditional strategy of purifying interventionism in religious life received a new impetus during the Enlightenment. The synchronic approach that emphasized cultural differences defined new areas for intervention, areas in both religion and society. It linked religious ideals and civic virtues to form a single and compelling justification for intervention. Social reform, not encyclopedism, drove the movement. And social reform determined the limits of interventionism. Therefore, the "people" as defined by these reformers were no longer constituted along structural or functional lines (for example, clergy versus laity) but on the sociocultural lines of approach traced by the new reformers.

In tracing these lines, the reformers benefited from new achievements of the Enlightenment era, more precisely its great design of a new social morality involving all social classes. They also had available to them increasing medical knowledge and the new preventionist attitude of the medical professionals. When the medical world discussed society, in treatises presented before learned societies or in the new genre of "topographic descriptions," it defined sectors of susceptibility for physical and social disease, the two being closely linked in the current miasmatic paradigm.[23] This approach drew up parameters and prescribed material and social remedies. Parameters of the social and religious disease called "popular culture" or "superstition" were a credulous mentality, the emotional tyranny of noisy and passionate behavior, a dissoluteness of manners, a constant overexcitement, a fixation on colors and outer appearances—in brief, all the characteristics of childhood. Popular culture was the childish phase of civilization and its remedy was education.[24] Is it surprising that medical care, national

22. Original cited in C. A. van Swigchem, T. Brouwer, and W. van Os, *Een huis voor het woord: Het Protestantse kerkinterieur in Nederland tot 1900* (The Hague, 1984), p. 5.

23. See, for example, the *Verhandelingen van de Natuur- en Geneeskundige Correspondentie-Societeit* (1779 et. sq.); H. F. J. M. van den Eerenbeemt, "Arts en sociaal besef in Nederland in historisch perspectief," *Sociale Wetenschappen* 12 (1969): 1–50.

24. As late as 1859, this is still the basic perspective of a socially progressive physician like S. Coronel, *Middelburg voorheen en thans* (Middelburg, 1859), pp. 226–227. On the other hand, it is quite striking to recognize this "infantilizing" view in the interpretations of present-day authors, such as the historian Eugen Weber in his *Peasants into Frenchmen: The Modernization of Rural France, 1870–1914* (London, 1972), especially chap. 1, and more

morals, and public education together formed the threefold subject of the new national "agent" (minister) Van Kooten, appointed according to Article 92 of the new constitution, the *staatsregeling* of 1798?

Defining areas of intervention required a search for the socio-cultural symptoms of disease. According to enlightened medical and sociohygienic convictions, the popular classes lived in a bestial state of ignorance and ferocity, far from the knowledge and self-restraint that marked civilization. Not every symptom of disease, however, called for immediate intervention. Mere superstitious errors might be harmless. In his inaugural lecture, *Oratio de prudenti Christi apostolorumque et evangelistarum consilio sermones et scripta ad captum atque intellectum vulgi quantum illud fieri potuit accomodantium*,[25] the newly appointed professor of divinity at the Remonstrant seminary, Paulus van Hemert (1756–1825), upheld the theory that Jesus Christ and his apostles had deliberately conformed themselves to the harmless superstitious errors of their time, although they knew better, and that they had even been able to take advantage of those superstitions and use them in their preaching to the vulgar.

It is important to realize that popular culture was not the only form of "social disease." The diagnosis did not simply follow the divisions of the current social stratification. Reflecting on what he called the nervous period (*zenuw-periode*) of the eighteenth century, the Amsterdam physician H. F. Thijssen (1787–1830) offered a diagnosis of the revolutionary disorder. Writing in 1824, he asserted that it was the disturbance of the equilibrium between reason and sentiment that had caused fanaticism (a fertile soil for revolution) and magnetism. He blamed, not the popular classes in particular, but the citizens as a whole. The real revolution was another one: "It is a good thing that now the seeds of the revolution germinate, that the hazes of prejudice, dissolved in the higher regions of society, will soon be equally removed in its lower regions by the sun of the civilization; and that the citizen, put on the road to civilization by all the schools of the city and the numerous institutions for public welfare, will follow the more distinguished on the path of morality."[26]

---

implicitly in the work of many advocates of the "civilizing offensive" hypothesis. See also J. Devlin, *The Superstitious Mind* (New Haven–London, 1986), p. 218.

25. (Amsterdam, 1791), with a Dutch translation.

26. H. F. Thijssen, *Geschiedkundige beschouwing der ziekten in de Nederlanden: In verband met de gesteldheid des lands en de leefwijze der inwoneren* (Amsterdam, 1824), pp. 70–71.

Therefore, when the enlightened elites stigmatized social groups for cultural backwardness, they did not do so merely because of their socioeconomic position and perspective. The definition the elite employed may also have been influenced by other factors, such as discrimination inflicted by some groups on others. As a matter of fact, the social reformers singled out three social sectors, each the target of a specific elite group. One sector was the mass of unemployed urban poor, which became the object of reform by local elites, who criticized their immoral way of life. A second sector was the superstitious peasantry of the inner provinces, who were to be civilized in a common offensive led by school teachers, clerics, and other representatives of those professions which, through their movement from one locality to another, were carriers and propagators of the supralocal patterns of culture called "civilization." A third sector was defined less along socioeconomic than religious lines; it concerned those people who lived in the darkness of Popery (Catholicism), who needed to be brought to civilized enlightenment. This concern led a broad group of interventionists to stigmatize all dissenting forms of belief and practice.[27]

One author in particular exemplifies the second and synchronic approach to cultural differences commonly proposed by the Enlightenment. Stephanus Hanewinkel (1776–1856) was the son of a Calvinist minister of Nuenen in the predominantly Catholic province of Brabant—the same village where, nearly a century later, Van Gogh, the son of one of his successors, painted his famous *Potato Eaters*. Hanewinkel was himself from 1790 onward a minister in several little parishes of the same province, a Calvinist rarity in a sky of Catholics. He used his leisure to make short trips around the province, observing all sorts of customs, speaking and sometimes debating with local people, but apparently always without revealing his identity; otherwise, the answers would have been too hostile to permit frank discussion about local beliefs. The account of his travels across the province, dated fictitiously to 1798–1799 (when he was a minister in Holland) and written as a series of letters to a friend in Holland, qualifies him as another protoethnologist in the northern Netherlands, but one of a rather dif-

27. See W. Frijhoff, "Problèmes d'une approche de la 'religion populaire' dans un pays de confession mixte: Le cas des Provinces-Unies," in *La Religion populaire: Colloques internationaux du CNRS, no. 576* (Paris, 1979); W. Frijhoff, "Katholieke toekomstverwachting ten tijde van de Republiek: Structuur, en grondlijnen tot een interpretatie," *Bijdragen en Mededelingen betreffende de Geschiedenis der Nederlanden* 98 (1983): 430–459; A. W. F. M. van de Sande, "Beeldvorming over Noord-Brabant en antipapisme in het begin van de negentiende eeuw," in *De periferie in het centrum*, ed. Rietbergen, pp. 95–108.

ferent kind from Le Francq.[28] Nothing escaped his attention: popular religious or magical practices, birth or funeral rituals, pilgrimages to holy shrines or sacred trees, living traditions about buildings, historical events or local heroes, forms of magic or witchcraft, prophecies about coming times.

Instead of trying systematically to recreate the social and cultural universe of the people observed, Hanewinkel employed another unifying principle. From the priests, teachers, and burgomasters to the simple faithful, he saw all Catholics and the whole range of their activities, beliefs, and practices under the common denominator of superstition, defined in another anonymous treatise, apparently written by the same author, as "the adoption as infallible truths of matters contrary to sound reason."[29] For Hanewinkel, the Catholic faith as a whole was simply an obscurantist superstition, and its priests, who willingly manipulated their flock, deserved no more respect than their faithful. On the contrary, the Brabant case was living proof of the need for enlightened instruction. Only after such instruction could toleration toward other (Protestant) opinions arise and a responsible people shape an adult nation. As long as the obscurantist Catholic clergy, educated at that hotbed of spiritual depravation, the University of Louvain (and similar Catholic institutions), remained in charge of the people's instruction, the enlightened Protestant elite would have to keep exclusive responsibility for the nation's destiny, planning at the same time an efficient fight against the darkness of all the Catholic beliefs.

Consequently, in the Enlightenment period and into the early nineteenth century, two approaches toward popular culture may be distinguished in the northern Netherlands: a more explanatory, anthropological approach, using a historical, or at least diachronic, method, and a more normative approach, using a synchronic method. Both approaches shared many characteristics but started from a fundamentally different preoccupation and led to even more different attitudes toward popular culture. The diachronic approach, rooted in encyclopedism, may be considered the starting point of what would soon be called folklore research.[30] Dutch folklorists of the early nineteenth century,

28. [S. Hanewinkel], *Reize door de Majorij van 's Hertogenbosch in den jaare 1798–1799*, 2 vols. (Amsterdam, 1799–1800). Of course, this whole travel account may be fictitious.

29. [S. Hanewinkel], *Gedachten over de Meiërij van 's Hertogenbosch en derzelver inwoners bij het begin der negentiende eeuw* (Amsterdam, 1801), p. 18.

30. For simultaneous evolutions abroad, see H. Bausinger, *Volkskunde: Von der Altertumswissenschaft zur Kulturanalyse* (Berlin, 1972); R. M. Dorson, *The British Folklorists: A History* (Chicago, 1968); J. Copans and J. Jamin, eds., *Aux origines de l'anthropologie française: Les Mémoires de la Société des Observateurs de l'Homme en l'an VIII* (Paris, 1978);

such as Nicolaas Westendorp (who in 1819 founded the first Dutch folklore periodical under the eloquent title *Antiquiteiten*), the landed proprietor and poet Anthony C. W. Staring, or the librarian L. Ph. C. van den Bergh, had an essentially antiquarian interest in the matter of popular culture. They constructed, invented, and discovered it, departing from the perceived difference of cultural forms, values, and beliefs produced by social groups they identified as popular from their educated point of view. They sought mainly to find a scientific explanation of existing cultural differences, with the help of all the resources of the historical method, including archaeology and ancient, classical, or Germanic mythology. For the folklorists, popular customs were historical customs, "survivals," deemed to disappear as time went on. Superstitions and popular beliefs were a consequence of unequal rhythms in the cultural evolution of social groups.[31] The advancing unification of society would resolve the problem.

The folklorists were not unaware of the problem posed to the cultural identity of their society by the very existence of something like popular culture. The most important folklorist of the first half of the nineteenth century, the Frisian Mennonite minister Joost Hiddes Halbertsma, wrote in 1837:

> Once and for all it should be said that, speaking of popular ideas, popular superstition, popular customs, the character or the idiom of the people, we always talk about the so-called common man. In a

M. de Certeau, D. Julia, and J. Revel, "La Beauté du mort: le Concept de culture populaire," *Politique Aujourd'hui* (December 1970): 3–23; M. Ozouf, "L'invention de l'ethnographie française: Le Questionnaire de l'Académie celtique," *Annales E.S.C.* 36 (1981): 210–230; H. Senn, "Folklore Beginnings in France: The Académie celtique, 1804–1813," *Journal of the Folklore Institute* 18 (1981): 23–33; B. Kilborn, "Anthropological Thought in the Wake of the French Revolution: La Société des Observateurs de l'Homme," *Archives Européennes de Sociologie* 23 (1982): 73–91; N. Belmont, *Paroles païennes: Mythe et folklore* (Paris, 1986).

31. Literally, *superstitio* means "what survives." The terminological change implies a rationalization and a secularization of the perspective; see P. Saintyves, "Les Origines de la méthode comparative et la naissance du folklore: Des superstitions aux survivances," *Revue de l'Histoire des Religions* 105 (1932): 44–70. The "survival" hypothesis has long remained a basic tool of folklore research. It was still an identifying instrument for P. J. Meertens, "Vorreformatorische Relikte in den reformatorischen Niederlanden," in *Festschrift Matthias Zender: Studien zu Volkskultur, Sprache und Landesgeschichte*, vol. 1, ed. F. Ennen and G. Wiegelmann (Bonn, 1972), pp. 395–411. I discuss some methodological implications in W. Frijhoff, "Vraagtekens bij het vroegmoderne kersteningsoffensief," in *Religieuze volkscultuur*, ed. Rooijakkers and Van der Zee, pp. 71–98. J. W. Buisman, "Secularisering en maatschappij in Nederland in de tweede helft van de achttiende eeuw," in *Rede, sentiment en ervaring: Sociale wetenschap in de achttiende eeuw*, ed. W. Arts and J. K. M. Gevers (Deventer, 1983), pp. 36–50, makes clear that the disenchantment of the world had to travel far before reaching the bulk of the Protestant ministers, who were obsessed by an interpretation of society and history in terms of guilt and punishment. That is why Balthasar Bekker, the late seven-

moral and a linguistic, and partly in a civic sense, the common people are properly speaking the people. Language, lifestyle, manners, and customs are a subject of agreement among the affluent people; there is not and cannot be anything national in it, because they conform to a standard that lies beyond the nation. The higher they climb, the more accurate they follow that standard and the more all the affluent people of Europe resemble each other.[32]

In this passage, Halbertsma constructed an opposition between the freely chosen standard of elite behavior (civilization) and the traditional culture of the people, imprisoned in space and time.

The representatives of the second approach directed their main effort at narrowing this gap, by liberating the people from their passions and their uncontrolled social condition and imposing on them the free choice of a strict system of social codes and cultural norms: a new, more rigid prison for the benefit of society. The individual would gain self-consciousness and the self-respect resulting from a free sacrifice on the altar of the societal edifice. During the whole nineteenth century, social hygienics departed from the synchronic approach of the "people" in order to intervene actively in the structuring of social and cultural ideals, practices, and relationships, in brief, to reform popular culture. Beginning with the *Maatschappij tot Nut van 't Algemeen* and its obstinate struggle against magical practices and superstitious convictions, the inadmissibility of the existence of popular beliefs and practices in a well-ordered society legitimized unremitting intervention in the lower social classes.[33] This interventionism covered the reality of those beliefs and practices with a thick, intellectual and normative dis-

---

teenth-century minister and fighter against a certain theological conception of demonology, can be praised by his enlightened colleague Jacobus Scheltema as a forerunner in his battle with superstition; see J. Scheltema, "Het leeven, de leer en lotgevallen van Balthasar Bekker," in *Algemeene vaderlandsche letteroefeningen* (1804), pt. 2, pp. 49–67, 97–111, 145–157.

32. J. H. Halbertsma, "De witte wiven," *Overijsselsche Volksalmanak* 2 (1837): 246–247. In his introduction to J. van Lennep, *Proeve van het Plat-Amsterdamsch* (Deventer, 1845), p. 37, the same Halbertsma gave a similar definition. See also M. F. Schatz, *Plat Amsterdams in Its Social Context: A Sociolinguistic Study of the Dialect of Amsterdam* (Amsterdam, 1986), p. 29.

33. See, for example, H. W. van der Ploeg, *Het belang der waare Volkverlichting* (Amsterdam, 1800); G. Bakker, *Betoog van het ongegronde, onzedelijke en schadelijke der vooroordeelen omtrend de waarzeggerijen, toverijen, spookerijen, enz.* (Amsterdam, 1802). On the concept of popular Enlightenment, see J. Voss, "Der gemeine Mann und die Volksaufklärung im späten 18. Jahrhundert," in *Vom Elend der Handarbeid,* ed. H. Mommsen and W. Schulze (Stuttgart, 1981), pp. 258–283; J. Voss, "Zur deutschen Aufklärungsdiskussion im späten 18. Jahrhundert," *Innsbrucker Historische Studien* 7/8 (1985): 263–283; R. Vierhaus, "'Aufklärung' et monde populaire," in *Histoire sociale, sensibilités collectives et*

course that makes it extremely difficult for us to reconstruct it from within. It would be exaggerated to deny the mere existence of elements and expressions of early modern or even modern popular culture. To what extent and at what moment that culture possessed its own autonomy and a proper, inner cohesion, one that was not derived from elite and hence unifying discourse about it—that of the folklorists and that of the interventionists—remains a subject of research. But that is quite another story.

---

*mentalités. Mélanges Robert Mandrou* (Paris, 1985), pp. 495–505. For the Netherlands, see the brief survey, beginning with the *Nut*, by H. Nijenhuis, *Volksopvoeding tussen elite en massa: Een geschiedenis van volwasseneneducatie in Nederland* (Meppel, 1981).

# 15

# Professors, Amateurs, and Learned Societies: The Organization of the Natural Sciences

## H. A. M. Snelders

T HE Dutch Republic in early modern times played a distinctive role as the Continental nursery for new scientific ideas from abroad. In the seventeenth century, René Descartes's philosophical ideas, for instance, were readily accepted in the republic, both in and outside universities and athenaea, and were subsequently propagated outside the country. Isaac Newton's empirical-mathematical natural science, too, spread across the Continent via the Netherlands, through the publications of a Dutch triumvirate: the physician and chemist Herman Boerhaave and the physicists Willem Jacob 's Gravesande and Petrus van Musschenbroek. When in 1715 Boerhaave delivered his *Sermo academicus de comparando certo in physicis* (Discourse on the Achievement of Certainty in Physics), Newtonianism gained a firm foothold at Leiden University. Two years later, 's Gravesande began lecturing on experimental physics, and in 1723 at Utrecht University Van Musschenbroek reformed the scientific curriculum according to the spirit of Newton.[1] The first scientists (although not professors) outside France to embrace and defend Antoine Laurent Lavoisier's antiphlogistic chemistry were Dutch, too: the Haarlem physician Martinus van Marum, the merchant Adriaan Paets van Troostwijk, and his friend, the physician Jan Rudolph Deiman, with their Amsterdam circle, the

1. C. de Pater, *Petrus van Musschenbroek (1692–1761), een Newtoniaans natuuronderzoeker* (Leiden, 1979). See also E. G. Ruestow, *Physics at Seventeenth- and Eighteenth-Century Leiden: Philosophy and the New Science in the University* (The Hague, 1973).

*Gezelschap der Hollandsche Scheikundigen* (Society of Dutch Chemists).[2]

The point of departure for a survey of Dutch scientific learning during the eighteenth century should be the realization that it was not until 1815 that a faculty of mathematics and natural sciences was established at the Dutch universities. During the Republic of the United Provinces, the Batavian Republic, and the French-oriented Kingdom of Holland, that is, until 1815, mathematics and natural sciences had been taught in the faculties of medicine and of natural philosophy. The faculty of natural philosophy taught both humanities and physics. Chemical-pharmaceutical and botanical education was given by medical professors, most of whom were practicing physicians. There were hardly any students in mathematics and physics; chemistry and botany were merely considered part of the medical curriculum and directly related to pharmacy and materia medica. Consequently, progress in these disciplines depended greatly on the interests of the medical professors who were required to teach them.

Preeminent in the medical faculty of the early eighteenth century was Boerhaave, who "cultivated chemistry with unbelievable devotion and taught it for some twenty-seven years with the greatest success."[3] Boerhaave's two-volume textbook, *Elementa chemiae* (1732), exerted a dominant influence on his contemporaries.[4] Unfortunately, there were few possibilities for establishing a career as a mathematician or natural scientist. In the second half of the century, scientific education and research at the universities lingered rather than flourished, while on the other hand there was an increasing interest in natural sciences among practitioners such as pharmacists and physicians.

## POPULARIZATION OF SCIENCE

The great interest that the well-to-do classes of society took in natural sciences forms another characteristic aspect of the Dutch Enlightenment. An example can be found in the diary of the Swedish astronomer Bengt Ferrner, which he kept from 12 February until 12 July 1759

2. H. A. M. Snelders, *Het gezelschap der Hollandsche Scheikundigen: Amsterdamse chemici uit het einde van de achttiende eeuw* (Amsterdam, 1980).

3. G. A. Lindeboom, *Herman Boerhaave: The Man and His Work* (London, 1968), p. 323.

4. F. Greenaway, "Boerhaave's Influence on Some 18th-Century Chemists," in *Boerhaave and His Time*, ed. G. A. Lindeboom (Leiden, 1979), pp. 102–113.

while staying in the Netherlands.[5] The wealthy Mennonite merchant Jacob de Clerq invited him to join the "Monday-evening society," so Ferrner attended lectures by the Mennonite teacher Klaas de Vries on vision and optics and by the physician Johannes Albertus Schlosser on salts. Ferrner found De Vries's lecture rather dull, partly because no experiments were performed and partly because he did not mention mathematics. But, then, not all members were sufficiently educated in that discipline. Ferrner also went to the "Thursday-evening society," where between fifteen and twenty gentlemen watched Benjamin Bosma's physical experiments on colliding and falling bodies. In 1752 Bosma had started lecturing on mathematics, metaphysics, and geography, and from 1757 onward he gave important courses on experimental physics.

A recently discovered subscription book shows that most of the 328 gentlemen attending Bosma's courses were merchants and booksellers.[6] Thirty-three of them were accompanied by their wives. For forty years, Bosma contributed greatly to the popularization of the natural sciences among the well-to-do in Amsterdam. Pieter Cramer, an eager, learned merchant who possessed a precious collection of physical and mathematical instruments as well as a remarkable shell cabinet, provided him with the necessary apparatus. Ferrner's diary reveals that many Amsterdammers had an active interest in natural sciences. Jacob de Clerq and the banker Theodoor de Smeth also had fine collections of physical instruments. De Smeth and the merchant Jacobus van de Wal each owned an astronomical observatory on top of his house; Van de Wal ground his own telescope mirrors.

Besides Bosma, there were other salaried lecturers on science. Daniel Gabriel Fahrenheit earned a living in Amsterdam making thermometers, barometers, and areometers. From 1718 until 1729, he lectured on mechanics, hydrodynamics, optics, and chemistry before an audience of laymen. In early 1720, at the request of some interested Mennonites, he began a series of lectures in experimental physics. The Leiden University library holds a collection of notes, taken by the mer-

---

5. "Bengt Ferrner's dagboek van zijne reis door Nederland in 1759, medegedeeld door G. W. Kernkamp," *Bijdragen en mededeelingen van het Historisch Genootschap* 31 (1910): 314–509.

6. M. Keyser, "Het intekenboek van Benjamin Bosma. Natuurwetenschappelijk en wijsgerig onderwijs te Amsterdam, 1752–1790: Een verkenning," *Jaarverslagen Koninklijk Oudheidkundig Genootschap* (1986): 65–81. On Bosma, see also Margaret C. Jacob, *The Cultural Meaning of the Scientific Revolution* (New York, 1988), pp. 185–186.

chant Jacob Ploos van Amstel, which provide a good insight into the contents of Fahrenheit's lectures.[7]

The popularization of natural sciences by professionals was not restricted to Dutch nationals. Benjamin Martin and James Ferguson, for example, were well-known English itinerant lecturers.[8] About 1730, the Huguenot John Theophilus Desaguliers came over from England to lecture on physical subjects in Rotterdam and The Hague. The Dutch physician Leonardus Stocke also lectured in Middelburg, Utrecht, and Rotterdam.

Bernard Nieuwentyt's *Het regt gebruik der wereltbeschouwingen ter overtuiginge van ongodisten en ongeloovigen aangetoont* (1715) exercised great influence in the Dutch Republic, and a heavily mutilated English translation appeared three years later under the title *The Religious Philosopher: or, the Right Use of Contemplating the Works of the Creator . . . Designed for the Conviction of Atheists and Infidels.* Nieuwentyt sought to prove the existence of God through teleological arguments. This Dutch version of Enlightenment thought, holding a strong Christian element, appears in several physico-theological works.[9] The study of creation not only furnished ample evidence of God's existence but also demonstrated the Creator's wisdom and omnipotence. According to his contemporary Petrus van Musschenbroek, Nieuwentyt's work in particular stimulated many people to investigate God's work in nature. Nieuwentyt's book, which resembles a manual of "modern" science, added greatly to the propagation of scientific knowledge. In 1736, Van Musschenbroek concluded: "Never were more devotees of physics in the United Netherlands met than in our present time; because not only does this science flourish among most scholars, but also among many prominent merchants and people of all rank and dignity." In 1739, he added that the interest had led to the foundation of informal learned societies "in which one is occupied to perform experiments and to revel in the contemplation of the properties and actions of a variety of bodies."[10] The scientific contributions of

7. *Fahrenheit's Letters to Leibniz and Boerhaave*, ed. P. van der Star (Leiden-Amsterdam, 1983), p. 105. University Library, Leiden; Western manuscripts department, BPL 772.

8. J. R. Millburn, "The London Evening Courses of Benjamin Martin and James Ferguson: Eighteenth-Century Lecturers on Experimental Philosophy," *Annals of Science* 40 (1983): 437–455.

9. J. Bots, *Tussen Descartes en Darwin: Geloof en natuurwetenschap in de 18e eeuw in Nederland* (Assen, 1972).

10. P. van Musschenbroek, *Beginselen der natuurkunde: Beschreven ten dienste der landgenooten* (Leiden, 1736), preface; P. van Musschenbroek, *Beginselen der natuurkunde: Beschreven ten dienste der landgenooten*, 2d ed. (Leiden, 1739), preface.

such men as Boerhaave, 's Gravesande, and Van Musschenbroek, with their ties to the universities, show that in the first half of the century the popularization of the natural sciences was not at the expense of university science.

This situation altered, however, in the second half of the century. For one thing, the level of scientific learning was simply higher in the first half of the century; Van Musschenbroek and 's Gravesande were more renowned and more original than later scientists such as Petrus Camper or Jan Hendrik van Swinden. The rise of learned societies was also a factor; they provided more practical and applied opportunities to study natural sciences than did the universities. The laymen's interests, however, did not lead to direct and original scientific progress. The experiments performed in the societies were simple and intended to instruct and amuse the spectators, not to gather new facts and insights, to contribute to the development of science. The learned societies did, however, become a strong stimulus for the construction and improvement of scientific instruments. This increasing interest in natural sciences outside the universities led to a process of institutionalization.

## LEARNED SOCIETIES

In the second half of the eighteenth century, many learned societies were established.[11] Some were more generally oriented and had dual aspirations: to acquaint their members with nature and to exchange scientific experiences and contribute to the development of the natural sciences. The societies had two kinds of members: directors, well-to-do regents, higher public servants and merchants, who governed and financed the society; and normal members (physicians, pharmacists, philosophers, and so on). The societies wanted to be officially recognized (like the Royal Society), which meant that the provincial estates would grant a patent and the stadholder would become their protector. The

11. R. Hooykaas, "De natuurwetenschappen in de eeuw der genootschappen," in *NG 200: Natuurkundig gezelschap te Utrecht, 1777–1977* (Utrecht, 1977), pp. 11–38; W. W. Mijnhardt, "Veertig jaar cultuurbevordering: Teylers Stichting, 1778–1815," in *Teyler 1778–1978: Studies en bijdragen over Teylers Stichting naar aanleiding van het tweede eeuwfeest* (Haarlem-Antwerp, 1978), pp. 58–111; W. W. Mijnhardt, "Het Nederlandse genootschap in de achttiende en vroege negentiende eeuw," *De Negentiende Eeuw* 7 (1983): 76–101; W. W. Mijnhardt, "Wetenschapsbevordering onder het Ancien Régime: Het Zeeuws Genootschap der Wetenschappen, 1765–1794," *Archief. Mededelingen van het Zeeuws Genootschap der Wetenschappen* (1985): 1–94; W. W. Mijnhardt, *Tot heil van 't menschdom: Culturele genootschappen in Nederland, 1750–1815* (Amsterdam, 1988).

first to be established was the *Hollandsche Maatschappij der Weten-schappen* (Holland Society of Sciences) at Haarlem (1752), followed by the *Zeeuwsch Genootschap der Wetenschappen* (Zeeland Society of Sciences) at Vlissingen (1765); then came the *Bataafsch Genootschap der Proefondervindelijke Wijsbegeerte* (Batavian Society of Experimental Philosophy) at Rotterdam (1769), the *Provinciaal Utrechtsch Genootschap van Kunsten en Wetenschappen* (Provincial Utrecht Society of Arts and Sciences) at Utrecht (1773), and *Teyler's Tweede Genootschap* (Teyler's Second Society) at Haarlem (1778).

The learned societies stimulated the study of natural sciences and their practical applications by offering prizes for the best essays on scientific subjects. These inducements were taken up by the scientists of the time, mainly physicians and pharmacists. Lavoisier's new chemistry, for instance, found more acceptance outside the universities and was stimulated by the prize essays of the learned societies.[12] Besides these general learned societies, local scientific societies were established in several Dutch towns: before 1770, there were two; two more in the period 1770–1779; four in 1780–1789; and nine in 1790–1799.[13] The members of these small societies of amateurs kept one another informed about their observations and experiments and they discussed and repeated the work of others. It is not surprising that most of these local societies (eleven) were established in cities in Holland, by far the wealthiest of the seven provinces.

The members of these social clubs—local ministers, physicians, pharmacists, and gentlemen from the upper and middle classes of town—were in general passively interested. They attended the weekly meetings to watch the experiments. The natural sciences of the time were interesting enough for laymen to consider participation and not so complicated as to preclude understanding. Interest in natural sciences even became fashionable. In their novel *Historie van den Heer Willem Leevend*, Elisabeth Bekker and Aagje Deken introduced a character who "has magic lanterns, illumination cases, and small air pumps, which he handles deftly; and on one occasion he also dissected a butterfly."[14] As a matter of course, the laymen's greatest interest focused on natural history (zoology, botany, mineralogy), because it was

12. H. A. M. Snelders, "The New Chemistry in the Netherlands," *Osiris* 4 (1988).

13. H. A. M. Snelders, "De natuurwetenschappen in de lokale wetenschappelijke genootschappen uit de eerste helft van de negentiende eeuw," *De Negentiende Eeuw* 7 (1983): 102–122.

14. E. Wolff and A. Deken, *Historie van den Heer Willem Leevend* (The Hague, 1784), vol. 2, pp. 50–51.

relatively easy to build up a collection of specimens. Physics, on the other hand, required a knowledge of mathematics. Emphasis therefore fell on visually appealing experiments with air pumps, magnets, prisms, and electrical machines. Besides the so-called *physique amusante*, observations with a telescope were made.

## THE NEW CHEMISTRY IN THE NETHERLANDS

In spite of these experimental trends, a lively interest in chemistry did not develop until about 1790. In the second half of the eighteenth century, scientists discovered and isolated several gases, which led to quantitative chemistry and Lavoisier's chemical revolution. Dutchmen outside the universities played a considerable role in the dissemination of the new theory of oxidation. Martinus van Marum, director of Teyler's Cabinet of Physical and Natural Curiosities and Library, became the first Lavoisierian in the Netherlands after being intensively indoctrinated by French chemists during a visit to Paris in July 1785. With the aid of the "very large electrical machine" at Teyler's museum, he interpreted his experiments according to the new chemical theory. In 1787, he published in Dutch "An Outline of the Teaching of M. Lavoisier, Concerning Pure Atmospheric Air and the Union of Its Fundamental Principle with Various Bodies," which was to play an important part in the spread of Lavoisier's ideas throughout the Netherlands.

In the spring of 1787, Lambertus Bicker, a physician and director and first secretary of the *Bataafsch Genootschap der Proefondervindelijke Wijsbegeerte* at Rotterdam, read Van Marum's "Outline" and was immediately converted to Lavoisier. Even earlier, in late 1786 or early 1787, the Utrecht professor of medicine, botany, chemistry, and physiology Alexander Petrus Nahuys was converted after he completed an independent and critical study of the antiphlogistic literature and repeated and extended the experiments described.[15] His criticism of the phlogistic ideas of the Amsterdam chemists Adriaan Paets van Troostwijk and Jan Rudolph Deiman eventually led to their conversion late 1789. In late 1790 or early 1791, Paets van Troostwijk and Deiman established a small organization, the *Gezelschap der Hollandsche Scheikundigen*, which carried out many original experiments in sup-

---

15. H. A. M. Snelders, "Lambertus Bicker (1732–1801): An Early Adherent of Lavoisier in the Netherlands," *Janus* 67 (1980): 101–123; H. A. M. Snelders, "De Utrechtse chemicus Alexander Petrus Nahuys (1737–1794)," *Jaarboek Oud Utrecht* (1980): 120–148.

port of Lavoisier's chemistry.[16] In 1798, Van Marum was able to say that "at first some chemists in this country showed anything but approbation of the fact that I had adopted the Lavoisierian theory so quickly and professed it publicly; and as far as I know, all of them without exception stuck to the theory of phlogiston. Since then, however, most of them have changed their minds so that in this country the new chemical theory no longer has opponents among chemists of any repute."[17]

After Van Marum had adopted Lavoisier's ideas in 1785, it took an incubation period of five years before the most influential members of the Dutch scientific community accepted the antiphlogistic theory. The acceptance of the new chemistry is one of the highlights in the history of eighteenth-century science in the Netherlands.

## PURE AND APPLIED SCIENCE

The interest in the new chemistry was of little importance in practical applications. The learned societies, however, were already worried about the low state of chemistry in the Netherlands. In 1784, the *Provinciaal Utrechtsch Genootschap van Kunsten en Wetenschappen* had offered a prize for the best essay on "the real causes as to why our neighbors, particularly the Germans, held chemistry in greater esteem and engage in more general study than in our country." The study of chemistry, especially applied chemistry, clearly needed improving. Although the two essays submitted for the prize did not entirely serve the purpose, the board of the society awarded a gold medal to the Groningen pharmacist Boudewijn Tieboel and a silver to his Amsterdam colleagues Theodorus Petrus Schonk and Petrus Johannes Kasteleyn.

Both prize-winning essays, published in the transactions of the society for 1786, indicated several reasons why the standard of chemistry in Germany was so much higher than in the Netherlands.[18] In the German states, the study of chemistry was encouraged for its applications in the chemical industry. The absence in the Netherlands of mine pits, ores, salt wells, and mineral waters was considered to be the main

16. Snelders, *Gezelschap der Hollandsche Scheikundigen.*

17. M. van Marum, *Life and Work*, vol. 5, ed. E. Lefebvre and J. G. de Bruijn (Leiden, 1974), p. 241.

18. B. Tieboel, *Verhandelingen van het Provinciaal Utrechtsch Genootschap van Kunsten en Wetenschappen*, vol. 4 (1786), pt. 1, pp. 1–107; Th. P. Schonk and P. J. Kasteleyn, pp. 109–183.

cause for the low state of chemistry. In Germany no fewer than thirty-two universities and high schools offered chemistry and the other natural sciences, taught by first-rank, well-paid scientists.

Tieboel and his colleagues outlined the benefits of chemistry for the education of pharmacists and pointed to its usefulness in commerce and manufacturing. They attributed the sad state of the Dutch cotton mills to the fact that no use had been made of the principles of chemistry to calculate the amounts of chemicals necessary in the manufacturing process. In the same way, it was necessary to apply agricultural chemistry to improve the soil. Even the china factory founded in 1774 by the reformed minister Johannes de Mol would have been more successful had a chemist been consulted.

Both answers on the Utrecht prize essay reveal the utilitarian ideology at work in the Dutch Enlightenment. In fact, many of the learned societies founded in the 1770s and 1780s were devoted to the arts and to social and economic correctives. The *Hollandsche Maatschappij der Wetenschappen* awarded prizes for the best essays on the welfare of the country as well as on pure science. More than 60 percent of the competitions in the period 1753–1799 covered practical topics.[19] Table 15.1

*Table 15.1* Prize competitions proposed by the *Hollandsche Maatschappij der Wetenschappen*, 1753–1799

| Subject | 1753–1759 | 1760–1769 | 1770–1779 | 1780–1789 | 1790–1799 | Total |
|---|---|---|---|---|---|---|
| General | — | 4(4)[a] | 7(5) | 6(2) | 3(1) | 20(12) |
| Pure science | | | | | | |
| astronomy | — | — | 1(1) | 1(0) | — | 2(1) |
| physics | — | — | — | 3(1) | 1(0) | 4(1) |
| chemistry | — | — | — | 1(1) | 2(0) | 3(1) |
| natural history | — | 1(1) | 1(0) | 6(1) | 3(1) | 11(3) |
| Applied science | | | | | | |
| agriculture | 2(0) | — | 4(2) | — | 5(0) | 11(2) |
| meteorology | — | — | 1(0) | — | — | 1(0) |
| medicine | 2(2) | 2(2) | 1(1) | 4(2) | 5(1) | 14(8) |
| technology | 3(3) | 4(3) | 5(3) | 4(3) | 5(3) | 21(15) |
| chemical technology | — | — | — | — | 2(0) | 2(0) |
| | 7(5) | 11(10) | 20(12) | 25(10) | 26(6) | 89(43) |

[a]The number of competitions for which prizes were awarded is given in parentheses.

19. J. G. de Bruijn, *Inventaris van de prijsvragen uitgeschreven door de Hollansche Maatschappij der Wetenschappen, 1753–1919* (Haarlem-Groningen, 1977); see also S. Schama, *Patriots and Liberators: Revolution in the Netherlands, 1780–1813* (New York, 1977), p. 73.

shows an increase of pure science between 1760 and 1799 (14.3 to 26.1 percent) and a decrease of applied science (85.7 to 73.9 percent). For the whole period 1753–1799, 32.3 percent of the competition were in pure science and 67.6 percent in applied science.

Most of the technical essays dealt with the maintenance of dikes and the navigability of rivers. In 1777, the *Hollandsche Maatschappij* decided to establish a special department for the promotion of national prosperity. In 1797, the *Oeconomische Tak* (Economic Branch) became an independent society, the *Nationale Nederlandsche Huishoudelijke Maatschappij* (National Netherlands Economic Society).[20] The decision to establish the *Oeconomische Tak* was stimulated by a contest of the *Hollandsche Maatschappij* of 1771 that had posed the question "What is the basis of Holland's commerce, its increase and prosperity?." In his answer, winner Hendrik Herman van den Heuvel, clerk of the court justice at Utrecht, suggested a plan for improving commerce.[21] He pointed to what had been done in England by the duke of Buckingham and by the society instituted in London for the encouragement of arts, manufacturing, and commerce: they had rewarded discoveries and inventions on behalf of commerce and industry. In 1788, the *Oeconomische Tak* offered no less than 55 prizes for the best essays on agriculture (15), commerce and colonial affairs (6), trade and factories (25), mechanics and chemistry (3), and navigation and fisheries (6). In 1779, the available prize money was divided as follows: 20 percent for agriculture, 20 percent for commerce and colonial affairs, 40 percent for trade and factories, 10 percent for mechanics and chemistry, and 10 percent for navigation and fisheries. Most support went to industry, particularly the textile industry; spinning schools were established and sheep farming was promoted.

The early activities of improvement societies such as the *Oeconomische Tak* met with great success. Within a short time, no less than fifty-five local branches were established all over the country, with some three thousand members. Soon, however, the enthusiasm decreased. This was also the case with the *Maatschappij ter bevordering van den landbouw* (Society for the Promotion of Agriculture) founded in Amsterdam in 1776. Between 1776 and 1801, this society published thirteen essays on topics such as the application of wood and peat

20. J. A. Bierens de Haan, *Van Oeconomische Tak tot Nederlandsche Maatschappij voor Nijverheid en Handel, 1777–1952* (Haarlem, 1952).

21. H. H. van den Heuvel, "Welke is de grond van Hollands koophandel, van zynen aanwasch en bloey?" in *Verhandelingen uitgegeeven door de Hollandsche Maatschappy der Weetenschappen*, vol. 16 (1774), pt. 1, pp. 1–160.

ashes as fertilizer, the improvement of the flax culture, the domestic breeding of horses, and the elimination of noxious plants and, of course, the rinderpest. Approximately seventy members were not farmers (most of them lived in Amsterdam and owned a house in the country), yet their interest focused on agriculture.[22]

In fact, the only learned society engaged in applied science was the *Bataafsch Genootschap* at Rotterdam. This society restricted itself to "experimental activities, which are founded a posteriori from observation, and which have been or can be affirmed by experiments or observations, or can lead to experiments, regardless of the branch of experimental philosophy or national economy they belong to." Of the competitions offered by the *Bataafsch Genootschap* between 1770 and 1800, 18.8 percent dealt with pure science and 81.2 percent with applied science. In the period 1770–1799, pure sciences decreased from 20.0 percent to zero in the last decade of the eighteenth century. Applied sciences increased from 80 to 100 percent (see Table 15.2).[23] The first prizes were offered for essays on the maintenance and improvement of rivers and dikes, in particulair in the vicinity of Rotterdam. Soon the society offered prizes for essays on the improvement of mills, and in 1778 of steam engines. The new developments in chemistry and physics were rapidly reflected in the prize essays, which discussed subjects such as the nature of lightning, the construction of a lightning conductor, the influence of atmospheric electricity on healthy and sick bodies, and new gases and their significance for medicine, to name only a few. The winter of 1788–1789 saw Lambertus Bicker lecture on the theory of steam engines—a direct result of the society's early interest in this apparatus.[24] In 1772, in defense of the steam engine, Bicker wrote *De groote voordeelen aangetoond, welken ons land genieten zou, indien men vuur-machines in plaatse van watermolens gebruikte* (The Great Advantages Proved, Which Our Country Would Enjoy, If One Used Fire Engines Instead of Water Mills). Bicker compared the power and cost of steam engines and water mills and noted especially the

22. P. van Schaik, "De Maatschappij ter bevordering van den landbouw (1776–1847)," *Landbouwkundig Tijdschrift* 74 (1962): 24–31; H. A. M. Snelders, "Landbouw en scheikunde in Nederland in de vóór-Wageningse periode (1800–1876)," *A.A.G. Bijdragen* 24 (1984): 59–104.

23. M. J. van Lieburg, *Het Bataafsch Genootschap der Proefondervindelijke Wijsbegeerte te Rotterdam, 1769–1984: Een bibliografisch en documenterend overzicht* (Amsterdam, 1985).

24. L. Bicker, "Natuurkundige leezingen, over de stoom-machine, en alles wat daartoe betrekkelijk is," in *Nieuwe verhandelingen van het Bataafsch Genootschap der Proefondervindelijke Wijsbegeerte*, vol. 1 (1800), pp. 297–538.

*Table 15.2* Prize competitions proposed by the *Bataafsch Genootschap der Proefondervindelijke Wijsbegeerte*, 1771–1799

| Subject | 1770–1779 | 1780–1789 | 1790–1799 | Total |
|---|---|---|---|---|
| General | — | 1(0)[a] | — | 1(0) |
| Pure science | | | | |
| physics | 1(1) | 3(1) | — | 4(2) |
| chemistry | 1(1) | 6(2) | — | 7(3) |
| natural history | 1(1) | — | — | 1(1) |
| Applied science | | | | |
| agriculture | — | 3(2) | — | 3(2) |
| meteorology | — | 2(0) | — | 2(0) |
| medicine | 3(3) | 11(3) | 3(3) | 17(9) |
| technology | 9(6) | 7(4) | 13(6) | 29(16) |
| chemical technology | — | 1(0) | — | 1(0) |
| | 15(12) | 34(12) | 16(9) | 65(33) |

[a]The number of competitions in which prizes were awarded is given in parentheses.

independence of the steam engine from the vagaries of wind. He rejected the argument that war with England might cause problems with the supply of coal, since that fuel could also be obtained in Liège and Ostend, and in case of emergency the country could provide peat and wood as substitutes. In spite of Dutch interest as early as the 1750s, the Newcomen engine was not introduced until 1774, when an atmospheric engine was purchased to regulate the level of Rotterdam's canal system. The engine entered service in 1776, but without success; a Watt engine for polder drainage introduced in 1778 also failed.[25]

Not all utilitarian endeavors led to a scientifically based industry. In 1786, Tieboel urged the appointment in each town of a well-paid teacher of chemistry (a physician or a pharmacist) to lecture on pharmaceutical chemistry. This would enable physicians and pharmacists to analyze the purity of chemical substances, and the increase in the general level of chemical knowledge would stimulate the investigation of natural substances and the building of chemical factories. The stimulus, however, never materialized. At the end of the eighteenth century, town lecturers in chemistry and pharmacy were eventually appointed, but they confined themselves to pharmaceutical chemistry for apprentice pharmacists. In 1784, five Amsterdam merchants proposed that

25. J. Tenn and M. J. Breckin, "The International Diffusion of the Watt Engine, 1775–1825," *Economic History Review* 31 (1978): 541–564; [L. Bicker], "Historie der vuur-machines, of stoom-werktuigen," in *Nieuwe verhandelingen van het Bataafsch Genootschap der Proefondervindelijke Wijsbegeerte*, vol. 1 (1800), pp. 133–153. See also K. van der Pols, *De ontwikkeling van het wateropvoerwerktuig in Nederland, 1770–1870* (Delft, 1984).

the town council establish a chair of chemistry at the Athenaeum Illustre.[26] They sought the teaching of chemistry to physicians, pharmacists, merchants, and manufacturers. On 26 November 1784, the town council consulted the Inspectores Collegii Medici, who did not feel the need for a professor who taught chemistry and pharmacy in the Dutch language. Chemistry, they declared, insofar as it served medicine and pharmacy, was already taught daily at the pharmacy. The advisers were not able to assess the benefit of chemistry for commerce.

A few months later, the merchants made the same request, now referring to the aforementioned prize the *Provinciaal Utrechtsch Genootschap* had offered on 6 December 1784.[27] They were willing to deposit 20,000 guilders to fund the chair, and so the town physician Dirk van Rhyn was appointed professor of chemistry, pharmacy, and materia medica. But he could not obtain a chemical laboratory, which he needed above all. Not until 1796, after the French occupation, did the Amsterdam town council order the pharmacists Anthonie Lauwerenburg and Schonk to design a chemical laboratory, but it was never built. The only possible conclusion is that the municipal government of Amsterdam left to its own devices did not really care to stimulate chemistry and the chemical industry.

Practical chemical research was done mainly outside the universities. The *Gezelschap der Hollandsche Scheikundigen* had a chemical laboratory of its own, in all probability at the home of Paets van Troostwijk, a well-to-do merchant. In 1788, the flourishing society *Felix Meritis* moved into a new building that contained physical and chemical laboratories as well as an observatory. The chemical laboratory had a fireplace, sinks, water taps, and ovens; the floor was covered with yellow bricks to prevent accidents. In this well-equiped laboratory, prominent Amsterdam scientists demonstrated the latest achievements in chemistry and physics before the society members, who could also carry out experiments themselves.[28]

Despite such facilities and interest, important industries remained few. An inventory made in 1800 by Johannes Goldberg, agent of national economy of the Batavian Republic, indicates that Amsterdam had refineries for borax, camphor, sulphur, and saltpeter; factories for

26. W. P. Jorissen, *Chemisch Weekblad* 8 (1911): 501–504.

27. *Verhandelingen van het Provinciaal Utrechtsch Genootschap van Kunsten en Wetenschappen*, vol. 3 (1785), pt. 1, pp. xiv–xvi.

28. H. A. M. Snelders, "Het departement natuurkunde van de Maatschappij van Verdiensten Felix Meritis in het eerste kwart van zijn bestaan," *Documentatieblad Werkgroep Achttiende Eeuw* 15 (1983): 197–214.

the manufacture of Prussian blue, sal ammoniac, nitric acid, vinegar, and dye stuffs; and many sugar refineries.[29] Although leading cities such as Amsterdam and Rotterdam had white lead factories, the chemical industry was never an important employer, because the finished products were usually sent elsewhere.[30]

But this economic development had little significance for the study of chemistry, despite frequent appeals for closer cooperation between the discipline of chemistry and trade and industry. In 1785, Kasteleyn edited the first Dutch journal on applied chemistry, *Chemische oefeningen voor de beminnaars der scheikunde in 't algemeen en de apothekers, fabrikanten en trafiekanten in 't bijzonder* (Chemical Exercises for Chemistry Lovers in General and Pharmacists, Manufacturers, and Processing Industrialists in Particular; three volumes between 1785 and 1788). Every issue of the journal had four sections, dealing with "chemical operation for pharmacy," "investigations on the authenticity or falsification of some natural products and chemical preparations," "chemical processes for economics, factories, and processing industries," and "newest discoveries and improvements in chemistry." Later, Kasteleyn published a continuation of the journal (1792–1793), wrote the three-volume *Beschouwende en werkende pharmaceutische-oeconomische en natuurkundige chemie* (Thoughts on Pharmaceutical-Economic and Physical Chemistry; 1786–1794), and edited the multi-volume *Volledige beschrijving van alle konsten, ambachten, handwerken, fabrieken, trafieken, derzelven werkhuizen, gereedschappen, enz* (Complete Description of All Arts, Crafts, Trades, Factories, Processing Industries, Workplaces, Tools, and so on; published beginning 1788). In March 1792, Kasteleyn lectured at a meeting of *Felix Meritis* about the influences of chemistry on commerce.[31] He showed in detail the significance of chemistry for society in general, and in particular for the different sectors of industry and commerce. His was a strong plea for an independent science of chemistry, but it failed to elicit any response. The city government showed no interest in providing financial assistance for the growth of chemical industries.

This situation did not alter substantially at the beginning of the

29. "Journaal der reize der agent van nationale oeconomie der Bataafsche Republiek (Ao.1800)," *Tijdschrift voor Staathuishoudkunde en Statistiek* 18 (1859): 194–217, 241–254, 313–337, 377–392, 441–459; 19 (1860): 1–18, 57–74, 121–141, 185–199, 249–263. On Amsterdam, 19 (1860): 185–186.

30. H. Diederiks, *Een stad in verval: Amsterdam omstreeks 1800* (Amsterdam, 1982), pp. 161–165.

31. P. J. Kasteleyn, *Chemische en physische oefeningen* (Leiden, 1793), vol. 2, pp. 1–30.

nineteenth century.[32] Trade and agriculture were of much greater economic importance than the chemical industry. As late as 1842, Antony Hendrik van der Boon Mesch, professor of chemistry at Leiden University, complained that in the Netherlands one had to look abroad for progress in the natural sciences.[33] He emphasized that manufacturers did not understand the principles of chemistry, a point already made half a century earlier. In 1791, Petrus Driessen, professor of materia medica, chemistry, and natural history at Groningen University, published *Natuur- en scheikundige waarnemingen over eenige gewigtige onderwerpen der geneeskunde en oeconomie in ons vaderland, ingerigt ter bevordering en uitbreiding van landbouw, kunsten en fabrieken, en ter meerdere bloei der artzenijmengkunde* (Physical and Chemical Observations about Some Important Medical and Economic Subjects in our Country, Arranged for the Promotion and Extension of Agriculture, Arts, and Factories, and for More Prosperity of Pharmacy). An anonymous reviewer in the weekly *Algemeene Konst- en Letter-Bode* doubted that Driessen's attempt to make chemistry more useful to industry would be successful: "The majority of those who prepare chemical products in our country do not understand a thing about the principles of chemistry and only work—wholly mechanically—according to the instructions of their predecessors. Like the country folk, they are wholly unfamiliar with the introduction of any novelty, with the perfection of their factories through discussions with chemists, or with the notion of consulting them on important matters."[34]

Not until 1815 did Reijer Hendrik van Someren start a litmus factory at Rotterdam, and in 1820 he prepared Prussian blue with the aid of technology he had learned in Germany.[35] Like most owners of factories of sulphuric acid, white lead, madder (a plant used for making red dye), and candles, Van Someren had not been educated at a university or a technical high school. This situation did not alter until 1840, when Gerrit Jan Mulder, professor of chemistry at Utrecht University, introduced practical chemical education in the Netherlands.[36]

32. J. MacLean, "De relatie tussen de natuurwetenschappen, de technologie en de industrialisatie in de Nederlanden, 1800–1850," *De Ingenieur* (1980) no. 30–31, pp. 19–24.

33. A. H. van der Boon Mesch, "Over het Nederlandsche fabrykwezen en de middelen, om hetzelve te bevorderen, en in bloei te doen toenemen," *Tijdschrift voor Nijverheid* 7 (1843): 527–608.

34. *Algemeene Konst- en Letter-Bode* 7 (1791): 36.

35. J. MacLean, "Reijer Hendrik van Someren (1787–1851), promotor van de Nederlandse scheikundige technologie," *Rotterdams Jaarboekje* (1977): 190–208.

36. H. A. M. Snelders, "Schei- en natuurkunde aan de Utrechtse Universiteit in de negentiende eeuw," *Tijdschrift voor de Geschiedenis der Geneeskunde, Natuurwetenschappen, Wiskunde en Techniek* 7 (1984): 32–48; H. A. M. Snelders, "Het chemisch laboratorium 'de Leeuwenbergh' te Utrecht (1845–1903)," ibid., 129–140.

As this survey of Dutch science in the eighteenth century has shown, decline, Enlightenment, and revolution—the key words of this volume—are also elements in the history of the natural sciences in the period. The study of natural sciences at Dutch universities, in particular the combination of teaching and research, shows an increasing decline. In the beginning of the century, the study of natural sciences flourished at the universities, in particular through the publications of the triumvirate Boerhaave, 's Gravesande, and Van Musschenbroek. By the end of the century, however, scientific activities had shifted mainly to the local scientific societies. Thus, the scientific activities of Jan Hendrik van Swinden, professor of philosophy, natural philosophy, mathematics, and astronomy at Amsterdam, were centered almost wholly at *Felix Meritis* and not at the Athenaeum Illustre. Natural sciences became a pastime for well-to-do gentlemen or a by-product of scientific education. A structural change in scientific teaching and research did not set in until 1840, when Gerrit Jan Mulder was appointed professor of chemistry at Utrecht University.

Enlightenment was reflected, although faintly, in the scientific societies with their prize essays on subjects of public welfare. A new interest in the natural sciences in the first half of the eighteenth century was characterized by the spread of Newtonianism, and in the course of the century emphasis shifted to experimental sciences related to heat, electricity, light, and chemistry.

There is, finally, no doubt that social and economic interests, and the desire for reform, stimulated the study of natural sciences at the end of the eighteenth century. The chemical revolution was immediately accepted in the Netherlands. But a stimulus by the government, something to increase financial opportunities, was lacking. Only in the middle of the nineteenth century would the situation change. Despite the activities of the late eighteenth-century scientific reformers, the state-sponsored application of science to the needs of industry happened very slowly in the Netherlands.

# 16

# A Myth of Decline

## Frans Grijzenhout

ACCORDING to a 1973 questionnaire investigating the behavior of visitors to the Amsterdam Rijksmuseum, some 50 percent claimed that they had visited the department of eighteenth- and nineteenth-century Dutch painting. Especially in summer and among foreigners, this department apparently attracted many people. Those who conducted the inquiry, however, never actually observed crowds of people walking into those rooms. On the contrary, anyone who has actually spent time in the department of eighteenth- and nineteenth-century Dutch art can vouch for the fact that it is one of the least visited areas in the entire museum.[1]

Anyone who wants to study Dutch eighteenth-century art in the Rijksmuseum will not have to fight through crowds of tourists, like those disturbing one another in front of Rembrandt's *Nightwatch* or the *The Love Letter* by Vermeer. The visitor can stroll through the eighteenth-century rooms at ease and take an unhampered look at the paintings. He or she will probably see many names of unfamiliar artists, with the possible exception of Cornelis Troost. This cannot, of course, be the fault of the eighteenth century. Many visitors go to that department in the Louvre in Paris or the National Gallery in London; there, they admire the works by Gainsborough, Hogarth, Constable,

1. O.Valkman, *Queuen voor de Nachtwacht: Het Rijksmuseum en zijn bezoekers* (Amsterdam, 1976), pp. 18, 72, 84.

Boucher, David, and Goya. No, it must be the Dutch eighteenth century that has a bad reputation or is unknown to the visitors.

As a matter of fact, this period in Dutch art history has had a bad
reputation until very recently. Most attention was given to the art of
the "Golden Age," the age of Rembrandt, Hals, Vermeer, and so many
others. Eighteenth-century art was thought to be too much influenced
by French taste to be compatible with national, Dutch character.[2] It
was only during and after World War II that the appraisal of and love
for Dutch eighteenth-century art began growing. This revaluation took
place outside the official art historical world, among critics such as A.
Staring and J. Knoef, who published several studies on eighteenth- and
early nineteenth-century Dutch art in the series "Unknown Fields of
Dutch Art History."[3] The introductory notes to some of the catalogues
of exhibitions devoted during the postwar years to eighteenth-century
art were, however, in a somewhat apologetic mood. In the catalogue of
the exhibition "Cornelis Troost and His Times" of 1946 one reads for
example:

> Organizing an exhibition on Dutch eighteenth-century art today may
> need some explanation. After the rise of culture in the seventeenth
> century, the eighteenth undoubtedly was an age of decline, nowhere
> to appear more clearly than in the visual arts. Comparing the art of
> the eighteenth to that of the seventeenth century may seem logical; it
> is also unfair and can even be dangerous: one cannot value the re-
> sults of one period with the standards of another. In doing so one
> could misjudge the intrinsic values and gains of that period. It is
> these values that make it acceptable to organize this exhibition; be-
> cause of the absence of these values in our own time, we learned to
> revaluate them, without being blinded to the evidence that these
> same features had some negative aspects and, indeed, were responsi-
> ble for much of the decline in the eighteenth century.[4]

Even ten years later, the catalogue for "Painters from an Era of Gal-
lantry" stated that eighteenth-century works of art were in "no way to

2. For an extreme view, see F. M. Huebner, *De romantische schilderkunst in de
Nederlanden* (The Hague, 1944), pp. 9, 14, 18; Huebner, writing from a national-socialist
point of view, stated that "the spirit of the Enlightenment, coming from the south" was
spoiling the national character of the Dutch, who combined the features of northern Frisians,
Saxons, and Franks.

3. J. Knoef, *Tusschen rococo en romantiek* (The Hague, 1943), and A. Staring,
*Kunsthistorische verkenningen*, (The Hague, 1948).

4. Exhibition catalogue, *Cornelis Troost en zijn tijd* (Rotterdam, Museum Boymans,
1946), p. 3.

be compared to the masterpieces of the seventeenth century. There is no original creativity; Holland did not see real masters of art in this period." The peculiar charm of the period was to be found in its airiness, grace, and *joie de vivre.*[5]

An extensive exhibition of Dutch eighteenth-century art was on display in three American museums in Minneapolis, Toledo, and Philadelphia in the years 1971–1972. The great connoisseur of eighteenth-century Dutch art, J. W. Niemeijer, formulated in an introductory essay to the exhibition's catalogue the ambiguous feelings of most of his fellow art historians on the subject:

> It has taken quite a while for historians to reconcile themselves to the fact that the seventeenth century was succeeded by the eighteenth century. As a matter of fact, they haven't really managed to do it yet. . . . The Dutch have been careful not to let foreigners see too many of the products of that century; they have always been more or less ashamed that the magnificent bloom of the seventeenth century was unable to sustain itself for another hundred years.

Niemeijer considered the American exhibition "a triumph for Dutch eighteenth-century painting and drawing that cannot fail to enhance their prestige mightily."[6] It may be ironic, though, that this collection of masterpieces was shown to the American public but has never been on show in a Dutch museum—although it should be said that recently more exhibitions and publications on Dutch eighteenth-century art and culture have appeared and appreciation of the period has grown.[7]

In a way, the appreciation of eighteenth-century art runs historically parallel to interest in political, economic, social, and cultural history in the Netherlands during this period. Some years ago it seemed that the sources of a negative view of the eighteenth century were to be found in that century itself. Especially in Dutch spectatorial writing, authors constantly complained about the decline of morals, economic activity, and political importance of the Dutch Republic compared to

5. Exhibition catalogue, *Schilders van het galante tijdperk* (Arnhem, Gemeentemuseum, 1956), p. 6.

6. Exhibition catalogue, *Dutch Masterpieces from the Eighteenth Century* (Minneapolis Institute of Arts, Toledo Museum of Art, Philadelphia Museum of Art, 1971–1972), p. 13.

7. E. G. J. W. Niemeijer, *Cornelis Troost, 1696–1750* (Assen, 1973); Th. Laurentius, J. W. Niemeijer, and G. Ploos van Amstel, *Cornelis Ploos van Amstel, 1726–1798: Kunstverzamelaar en prentuitgever,* 2 vols. (Assen, 1984); *Achttiende-eeuwse Nederlandse kunst in de Nederlanden, Leids Kunsthistorisch Jaarboek* 4 (1985); exhibition catalogue, *Tussen zonnegoud en kaarslicht: Dordtse meesters, 1780–1840* (Dordrechts Museum, 1986).

the seventeenth-century situation and to foreign countries. One must ask if contemporary authors complained about the quality of Dutch eighteenth-century art as well. How did those in the eighteenth century evaluate the art of their time?

No systematic research has been done on this question so far. One approach might be to consult artist biographies of the eighteenth century. The classic example of collected biographies is, of course, Giorgio Vasari's *Le vite de' più eccellenti pittori, scultori e architettori* (1550, 2d ed. 1568), which gives an organic picture of the rise, flowering, and decline of Italian art from 1300 on to Vasari's own time. Given the outright negative and fatalistic view in the Dutch spectatorial magazines of the decline of Dutch culture in the eighteenth century, one would expect Dutch eighteenth-century authors to use the same model in writing on their own art history. A critical note can already be read in the second volume of Arnold Houbraken's *Schouburg der Nederlantsche kunstschilders* (1719). Houbraken clearly defines the period 1560–1660 as the summit in the development of Dutch painting. In his days, he complains, the artistic sky is filled with many stars that shine much less brilliantly than did their seventeenth-century predecessors. In Pictura's academy, more and more places remain vacant. Houbraken knows the reasons for this decay: want of money, absence of real art lovers, and a decline in the education of the children of the well-to-do, which now teaches the rules of gain more than those of the arts.[8] Houbraken's criticism was resumed at the middle of the eighteenth century, when Jan van Gool published, as a sequel to Houbraken's *Schouburg*, his *De nieuwe schouburg der Nederlantsche kunstschilders en schilderessen*. Although Van Gool states proudly in his first volume that Holland was not inferior to any other nation in the field of the arts,[9] in the second volume, published only one year later, he strikes another note. The poem by Dirk Smits, "The Crown of Painting for Mr. Gerard Braamcamp," which introduces the volume makes the point sharp. Braamcamp, to whom Van Gool had dedicated this second volume of his work, was a wealthy wood merchant, and one of the main patrons of mid-eighteenth-century Amsterdam.[10] Smits's poem describes how the lilies and roses that normally adorn the cheeks of Art

8. A. Houbraken, *De groote Schouburg der Nederlantsche kunstschilders*, vol. 2 (The Hague, 1719), pp. 103–105.

9. J. van Gool, *De nieuwe schouburg der Nederlantsche kunstschilders en schilderessen*, 2 vols. (The Hague, 1750–1751), vol. 1, p. 2.

10. On Braamcamp, see C. Bille, *De tempel der kunst of het kabinet van den heer Braamcamp*, vol. 1 (Amsterdam, 1761), pp. 13, 31–59.

were fading away. To sustain Art, Minerva sends Mercury to Amsterdam to find in the eighteenth-century world trade center, the treasury of painting that had been lost in palaces, churches, homes, and courts. In Amsterdam only, the center of the world's trade, as opposed to the aristocratic and ecclesiastical circles where the arts had died, could art be rescued. Braamcamp, sustained by Minerva and Mercury, was to be the one to look after the declining arts. It is interesting to see, in the following lines of the poem, that Braamcamp is mentioned not because of his support of living artists, like Troost, De Wit, and Cresant— whom he did protect—but mainly because of his activities as a collector of seventeenth-century Dutch art! Of the works of art collected by Braamcamp, Smits mentions Dou, Van Mieris, Wouwerman, Ostade, Berchem, Weenix, Lairesse, Metsu, Terborch, Van der Velde, and Rembrandt, all popular masters among eighteenth-century collectors of Dutch art. The only eighteenth-century artist mentioned by Smits in this connection is Jan van Huysum, the famous painter of flower and fruit still life. Apparently "saving the arts" in 1751 meant "collecting seventeenth-century art."

Van Gool himself notices that "Dutch Pictura" had climbed its highest step in the previous century, rightly called "the felicitous age of painting." But in contrast to the theory of Vasari (and the eighteenth-century philosopher Vico), Van Gool does not think the decline of art in his times to be the result of an inherent, inevitable law of nature. The chief fault lies with the art dealers, who are blamed by Van Gool for advising the art collectors of his time to buy seventeenth-century art. As a result of this tendency, contemporary artists are not stimulated enough and the decay of art is inevitable. Still, he thinks that there are possibilities for young artists to follow their illustrious predecessors "on that noble track" that had led them to their outstanding results. Some of his contemporaries had even reached the same high level in painting as their seventeenth-century predecessors, one example being Jan van Huysum, whom Van Gool considers one of the great artists of his time.[11] Although Van Gool claims to remain strictly neutral on the merits of living artists, one can conclude from some of his remarks that he certainly likes the work of, for example, Balthasar Denner, Philips van Dyk, Hendrik van Limborch, Rachel Ruysch, Jacob de Wit, and Aert Schouman. In general, he defends history painting, but he has an open eye for the qualities of other genres. The only style Van

11. Van Gool, *Nieuwe schouburg*, vol. 2, introduction and pp. 2, 12ff.

Gool apparently dislikes is the highly finished genre painting in the tradition of the Leiden school, with such artists as Willem van Mieris and Frans van Mieris II.[12] Van Gool's opinion about the cause of decay was disputed by the artist and art trader Gerard Hoet, who stated that only the artists themselves could be blamed for a loss of quality. He refused to take the easy way out and simply criticize the so-called amoral behavior of his contemporaries.[13]

Although Van Gool was not extremely negative about the accomplishments of most of his contemporaries, it is clear that he was preoccupied with the state of the arts. One should not forget that in the years in which Van Gool published his book the whole generation of artists whom he had cherished was fading away. Philips van Dyk, painting portraits in the style of Netscher, was to pass away in 1753; Jan van Huysum and Rachel Ruysch, both still-life painters, died in 1749 and 1750, respectively. Cornelis Troost, an artist who had contributed something really new to Dutch art—an original, eighteenth-century version of Dutch portraiture and a refreshing element of satire and humor—died in 1750. Jacob de Wit, masterly painter of trompe l'oeil decorations of ceilings and of history painting, would die in 1754.[14] These were the only living artists who could be and were compared to the seventeenth-century masters. Van Gool had apparently seen no young, promising artists who could take over the torch of the elder generation.

In the next twenty years, no one heard remarks on the quality of contemporary Dutch art. During this period, there were good craftsmen in the republic, such as Tibout Regters and Hendrik Pothoven, who could produce a nice portrait for members of the bourgeoisie. It is a striking fact, however, that most members of the patriciate and aristocracy had their portraits done by foreign, mostly French-speaking, painters visiting the republic. These artists, such as J. E. Liotard, J. B. Perronneau, J. F. de la Croix, G. de Spinny, B. S. Bolomey, and J. Humbert, stayed for some years or even settled in the Netherlands and

12. L. de Vries, "Jan van Gool als kunstcriticus," *Oud-Holland* 97 (1983): 266–283; see also *Oud-Holland* 99 (1985): 165–190.

13. L. de Vries, "'De kunsthandel is zoo edel als eenigen, vermits "er geen bedrog in is"': De pamflettenstrijd tussen Gerard Hoet en Johan van Gool," *Leids Kunsthistorisch Jaarboek* 4 (1985): 1–16.

14. For Troost's fame, see Niemeijer, *Troost*, pp. 112–113. For remarks on the appraisal of Jacob de Wit, see exhibition catalogue, *Jacob de Wit: Titian of the Amstel* (Amsterdam, Royal Palace, 1986).

influenced Dutch portraiture.[15] One hears no explicit comments on this influence until around 1770, however.

We might expect to find some commentary on the quality of contemporary Dutch art in spectatorial literature, where there is an exhausting number of essays on the decline of morals, commerce, and science. I consulted some spectators at random but could not find relevant commentary for those years.[16] In 1767, however, *De Philosooph* published a "letter by a Mr. C. about the absence of taste in the Netherlands." Mr. C. reproaches the Dutch for a lack of taste, especially in literature and music but also in the visual arts. He concentrates on the style of the Amsterdam houses, which follow too eagerly, in his view, the example set by the Italians and, later, the French. Much of his critical essay is devoted to the Amsterdam town hall, built in 1648 by Jacob van Campen. This building, once considered the world's eighth miracle, is severely criticized by C. because of its lack of right proportions. He also criticizes many of the paintings in the building: the figures in the paintings are not proportional to the rooms they are in. The only artist mentioned by C. in a positive way is Rembrandt, whose *Nightwatch* is largely praised. Other painters receive credit only because of their way of coloring, an example for the present generation to follow. Eighteenth-century painting is mentioned by C. in the context of the decline of architecture in his day. His main criticism, again, is the lack of proportion in decorative painting. As a representative of that tendency, he mentions Isaac de Moucheron, "who had no more merit than stealing a landscape from some prints, without bringing any coherence into it. As monstrously large as Ferdinand Bol, Govert Flinck, and Jacob de Wit painted their figures in the small rooms in the town hall, tiny, doll-like landscapes are being painted nowadays for the large rooms of the wealthy merchants."[17] In a reaction to C.'s letter, Cornelis Ploos van Amstel stated that the author, known by him to be the famous physician Petrus Camper, unjustly criticized the Amsterdam town hall for its lack of proportion. As far as the figures in its paint-

---

15. A. Staring, *Fransche kunstenaars en hun Hollandsche modellen* (The Hague, 1947); F. Grijzenhout, *Liotard in Nederland* (Utrecht, 1985); N. Dekking et al., *Tischbein: Een reizend portrettist in Nederland* (Utrecht, 1987).

16. I consulted J. van Effen, *De Hollandsche Spectator*, 2d ed. (Amsterdam, 1756; orig. 1731–1735); *De Philanthrope of de Menschenvriend* (Amsterdam, 1757–1762); *De Philosooph* (Amsterdam, 1766–1769); *De Gryzaard* (Monnikendam-Hoorn, 1768–1769). *De Gryzaard*, no. 86 (17 February 1769) mentions "our outstanding Troost" as a painter of realistic scenes.

17. "Brief van den Heer C. over het gebrek aan Smaak in de Nederlanders," *De Philosooph*, no. 93 (12 October 1767): 321–328.

ings, Ploos defended their iconography as being original and therefore purely Dutch.[18]

Much more explicit on the quality of Dutch eighteenth-century art, and from another point of view, is the well-known woman novelist Betje Wolff. In her letter of 5 March 1777 to Jan Everhard Grave she writes:

> There is a trifling spirit in our age, extending itself to our way of dressing, our amusement itself. Nice, cosy, and tiny cabinet pictures are being painted, but one has lost the skill of a Rubbens [sic], a Frans Hals, a Potter. Look for example, to say something more of painting, at a picture by Van Dyck: nothing more tender, tasty, sensual, lifely than his women and children. Nowadays, the proverb still goes: "That woman has nice soft hands, they look like hands by Van Dyck!" Now, look at the portraits of our time. What do they look alike? like wax? like polished card-paper! And when we come to the forceful, strong, miraculous image of men, it is still worse.[19]

It becomes clear from these words that Wolff's criticism was not confined to the aesthetic and artistic quality of eighteenth-century painters. Her remarks match her criticism of the Dutch, especially Dutch patrician and aristocratic culture. Following spectatorial literature with its ceaseless complaint about the effeminacy of the Dutch, the decline of morals, and the gratuitous imitation of French taste, Wolff chastised her fellow countrymen. For her, examples to be emulated in a moral and aesthetic way were the portraits of their seventeenth-century ancestors. By glorifying these, she glorified seventeenth-century society and painting as well. Two things in her remarks on painting are striking. First, she mentions not only painters from the northern Netherlands, such as Hals and Potter, but also Rubens and Van Dyck from Flanders. Thus, Betje Wolff's art criticism is not yet dictated by feelings of severe nationalism. Second, her preference for Frans Hals is remarkable. In Wolff's time, Hals was not a painter whom people would mention as

18. Anonymous, *De bouworde van 't stadhuis van Amsterdam, en de smaak der Nederlanderen ten opzigte der konsten en wetenschappen, verdedigd, tegen de ongegronde berispingen van den heer C.* (Amsterdam, 1767). See also J. B. Bedaux, "Een 18de-eeuwse kunsttheoretische discussie," *Kunstlicht*, no. 15 (1985): 25–28; E. A. Koolhaas-Grosfeld, "De negentiende eeuw en de zeventiende-eeuwse schilderkunst, als een vraagstuk van Ouden en Modernen. I," *De Negentiende Eeuw* 9 (1985): 145–170, especially p. 165.

19. J. Dyserinck, *Brieven van Betje Wolff en Aagje Deken* (The Hague, 1904), p. 208. Grave was a sugar refiner in Amsterdam and belonged to the group who founded *Felix Meritis* in 1777. For his relationship with Betje Wolff, see P. J. Buijnsters, *Wolff en Deken: Een biografie* (The Hague, 1984), pp. 149, 154–157, and passim.

an outstanding example of Dutch seventeenth-century art. Contrary to most of her contemporaries, Wolff loved Hals because of his rough technique, impressionistic and realistic at the same time.[20] The only eighteenth-century painter mentioned by Wolff in a positive way is Cornelis Troost. In the famous novel *Sara Burgerhart* (1784), which Wolff wrote with Aagje Deken, the positive hero of the novel, Abraham Blankaart, states in a letter to the widow Spilgoed: "I wished, that our painter Cornelis Troost would be still alive; I'd have him make that group, to make my family portrait of it, provided I could be in it, with Snap, my dog, with me."[21] Obviously Blankaart, and with him Wolff and Deken, did not think any contemporary artist capable of painting a nice conversation piece.

In the 1780s, strong feelings of nationalism began to arise in the republic. The cause lay in the war with the English of 1780–1784. During these years, the lost greatness of the seventeenth-century republic was stressed repeatedly. It seems only logical that, at the same time, we would find defenders of a national Dutch school of painting. On 18 November 1783, Jacob Otten Husly, Amsterdam architect of the new *Felix Meritis* building at the Keizersgracht, gave a lecture titled "The Honor of Dutch Painters Defended against the General Prejudice That They Could Not Be Compared to the Painters of Other Nations, Let Alone to the Ancients."[22] Husly's provoking hypothesis was that Dutch painting was not inferior to that in other countries, for example to that in England, but, on the contrary, was superior to it. Husly begins his argument with the fact that the Italians, whose work was normally presented as the criterion of excellence, had had their great artists in Raphael, Michelangelo, and Caracci, artists who had justly followed the example set by the ancients. Their followers, however, had not managed to surpass the phase of sheer imitation. The Dutch nation, on the other hand, with its age-old inclination toward freedom, could not bear "the slavish imitation of the ancients in the arts" and had returned to the source of all art, to the nature of creation itself. This nature was

20. Buijnsters, *Wolff en Deken*, pp. 77, 219; see also A. Loosjes, *Haarlems schilder-lof* (Haarlem, 1788), and A. Loosjes, *Frans Hals, lierzang* (Haarlem, 1789).
21. B. Wolff and A. Deken, *Historie van Mejuffrouw Sara Burgerhart*, ed. P. J. Buijnsters (The Hague, 1980), vol. 2, p. 622. See also Buijnsters, *Wolff en Deken*, p. 219.
22. Municipal Archive, Amsterdam, coll. *Concordia et Libertate*, no. 9. The text was published with the signature "H" in the *Algemeen Magazyn van Wetenschap, Konst en Smaak*, vol. 2 (1787), pp. 341–376. See also E. Koolhaas-Grosfeld, "Nationale versus goede smaak: Bevordering van nationale kunst in Nederland, 1780–1840," *Tijdschrift voor Geschiedenis* 95 (1982): 612–613, and E. Koolhaas-Grosfeld, "Op zoek naar de Gouden Eeuw," in *Op zoek naar de Gouden Eeuw* (Haarlem, Frans Hals Museum, 1986), p. 41.

put on a higher level than the idealized nature in ancient and Italian art. Dutch painting excelled in variety, and each genre had its own specialists. The artists mentioned by Husly to clarify his argument were generally from the seventeenth century: Van der Werff, De Wit, and Walraven (history painting), Troost ("modern," that is, contemporary subject painting). Rachel Ruysch and Jan van Huysum (fruit and flowers) were the familiar eighteenth-century exceptions. In coloring, Dutch masters were considered by Husly to be far superior to the Italians, English, Germans (they had never come any farther than calligraphy), and French (too much inclined toward "riggish playfulness").

Roelof van Eijnden made a more classicist approach to the problem some years later, in 1787, in a prize-winning essay on the question "How far the national taste of the Dutch school had reached the aim of painting and drawing." He criticized the simple imitation of nature by the Dutch but praised their coloring, still lifes, realistic landscapes, and modern representations. Van Eijnden did not agree with Husly that the Dutch could ever come near the quality of Italian painting, but Dutch art was definitely better than English art![23]

By the 1780s, Dutch art theory and art practice had come to a strange crossroads. First there was the neoclassicist ideal, which dominated much of European art theory in those days and was taught at several art academies in the republic. On the other hand, some critics referred to the characteristic, national stroke in Dutch art, described as simply realistic, a highly praised imitation of nature. In the writings of Cornelis Ploos van Amstel, one of the most important theorists of his time, this dilemma becomes obvious. Ploos, as a director of the Amsterdam Academy of Drawing, explicitly defended and hence furthered classicist drawing as the basis of all art. Conversely, from 1767 onward, he pleaded for a "Dutch iconography" and edited colored prints after Dutch seventeenth-century paintings. In his theoretical writings and lectures at the academy in the 1780s, he defended—as an antagonist of the famous Sir Joshua Reynolds—the poetry and invention of Dutch art by pointing to its originality and quality of color and clairobscur. In so doing, he transposed some classicist standards, formally applied to the content of painting, to its style. Thus Ploos became the Dutch herald of the romantic interpretation of Dutch seventeenth-cen-

---

23. R. van Eijnden, "Antwoord op de vraag in hoeverre de *Nationale Smaak* van de *Hollandsche* School 't doelwit der *Schilder-* en *Tekenkunde* bereike," *Verhandelingen uitgegeven door Teylers Tweede Genootschap*, vol. 5 (Haarlem, 1787).

tury painting.[24] The visual arts at the end of the eighteenth century, then, mirror Ploos's dilemma. Especially in architecture and the decorative arts, artists were aiming at a clearly neoclassicist ideal. On the other hand, decorative and easel painting in the last twenty years of the century showed some influence of neoclassicism but more often followed seventeenth-century examples in landscape, still life, interior, and genre.[25]

According to some art historians, however, we should not speak of a dilemma in eighteenth-century Dutch art. Both tendencies, one toward neoclassicism and one toward a reappraisal of seventeenth-century painting and subject matter, were in harmony with each other. Dutch theorists of the late eighteenth century admired the glorious examples of Dutch seventeenth-century history and Dutch seventeenth-century realistic painting as well. The common base for this mixed aesthetic preference, it is claimed, lay in the enlightened, even patriotic feelings of the theorists who tried to connect Dutch seventeenth-century history and art with the ideals of liberty and ancient republicanism; thus, they tried to make Dutch seventeenth-century art fit classicist standards.[26]

With the evidence presented in this chapter, one would expect the Patriots to offer the most sustained defense of seventeenth-century Dutch art. In their political writings, Dutch Patriots more than once criticized the morals of their age and naively glorified the seventeenth century. In these Patriotic writings, however, most references are to seventeenth-century (anti-Orangist) statesmen such as Van Oldenbarneveldt, Hugo de Groot, Hogerbeets, and Johan and Cornelis de Witt and to Dutch triumphant admirals such as Michiel de Ruyter. Literary writers and artists are seldom mentioned in their works. And typically enough, those works of art connected to Patriotism almost all show strong neoclassicist influences. We can consider a few examples.

On 13 May 1786, new banners were presented to the Amsterdam arms society *Tot Nut der Schutterij*. They had been painted by one of the members of the society, Isaac van 't Hoff. One of the representations clearly referred to the classicist background of Patriot imagery. It shows a young man in Roman armor trampling on the enemy's arms

24. P. Knolle, "Cornelis Ploos van Amstel, pleitbezorger van de 'Hollandse' iconografie," *Oud-Holland* 98 (1984): 43–52.

25. Exhibition catalogue, *Tussen zonnegoud en kaarslicht: Dordtse meesters, 1780–1840* (Dordrechts Museum, 1986).

26. Koolhaas-Grosfeld, *Op zoek*, p. 40.

(symbol of Patriotism) and holding a crown of grass (for him who liberates a city from its enemy) and one of oak leaf (for the soldier who protects the citizens). He explicitly disregards the danger of a threatening pool or hole and a fire. A monument in the background with the old and new coats of arms of the city of Amsterdam refers to those who had died to defend the city's rights and prosperity. The device "Follow!" is explained in an accompanying booklet as to be read as "Follow the many examples antiquity is teaching you," follow the lessons of Patriotism taught by the ancients. The examples mentioned by the booklet's author are the famous republican exempla of the Fabii, the Decii, and Marcus Curtius, who gave his life to save the Roman Republic by throwing himself in a cleft on the Roman forum: perhaps the pool should be seen as a reference to this example.[27]

In Patriotic allegorical engravings, elements from antiquity are prominent. The engraving *Temple for the Netherlands* (1794) by J. G. Visser is a fine example of this genre. It shows the Temple of the Netherlands as a second temple of Vesta, hung with representations of the glorious deeds of the Batavians, the legendary ancestors of the Dutch and of seventeenth- and eighteenth-century Patriotic heroes. In the temple itself, Dutch Freedom is assisted by Religion, Justice and the Laws, Gratitude, Abundance, and some Batavians as sentinels. In the background, one sees agriculture and commerce, the cornerstones of Dutch wealth. In this engraving, elements from the classics and from Dutch antiquity have been united strikingly with the images of persons and events from Dutch history in the sixteenth, seventeenth, and late eighteenth centuries. There was continuity from the Roman Republic through the Batavians to the Dutch Republic and the Patriots—a continuity based on republicanism, thirst for freedom, and patriotism.[28] That was the message of the engraving.

The last example I mention here is a painting by Nicolas-Jean Delin, *Hercules and Omphale* (see p. 270).[29] The story of Hercules and

---

27. Th. van Leeuwen, *Aan de wel edele heren bestuurderen, exerceerende en honoraire leden . . . van het wapengenootschap, onder de spreuk tot nut der schuttery* (Amsterdam, [1786]).

28. I. Schöffer, "The Batavian Myth during the Sixteenth and Seventeenth Centuries," in *Britain and the Netherlands*, vol. 5, ed. J. S. Bromley and E. H. Kossmann (The Hague, 1975), pp. 78–101. The tradition was confirmed by E. M. Engelberts, *De aloude staat en geschiedenissen der Vereenigde Nederlanden*, 4 vols. (Amsterdam, 1784–1799). See F. Grijzenhout, "Tempel voor Nederland: De Nationale Konst-Gallerij in 's-Gravenhage," *Nederlands Kunsthistorisch Jaarboek* 35 (1984), especially p. 32ff.

29. Canvas, 182 × 120 cm (oval), signed and dated "N. Delin pinxit 1786"; Stedelijk Museum "De Lakenhal," Leiden, inv. no. 1367.

Omphale runs as follows. Hercules was sold to Omphale, queen of Lydia, as a slave for three years, because he had murdered his friend Iphitus in a fit of madness. She, however, soon alleviated his lot by making him her lover. While in her service, Hercules grew effeminate, wearing women's clothes and adornments and spinning yarn.[30] Delin's picture shows the most conventional representation of the story. Hercules is sitting next to Omphale, who is accompanied by Cupid. Obviously, the partners have changed their traditional attributes: Hercules is shown spinning with his mighty hands, while Omphale is holding Hercules' club in her left hand, his lion skin on her head; with her left foot she tramples on an animal's jaw, probably of the Nemean lion once killed by Hercules.

The myth of Hercules and Omphale dates from the sixth century B.C. and was depicted many times from the Hellenistic period onward. The popularity of the theme is usually explained by suggesting that in several periods of human history we became aware of the relativity of manly virtue and military power and favored the blessings of love as a feminine virtue. Depending on the spirit of the age, Hercules could be represented as passive, acquiescent, or equal to Omphale. Especially in the period of rococo, the theme would seem to be the perfect expression of effeminate culture. This general interpretation is, of course, based on a sociopsychological vision of history.[31]

Delin's *Hercules and Omphale*, however, was painted in 1786 for a Dutch Patriot, Johannes Hartevelt, distiller of jenever (gin) in Leiden. Hartevelt installed the painting in his house on Oude Singel 144 together with another, an allegory of the alliance between Holland and France in 1785, also by Delin. Rather than confirm this reading of feminine love triumphing over military power, a museum catalogue at De Lakenhal in Leiden states, correctly in my view, that the subject of the painting must be the decline of morals of the Dutch in the eighteenth century. This interpretation is confirmed by several statements in the spectatorial press. The *Nederlandsche Spectator* of 1751, for example, tells the story of an argument in heaven between Hercules and "Formosus Argus." Hercules has seen the *petits-maitres*, the fashionable, French-speaking, aristocratic, arrogant young men of the mid-century wearing furs. He is outraged to see these dandies dressed in his

30. J. Hall, *Dictionary of Subjects and Symbols in Art* (New York, 1974), p. 151.

31. For example, see H. Poensgen, "Herkules und Omphale: Zu einem neu erworbenen Gemälde der Kurpfälzischen Museum," in *Bibliotheca docet: Festgabe für Carl Wehmer* (Amsterdam, 1963), pp. 303–334.

own traditional attribute, but Father Jupiter tells him that it is not lion's fur these men are wearing but rabbit's. Argus, the barrister of the *petits-maitres*, plays his master card against Hercules. He reminds him of his affair with Omphale: had the *petits-maitres* been so rude to Hercules when he was under the spell of Omphale's love? Hercules can do nothing but leave the room, ashamed. This story of Hercules and Omphale, then, was told as a parable of the decline of morals among the young Dutchmen of mid-century.[32] More than thirty years later, the same story appears in Delin's painting as a warning to young men not to concede to effeminacy and luxury.

Hercules and Omphale really was a myth of decline, a gendered parable with a message told by a painter for a Patriotic employer. This myth, with all its implicit rejection of contemporary culture and longing for the good old days that never were, was expressed by Delin in one of the rare examples of Dutch history painting in these years, be it with some evocations of baroque style. Very little is seen of a "seventeenth-century revival" in Patriot art. On the contrary, the Patriots followed the neoclassicist track in expressing their political and moral views. And in this regard, they were by no means unique: for their political propaganda, both Orangists and Patriots made use of the methods of history painting—with its traditional classical and biblical examples and allegorical apparatus adapted to the style of the day, neoclassicism.[33] Neither side sought to bring back the style of that "lost" golden century.

32. Another reference to Hercules and Omphale is to be found in *De Nederlandsche Spectator* 7 (1755): 91. See also J. Hartog, *De spectatoriale geschriften van 1741–1800*, 2d ed. (Utrecht, 1890), p. 91. I am grateful to N. C. F. van Sas for this reference, which led me to the one mentioned in the text.

33. For an Orangist example, see B. Bolomey's *Sophia Wilhelmina of Prussia, Wife of Prince Willem V, in the Temple of the Arts* (probably 1787–1788), Rijksmuseum Amsterdam, inv. no. A 965.

# Glossary

*Aan het volk van Nederland* (To the People of the Netherlands, 1781)   One of the most influential pamphlets of the Patriot period. In this tract, Joan Derk van der Capellen tot den Pol (1741–1784) denounced the stadholdership as tyrannical and urged political reform on the basis of sovereignty of the people. He also advocated the foundation of *vrijkorpsen* (free corps) to enable the enlightened citizenry to defend itself against the military machine of the stadholder.

Anglo-Dutch war of 1780–1784   This commerical conflict with England, the fourth of a series (the first three in 1650–1678), created a power vacuum in the Dutch Republic that triggered the Patriots into action and culminated in the 1787 revolution.

Barrier   A series of forts placed in the Austrian Netherlands as a result of the War of the Spanish Succession and intended to provide a barrier against French invasion of the Low Countries. After 1714, the Dutch were supposed to pay for their upkeep, which they did only fitfully.

Batavians   The Batavian myth postulated the independence of Holland from the time of the Batavian tribe of the Roman period and defined the medieval count of Holland as a predecessor of the stadholder and as a creation of the representatives of the nobility. In the Patriot period, the term "Batavus" also came to include all noble, fatherland-loving patriots who were prepared to oppose the Dutch ancien régime. The name of the Batavian revolution of 1795 derived from this usage.

Bayle, Pierre (1647–1706)   Of the many French Huguenot refugees who fled
to the Netherlands after the revocation of the Edict of Nantes (1685), Bayle
became the most famous. He supported William of Orange and religious
toleration and was an early contributor to the Enlightenment. In 1697 he
published his *Dictionnaire*, which was the first encyclopedia.

Bentinck, William (1704–1774)   William Bentinck, Heer van Rhoon en Pen-
drecht, was the eldest son of the second marriage of Hans Willem Bentinck,
the closest friend of stadholder-king William III. William Bentinck pursued a
career in Dutch politics and diplomacy and was one of the chief engineers of
the elevation of William IV to the stadholdership in 1747.

Burgomaster   Chief official of Dutch town administration. The burgomasters
of the larger towns, who represented the town in the provincial estates and
in the Estates General, wielded enormous power (see also *Regenten*).

Capellen tot den Pol, Joan Derk van der (1741–1784)   Van der Capellen, a
nobleman from the province of Overijssel, was one of the major leaders of
the Patriot opposition in its early stage. His pamphlet *Aan het volk van
Nederland* (1781), in which he advocated the creation of the *vrijkorpsen*,
was responsible for the arming of the opposition.

Contracten van correspondentie   Secret agreements for the rotation of political office, by which sometimes even perpetual calendars established the distribution of offices. These agreements served to reduce the numbers of an
already diminishing oligarchy.

Court, Pieter de la (1618–1685)   Leiden merchant and political philosopher.
De la Court was one of the the most important Dutch political theorists of
the seventeenth century. He defended the policies of the estates of Holland
against those of the stadholders. His publications laid the foundation for the
*Waare Vrijheid* ideology.

Den Haag (The Hague)   On the coast of the province of Holland, the capital
of the Dutch Republic and seat of the Estates General and the provincial
estates of Holland as well. In the eighteenth century, this city of 35,000 was
a cultural and publishing center and the site of the stadholder's court.

*Doelen*   In major Dutch towns, the shooting range and seat of the armed
militia, made up of local citizens.

*Doelistenbeweging*   Opposition movement against the Amsterdam regents in
1748. The *Doelisten* defended democratic positions disguised in the language and form of early-modern guild democracy based on ancient privileges. These rebels convened in the *Doelen*.

Estates General (*Staten-Generaal*)   The Estates General, the central governing
body of the Dutch Republic, originated in the later Middle Ages and had
only a limited political function in the Habsburg period. In the Union of
Utrecht (1579), the constitutional base of the United Provinces, the Estates
General was seen as the main instrument of the union. But because most
provinces, especially Holland and Zeeland, were extremely jealous of their

own sovereignty, the Estates General in time was stripped of most of its union powers. Until the end of the republic, the executive powers of the Estates General remained limited. It exercised full rights only in governing the Generality lands.

**Frederick Hendrik** (1584–1647)   Count of Nassau, Prince of Orange, son of William the Silent and Louise de Coligny. In 1625, Frederick succeeded his elder brother Prince Maurice as stadholder of most of the provinces of the Dutch Republic.

**Generality lands**   These parts of the Low Countries, conquered by the Dutch Republic in the Eighty Years' War, were denied the right of self-rule and administered by the Estates General. The most important were Staats-Brabant, Staats-Limburg, and Staats-Vlaanderen.

**'s Gravesande, Willem J.** (1688–1742)   The most important Dutch scientist of the first half of the eighteenth century, 's Gravesande taught physics at Leiden University and helped to establish Newton's science in the Dutch Republic.

***Grietenijen***   Country districts in the province of Friesland and the western part of Groningen, each consisting of several villages. The *grietenijen* were each administered by a *grietman*, who also was the chief juridical officer of the district. All *grietenijen* had the right to send delegates to the estates of the province.

***Grondwettige herstelling*** (Constitutional Restoration), 1784   This central political tract of the Patriot movement consisted of a detailed analysis of the original rights and privileges of the various political bodies in the republic, discussed by province, and of the ways to restore these. The third part (never published) was intended to deal with cultural, religious, and educational issues.

**Grotius, Hugo** (1583–1645)   The most important Dutch political theorist of the seventeenth century. No friend of absolute monarchy, Grotius left a legacy of theory on the working of natural law in society and government; among his writings, *Het regt van oorlog en vrede* (1625).

***Hollandsche Spectator***   Influential Dutch periodical, modeled after its English counterpart, the *Spectator*. Founded by Justus van Effen (1684–1735), a Dutch journalist prolific in both French and Dutch. The *Hollandsche Spectator* was the first of a host of spectatorial periodicals that were to dominate Dutch enlightened journalism in the period 1730–1780.

**King William I** (1772–1843)   Son of William V, the last stadholder of the Dutch Republic. The young William became the first king of the Netherlands when, in 1814 after the defeat of Napoleon, the monarchy was introduced. During his reign, William adopted most of the economic and cultural proposals of the Patriots.

**Kluit, Adriaan** (1735–1807)   Dutch professor of history at the University of Leiden. Kluit was the first to demolish on historical grounds the Batavian myth, according to which the provincial estates were the depositories of sovereignty. Kluit was a staunch defender of the stadholdership and an active political pamphleteer in the Patriot period.

*Landdag*   Meeting of the estates of the northern and eastern provinces.

Luzac, Elie (1721–1796)   Leiden publisher and political theorist of Huguenot origins. Luzac published Voltaire and La Mettrie, translated Montesquieu, and became the leading defender of the Orangist cause in the Patriot revolution.

Mennonites   Followers of Menno Simonsz (1496–1561), irenic disciple of the Anabaptists of the Radical Reformation. The Mennonites were treated as second-rate citizens in the Dutch Republic. Just like their English counterparts, the dissenters, they were not allowed to enter public office because of their religion. In the eighteenth century, a disproportionately large number of Mennonites were active in spreading Dutch Enlightenment ideals and in political opposition movements such as Patriotism.

Oldenbarnevelt, Johan van (1547–1619)   First grand pensionary of the province of Holland and significant agent in the formation of the Dutch Republic. In 1619, Van Oldenbarnevelt was put to death on the scaffold with the knowledge of Prince Maurice. As a result of this judicial murder, in the seventeenth and eighteenth centuries Van Oldenbarnevelt was considered the champion of *Waare Vrijheid*, the ideology of the *Staatsgezinden* who opposed the stadholder. He became one of the Patriots' major historical examples.

Orangists   Adherents of the princes of Orange, who served as stadholders in the Dutch Republic; the principal opponents of the *staatsgezinden*. The Orangists were predominately from the church and the army. Calvinist ministers saw the stadholders as the custodians of true religion, and army officers regarded the stadholders, who favored an active foreign policy and strong army, as a source of patronage.

Outer provinces   In the Dutch Republic, there existed a strong political and cultural division between the seaward provinces, such as Holland and Zeeland, which were mainly commerce and industry oriented, and the outer provinces, such as Overijssel and Gelderland—agrarian regions oriented toward the Continent and often opposed to the mercantile policies of the seaward provinces.

Patriotism   Revolutionary movement in the late eighteenth-century Dutch Republic. In various tracts, pamphlets, and periodicals, the Patriots offered a scheme to reform the political and cultural system of the republic. They considered the stadholder and his clients their main opponents. In 1787, the stadholder, assisted by Prussian troops, crushed the movement. Many patriots went into exile in France, only to return in 1795 to complete the reform of the Dutch state.

*Patriottentijd*   Period in Dutch history in which the Patriots tried to reform the political institutions of the republic.

*Predikanten*    Ministers of the Calvinist Dutch church. The *predikanten* often supported the stadholders, whom they saw as the principal defenders of Calvinism, in their continual struggle with the regents.

Prince Maurice (1567–1625)    Second son of William the Silent and first stadholder of the Dutch Republic. Maurice's opposition to the estates of Holland and especially his role in the lawsuit against Johan van Oldenbarnevelt made him a villain in Patriotic discourse.

Provincial estates    The governing body of each of the confederation of sovereign provinces that made up the Dutch Republic. These estates sent delegates to the meetings of the Estates General. The Estates General could not reach decisions unless all provinces concurred, so the center of gravity of the policy-making process in the republic was situated in the provincial estates.

*Pruikentijd*    Nickname for the eighteenth century in Dutch historiography. Until recently, it was accepted practice to contrast the seventeenth-century Golden Age with the *Pruikentijd* (periwig period), in which politics, economy, and culture were in decline.

*Raadpensionaris* (grand pensionary)    Originally the *raadpensionaris* was the legal adviser of the provincial estates. Because of the dominance of the province of Holland, the office of Holland's *raadpensionaris* evolved quickly into a central position in the Dutch political machinery. In the hands of extremely capable politicians such as Johan van Oldenbarnevelt and Johan de Witt, the *raadpensionaris* was almost tantamount to a dictator.

*Regenten* (regents)    Members of the Dutch governing class, the *regentenpatriciaat*, from which almost all political and juridical officials were recruited. Because of the peculiar political system of the Dutch Republic, the towns, especially the larger ones such as Amsterdam and Middelburg, were the crucial components of the Dutch policy-making process. The number of town regents active in national politics was, however, always limited. Only five hundred on an average of two thousand regents fulfilled such a national role. The large majority should be considered administrators rather than politicians.

*Regerings reglementen* (governmental regulation, 1674–1675)    During the 1672 invasion by Louis XIV, the French Sun King, the provinces of Utrecht, Gelderland, and Overijssel surrendered to the French. After the defeat of the Sun King, however, these provinces were admitted into the union only on the condition that their provincial estates accept the *regerings reglementen*, drafted by stadhouder William III. These regulations gave the stadholder the right to appoint all major local and provincial officials, which enhanced his political influence enormously. At the elevation of William IV to the position stadholder in 1747, similar regulations were imposed on the other provinical estates.

Remonstrants (Arminians)    Dissenting religious group; followers of the Leiden professor of theology Arminius in a 1618–1619 religious controversy. Although the Remonstrants were persecuted in the first half of the seventeenth century, they became a respectable religious minority to whom, however, political rights were denied. They played an important part in creating the Dutch Enlightenment.

**Revolutions of 1672, 1702, and 1747** The political conflict underlying these three revolutions was chiefly that between two views on the function of the political machinery of the Dutch state, put forward by the Orangists and the *staatsgezinden*. The Orangists favored an active foreign policy, a strong army, and a strong executive, controlled by the stadholder; the provincial estates, especially that of Holland, preferred a neutral stand in international affairs and a small army. In 1702 and 1747, new elements, disguised as a plea for the reconstruction of older civic democratic procedures, came into play.

**Rousset de Missy, Jean (1686–1762)** Another of the many talented French Protestants who fled to the Dutch Republic, Rousset de Missy became a school teacher, translator, journalist, political propagandist, historian, spy, leading freemason, and in 1748 radical leader of discontented groups in Amsterdam. He knew Dutch, although he generally wrote in French.

*Schutterij* (municipal militia) In late medieval Dutch towns, civic militias had served important roles both in the defense of the cities and in municipal government. In the sixteenth century, their importance dwindled. Much of the democratically inspired political protest of the eighteenth-century Dutch Republic strove to reimplement or reconstruct the original political rights, supposed or real, of the municipal militias.

**Slingelandt, Simon van (1664–1736)** In the aftermath of the War of the Spanish Succession, Van Slingelandt, as secretary to the council of state, tried to introduce radical reforms into the outdated political machinery of the Dutch Republic. His *Discours over de defecten in de tegenwoordige constitutie der regering van den Staat der Vereenigde Nedelanden* (1716) was widely read, but on accepting the grand pensionaryship of the estates of Holland in 1727 Van Slingelandt was forced to renounce his reformist proposals.

**Sociability** A phenomenon widespread in eighteenth-century Europe but particularly commonplace in the Dutch Enlightenment. In the Netherlands there were over five hundred societies—salons, masonic lodges, philosophical societies, reading clubs could be found in every city and major village.

**Southern Netherlands** Part of the territory of the Low Countries roughly corresponding to modern Belgium. Until 1568, the Low Countries were one of the main possessions of the Habsburg Empire of Charles V and Philip II. As a result of the Dutch revolt against Spain (1568–1579), the Low Countries split: the northern Netherlands became the Dutch Republic, the south remained under Spanish rule. After the War of the Spanish Succession (1702–1714), the Southern Netherlands were incorporated into the Austrian Empire and called the Austrian Netherlands.

*Staatsgezinden*   Those regents who strongly defended the sovereign rights of the provinces, usually led by grand pensionaries of Holland. The stadholders, who strove to strengthen the position of the Estates General and the unity of the provinces, were the natural opponents of the *staatsgezinden*. All major conflicts in Dutch seventeenth- and eighteenth-century history focused on this opposition. In practice, then, the personalities of the combatants, stadholders and grand pensionaries, decided political issues. In two stadholderless periods (1650–1672 and 1702–1747), the *staatsgezinden* enjoyed full power. Strong-headed stadholders such as Frederick Hendrik and William III succeeded in turning the balance to their own favor. In the *Patriottentijd*, some of the *staatsgezinden* joined the Patriot movement while others offered their services to the stadholder.

Stadholder   The office of stadholder was an anomaly in the political structure of the Dutch state. Originally, the stadholder was the representative of the Habsburg kings and watched over the royal interests in the various provinces. In many provinces, the stadholder acquired the right to appoint members to the town councils. After the successful Dutch revolt against Spain, the provincial estates assumed sovereignty and with it acquired the right to appoint the stadholder. As a result, the stadholder became a servant as well as a master of the provincial estates (see also Orangists).

Tax farming   A system widely practiced on the Continent in which governments gave individuals the concession to collect taxes in their district. The system was fraught with abuses yet convenient and relatively inexpensive as a method of collection.

*Vrijkorpsen* (free corps)   The foundation of free corps, or *exercitiegenootschappen*, was advocated by Joan van der Capellen, who urged the enlightened citizenry to practice the use of weaponry to be able to defend themselves against the stadholders and the military in his control. Although the military significance of the *vrijkorpsen* was minimal, its political impact was enormous. The local *vrijkorpsen* united in a national movement based in Utrecht, stimulated political discussion, and enhanced nationalist feelings.

*Vroedschap* (town council)   The core of local political government in the Dutch Republic. *Vroedschap* members were chosen by cooptation and sat for life. In most towns, however, real power was in the hands of the burgomasters, who often represented the town in the provincial estates. The majority of the members of the *vroedschap* contented themselves with administrative rather than political tasks (see also Burgomaster and *Regenten*).

*Waare Vrijheid* (True Liberty)   The ideology of the staatsgezinden, *Waare Vrijheid* stressed the autonomy of the provinces. The ideology was developed during the first stadholderless period (1650–1672) by political theorists such as Pieter de la Court.

War of the Austrian Succession (1740–1748)   In 1740 Prussia invaded the Austrian territory of Silesia, and France supported its aggression. French involvement brought Britain into the war on the Austrian side. At stake for the British was the continuing Austrian presence in the Southern Netherlands and hence the safety of the Dutch Republic. France invaded the Austrian Netherlands in 1744 and Zeeland in the Dutch Republic in 1747. France lost the war but not without exposing Dutch weakness and causing the restoration of the stadholder, William IV.

War of the Spanish Succession (1702–1714)   At his death, the king of Spain, Charles II, left his kingdom to France. To prevent this spectacular growth in French power, an alliance of Britain, the Netherlands, and the Austrian Holy Roman Empire made war against France. Peace was proclaimed in 1712 at Utrecht, the Netherlands both north and south having been the scene of fierce fighting. Austria acquired the Southern Netherlands (modern Belgium), and Britain emerged as a major power as a result of its victories over the French.

Wilhelmina of Prussia (1751–1820)   Wife of stadholder William V and daughter of August Wilhelm of Prussia. In June 1787, Wilhelmina tried to travel from the town of Nijmegen in the eastern part of the Netherlands to The Hague in order to prepare the ground for a return of her husband. She was arrested by Patriot soldiers at Goejanverwellesluis, which prompted her Prussian relatives into action. In the autumn of 1787, William V, assisted by Prussian troops, defeated the Patriot armies and regained his powers.

William III (1650–1702)   Prince of Orange and son of stadholder William II and Mary Stuart. First Orange to become stadholder of all the provinces of the Dutch Republic. William's elevation to the stadholdership in 1672 ended the first stadholderless period and brought the downfall and death of his great opponent Johan de Witt. During his reign, William strengthened the position of the office of stadholder, but he did not try to reform the political structure of the republic by increasing the powers of the executive; European politics and the struggle against France remained his chief political aims. He became king of England in 1689.

William IV (1711–1751)   Son of Johan Willem Friso, the Frisian stadholder and descendant of the Frisian branch of the Nassau family. The ruinous outcome of the War of the Austrian Succession (1740–1748) created a revolution in which William IV was able to secure the stadholdership of all provinces, which had become hereditary for the first time in Dutch history. Nevertheless, he failed to impose the reforms his secure position enabled.

William V (1751–1795)   Prince of Orange-Nassau and son of stadholder William IV and Anne of Hanover. William V was a meticulous administrator but hardly a shrewd politician. His hesitancy kept him from seizing the initiative in the power vacuum at the beginning of the fourth Anglo-Dutch War of 1780–1784. In 1787, he was restored to his original position, but in 1795 he was forced to flee the country. His son William Frederick would become the first king of the Netherlands in 1814.

Witt, Johan de (1625–1672)   One of the greatest grand pensionaries of the

Dutch Republic. De Witt was one of the creators of *Waare Vrijheid* and a fierce opponent of the policies of the House of Orange. He saw their bellicosity as a fundamental threat to the commercial interests of the republic. In the 1672 revolution that caused the elevation of William III to the stadholdership, De Witt was jailed. While awaiting trial, he was taken from his cell and murdered by an Orangist mob. Both his political stand and his fate made him a martyr of the Patriot cause in the revolution of 1780–1787.

Wolff, Elizabeth (Betje) (1738–1804)   The first important Dutch novelist. With her friend and companion, Aagje Deken, Wolff wrote *De historie van Mejuffrouw Sara Burgerhart*. She was also an ardent Patriot and a promoter of the new science.

# Contributors

W. VAN DEN BERG is professor of modern Dutch literature at the University of Amsterdam. Included among his publications are *De ontwikkeling van de term "romantisch" en zijn varianten in Nederland tot 1840* (Assen, 1973). He has also published on the literary novel, the concept of preromanticism, and literary sociability.

CHRISTINE VAN BOHEEMEN-SAAF is professor of English and American literature at the University of Amsterdam. Among her many books is *The Novel as Family Romance* (Ithaca, 1987).

WAYNE PH. TE BRAKE is associate professor of history at the State University of New York at Purchase and affiliate of the Center for the Study of Social Change at the New School for Social Research. He is author of *Regents and Rebels: The Revolutionary World of an Eighteenth-Century Dutch City* (Oxford, 1989).

WILLEM TH. M. FRIJHOFF is professor of cultural history at the Erasmus University of Rotterdam. He has published numerous books and articles on the cultural history of early modern Europe, among them *La société Neérlandaise et ses gradués, 1574–1814* (Amsterdam, 1981).

FRANS GRIJZENHOUT, member of the staff at the Netherlands Office of Fine Arts, is a specialist on eighteenth-century art history. He has published several books and articles, among them *Feesten voor het Vaderland: Patriotse en Bataafse feesten, 1780–1806* (Zwolle, 1989).

MARGARET C. JACOB is professor of history in the university at the New School for Social Research. Her most recent book is *Living the Enlightenment: Freemasonry and Politics in Eighteenth Century Europe* (New York, 1991). She writes on cultural and intellectual history of Britain, the Netherlands, Belgium, and France in the eighteenth century.

JAN A. F. DE JONGSTE is associate professor in Dutch history at the University of Leiden. He has published on eighteenth-century Dutch political history, including *Onrust aan het Spaarne: Haarlem in de jaren 1747–1751* (Dieren, 1984).

E. H. KOSSMANN is emeritus professor of modern history at the University of Groningen. He is a member of the Royal Netherlands Academy of Arts and Sciences. He has published numerous books and articles on European and Dutch history, among them *La Fronde* (Leiden, 1954) and *The Low Countries, 1780–1940* (Oxford, 1978).

WIJNAND W. MIJNHARDT, professor of cultural history at the University of Utrecht, is author of *Tot heil van 't menschdom: Culturele genootschappen in Nederland, 1750–1815* (Amsterdam, 1988), a history of eighteenth-century Dutch sociability. He is currently completing a book on the revolution in publishing and reading in the Netherlands of 1780–1850.

ECO O. G. HAITSMA MULIER is professor of modern history at the University of Amsterdam. He is interested primarily in the history of political thought and the history of historiography. His publications include *The Myth of Venice and Dutch Republican Thought in the Seventeenth Century* (Assen, 1980) and (with G. A. C. van der Lem) *Repertorium van geschiedschijvers in Nederland, 1500–1800* (The Hague 1990).

J. G. A. POCOCK is professor of history at The Johns Hopkins University. He is the author of many books, in particular, *The Machiavellian Moment* (Princeton, 1975), and numerous essays on the English republican tradition. He is currently at work on a study of the historian Gibbon.

JEREMY D. POPKIN is professor of history at the University of Kentucky. He is the author of *News and Politics in the Age of Revolution: Jean Luzac's 'Gazette de Leyde'* (Ithaca, 1989), *Revolutionary News: The Press in France, 1789–1799* (Durham, N.C., 1990), and several articles on journalism and publishing in western Europe from 1770 to 1815.

NICOLAAS C. F. VAN SAS is associate professor of modern history at the University of Amsterdam. He is the author of *Onze natuurlijke bondgenoot: Nederland, Engeland en Europa, 1813–1831* (Groningen, 1985), and of many articles, especially on political culture in the Netherlands during the "long" nineteenth century. His research interests include problems of nation building, nationalism, and images and self-images of nations.

H. A. M. Snelders is professor of the history of science at the University of Utrecht and at the Vrije Universiteit at Amsterdam. He has written extensively on chemistry and physics in the Netherlands and on the relations between science and *Naturphilosophie*. He is presently working on a history of physical chemistry in the Netherlands.

Wyger R. E. Velema is a fellow of the Royal Dutch Academy of Sciences. He specializes in eighteenth-century Dutch political theory and has recently completed a dissertation titled *Enlightenment and Conservatism in the Dutch Republic: The Political Thought of Elie Luzac*.

I. J. H. Worst is a fellow of the Netherlands Organisation for Scientific Research. He is currently completing a dissertation on Dutch political theory in the late eighteenth and early nineteenth centuries, and has published articles on Dutch political theory and historiography.

# Index

*Library of Congress Cataloging-in-Publication Data*

The Dutch Republic in the eighteenth century : decline, Enlightenment,
and revolution / edited by Margaret C. Jacob and Wijnand W.
Mijnhardt.
    p.  cm.
  Includes bibliographical references and index.
  ISBN 0-8014-2624-3
  1. Netherlands—History—1714–1795.  2. Enlightenment—
Netherlands.  I. Jacob, Margaret C., 1943– .  II. Mijnhardt, W.
W., 1950– .
DJ202.D44  1992
949.2.'04—dc20                            91-55551